Alexis De Tocqueville
Democracy in America, Vol. II

Édition de Grand Luxe

THE CAPITOL AT WASHINGTON.

Photogravure from a photograph.

Democracy in America

By
Alexis De Tocqueville

Translated by Henry Reeve

With a Critical and Biographical Introduction
by John Bigelow

Illustrated
Volume II

New York
D. Appleton and Company
1899

CONTENTS

CHAPTER XIX

PAGE

THE CHANCES OF THE DURATION OF THE UNION . . . 419

CHAPTER XX

THE CAUSES OF THE COMMERCIAL PROSPERITY OF THE
UNITED STATES 467

CHAPTER XXI

FUTURE PROSPECTS OF THE UNITED STATES 477

CHAPTER XXII

THE INFLUENCES OF DEMOCRACY UPON PHILOSOPHY . . 484

CHAPTER XXIII

THE INFLUENCES OF DEMOCRACY UPON RELIGION . . . 502

CHAPTER XXIV

THE INFLUENCES OF DEMOCRACY UPON SCIENCE AND THE
ARTS 517

CHAPTER XXV

THE INFLUENCES OF DEMOCRACY UPON LANGUAGE AND
LITERATURE 539

CHAPTER XXVI

INDIVIDUALISM IN DEMOCRATIC COUNTRIES 580

CHAPTER XXVII
PAGE
PUBLIC ASSOCIATIONS 593

CHAPTER XXVIII
THE PRINCIPLE OF INTEREST RIGHTLY UNDERSTOOD . . 608

CHAPTER XXIX
THE DESIRE FOR WEALTH AND FOR PHYSICAL PROSPERITY . 615

CHAPTER XXX
OCCUPATIONS AND BUSINESS CALLINGS 639

CHAPTER XXXI
INFLUENCE OF DEMOCRACY UPON MANNERS 650

CHAPTER XXXII
INFLUENCE OF DEMOCRACY UPON SOCIAL AND DOMESTIC
RELATIONS 664

CHAPTER XXXIII
INFLUENCE OF DEMOCRACY UPON PUBLIC RELATIONS . . 709

CHAPTER XXXIV
WARFARE AND REVOLUTIONS AMONG DEMOCRATIC PEOPLES 741

CHAPTER XXXV
INFLUENCE OF DEMOCRATIC OPINIONS AND SENTIMENTS
UPON POLITICAL SOCIETY 780
APPENDIX 830

ILLUSTRATIONS

FACING PAGE

THE CAPITOL AT WASHINGTON . . . . *Frontispiece*
Photogravure from a photograph

MEXICAN PICTURE CHRONICLE OF CEMPOALLA . . . vi
Page from an illuminated manuscript history written about
1530 A. D. for the Aztec Prince known as Ixtlilxochitl II

ANDREW JACKSON 454
Photogravure from a lithograph after a daguerreotype by Brady

AN EAST RIVER PALACE 536
Photogravure from a photograph

STUMP SPEAKING 562
Photogravure from an engraving after a painting by G. C.
Bingham

WAR NEWS 760
Photogravure from a painting by Richard Caton Woodville, now
in the Metropolitan Museum of Art, New York City

A JURY 856
Photogravure from an engraving after a painting by J. Morgan

FAMOUS AND UNIQUE MANUSCRIPT AND BOOK ILLUSTRATIONS.

A series of fac-similes, showing the development of manuscript and book illustrating during four thousand years.

MEXICAN PICTURE CHRONICLE OF CEMPOALLA.

Page from an illuminated manuscript history written about 1530 A. D. for the Aztec Prince known as Ixtlilxochitl II.

FAMOUS AND UNIQUE MANUSCRIPT AND
BOOK ILLUSTRATIONS

A series of fac-similes showing the development of manuscript and
book illustrating during four thousand years

CEMPOALLA

Page from an illuminated manuscript history written about 1530 A.D.

DEMOCRACY IN AMERICA

CHAPTER XIX

THE CHANCES OF THE DURATION OF THE UNION

What the chances are in favour of the duration of the American Union,
and what dangers threaten it—Of the republican institutions of the
United States, and what their chances of duration are.

THE maintenance of the existing institutions of the
several States depends in some measure upon the
maintenance of the Union itself. It is therefore important in the first instance to inquire into the probable
fate of the Union. One point may indeed be assumed at
once: if the present confederation were dissolved, it appears to me to be incontestable that the States of which
it is now composed would not return to their original isolated condition, but that several Unions would then be
formed in the place of one. It is not my intention to inquire into the principles upon which these new Unions
would probably be established, but merely to show what
the causes are which may effect the dismemberment of
the existing confederation.

With this object I shall be obliged to retrace some of
the steps which I have already taken, and to revert to
topics which I have before discussed. I am aware that the
reader may accuse me of repetition, but the importance of
the matter which still remains to be treated is my excuse;

I had rather say too much than say too little to be thoroughly understood, and I prefer injuring the author to slighting the subject.

The legislators who formed the Constitution of 1789 endeavoured to confer a distinct and preponderating authority upon the Federal power. But they were confined by the conditions of the task which they had undertaken to perform. They were not appointed to constitute the government of a single people, but to regulate the association of several States; and, whatever their inclinations might be, they could not but divide the exercise of sovereignty in the end.

In order to understand the consequences of this division, it is necessary to make a short distinction between the affairs of the Government. There are some objects which are national by their very nature—that is to say, which affect the nation as a body, and can only be intrusted to the man or the assembly of men who most completely represent the entire nation. Among these may be reckoned war and diplomacy. There are other objects which are provincial by their very nature—that is to say, which only affect certain localities, and which can only be properly treated in that locality. Such, for instance, is the budget of a municipality. Lastly, there are certain objects of a mixed nature, which are national inasmuch as they affect all the citizens who compose the nation, and which are provincial inasmuch as it is not necessary that the nation itself should provide for them all. Such are the rights which regulate the civil and political condition of the citizens. No society can exist without civil and political rights. These rights, therefore, interest all the citizens alike; but it is not always necessary to the existence and the prosperity of the nation that these rights should be uniform, nor, consequently, that they should be regulated by the central authority.

There are, then, two distinct categories of objects which are submitted to the direction of the sovereign power; and these categories occur in all well-constituted communities, whatever the basis of the political constitution may otherwise be. Between these two extremes the objects which I have termed mixed may be considered to lie. As these objects are neither exclusively national nor entirely provincial, they may be obtained by a national or by a provincial government, according to the agreement of the contracting parties, without in any way impairing the contract of association.

The sovereign power is usually formed by the union of separate individuals, who compose a people; and individual powers or collective forces, each representing a very small portion of the sovereign authority, are the sole elements which are subjected to the general Government of their choice. In this case the general Government is more naturally called upon to regulate, not only those affairs which are of essential national importance, but those which are of a more local interest; and the local governments are reduced to that small share of sovereign authority which is indispensable to their prosperity.

But sometimes the sovereign authority is composed of preorganized political bodies, by virtue of circumstances anterior to their union; and in this case the provincial Governments assume the control, not only of those affairs which more peculiarly belong to their province, but of all or of a part of the mixed affairs to which allusion has been made. For the confederate nations which were independent sovereign States before their union, and which still represent a very considerable share of the sovereign power, have only consented to cede to the general Government the exercise of those rights which are indispensable to the Union.

When the national Government, independently of the prerogatives inherent in its nature, is invested with the right of regulating the affairs which relate partly to the general and partly to the local interests, it possesses a preponderating influence. Not only are its own rights extensive, but all the rights which it does not possess exist by its sufferance, and it may be apprehended that the provincial Governments may be deprived of their natural and necessary prerogatives by its influence.

When, on the other hand, the provincial Governments are invested with the power of regulating those same affairs of mixed interest, an opposite tendency prevails in society. The preponderating force resides in the province, not in the nation; and it may be apprehended that the national Government may in the end be stripped of the privileges which are necessary to its existence.

Independent nations have therefore a natural tendency to centralization, and confederations to dismemberment.

It now only remains for us to apply these general principles to the American Union. The several States were necessarily possessed of the right of regulating all exclusively provincial affairs. Moreover, these same States retained the rights of determining the civil and political competency of the citizens, or regulating the reciprocal relations of the members of the community, and of dispensing justice; rights which are of a general nature, but which do not necessarily appertain to the national Government. We have shown that the Government of the Union is invested with the power of acting in the name of the whole nation in those cases in which the nation has to appear as a single and undivided power; as, for instance, in foreign relations, and in offering a common resistance to a common enemy; in short, in conducting those affairs which I have styled exclusively national.

In this division of the rights of sovereignty, the share of the Union seems at first sight to be more considerable than that of the States; but a more attentive investigation shows it to be less so. The undertakings of the Government of the Union are more vast, but their influence is more rarely felt. Those of the provincial Governments are comparatively small, but they are incessant, and they serve to keep alive the authority which they represent. The Government of the Union watches the general interests of the country; but the general interests of a people have a very questionable influence upon individual happiness, while provincial interests produce a most immediate effect upon the welfare of the inhabitants. The Union secures the independence and the greatness of the nation, which do not immediately affect private citizens; but the several States maintain the liberty, regulate the rights, protect the fortune, and secure the life and the whole future prosperity of every citizen.

The Federal Government is very far removed from its subjects, while the provincial Governments are within the reach of them all, and are ready to attend to the smallest appeal. The central Government has upon its side the passions of a few superior men who aspire to conduct it; but upon the side of the provincial Governments are the interests of all those second-rate individuals who can only hope to obtain power within their own State, and who nevertheless exercise the largest share of authority over the people because they are placed nearest to its level. The Americans have therefore much more to hope and to fear from the States than from the Union; and, in conformity with the natural tendency of the human mind, they are more likely to attach themselves to the former than to the latter. In this respect their habits and feelings harmonize with their interests.

When a compact nation divides its sovereignty, and adopts a confederate form of government, the traditions, the customs, and the manners of the people are for a long time at variance with their legislation; and the former tend to give a degree of influence to the central Government which the latter forbids. When a number of confederate States unite to form a single nation, the same causes operate in an opposite direction. I have no doubt that if France were to become a confederate republic like that of the United States the Government would at first display more energy than that of the Union; and if the Union were to alter its constitution to a monarchy like that of France, I think that the American Government would be a long time in acquiring the force which now rules the latter nation. When the national existence of the Anglo-

Americans began, their provincial existence was already of long standing; necessary relations were established between the townships and the individual citizens of the same States; and they were accustomed to consider some objects as common to them all, and to conduct other affairs as exclusively relating to their own special interests.

The Union is a vast body which presents no definite object to patriotic feeling. The forms and limits of the State are distinct and circumscribed; since it represents a certain number of objects which are familiar to the citizens and beloved by all. It is identified with the very soil, with the right of property and the domestic affections, with the recollections of the past, the labours of the present, and the hopes of the future. Patriotism, then, which is frequently a mere extension of individual egotism, is still directed to the State, and is not excited by the Union. Thus the tendency of the interests, the habits, and the feelings of the people is to centre political activity in the States in preference to the Union.

It is easy to estimate the different forces of the two Governments by remarking the manner in which they fulfil their respective functions. Whenever the Government of a State has occasion to address an individual or an assembly of individuals, its language is clear and imperative; and such is also the tone of the Federal Government in its intercourse with individuals; but no sooner has it anything to do with a State than it begins to parley, to explain its motives and to justify its conduct, to argue, to advise, and, in short, anything but to command. If doubts are raised as to the limits of the constitutional powers of each Government, the provincial Government prefers its claim with boldness, and takes prompt and energetic steps to support it. In the meanwhile the Government of the Union reasons; it appeals to the interests, to the good sense, to the glory of the nation; it temporizes, it negotiates, and does not consent to act until it is reduced to the last extremity. At first sight it might readily be imagined that it is the provincial Government which is armed with the authority of the nation, and that Congress represents a single State.

The Federal Government is, therefore, notwithstanding the precautions of those who founded it, naturally so weak that it more peculiarly requires the free consent of the governed to enable it to subsist. It is easy to perceive that its object is to enable the States to realize with facility their determination of remaining united; and, as long as this preliminary condition exists, its authority is great, temperate, and effective. The Constitution fits the Government to control individuals, and easily to surmount such obstacles as they may be inclined to offer; but it was by no means established with a view to the possible separation of one or more of the States from the Union.

If the sovereignty of the Union were to engage in a struggle with that of the States at the present day, its defeat may be confidently predicted; and it is not probable that such a struggle would be seriously undertaken. As often as a steady resistance is offered to the Federal Government it will be found to yield. Experience has hitherto shown that whenever a State has demanded anything with perseverance and resolution it has invariably succeeded; and that if a separate Government has distinctly refused to act, it was left to do as it thought fit.[1]

But even if the Government of the Union had any strength inherent in itself, the physical situation of the country would render the exercise of that strength very difficult.[2] The United States cover an immense territory; they are separated from each other by great distances; and the population is disseminated over the surface of a country which is still half a wilderness. If the Union were to undertake to enforce the allegiance of the confederate States by military means, it would be in a position very analogous to that of England at the time of the War of Independence.

However strong a Government may be, it can not easily escape from the consequences of a principle which it has once admitted as the foundation of its constitution.

The Union was formed by the voluntary agreement of the States; and, in uniting together, they have not forfeited their nationality, nor have they been reduced to the condition of one and the same people. If one of the States chose to withdraw its name from the contract, it would be difficult to disprove its right of doing so; and the Federal Government would have no means of maintaining its claims directly, either by force or by right. In order to enable the Federal Government easily to conquer the resistance which may be offered to it by any one of its subjects, it would be necessary that one or more of them should be specially interested in the existence of the Union, as has frequently been the case in the history of confederations.

If it be supposed that among the States which are united by the Federal tie there are some which exclusively enjoy the principal advantages of union, or whose prosperity depends on the duration of that union, it is unquestionable that they will always be ready to support the central Government in enforcing the obedience of the others. But the Government would then be exerting a force not derived from itself, but from a principle contrary to its nature. States form confederations in order to derive equal advantages from their union; and in the case just alluded to the Federal Government would derive its power from the unequal distribution of those benefits among the States.

If one of the confederate States have acquired a preponderance sufficiently great to enable it to take exclusive possession of the central authority, it will consider the other States as subject provinces, and it will cause its own supremacy to be respected under the borrowed name of the sovereignty of the Union. Great things may then be done in the name of the Federal Government, but in reality that Government will have ceased to exist.[3] In both these cases the power which acts in the name of the confederation becomes stronger the more it abandons the natural state and the acknowledged principles of confederations. In America the existing Union is advantageous to all the States, but it is not indispensable to any one of them. Several of them might break the Federal tie without compromising the welfare of the others, although their own prosperity would be lessened. As the existence and the happiness of none of the States are wholly dependent on the present Constitution, they would none of them be disposed to make great personal sacrifices to maintain it. On the other hand, there is no State which seems hitherto to have its ambition much interested in the maintenance of the existing Union. They certainly do not all exercise the same influence in the Federal Councils, but no one of them can hope to domineer over the rest, or to treat them as its inferiors or as its subjects.

It appears to me unquestionable that if any portion of the Union seriously desired to separate itself from the other States they would not be able, nor indeed would they attempt, to prevent it; and that the present Union will only last as long as the States which compose it choose to continue members of the confederation. If this point be admitted, the question becomes less difficult; and our object is, not to inquire whether the States of the existing Union are capable of separating, but whether they will choose to remain united.

Among the various reasons which tend to render the existing Union useful to the Americans, two principal causes are peculiarly evident to the observer. Although the Americans are, as it were, alone upon their continent, their commerce makes them the neighbours of all the nations with which they trade. Notwithstanding their apparent isolation, the Americans require a certain degree of strength, which they can not retain otherwise than by remaining united to each other. If the States were to split, they would not only diminish the strength which they are now able to display toward foreign nations, but they would soon create foreign powers upon their own territory. A system of inland custom-houses would then be established; the valleys would be divided by imaginary boundary lines; the courses of the rivers would be confined by territorial distinctions; and a multitude of hindrances would prevent the Americans from exploring the whole of that vast continent which Providence has allotted to them for a dominion. At present they have no invasion to fear, and consequently no standing armies to maintain, no taxes to levy. If the Union were dissolved, all these burdensome measures might ere long be required. The Americans are then very powerfully interested in the maintenance of their Union. On the other hand, it is almost impossible to discover any sort of material interest which might at present tempt a portion of the Union to separate from the other States.

When we cast our eyes upon the map of the United States, we perceive the chain of the Alleghany Mountains, running from the northeast to the southwest, and crossing nearly one thousand miles of country; and we are led to imagine that the design of Providence was to raise between the valley of the Mississippi and the coasts of the Atlantic Ocean one of those natural barriers which break the mutual intercourse of men, and form the necessary limits of different States. But the average height of the Alleghanies does not exceed twenty-five hundred feet; their greatest elevation is not above four thousand feet; their rounded summits, and the spacious valleys which they conceal within their passes, are of easy access from several sides. Besides which, the principal rivers which fall into the Atlantic Ocean—the Hudson, the Susquehanna, and the Potomac—take their rise beyond the Alleghanies, in an open district, which borders upon the valley of the Mississippi. These streams quit this tract of country, make their way through the barrier which would seem to turn them westward, and as they wind through the mountains they open an easy and natural passage to man. No natural barrier exists in the regions which are now inhabited by the Anglo-Americans; the Alleghanies are so far from serving as a boundary to separate nations that they do not even serve as a frontier to the States. New York, Pennsylvania, and Virginia comprise them within their borders, and extend as much to the west as to the east of the line. The territory now occupied by the twenty-four States of the Union, and the three great districts which have not yet acquired the rank of States, although they already contain inhabitants, covers a surface of 1,002,600 square miles, which is about equal to five times the extent of France. Within these limits the qualities of the soil, the temperature, and the produce of the country, are extremely various. The vast extent of territory occupied by the Anglo-American republics has given rise to doubts as to the maintenance of their Union. Here a distinction must be made; contrary interests sometimes arise in the different provinces of a vast empire, which often terminate in open dissensions; and the extent of the country is then most prejudicial to the power of the State. But if the inhabitants of these vast regions are not divided by contrary interests, the extent of the territory may be favourable to their prosperity; for the unity of the Government promotes the interchange of the different productions of the soil, and increases their value by facilitating their consumption.

It is indeed easy to discover different interests in the different parts of the Union, but I am unacquainted with any which are hostile to each other. The Southern States are almost exclusively agricultural. The Northern States are more peculiarly commercial and manufacturing. The States of the West are at the same time agricultural and manufacturing. In the South, the crops consist of tobacco, of rice, of cotton, and of sugar; in the North and the West, of wheat and maize. These are different sources of wealth; but union is the means by which these sources are opened to all, and rendered equally advantageous to the several districts.

The North, which ships the produce of the Anglo-Americans to all parts of the world, and brings back the produce of the globe to the Union, is evidently interested in maintaining the confederation in its present condition, in order that the number of American producers and consumers may remain as large as possible. The North is the most natural agent of communication between the South and the West of the Union on the one hand, and the rest of the world upon the other; the North is therefore interested in the union and prosperity of the South and the West, in order that they may continue to furnish raw materials for its manufactures, and cargoes for its shipping.

The South and the West, on their side, are still more directly interested in the preservation of the Union, and the prosperity of the North. The produce of the South is, for the most part, exported beyond seas; the South and the West consequently stand in need of the commercial resources of the North. They are likewise interested in the maintenance of a powerful fleet by the Union, to protect them efficaciously. The South and the West have no vessels, but they can not refuse a willing subsidy to defray the expenses of the navy; for if the fleets of Europe were to blockade the ports of the South and the delta of the Mississippi, what would become of the rice of the Carolinas, the tobacco of Virginia, and the sugar and cotton which grow in the valley of the Mississippi? Every portion of the Federal budget therefore contributes to the maintenance of material interests which are common to all the confederate States.

Independently of this commercial utility, the South and the West of the Union derive great political advantages from their connection with the North. The South contains an enormous slave population; a population which is already alarming, and still more formidable for the future. The States of the West lie in the remoter parts of a single valley; and all the rivers which intersect their territory rise in the Rocky Mountains or in the Alleghanies, and fall into the Mississippi, which bears them onward to the Gulf of Mexico. The Western States are consequently entirely cut off, by their position, from the traditions of Europe and the civilization of the Old World. The inhabitants of the South, then, are induced to support the Union in order to avail themselves of its protection against the blacks; and the inhabitants of the West in order not to be excluded from a free communication with the rest of the globe, and shut up in the wilds of central America. The North can not but desire the maintenance of the Union, in order to remain, as it now is, the connecting link between that vast body and the other parts of the world.

The temporal interests of all the several parts of the Union are, then, intimately connected; and the same assertion holds true respecting those opinions and sentiments which may be termed the immaterial interests of men.

The inhabitants of the United States talk a great deal of their attachment to their country; but I confess that I do not rely upon that calculating patriotism which is founded upon interest, and which a change in the interests at stake may obliterate. Nor do I attach much importance to the language of the Americans, when they manifest, in their daily conversation, the intention of maintaining the Federal system adopted by their forefathers. A government retains its sway over a great number of citizens, far less by the voluntary and rational consent of the multitude, than by that instinctive, and to a certain extent involuntary agreement, which results from similarity of feelings and resemblances of opinion. I will never admit that men constitute a social body, simply because they obey the same head and the same laws. Society can only exist when a great number of men consider a great number of things in the same point of view; when they hold the same opinions upon many subjects, and when the same occurrences suggest the same thoughts and impressions to their minds.

The observer who examines the present condition of the United States upon this principle, will readily discover that, although the citizens are divided into twenty-four distinct sovereignties, they nevertheless constitute a single people; and he may perhaps be led to think that the state

432   DEMOCRACY IN AMERICA

of the Anglo-American Union is more truly a state of
society than that of certain nations of Europe which live
under the same legislation and the same prince.

Although the Anglo-Americans have several religious
sects, they all regard religion in the same manner. They
are not always agreed upon the measures which are most
conducive to good government, and they vary upon some
of the forms of government which it is expedient to adopt;
but they are unanimous upon the general principles which
ought to rule human society. From Maine to the Floridas,
and from the Missouri to the Atlantic Ocean, the people
is held to be the legitimate source of all power. The same
notions are entertained respecting liberty and equality, the
liberty of the press, the right of association, the jury, and
the responsibility of the agents of Government.

If we turn from their political and religious opinions
to the moral and philosophical principles which regulate
the daily actions of life and govern their conduct, we shall
still find the same uniformity. The Anglo-Americans [4]
acknowledge the absolute moral authority of the reason
of the community, as they acknowledge the political authority of the mass of citizens; and they hold that public
opinion is the surest arbiter of what is lawful or forbidden,
true or false. The majority of them believe that a man
will be led to do what is just and good by following his
own interest rightly understood. They hold that every
man is born in possession of the right of self-government,
and that no one has the right of constraining his fellow-
creatures to be happy. They have all a lively faith in the
perfectibility of man; they are of opinion that the effects
of the diffusion of knowledge must necessarily be advantageous, and the consequences of ignorance fatal; they all
consider society as a body in a state of improvement, humanity as a changing scene, in which nothing is, or ought
to be, permanent; and they admit that what appears to
them to be good to-day may be superseded by something
better to-morrow. I do not give all these opinions as
true, but I quote them as characteristic of the Americans.

The Anglo-Americans are not only united together by these common opinions, but they are separated from all other nations by a common feeling of pride. For the last fifty years no pains have been spared to convince the inhabitants of the United States that they constitute the only religious, enlightened, and free people. They perceive that, for the present, their own democratic institutions succeed, while those of other countries fail; hence they conceive an overweening opinion of their superiority, and they are not very remote from believing themselves to belong to a distinct race of mankind.

The dangers which threaten the American Union do not originate in the diversity of interests or of opinions, but in the various characters and passions of the Americans. The men who inhabit the vast territory of the United States are almost all the issue of a common stock; but the effects of the climate, and more especially of slavery, have gradually introduced very striking differences between the British settler of the Southern States and the British settler of the North. In Europe it is generally believed that slavery has rendered the interests of one part of the Union contrary to those of another part; but I by no means remarked this to be the case: slavery has not created interests in the South contrary to those of the North, but it has modified the character and changed the habits of the natives of the South.

I have already explained the influence which slavery has exercised upon the commercial ability of the Americans in the South; and this same influence equally extends to their manners. The slave is a servant who never remonstrates, and who submits to everything without complaint. He may sometimes assassinate, but he never withstands, his master. In the South there are no families so poor as not to have slaves. The citizen of the Southern States of the Union is invested with a sort of domestic dictatorship from his earliest years; the first notion he acquires in life is that he is born to command, and the first habit which he contracts is that of being obeyed without resistance.

His education tends, then, to give him the character of a supercilious and a hasty man; irascible, violent, and ardent in his desires, impatient of obstacles, but easily discouraged if he can not succeed upon his first attempt.

The American of the Northern States is surrounded by no slaves in his childhood; he is even unattended by free servants, and is usually obliged to provide for his own wants. No sooner does he enter the world than the idea of necessity assails him on every side: he soon learns to know exactly the natural limit of his authority; he never expects to subdue those who withstand him by force; and he knows that the surest means of obtaining the support of his fellow-creatures is to win their favour. He therefore becomes patient, reflecting, tolerant, slow to act, and persevering in his designs.

In the Southern States the more immediate wants of life are always supplied; the inhabitants of those parts are not busied in the material cares of life, which are always provided for by others; and their imagination is diverted to more captivating and less definite objects. The American of the South is fond of grandeur, luxury, and renown, of gaiety, of pleasure, and, above all, of idleness; nothing obliges him to exert himself in order to subsist; and as he has no necessary occupations, he gives way to indolence, and does not even attempt what would be useful.

But the equality of fortunes, and the absence of slavery in the North, plunge the inhabitants in those same cares of daily life which are disdained by the white population of the South. They are taught from infancy to combat want, and to place comfort above all the pleasures of the intellect or the heart. The imagination is extinguished by the trivial details of life, and the ideas become less numerous and less general, but far more practical and more precise. As prosperity is the sole aim of exertion, it is excellently well attained; Nature and mankind are turned to the best pecuniary advantage, and society is dexterously made to contribute to the welfare of each of its members, while individual egotism is the source of general happiness.

The citizen of the North has not only experience, but knowledge: nevertheless he sets but little value upon the pleasures of knowledge; he esteems it as the means of attaining a certain end, and he is only anxious to seize its more lucrative applications. The citizen of the South is more given to act upon impulse; he is more clever, more frank, more generous, more intellectual, and more brilliant. The former, with a greater degree of activity, of common sense, of information, and of general aptitude, has the characteristic good and evil qualities of the middle classes. The latter has the tastes, the prejudices, the weaknesses, and the magnanimity of all aristocracies. If two men are united in society, who have the same interests, and to a certain extent the same opinions, but different characters, different acquirements, and a different style of civilization, it is probable that these men will not agree. The same remark is applicable to a society of nations. Slavery, then, does not attack the American Union directly in its interests, but indirectly in its manners.

The States which gave their assent to the Federal Contract in 1790 were thirteen in number; the Union now consists of thirty-four members. The population, which amounted to nearly four millions in 1790, had more than trebled in the space of forty years; and in 1830 it amounted to nearly thirteen millions.[5] Changes of such magnitude can not take place without some danger.

A society of nations, as well as a society of individuals, derives its principal chances of duration from the wisdom of its members, their individual weakness, and their limited number. The Americans who quit the coasts of the Atlantic Ocean to plunge into the western wilderness are adventurers impatient of restraint, greedy of wealth, and frequently men expelled from the States in which they were born. When they arrive in the deserts they are unknown to each other, and they have neither traditions, family feeling, nor the force of example to check

30

their excesses. The empire of the laws is feeble among them; that of morality is still more powerless. The settlers who are constantly peopling the valley of the Mississippi are, then, in every respect very inferior to the Americans who inhabit the older parts of the Union. Nevertheless, they already exercise a great influence in its councils; and they arrive at the government of the commonwealth before they have learned to govern themselves.[6]

The greater the individual weakness of each of the contracting parties, the greater are the chances of the duration of the contract; for their safety is then dependent upon their union. When, in 1790, the most populous of the American republics did not contain five hundred thousand inhabitants,[7] each of them felt its own insignificance as an independent people, and this feeling rendered compliance with the Federal authority more easy. But when one of the confederate States reckons, like the State of New York, two millions of inhabitants, and covers an extent of territory equal in surface to a quarter of France,[8] it feels its own strength; and although it may continue to support the Union as advantageous to its prosperity, it no longer regards that body as necessary to its existence; and as it continues to belong to the Federal compact, it soon aims at preponderance in the Federal assemblies. The probable unanimity of the States is diminished as their number increases. At present the interests of the different parts of the Union are not at variance; but who is able to foresee the multifarious changes of the future in a country in which towns are founded from day to day, and States almost from year to year?

Since the first settlement of the British colonies, the number of inhabitants has about doubled every twenty-two years. I perceive no causes which are likely to check this progressive increase of the Anglo-American population for the next hundred years; and before that space of time has elapsed, I believe that the territories and dependencies of the United States will be covered by more than a hundred millions of inhabitants, and divided into

forty States.[9] I admit that these hundred millions of men
have no hostile interests. I suppose, on the contrary, that
they are all equally interested in the maintenance of the
Union; but I am still of opinion that where there are
a hundred millions of men, and forty distinct nations, un-
equally strong, the continuance of the Federal Government can only be a fortunate accident.

Whatever faith I may have in the perfectibility of man,
until human nature is altered, and men wholly transformed, I shall refuse to believe in the duration of a government which is called upon to hold together forty different peoples, disseminated over a territory equal to one
half of Europe in extent; to avoid all rivalry, ambition,
and struggles between them, and to direct their independent activity to the accomplishment of the same designs.

But the greatest peril to which the Union is exposed
by its increase arises from the continual changes which
take place in the position of its internal strength. The
distance from Lake Superior to the Gulf of Mexico extends from the forty-seventh to the thirtieth degree of
latitude, a distance of more than twelve hundred miles as
the bird flies. The frontier of the United States winds
along the whole of this immense line, sometimes falling
within its limits, but more frequently extending far beyond it, into the waste. It has been calculated that the
whites advance every year a mean distance of seventeen
miles along the whole of this vast boundary. Obstacles,
such as an unproductive district, a lake or an Indian nation unexpectedly encountered, are sometimes met with.
The advancing column then halts for a while; its two extremities fall back upon themselves, and as soon as they
are reunited they proceed onward. This gradual and continuous progress of the European race toward the Rocky
Mountains has the solemnity of a providential event; it
is like a deluge of men rising unabatedly, and daily driven
onward by the hand of God.

Within this first line of conquering settlers towns are
built, and vast States founded. In 1790 there were only

a few thousand pioneers sprinkled along the valleys of the
Mississippi; and at the present day these valleys contain
as many inhabitants as were to be found in the whole
Union in 1790. Their population amounts to nearly four
millions.[10] The city of Washington was founded in 1800,
in the very centre of the Union; but such are the changes
which have taken place that it now stands at one of the
extremities; and the delegates of the most remote Western States are already obliged to perform a journey as
long as that from Vienna to Paris.[11]

All the States are borne onward at the same time in
the path of fortune, but of course they do not all increase
and prosper in the same proportion. To the North of
the Union the detached branches of the Alleghany chain,
which extend as far as the Atlantic Ocean, form spacious
roads and ports, which are constantly accessible to vessels
of the greatest burden. But from the Potomac to the
mouth of the Mississippi the coast is sandy and flat. In
this part of the Union the mouths of almost all the rivers
are obstructed; and the few harbours which exist among
these lagoons afford much shallower water to vessels, and
much fewer commercial advantages than those of the
North.

This first natural cause of inferiority is united to
another cause proceeding from the laws. We have
already seen that slavery, which is abolished in the North,
still exists in the South; and I have pointed out its
fatal consequences upon the prosperity of the planter
himself.

The North is therefore superior to the South both in
commerce [12] and manufacture; the natural consequence
of which is the more rapid increase of population and of
wealth within its borders. The States situated upon the
shores of the Atlantic Ocean are already half peopled.
Most of the land is held by an owner; and these districts
can not, therefore, receive so many emigrants as the Western States, where a boundless field is still open to their
exertions. The valley of the Mississippi is far more fertile

than the coast of the Atlantic Ocean. This reason, added to all the others, contributes to drive the Europeans westward—a fact which may be rigorously demonstrated by figures. It is found that the sum total of the population of all the United States has about trebled in the course of forty years. But in the recent States adjacent to the Mississippi the population has increased thirty-one fold within the same space of time.

The relative position of the central Federal power is continually displaced. Forty years ago the majority of the citizens of the Union was established upon the coast of the Atlantic, in the environs of the spot upon which Washington now stands; but the great body of the people is now advancing inland and to the North, so that in twenty years the majority will unquestionably be on the western side of the Alleghanies. If the Union goes on to subsist, the basin of the Mississippi is evidently marked out, by its fertility and its extent, as the future centre of the Federal Government. In thirty or forty years that tract of country will have assumed the rank which naturally belongs to it. It is easy to calculate that its population, compared to that of the coast of the Atlantic, will be, in round numbers, as 40 to 11. In a few years the States which founded the Union will lose the direction of its policy, and the population of the valleys of the Mississippi will preponderate in the Federal assemblies.

This constant gravitation of the Federal power and influence toward the Northwest is shown every ten years, when a general census of the population is made, and the number of delegates which each State sends to Congress is settled afresh.[13] In 1790 Virginia had nineteen representatives in Congress. This number continued to increase until the year 1813, when it reached to twenty-three; from that time it began to decrease, and in 1833 Virginia elected only twenty-one representatives.[14] During the same period the State of New York progressed in the contrary direction: in 1790 it had ten representatives in Congress; in 1813, twenty-seven; in 1823, thirty-four;

and in 1833, forty. The State of Ohio had only one representative in 1803, and in 1833 it had already nineteen.

It is difficult to imagine a durable union of a people which is rich and strong with one which is poor and weak, even if it were proved that the strength and wealth of the one are not the causes of the weakness and poverty of the other. But union is still more difficult to maintain at a time at which one party is losing strength, and the other is gaining it. This rapid and disproportionate increase of certain States threatens the independence of the others. New York might perhaps succeed, with its two millions of inhabitants and its forty representatives, in dictating to the other States in Congress. But even if the more powerful States make no attempt to bear down the lesser ones, the danger still exists; for there is almost as much in the possibility of the act as in the act itself. The weak generally mistrust the justice and the reason of the strong. The States which increase less rapidly than the óthers look upon those which are more favoured by fortune with envy and suspicion. Hence arise the deep-seated uneasiness and ill-defined agitation which are observable in the South, and which form so striking a contrast to the confidence and prosperity which are common to other parts of the Union. I am inclined to think that the hostile measures taken by the Southern provinces upon a recent occasion are attributable to no other cause. The inhabitants of the Southern States are, of all the Americans, those who are most interested in the maintenance of the Union; they would assuredly suffer most from being left to themselves; and yet they are the only citizens who threaten to break the tie of confederation. But it is easy to perceive that the South, which has given four Presidents—Washington, Jefferson, Madison, and Monroe—to the Union, which perceives that it is losing its Federal influence, and that the number of its representatives in Congress is diminishing from year to year, while those of the Northern and Western States are increasing; the South, which is peopled with ardent and irascible beings, is becoming more and more irritated and alarmed. The citizens reflect upon their present position and remember their past influence, with the melancholy uneasiness of men who suspect oppression: if they discover a law of the Union which is not unequivocally favourable to their interests, they protest against it as an abuse of force; and if their ardent remonstrances are not listened to, they threaten to quit an association which loads them with burdens while it deprives them of their due profits. " The tariff," said the inhabitants of Carolina in 1832, " enriches the North, and ruins the South; for if this were not the case, to what can we attribute the continually increasing power and wealth of the North, with its inclement skies and arid soil; while the South, which may be styled the garden of America, is rapidly declining? " [15]

If the changes which I have described were gradual, so that each generation at least might have time to disappear with the order of things under which it had lived, the danger would be less; but the progress of society in America is precipitate, and almost revolutionary. The same citizen may have lived to see his State take the lead in the Union, and afterward become powerless in the Federal assemblies; and an Anglo-American republic has been known to grow as rapidly as a man passing from birth and infancy to maturity in the course of thirty years. It must not be imagined, however, that the States which lose their preponderance also lose their population or their riches: no stop is put to their prosperity, and they even go on to increase more rapidly than any kingdom in Europe.[16] But they believe themselves to be impoverished because their wealth does not augment as rapidly as that of their neighbours; and they think that their power is lost, because they suddenly come into collision with a power greater than their own:[17] thus they are more hurt in their feelings and their passions than in their interests. But this is amply sufficient to endanger the maintenance of the Union. If kings and peoples had only had their true interests in view ever since the beginning of the world, the name of war would scarcely be known among mankind.

Thus the prosperity of the United States is the source of the most serious dangers that threaten them, since it tends to create in some of the confederate States that over-excitement which accompanies a rapid increase of fortune; and to awaken in others those feelings of envy, mistrust, and regret which usually attend upon the loss of it. The Americans contemplate this extraordinary and hasty progress with exultation; but they would be wiser to consider it with sorrow and alarm. The Americans of the United States must inevitably become one of the greatest nations in the world; their offset will cover almost the whole of North America; the continent which they inhabit is their dominion, and it can not escape them. What urges them to take possession of it so soon? Riches, power, and renown can not fail to be theirs at some future time, but they rush upon their fortune as if but a moment remained for them to make it their own.

I think that I have demonstrated that the existence of the present confederation depends entirely on the continued assent of all the confederates; and, starting from this principle, I have inquired into the causes which may induce the several States to separate from the others. The Union may, however, perish in two different ways: one of the confederate States may choose to retire from the compact, and so forcibly to sever the Federal tie; and it is to this supposition that most of the remarks that I have made apply: or the authority of the Federal Government may be progressively intrenched on by the simultaneous tendency of the united republics to resume their independence. The central power, successively stripped of all its prerogatives, and reduced to impotence by tacit consent, would become incompetent to fulfil its purpose; and the second Union would perish, like the first, by a sort of senile inaptitude. The gradual weakening of the Federal tie, which may finally lead to the dissolution of the Union, is a distinct circumstance, that may produce a variety of minor consequences before it operates so violent a change. The confederation might still subsist, although its Government were reduced to such a degree of inanition as to paralyze the nation, to cause internal anarchy, and to check the general prosperity of the country.

After having investigated the causes which may induce the Anglo-Americans to disunite, it is important to inquire whether, if the Union continues to subsist, their Government will extend or contract its sphere of action, and whether it will become more energetic or more weak.

The Americans are evidently disposed to look upon their future condition with alarm. They perceive that in most of the nations of the world the exercise of the rights of sovereignty tends to fall under the control of a few individuals, and they are dismayed by the idea that such will also be the case in their own country. Even the statesmen feel, or affect to feel, these fears; for, in America, centralization is by no means popular, and there is no surer means of courting the majority than by inveighing against the encroachments of the central power. The Americans do not perceive that the countries in which this alarming tendency to centralization exists are inhabited by a single people; while the fact of the Union being composed of different confederate communities is sufficient to baffle all the inferences which might be drawn from analogous circumstances. I confess that I am inclined to consider the fears of a great number of Americans as purely imaginary; and far from participating in their dread of the consolidation of power in the hands of the Union, I think that the Federal Government is visibly losing strength.

To prove this assertion I shall not have recourse to any remote occurrences, but to circumstances which I have myself witnessed, and which belong to our own time.

An attentive examination of what is going on in the United States will easily convince us that two opposite tendencies exist in that country, like two distinct currents

flowing in contrary directions in the same channel. The
Union has now existed for forty-five years, and in the
course of that time a vast number of provincial prejudices,
which were at first hostile to its power, have died away.
The patriotic feeling which attached each of the Americans
to his own native State is become less exclusive; and the
different parts of the Union have become more intimately
connected the better they have become acquainted with
each other. The Post,[18] that great instrument of intellectual intercourse, now reaches into the backwoods; and
steamboats have established daily means of communication between the different points of the coast. An inland
navigation of unexampled rapidity conveys commodities
up and down the rivers of the country.[19] And to these
facilities of Nature and art may be added those restless
cravings, that busy-mindedness, and love of pelf, which are
constantly urging the American into active life, and bringing him into contact with his fellow-citizens. He crosses
the country in every direction; he visits all the various
populations of the land; and there is not a province in
France in which the natives are so well known to each
other as the thirteen millions of men who cover the territory of the United States.

But while the Americans intermingle, they grow in resemblance of each other; the differences resulting from
their climate, their origin, and their institutions, diminish;
and they all draw nearer and nearer to the common type.
Every year thousands of men leave the North to settle in
different parts of the Union: they bring with them their
faith, their opinions, and their manners; and as they are
more enlightened than the men among whom they are
about to dwell, they soon rise to the head of affairs, and
they adapt society to their own advantage. This continual
emigration of the North to the South is peculiarly favourable to the fusion of all the different provincial characters
into one national character. The civilization of the North
appears to be the common standard, to which the whole
nation will one day be assimilated.

The commercial ties which unite the confederate States are strengthened by the increasing manufactures of the Americans, and the union which began to exist in their opinions gradually forms a part of their habits: the course of time has swept away the bugbear thoughts which haunted the imaginations of the citizens in 1789. The Federal power is not become oppressive; it has not destroyed the independence of the States; it has not subjected the confederates to monarchical institutions; and the Union has not rendered the lesser States dependent upon the larger ones; but the confederation has continued to increase in population, in wealth, and in power. I am therefore convinced that the natural obstacles to the continuance of the American Union are not so powerful at the present time as they were in 1789; and that the enemies of the Union are not so numerous.

Nevertheless, a careful examination of the history of the United States for the last forty-five years will readily convince us that the Federal power is declining; nor is it difficult to explain the causes of this phenomenon. When the Constitution of 1789 was promulgated, the nation was a prey to anarchy; the Union, which succeeded this confusion, excited much dread and much animosity; but it was warmly supported because it satisfied an imperious want. Thus, although it was more attacked than it is now, the Federal power soon reached the maximum of its authority, as is usually the case with a government which triumphs after having braced its strength by the struggle. At that time the interpretation of the Constitution seemed to extend, rather than to repress, the Federal sovereignty; and the Union offered, in several respects, the appearance of a single and undivided people, directed in its foreign and internal policy by a single Government. But to attain this point the people had risen, to a certain extent, above itself.

The Constitution had not destroyed the distinct sovereignty of the States; and all communities, of whatever nature they may be, are impelled by a secret propensity to assert their independence. This propensity is still more decided in a country like America, in which every village forms a sort of republic accustomed to conduct its own affairs. It therefore cost the States an effort to submit to the Federal supremacy; and all efforts, however successful they may be, necessarily subside with the causes in which they originated.

As the Federal Government consolidated its authority, America resumed its rank among the nations, peace returned to its frontiers, and public credit was restored; confusion was succeeded by a fixed state of things, which was favourable to the full and free exercise of industrious enterprise. It was this very prosperity which made the Americans forget the cause to which it was attributable; and when once the danger was passed, the energy and the patriotism which had enabled them to brave it disappeared from among them. No sooner were they delivered from the cares which oppressed them than they easily returned to their ordinary habits, and gave themselves up without resistance to their natural inclinations. When a powerful Government no longer appeared to be necessary, they once more began to think it irksome. The Union encouraged a general prosperity, and the States were not inclined to abandon the Union; but they desired to render the action of the power which represented that body as light as possible. The general principle of Union was adopted, but in every minor detail there was an actual tendency to independence. The principle of confederation was every day more easily admitted, and more rarely applied; so that the Federal Government brought about its own decline, while it was creating order and peace.

As soon as this tendency of public opinion began to be manifested externally, the leaders of parties, who live by the passions of the people, began to work it to their own advantage. The position of the Federal Government then became exceedingly critical. Its enemies were in possession of the popular favour; and they obtained the right of conducting its policy by pledging themselves to lessen its influence. From that time forward the Government of the Union has invariably been obliged to recede as often as it has attempted to enter the lists with the Governments of the States. And whenever an interpretation of the terms of the Federal Constitution has been called for, that interpretation has most frequently been opposed to the Union, and favourable to the States.

The Constitution invested the Federal Government with the right of providing for the interests of the nation; and it had been held that no other authority was so fit to superintend the "internal improvements" which affected the prosperity of the whole Union; such, for instance, as the cutting of canals. But the States were alarmed at a power, distinct from their own, which could thus dispose of a portion of their territory; and they were afraid that the central Government would, by this means, acquire a formidable extent of patronage within their own confines, and exercise a degree of influence which they intended to reserve exclusively to their own agents. The democratic party, which has constantly been opposed to the increase of the Federal authority, then accused the Congress of usurpation, and the Chief Magistrate of ambition. The central Government was intimidated by the opposition; and it soon acknowledged its error, promising exactly to confine its influence for the future within the circle which was prescribed to it.

The Constitution confers upon the Union the right of treating with foreign nations. The Indian tribes, which border upon the frontiers of the United States, had usually been regarded in this light. As long as these savages consented to retire before the civilized settlers, the Federal right was not contested: but as soon as an Indian tribe attempted to fix its dwelling upon a given spot, the adjacent States claimed possession of the lands and the rights of sovereignty over the natives. The central Government soon recognised both these claims; and after it had concluded treaties with the Indians as independent nations, it gave them up as subjects to the legislative tyranny of the States.[20]

Some of the States which had been founded upon the coast of the Atlantic extended indefinitely to the West, into wild regions where no European had ever penetrated. The States whose confines were irrevocably fixed looked with a jealous eye upon the unbounded regions which the future would enable their neighbours to explore. The latter then agreed, with a view to conciliate the others, and to facilitate the Act of Union, to lay down their own boundaries, and to abandon all the territory which lay beyond those limits to the confederation at large.[21]   Thenceforward the Federal Government became the owner of all the uncultivated lands which lie beyond the borders of the thirteen States first confederated. It was invested with the right of parcelling and selling them, and the sums derived from this source were exclusively reserved to the public treasure of the Union, in order to furnish supplies for purchasing tracts of country from the Indians, for opening roads to the remote settlements, and for accelerating the increase of civilization as much as possible. New States have, however, been formed in the course of time, in the midst of those wilds which were formerly ceded by the inhabitants of the shores of the Atlantic. Congress has gone on to sell, for the profit of the nation at large, the uncultivated lands which those new States contained. But the latter at length asserted that, as they were now fully constituted, they ought to enjoy the exclusive right of converting the produce of these sales to their own use. As their remonstrances became more and more threatening, Congress thought fit to deprive the Union of a portion of the privileges which it had hitherto enjoyed; and at the end of 1832 it passed a law by which the greatest part of the revenue derived from the sale of lands was made over to the new western republics, although the lands themselves were not ceded to them.[22]

The slightest observation in the United States enables one to appreciate the advantages which the country de-

rives from the Bank.   These advantages are of several
kinds, but one of them is peculiarly striking to the stranger.
The bank-notes of the United States are taken upon the
borders of the deserts for the same value as at Philadelphia,
where the Bank conducts its operations.[23]

The Bank of the United States is nevertheless the object of great animosity.   Its directors have proclaimed their
hostility to the President: and they are accused, not without some show of probability, of having abused their influence to thwart his election.   The President, therefore,
attacks the establishment which they represent with all the
warmth of personal enmity; and he is encouraged in the
pursuit of his revenge by the conviction that he is supported by the secret propensities of the majority.   The
Bank may be regarded as the great monetary tie of the
Union, just as Congress is the great legislative tie; and the
same passions which tend to render the States independent of the central power contribute to the overthrow of
the Bank.

The Bank of the United States always holds a great
number of the notes issued by the provincial banks, which
it can at any time oblige them to convert into cash.   It has
itself nothing to fear from a similar demand, as the extent
of its resources enables it to meet all claims.   But the existence of the provincial banks is thus threatened, and their
operations are restricted, since they are only able to issue
a quantity of notes duly proportioned to their capital.
They submit with impatience to this salutary control.   The
newspapers which they have bought over, and the President, whose interest renders him their instrument, attack
the Bank with the greatest vehemence.   They rouse the
local passions and the blind democratic instinct of the
country to aid their cause; and they assert that the Bank
directors form a permanent aristocratic body, whose influence must ultimately be felt in the Government, and
must affect those principles of equality upon which society
rests in America.

The contest between the Bank and its opponents is

only an incident in the great struggle which is going on in America between the provinces and the central power; between the spirit of democratic independence and the spirit of gradation and subordination. I do not mean that the enemies of the Bank are identically the same individuals who, on other points, attack the Federal Government; but I assert that the attacks directed against the Bank of the United States originate in the same propensities which militate against the Federal Government; and that the very numerous opponents of the former afford a deplorable symptom of the decreasing support of the latter.

The Union has never displayed so much weakness as in the celebrated question of the tariff. The wars of the French Revolution and of 1812 had created manufacturing establishments in the North of the Union by cutting off all free communication between America and Europe. When peace was concluded, and the channel of intercourse re-opened by which the produce of Europe was transmitted to the New World, the Americans thought fit to establish a system of import duties, for the twofold purpose of protecting their incipient manufactures and of paying off the amount of the debt contracted during the war. The Southern States, which have no manufactures to encourage, and which are exclusively agricultural, soon complained of this measure. Such were the simple facts, and I do not pretend to examine in this place whether their complaints were well founded or unjust.

As early as the year 1820 South Carolina declared, in a petition to Congress, that the tariff was " unconstitutional, oppressive, and unjust." And the States of Georgia, Virginia, North Carolina, Alabama, and Mississippi subsequently remonstrated against it with more or less vigour. But Congress, far from lending an ear to these complaints, raised the scale of tariff duties in the years 1824 and 1828, and recognised anew the principle on which it was founded. A doctrine was then proclaimed, or rather revived, in the South, which took the name of Nullification.

I have shown in the proper place that the object of the

Federal Constitution was not to form a league, but to create a national Government. The Americans of the United States form a sole and undivided people, in all the cases which are specified by that Constitution; and upon these points the will of the nation is expressed, as it is in all constitutional nations, by the voice of the majority. When the majority has pronounced its decision, it is the duty of the minority to submit. Such is the sound legal doctrine, and the only one which agrees with the text of the Constitution, and the known intention of those who framed it.

The partisans of Nullification in the South maintain, on the contrary, that the intention of the Americans in uniting was not to reduce themselves to the condition of one and the same people; that they meant to constitute a league of independent States; and that each State, consequently, retains its entire sovereignty, if not de facto, at least de jure; and has the right of putting its own construction upon the laws of Congress, and of suspending their execution within the limits of its own territory, if they are held to be unconstitutional and unjust.

The entire doctrine of nullification is comprised in a sentence uttered by Vice-President Calhoun, the head of that party in the South, before the Senate of the United States, in the year 1833: " The Constitution is a compact to which the States were parties in their sovereign capacity; now, whenever a compact is entered into by parties which acknowledge no tribunal above their authority to decide in the last resort, each of them has a right to judge for itself in relation to the nature, extent, and obligations of the instrument." It is evident that a similar doctrine destroys the very basis of the Federal Constitution, and brings back all the evils of the old Confederation, from which the Americans were supposed to have had a safe deliverance.

When South Carolina perceived that Congress turned a deaf ear to its remonstrances, it threatened to apply the doctrine of nullification to the Federal tariff bill. Congress persisted in its former system; and at length the storm

31

broke out. In the course of 1832 the citizens of South
Carolina [24] named a National Convention to consult upon
the extraordinary measures which they were called upon
to take; and on the 24th of November of the same year
this convention promulgated a law, under the form of a
decree, which annulled the Federal law of the tariff, forbade the levy of the imposts which that law commands,
and refused to recognise the appeal which might be made
to the Federal courts of law.[25] This decree was only to
be put in execution in the ensuing month of February, and
it was intimated that if Congress modified the tariff before
that period South Carolina might be induced to proceed
no further with her menaces; and a vague desire was
afterward expressed of submitting the question to an extraordinary assembly of all the confederate States.

In the meantime South Carolina armed her militia, and
prepared for war. But Congress, which had slighted its
suppliant subjects, listened to their complaints as soon as
they were found to have taken up arms.[26] A law was
passed, by which the tariff duties were to be progressively
reduced for ten years, until they were brought so low as
not to exceed the amount of supplies necessary to the
Government.[27] Thus Congress completely abandoned the
principle of the tariff, and substituted a mere fiscal impost
for a system of protective duties.[28] The Government of
the Union, in order to conceal its defeat, had recourse to
an expedient which is very much in vogue with feeble governments. It yielded the point de facto, but it remained
inflexible upon the principles in question; and while Congress was altering the tariff law, it passed another bill, by
which the President was invested with extraordinary powers, enabling him to overcome by force a resistance which
was then no longer to be apprehended.

But South Carolina did not consent to leave the Union
in the enjoyment of these scanty trophies of success: the
same national convention which had annulled the tariff
bill met again, and accepted the proffered concession; but
at the same time it declared its unabated perseverance in

the doctrine of nullification: and to prove what it said, it annulled the law investing the President with extraordinary powers, although it was very certain that the clauses of that law would never be carried into effect.

Almost all the controversies of which I have been speaking have taken place under the presidency of General Jackson; and it can not be denied that in the question of the tariff he has supported the claims of the Union with vigour and with skill. I am, however, of opinion that the conduct of the individual who now represents the Federal Government may be reckoned as one of the dangers which threaten its continuance.

Some persons in Europe have formed an opinion of the possible influence of General Jackson upon the affairs of his country, which appears highly extravagant to those who have seen more of the subject. We have been told that General Jackson has won sundry battles, that he is an energetic man, prone by nature and by habit to the use of force, covetous of power, and a despot by taste. All this may perhaps be true; but the inferences which have been drawn from these truths are exceedingly erroneous. It has been imagined that General Jackson is bent on establishing a dictatorship in America, on introducing a military spirit, and on giving a degree of influence to the central authority which can not but be dangerous to provincial liberties. But in America the time for similar undertakings, and the age for men of this kind, is not yet come: if General Jackson had entertained a hope of exercising his authority in this manner, he would infallibly have forfeited his political station, and compromised his life; accordingly, he has not been so imprudent as to make any such attempt.

Far from wishing to extend the Federal power, the President belongs to the party which is desirous of limiting that power to the bare and precise letter of the Constitution, and which never puts a construction upon that act favourable to the Government of the Union; far from standing forth as the champion of centralization, General

Jackson is the agent of all the jealousies of the States; and
he was placed in the lofty station he occupies by the passions of the people which are most opposed to the central
Government. It is by perpetually flattering these passions
that he maintains his station and his popularity. General
Jackson is the slave of the majority: he yields to its wishes,
its propensities, and its demands; say rather, that he an-
ticipates and forestalls them.

Whenever the Governments of the States come into
collision with that of the Union, the President is generally
the first to question his own rights: he almost always out-
strips the legislature; and when the extent of the Federal
power is controverted, he takes part, as it were, against
himself; he conceals his official interests, and extinguishes
his own natural inclinations. Not, indeed, that he is naturally weak or hostile to the Union; for when the majority
decided against the claims of the partisans of nullification,
he put himself at its head, asserted the doctrines which
the nation held distinctly and energetically, and was the
first to recommend forcible measures; but General Jackson appears to me, if I may use the American expressions,
to be a Federalist by taste and a Republican by calculation.

General Jackson stoops to gain the favour of the majority, but when he feels that his popularity is secure, he
overthrows all obstacles in the pursuit of the objects which
the community approves, or of those which it does not
look upon with a jealous eye. He is supported by a power
with which his predecessors were unacquainted; and he
tramples on his personal enemies whenever they cross his
path with a facility which no former President ever enjoyed; he takes upon himself the responsibility of measures
which no one before him would have ventured to attempt:
he even treats the national representatives with disdain
approaching to insult; he puts his veto upon the laws of
Congress, and frequently neglects to reply to that powerful body. He is a favourite who sometimes treats his
master roughly. The power of General Jackson perpetually increases; but that of the President declines; in his

ANDREW JACKSON.

Photogravure from a lithograph after a daguerreotype by Brady.

hands the Federal Government is strong, but it will pass enfeebled into the hands of his successor.

I am strangely mistaken if the Federal Government of the United States be not constantly losing strength, retiring gradually from public affairs, and narrowing its circle of action more and more. It is naturally feeble, but it now abandons even its pretensions to strength. On the other hand, I thought that I remarked a more lively sense of independence, and a more decided attachment to provincial government, in the States. The Union is to subsist, but to subsist as a shadow; it is to be strong in certain cases, and weak in all others; in time of warfare, it is to be able to concentrate all the forces of the nation and all the resources of the country in its hands; and in time of peace its existence is to be scarcely perceptible: as if this alternate debility and vigour were natural or possible.

I do not foresee anything for the present which may be able to check this general impulse of public opinion; the causes in which it originated do not cease to operate with the same effect. The change will therefore go on, and it may be predicted that, unless some extraordinary event occurs, the Government of the Union will grow weaker and weaker every day.

I think, however, that the period is still remote at which the Federal power will be entirely extinguished by its inability to protect itself and to maintain peace in the country. The Union is sanctioned by the manners and desires of the people; its results are palpable, its benefits visible. When it is perceived that the weakness of the Federal Government compromises the existence of the Union, I do not doubt that a reaction will take place with a view to increase its strength.

The Government of the United States is, of all the Federal Governments which have hitherto been established, the one which is most naturally destined to act. As long as it is only indirectly assailed by the interpretation of its laws, and as long as its substance is not seriously altered, a change of opinion, an internal crisis, or a war, may restore all the vigour which it requires. The point which I have been most anxious to put in a clear light is simply this: Many people, especially in France, imagine that a change in opinion is going on in the United States, which is favourable to a centralization of power in the hands of the President and the Congress. I hold that a contrary tendency may distinctly be observed. So far is the Federal Government from acquiring strength, and from threatening the sovereignty of the States, as it grows older, that I maintain it to be growing weaker and weaker, and that the sovereignty of the Union alone is in danger. Such are the facts which the present time discloses. The future conceals the final result of this tendency, and the events which may check, retard, or accelerate the changes I have described; but I do not affect to be able to remove the veil which hides them from our sight.

The dismemberment of the Union, by the introduction of war into the hearts of those States which are now confederate, with standing armies, a dictatorship, and a heavy taxation, might eventually compromise the fate of the republican institutions. But we ought not to confound the future prospects of the republic with those of the Union. The Union is an accident, which will only last as long as circumstances are favourable to its existence; but a republican form of Government seems to me to be the natural state of the Americans; which nothing but the continued action of hostile causes, always acting in the same direction, could change into a monarchy. The Union exists principally in the law which formed it; one revolution, one change in public opinion, might destroy it forever; but the republic has a much deeper foundation to rest upon.

What is understood by a republican government in the United States is the slow and quiet action of society upon itself. It is a regular state of things really founded upon the enlightened will of the people. It is a conciliatory government under which resolutions are allowed time to ripen; and in which they are deliberately discussed, and executed with mature judgment. The republicans in the

United States set a high value upon morality, respect religious belief, and acknowledge the existence of rights. They profess to think that a people ought to be moral, religious, and temperate, in proportion as it is free. What is called the republic in the United States is the tranquil rule of the majority, which, after having had time to examine itself, and to give proof of its existence, is the common source of all the powers of the State. But the power of the majority is not of itself unlimited. In the moral world humanity, justice, and reason enjoy an undisputed supremacy; in the political world vested rights are treated with no less deference. The majority recognises these two barriers; and if it now and then oversteps them, it is because, like individuals, it has passions, and, like them, it is prone to do what is wrong, while it discerns what is right.

But the demagogues of Europe have made strange discoveries. A republic is not, according to them, the rule of the majority, as has hitherto been thought, but the rule of those who are strenuous partisans of the majority. It is not the people who preponderates in this kind of government, but those who are best versed in the good qualities of the people. A happy distinction, which allows men to act in the name of nations without consulting them, and to claim their gratitude while their rights are spurned. A republican government, moreover, is the only one which claims the right of doing whatever it chooses, and despising what men have hitherto respected, from the highest moral obligations to the vulgar rules of common sense. It had been supposed, until our time, that despotism was odious, under whatever form it appeared. But it is a discovery of modern days that there are such things as legitimate tyranny and holy injustice, provided they are exercised in the name of the people.

The ideas which the Americans have adopted respecting the republican form of government, render it easy for them to live under it, and endure its duration. If, in their country, this form often be practically bad, it is at least theoretically good; and, in the end, the people always acts in conformity to it.

It was impossible at the foundation of the States, and it would still be difficult, to establish a central administration in America. The inhabitants are dispersed over too great a space, and separated by too many natural obstacles, for one man to undertake to direct the details of their existence. America is therefore pre-eminently the country of provincial and municipal government. To this cause, which was plainly felt by all the Europeans of the New World, the Anglo-Americans added several others peculiar to themselves.

At the time of the settlement of the North American colonies, municipal liberty had already penetrated into the laws as well as the manners of the English; and the emigrants adopted it, not only as a necessary thing, but as a benefit which they knew how to appreciate. We have already seen the manner in which the colonies were founded: every province, and almost every district, was peopled separately by men who were strangers to each other, or who associated with very different purposes. The English settlers in the United States, therefore, early perceived that they were divided into a great number of small and distinct communities which belonged to no common centre; and that it was needful for each of these little communities to take care of its own affairs, since there did not appear to be any central authority which was naturally bound and easily enabled to provide for them. Thus, the nature of the country, the manner in which the British colonies were founded, the habits of the first emigrants, in short, everything, united to promote, in an extraordinary degree, municipal and provincial liberties.

In the United States, therefore, the mass of the institutions of the country is essentially republican; and in order permanently to destroy the laws which form the basis of the republic, it would be necessary to abolish all the laws at once. At the present day it would be even more difficult for a party to succeed in founding a monarchy in the

United States than for a set of men to proclaim that France should henceforward be a republic. Royalty would not find a system of legislation prepared for it beforehand; and a monarchy would then exist, really surrounded by republican institutions. The monarchical principle would likewise have great difficulty in penetrating into the manners of the Americans.

In the United States, the sovereignty of the people is not an isolated doctrine bearing no relation to the prevailing manners and ideas of the people: it may, on the contrary, be regarded as the last link of a chain of opinions which binds the whole Anglo-American world. That Providence has given to every human being the degree of reason necessary to direct himself in the affairs which interest him exclusively; such is the grand maxim upon which civil and political society rests in the United States. The father of a family applies it to his children; the master to his servants; the township to its officers; the province to its townships; the State to the provinces; the Union to the State; and when extended to the nation, it becomes the doctrine of the sovereignty of the people.

Thus, in the United States, the fundamental principle of the republic is the same which governs the greater part of human actions; republican notions insinuate themselves into all the ideas, opinions, and habits of the Americans, while they are formally recognised by the legislation: and before this legislation can be altered the whole community must undergo very serious changes. In the United States, even the religion of most of the citizens is republican, since it submits the truths of the other world to private judgment: as in politics the care of its temporal interests is abandoned to the good sense of the people. Thus every man is allowed freely to take that road which he thinks will lead him to heaven; just as the law permits every citizen to have the right of choosing his government.

It is evident that nothing but a long series of events, all having the same tendency, can substitute for this combination of laws, opinions, and manners a mass of opposite opinions, manners, and laws.

If republican principles are to perish in America, they can only yield after a laborious social process, often interrupted, and as often resumed; they will have many apparent revivals, and will not become totally extinct until an entirely new people shall have succeeded to that which now exists. Now, it must be admitted that there is no symptom or presage of the approach of such a revolution. There is nothing more striking to a person newly arrived in the United States than the kind of tumultuous agitation in which he finds political society. The laws are incessantly changing, and at first sight it seems impossible that a people so variable in its desires should avoid adopting, within a short space of time, a completely new form of government. Such apprehensions are, however, premature; the instability which affects political institutions is of two kinds, which ought not to be confounded: the first, which modifies secondary laws, is not incompatible with a very settled state of society; the other shakes the very foundations of the Constitution, and attacks the fundamental principles of legislation; this species of instability is always followed by troubles and revolutions, and the nation which suffers under it is in a state of violent transition.

Experience shows that these two kinds of legislative instability have no necessary connection; for they have been found united or separate, according to times and circumstances. The first is common in the United States, but not the second: the Americans often change their laws, but the foundation of the Constitution is respected.

In our days the republican principle rules in America, as the monarchical principle did in France under Louis XIV. The French of that period were not only friends of the monarchy, but they thought it impossible to put anything in its place; they received it as we receive the rays of the sun and the return of the seasons. Among them the royal power had neither advocates nor opponents. In like manner does the republican Government exist in

America, without contention or opposition; without proofs
and arguments, by a tacit agreement, a sort of consensus
universalis. It is, however, my opinion that by changing
their administrative forms as often as they do, the inhabitants of the United States compromise the future stability
of their Government.

It may be apprehended that men, perpetually thwarted
in their designs by the mutability of the legislation, will
learn to look upon republican institutions as an inconvenient form of society; the evil resulting from the instability of the secondary enactments might then raise a doubt
as to the nature of the fundamental principles of the Constitution, and indirectly bring about a revolution; but this
epoch is still very remote.

It may, however, be foreseen even now that when the
Americans lose their republican institutions they will speedily arrive at a despotic Government, without a long interval of limited monarchy.   Montesquieu remarked that
nothing is more absolute than the authority of a prince
who immediately succeeds a republic, since the powers
which had fearlessly been intrusted to an elected magistrate are then transferred to an hereditary sovereign. This
is true in general, but it is more peculiarly applicable to a
democratic republic.   In the United States, the magistrates
are not elected by a particular class of citizens, but by the
majority of the nation; they are the immediate representatives of the passions of the multitude; and as they are
wholly dependent upon its pleasure, they excite neither hatred nor fear: hence, as I have already shown, very little care
has been taken to limit their influence, and they are left in
possession of a vast deal of arbitrary power. This state of
things has engendered habits which would outlive itself; the
American magistrate would retain his power, but he would
cease to be responsible for the exercise of it; and it is impossible to say what bounds could then be set to tyranny.

Some of our European politicians expect to see an aristocracy arise in America, and they already predict the
exact period at which it will be able to assume the reins

of government. I have previously observed, and I repeat my assertion, that the present tendency of American society appears to me to become more and more democratic. Nevertheless, I do not assert that the Americans will not, at some future time, restrict the circle of political rights in their country, or confiscate those rights to the advantage of a single individual; but I can not imagine that they will ever bestow the exclusive exercise of them upon a privileged class of citizens, or, in other words, that they will ever found an aristocracy.

An aristocratic body is composed of a certain number of citizens who, without being very far removed from the mass of the people are, nevertheless, permanently stationed above it: a body which it is easy to touch and difficult to strike; with which the people are in daily contact, but with which they never can combine. Nothing can be imagined more contrary to Nature and to the secret propensities of the human heart than a subjection of this kind; and men who are left to follow their own bent will always prefer the arbitrary power of a king to the regular administration of an aristocracy. Aristocratic institutions can not subsist without laying down the inequality of men as a fundamental principle, as a part and parcel of the legislation, affecting the condition of the human family as much as it affects that of society; but these are things so repugnant to natural equity that they can only be extorted from men by constraint.

I do not think a single people can be quoted, since human society began to exist, which has, by its own free will and by its own exertions, created an aristocracy within its own bosom. All the aristocracies of the Middle Ages were founded by military conquest; the conqueror was the noble, the vanquished became the serf. Inequality was then imposed by force; and after it had been introduced into the manners of the country it maintained its own authority, and was sanctioned by the legislation. Communities have existed which were aristocratic from their earliest origin, owing to circumstances anterior to that event, and which became more democratic in each succeeding age. Such was the destiny of the Romans, and of the barbarians after them. But a people, having taken its rise in civilization and democracy, which should gradually establish an inequality of conditions, until it arrived at inviolable privileges and exclusive castes, would be a novelty in the world; and nothing intimates that America is likely to furnish so singular an example.

NOTES

[1] See the conduct of the Northern States in the War of 1812. "During that war," says Jefferson in a letter to General Lafayette, "four of the Eastern States were only attached to the Union, like so many inanimate bodies to living men."

[2] The profound peace of the Union affords no pretext for a standing army; and without a standing army a government is not prepared to profit by a favourable opportunity to conquer resistance, and take the sovereign power by surprise.

[3] Thus the province of Holland in the republic of the Low Countries, and the Emperor in the Germanic Confederation, have sometimes put themselves in the place of the Union, and have employed the Federal authority to their own advantage.

[4] It is scarcely necessary for me to observe that by the expression Anglo-Americans I only mean to designate the great majority of the nation; for a certain number of isolated individuals are of course to be met with holding very different opinions.

[5] Census of 1790, 3,929,328; census of 1830, 12,856,165; census of 1860, 31,443,321; census of 1890, 62,622,250.

[6] This indeed is only a temporary danger. I have no doubt that in time society will assume as much stability and regularity in the West as it has already done upon the coast of the Atlantic Ocean.

[7] Pennsylvania contained 431,373 inhabitants in 1790.

[8] The area of the State of New York is about 46,000 square miles.

[9] If the population continues to double every twenty-two years, as it has done for the last two hundred years, the number of inhabitants in the United States in 1852 will be twenty millions; in 1874, forty-eight millions; and in 1896, ninety-six millions. This may still be the case even if the lands on the western slope of the Rocky Mountains should be found to be unfit for cultivation. The territory which is already occupied can easily contain this number of inhabitants. One hundred millions of men disseminated over the surface of the twenty-four States and the three dependencies, which constitute the Union, would only give 762 inhabitants to the square league; this would be far below the mean population of France, which is 1,063 to the square league; or of England, which is 1,457; and it would even be below the population of Switzerland, for that country, notwithstanding its lakes and mountains, contains 783 inhabitants to the square league.

[10] 3,672,317; census of 1830.

[11] The distance from Jefferson, the capital of the State of Missouri, to Washington is 1,019 miles.

[12] The following statements will suffice to show the difference which exists between the commerce of the South and that of the North:

"In 1829 the tonnage of all the merchant vessels belonging to Virginia, the two Carolinas, and Georgia (the four great Southern States), amounted to only 5,243 tons. In the same year the tonnage of the vessels of the State of Massachusetts alone amounted to 17,322 tons. Thus the State of Massachusetts had three times as much shipping as the four above-mentioned States. Nevertheless the area of the State of Massachusetts is only 7,335 square miles, and its population amounts to 610,014 inhabitants; while the area of the four other States I have quoted is 210,000 square miles, and their population 3,047,767. Thus the area of the State of Massachusetts forms only one-thirtieth part of the area of the four States, and its population is five times smaller than theirs. Slavery is prejudicial to the commercial prosperity of the South in several different ways; by diminishing the spirit of enterprise among the whites, and by preventing them from meeting with as numerous a class of sailors as they require. Sailors are usually taken from the lowest ranks of the population. But in the Southern States these lowest ranks are composed of slaves, and it is very difficult to employ them at sea. They are unable to serve as well as a white crew, and apprehensions would always be entertained of their mutinying in the middle of the ocean, or of their escaping in the foreign countries at which they might touch.

[13] It may be seen that in the course of the last ten years (1820–1830) the population of one district—as, for instance, the State of Delaware—has increased in the proportion of 5 per cent.; while that of another—as the Territory of Michigan—has increased 250 per cent. Thus the population of Virginia had augmented 13 per cent., and that of the border State of Ohio 61 per cent., in the same space of time. The general table of these changes, which is given in the "National Calendar," displays a striking picture of the unequal fortunes of the different States.

[14] It has just been said that in the course of the last term the population of Virginia has increased 13 per cent.; and it is necessary to explain how the number of representatives for a State may decrease, when the population of that State, far from diminishing, is actually upon the increase. I take the State of Virginia, to which I have already alluded, as my term of comparison. The number of representatives of Virginia in 1823 was proportionate to the total number of representatives of the Union, and to the relation which the population bore to that of the whole Union: in 1833 the number of representatives of Virginia was likewise proportionate to the total number of the representatives of the Union, and to the relation which its population, augmented in the course of ten years, bore to the augmented population of the Union in the same space of time. The new number of Virginian representatives will then be to the old number, on the one hand, as the new number of all the representatives is to the old number; and, on the other hand, as the augmentation of the population of Virginia is to that of the whole population of the country. Thus, if the increase of the population of the lesser country be to that of

the greater in an exact inverse ratio of the proportion between the new and the old numbers of all the representatives, the number of the representatives of Virginia will remain stationary ; and if the increase of the Virginian population be to that of the whole Union in a feebler ratio than the new number of the representatives of the Union to the old number, the number of the representatives of Virginia must decrease.

[15] See the report of its committee to the Convention which proclaimed the nullification of the tariff in South Carolina.

[16] The population of a country assuredly constitutes the first element of its wealth. In the ten years (1820–1830) during which Virginia lost two of its representatives in Congress, its population increased in the proportion of 13.7 per cent. ; that of Carolina in the proportion of 15 per cent. ; and that of Georgia 15.5 per cent. But the population of Russia, which increases more rapidly than that of any other European country, only augments in ten years at the rate of 9.5 per cent. ; in France, at the rate of 7 per cent. ; and in Europe in general at the rate of 4.7 per cent.

[17] It must be admitted, however, that the depreciation which has taken place in the value of tobacco during the last fifty years has notably diminished the opulence of the Southern planters ; but this circumstance is as independent of the will of their Northern brethren as it is of their own.

[18] In 1832, the district of Michigan, which only contains 31,639 inhabitants, and is still an almost unexplored wilderness, possesses 940 miles of mail-roads. The Territory of Arkansas, which is still more uncultivated, was already intersected by 1,938 miles of mail-roads. The postage of newspapers alone in the whole Union amounted to 254,796 dollars.

[19] In the course of ten years, from 1821 to 1831, 271 steamboats have been launched upon the rivers which water the valley of the Mississippi alone. In 1829, 259 steamboats existed in the United States.

[20] See in the " Legislative Documents." already quoted in speaking of the Indians, the letter of the President of the United States to the Cherokees, his correspondence on this subject with his agents, and his messages to Congress.

[21] The first act of cession was made by the State of New York in 1780 ; Virginia, Massachusetts, Connecticut, South and North Carolina, followed this example at different times, and, lastly, the act of cession of Georgia was made as recently as 1802.

[22] It is true that the President refused his assent to this law, but he completely adopted it in principle.

[23] The present Bank of the United States was established in 1816, with a capital of 35,000,000 dollars ; its charter expires in 1836. Last year Congress passed a law to renew it, but the President put his veto upon the bill. The struggle is still going on with great violence on either side, and the speedy fall of the Bank may easily be foreseen.

[24] That is to say, the majority of the people ; for the opposite party, called the Union party, always formed a very strong and active minority. Carolina may contain about 47,000 electors ; 30,000 were in favour of nullification, and 17,000 opposed to it.

[25] This decree was preceded by a report of the committee by which it was framed, containing the explanation of the motives and object of the

law.   The following passage occurs in it : " When the rights reserved by the Constitution to the different States are deliberately violated, it is the duty and the right of those States to interfere, in order to check the progress of the evil ; to resist usurpation, and to maintain within their respective limits those powers and privileges which belong to them as independent sovereign States.   If they were destitute of this right, they would not be sovereign.   South Carolina declares that she acknowledges no tribunal upon earth above her authority.   She has indeed entered into a solemn compact of union with the other States ; but she demands, and will exercise, the right of putting her own construction upon it ; and when this compact is violated by her sister States, and by the Government which they have created, she is determined to avail herself of the unquestionable right of judging what is the extent of the infraction, and what are the measures best fitted to obtain justice."

[26] Congress was finally decided to take this step by the conduct of the powerful State of Virginia, whose legislature offered to serve as mediator between the Union and South Carolina.   Hitherto the latter State had appeared to be entirely abandoned, even by the States which had joined in her remonstrances.

[27] This law was passed on March 2, 1833.

[28] This bill was brought in by Mr. Clay, and it passed in four days through both Houses of Congress by an immense majority.

CHAPTER XX

The Americans destined by Nature to be a great maritime people—Commercial superiority of the Anglo-Americans less attributable to physical circumstances than to moral and intellectual causes—Future destiny of the Anglo-Americans as a commercial nation.

THE coast of the United States, from the Bay of Fundy to the Sabine River in the Gulf of Mexico, is more than two thousand miles in extent. These shores form an unbroken line, and they are all subject to the same Government. No nation in the world possesses vaster, deeper, or more secure ports for shipping than the Americans.

The inhabitants of the United States constitute a great civilized people, which fortune has placed in the midst of an uncultivated country at a distance of three thousand miles from the central point of civilization. America consequently stands in daily need of European trade. The Americans will, no doubt, ultimately succeed in producing or manufacturing at home most of the articles which they require; but the two continents can never be independent of each other, so numerous are the natural ties which exist between their wants, their ideas, their habits, and their manners.

The Union produces peculiar commodities which are now become necessary to us, but which can not be cultivated, or can only be raised at an enormous expense, upon the soil of Europe. The Americans only consume a small portion of this produce, and they are willing to sell us the rest. Europe is therefore the market of America, as Amer-

ica is the market of Europe; and maritime commerce is no
less necessary to enable the inhabitants of the United States
to transport their raw materials to the ports of Europe
than it is to enable us to supply them with our manufactured produce. The United States were therefore necessarily reduced to the alternative of increasing the business
of other maritime nations to a great extent if they had
themselves declined to enter into commerce, as the Spaniards of Mexico have hitherto done; or, in the second place,
of becoming one of the first trading powers of the globe.

The Anglo-Americans have always displayed a very
decided taste for the sea. The Declaration of Independence broke the commercial restrictions which united them
to England, and gave a fresh and powerful stimulus to
their maritime genius. Ever since that time the shipping
of the Union has increased in almost the same rapid proportion as the number of its inhabitants. The Americans
themselves now transport to their own shores nine tenths
of the European produce which they consume.[1] And they
also bring three quarters of the exports of the New World
to the European consumer.[2] The ships of the United
States fill the docks of Havre and of Liverpool; while the
number of English and French vessels which are to be seen
at New York is comparatively small.[3]

Thus, not only does the American merchant face the
competition of his own countrymen, but he even supports
that of foreign nations in their own ports with success.
This is readily explained by the fact that the vessels of the
United States can cross the seas at a cheaper rate than any
other vessels in the world. As long as the mercantile shipping of the United States preserves this superiority, it will
not only retain what it has acquired, but it will constantly
increase in prosperity.

It is difficult to say for what reason the Americans can
trade at a lower rate than other nations; and one is at first
led to attribute this circumstance to the physical or natural
advantages which are within their reach; but this supposition is erroneous. The American vessels cost almost as

much to build as our own;[4] they are not better built, and they generally last for a shorter time. The pay of the American sailor is more considerable than the pay on board European ships; which is proved by the great number of Europeans who are to be met with in the merchant vessels of the United States. But I am of opinion that the true cause of their superiority must not be sought for in physical advantages, but that it is wholly attributable to their moral and intellectual qualities.

The following comparison will illustrate my meaning: During the campaigns of the Revolution the French introduced a new system of tactics into the art of war, which perplexed the oldest generals, and very nearly destroyed the most ancient monarchies in Europe. They undertook (what never before had been attempted) to make shift without a number of things which had always been held to be indispensable in warfare; they required novel exertions on the part of their troops which no civilized nations had ever thought of; they achieved great actions in an incredibly short space of time; and they risked human life without hesitation to obtain the object in view. The French had less money and fewer men than their enemies; their resources were infinitely inferior; nevertheless they were constantly victorious, until their adversaries chose to imitate their example.

The Americans have introduced a similar system into their commercial speculations; and they do for cheapness what the French did for conquest. The European sailor navigates with prudence; he only sets sail when the weather is favourable; if an unforeseen accident befalls him, he puts into port; at night he furls a portion of his canvas; and when the whitening billows intimate the vicinity of land, he checks his way, and takes an observation of the sun. But the American neglects these precautions and braves these dangers. He weighs anchor in the midst of tempestuous gales; by night and by day he spreads his sheets to the wind; he repairs as he goes along such damage as his vessel may have sustained from the storm; and when

he at last approaches the term of his voyage, he darts onward to the shore as if he already descried a port. The
Americans are often shipwrecked, but no trader crosses the
seas so rapidly. And as they perform the same distance in
a shorter time, they can perform it at a cheaper rate.

The European touches several times at different ports
in the course of a long voyage; he loses a good deal of
precious time in making the harbour, or in waiting for a
favourable wind to leave it; and he pays daily dues to be
allowed to remain there. The American starts from Boston to go to purchase tea in China; he arrives at Canton,
stays there a few days, and then returns. In less than two
years he has sailed as far as the entire circumference of
the globe, and he has seen land but once. It is true that
during a voyage of eight or ten months he has drunk
brackish water and lived upon salt meat; that he has been
in a continual contest with the sea, with disease, and with
a tedious existence; but upon his return he can sell a
pound of his tea for a halfpenny less than the English merchant, and his purpose is accomplished.

I can not better explain my meaning than by saying
that the Americans affect a sort of heroism in their manner
of trading. But the European merchant will always find
it very difficult to imitate his American competitor, who,
in adopting the system which I have just described, follows
not only a calculation of his gain, but an impulse of his
nature.

The inhabitants of the United States are subject to all
the wants and all the desires which result from an advanced
stage of civilization; but as they are not surrounded by a
community admirably adapted, like that of Europe, to
satisfy their wants, they are often obliged to procure for
themselves the various articles which education and habit
have rendered necessaries. In America it sometimes happens that the same individual tills his field, builds his dwelling, contrives his tools, makes his shoes, and weaves the
coarse stuff of which his dress is composed. This circumstance is prejudicial to the excellence of the work; but it

powerfully contributes to awaken the intelligence of the workman. Nothing tends to materialize man, and to deprive his work of the faintest trace of mind, more than extreme division of labour. In a country like America, where men devoted to special occupations are rare, a long apprenticeship can not be required from any one who embraces a profession. The Americans, therefore, change their means of gaining a livelihood very readily; and they suit their occupations to the exigencies of the moment, in the manner most profitable to themselves. Men are to be met with who have successively been barristers, farmers, merchants, ministers of the Gospel, and physicians. If the American be less perfect in each craft than the European, at least there is scarcely any trade with which he is utterly unacquainted. His capacity is more general, and the circle of his intelligence is enlarged.

The inhabitants of the United States are never fettered by the axioms of their profession; they escape from all the prejudices of their present station; they are not more attached to one line of operation than to another; they are not more prone to employ an old method than a new one; they have no rooted habits, and they easily shake off the influence which the habits of other nations might exercise upon their minds from a conviction that their country is unlike any other, and that its situation is without a precedent in the world. America is a land of wonders, in which everything is in constant motion, and every movement seems an improvement. The idea of novelty is there indissolubly connected with the idea of amelioration. No natural boundary seems to be set to the efforts of man; and what is not yet done is only what he has not yet attempted to do.

This perpetual change which goes on in the United States, these frequent vicissitudes of fortune, accompanied by such unforeseen fluctuations in private and in public wealth, serve to keep the minds of the citizens in a perpetual state of feverish agitation, which admirably invigorates their exertions, and keeps them in a state of excitement above the ordinary level of mankind. The whole life of an American is passed like a game of chance, a revolutionary crisis, or a battle. As the same causes are continually in operation throughout the country, they ultimately impart an irresistible impulse to the national character. The American, taken as a chance specimen of his countrymen, must then be a man of singular warmth in his desires, enterprising, fond of adventure, and, above all, of innovation. The same bent is manifest in all that he does; he introduces it into his political laws, his religious doctrines, his theories of social economy, and his domestic occupations; he bears it with him in the depths of the backwoods, as well as in the business of the city. It is this same passion, applied to maritime commerce, which makes him the cheapest and the quickest trader in the world.

As long as the sailors of the United States retain these inspiriting advantages, and the practical superiority which they derive from them, they will not only continue to supply the wants of the producers and consumers of their own country, but they will tend more and more to become, like the English, the factors of all other peoples.[5] This prediction has already begun to be realized; we perceive that the American traders are introducing themselves as intermediate agents in the commerce of several European nations;[6] and America will offer a still wider field to their enterprise.

The great colonies which were founded in South America by the Spaniards and the Portuguese have since become empires. Civil war and oppression now lay waste those extensive regions. Population does not increase, and the thinly scattered inhabitants are too much absorbed in the cares of self-defence even to attempt any amelioration of their condition. Such, however, will not always be the case. Europe has succeeded by her own efforts in piercing the gloom of the Middle Ages; South America has the same Christian laws and Christian manners as we have; she contains all the germs of civilization which have grown amid the nations of Europe or their offsets, added to the advantages to be derived from our example: why, then, should she always remain uncivilized? It is clear that the question is simply one of time; at some future period, which may be more or less remote, the inhabitants of South America will constitute flourishing and enlightened nations.

But when the Spaniards and Portuguese of South America begin to feel the wants common to all civilized nations, they will still be unable to satisfy those wants for themselves; as the youngest children of civilization, they must perforce admit the superiority of their elder brethren. They will be agriculturists long before they succeed in manufactures or commerce, and they will require the mediation of strangers to exchange their produce beyond seas for those articles for which a demand will begin to be felt.

It is unquestionable that the Americans of the North will one day supply the wants of the Americans of the South. Nature has placed them in contiguity; and has furnished the former with every means of knowing and appreciating those demands, of establishing a permanent connection with those States, and of gradually filling their markets. The merchant of the United States could only forfeit these natural advantages if he were very inferior to the merchant of Europe; to whom he is, on the contrary, superior in several respects. The Americans of the United States already exercise a very considerable moral influence upon all the peoples of the New World. They are the source of intelligence, and all the nations which inhabit the same continent are already accustomed to consider them as the most enlightened, the most powerful, and the most wealthy members of the great American family. All eyes are therefore turned toward the Union; and the States of which that body is composed are the models which the other communities try to imitate to the best of their power; it is from the United States that they borrow their political principles and their laws.

The Americans of the United States stand in precisely

the same position with regard to the peoples of South America as their fathers, the English, occupy with regard to the Italians, the Spaniards, the Portuguese, and all those nations of Europe which receive their articles of daily consumption from England, because they are less advanced in civilization and trade. England is at this time the natural emporium of almost all the nations which are within its reach; the American Union will perform the same part in the other hemisphere; and every community which is founded, or which prospers in the New World, is founded and prospers to the advantage of the Anglo-Americans.

If the Union were to be dissolved, the commerce of the States which now compose it would undoubtedly be checked for a time; but this consequence would be less perceptible than is generally supposed. It is evident that, whatever may happen, the commercial States will remain united. They are all contiguous to each other; they have identically the same opinions, interests, and manners; and they are alone competent to form a very great maritime power. Even if the South of the Union were to become independent of the North, it would still require the services of those States. I have already observed that the South is not a commercial country, and nothing intimates that it is likely to become so. The Americans of the South of the United States will therefore be obliged, for a long time to come, to have recourse to strangers to export their produce, and to supply them with the commodities which are requisite to satisfy their wants. But the Northern States are undoubtedly able to act as their intermediate agents cheaper than any other merchants. They will therefore retain that employment, for cheapness is the sovereign law of commerce. National claims and national prejudices can not resist the influence of cheapness. Nothing can be more virulent than the hatred which exists between the Americans of the United States and the English. But notwithstanding these inimical feelings, the Americans derive the greater part of their manufactured commodities from England, because England supplies them at a cheaper rate than any other nation. Thus the increasing prosperity of America turns, notwithstanding the grudges of the Americans, to the advantage of British manufactures.

Reason shows and experience proves that no commercial prosperity can be durable if it can not be united, in case of need, to naval force. This truth is as well understood in the United States as it can be anywhere else: the Americans are already able to make their flag respected; in a few years they will be able to make it feared. I am convinced that the dismemberment of the Union would not have the effect of diminishing the naval power of the Americans, but that it would powerfully contribute to increase it. At the present time the commercial States are connected with others which have not the same interests, and which frequently yield an unwilling consent to the increase of a maritime power by which they are only indirectly benefited. If, on the contrary, the commercial States of the Union formed one independent nation, commerce would become the foremost of their national interests; they would consequently be willing to make very great sacrifices to protect their shipping, and nothing would prevent them from pursuing their designs upon this point.

Nations, as well as men, almost always betray the most prominent features of their future destiny in their earliest years. When I contemplate the ardour with which the Anglo-Americans prosecute commercial enterprise, the advantages which befriend them, and the success of their undertakings, I can not refrain from believing that they will one day become the first maritime power of the globe. They are born to rule the seas, as the Romans were to conquer the world.

NOTES

[1] The total value of goods imported during the year which ended on September 30, 1832, was 101,429,266 dollars. The value of the cargoes of foreign vessels did not amount to 10,731,039 dollars, or about one tenth of the entire sum.

[2] The value of goods exported during the same year amounted to 87,-176,943 dollars; the value of goods exported by foreign vessels amounted

to 21,036,183 dollars, or about one quarter of the whole sum. (" Williams's Register," 1833, p. 398.)

[3] The tonnage of the vessels which entered all the ports of the Union in the years 1829, 1830, and 1831, amounted to 3,307,719 tons, of which 544,571 tons were foreign vessels; they stood therefore to the American vessels in a ratio of about 16 to 100. (" National Calendar," 1833, p. 304.) The tonnage of the English vessels which entered the ports of London, Liverpool, and Hull, in the years 1820, 1826, and 1831, amounted to 443,-800 tons. The foreign vessels which entered the same ports during the same years amounted to 159,431 tons. The ratio between them was therefore about 36 to 100. (" Companion to the Almanac," 1834, p. 169.) In the year 1832 the ratio between the foreign and British ships which entered the ports of Great Britain was 29 to 100.

[4] Materials are, generally speaking, less expensive in America than in Europe, but the price of labour is much higher.

[5] It must not be supposed that English vessels are exclusively employed in transporting foreign produce into England, or British produce to foreign countries: at the present day the merchant shipping of England may be regarded in the light of a vast system of public conveyances, ready to serve all the producers of the world, and to open communications between all peoples. The maritime genius of the Americans prompts them to enter into competition with the English.

[6] Part of the commerce of the Mediterranean is already carried on by American vessels.

CHAPTER XXI

FUTURE PROSPECTS OF THE UNITED STATES

I HAVE now nearly reached the close of my inquiry; hitherto, in speaking of the future destiny of the United States, I have endeavoured to divide my subject into distinct portions, in order to study each of them with more attention. My present object is to embrace the whole from one single point; the remarks I shall make will be less detailed, but they will be more sure. I shall perceive each object less distinctly, but I shall descry the principal facts with more certainty. A traveller who has just left the walls of an immense city climbs the neighbouring hill; as he goes farther off he loses sight of the men whom he has so recently quitted; their dwellings are confused in a dense mass; he can no longer distinguish the public squares, and he can scarcely trace out the great thoroughfares; but his eye has less difficulty in following the boundaries of the city, and for the first time he sees the shape of the vast whole. Such is the future destiny of the British race in North America to my eye; the details of the stupendous picture are overhung with shade, but I conceive a clear idea of the entire subject.

The territory now occupied or possessed by the United States of America forms about one-twentieth part of the habitable earth. But extensive as these confines are, it must not be supposed that the Anglo-American race will always remain within them; indeed, it has already far overstepped them.

There was once a time at which we also might have created a great French nation in the American wilds, to counterbalance the influence of the English upon the destinies of the New World. France formerly possessed a territory in North America scarcely less extensive than the whole of Europe. The three greatest rivers of that continent then flowed within her dominions. The Indian tribes which dwelt between the mouth of the St. Lawrence and the delta of the Mississippi were unaccustomed to any other tongue but ours; and all the European settlements scattered over that immense region recalled the traditions of our country. Louisbourg, Montmorency, Duquesne, Saint-Louis, Vincennes, New Orleans (for such were the names they bore) are words dear to France and familiar to our ears.

But a concourse of circumstances, which it would be tedious to enumerate,[1] have deprived us of this magnificent inheritance. Wherever the French settlers were numerically weak and partially established, they have disappeared: those who remain are collected on a small extent of country, and are now subject to other laws. The four hundred thousand French inhabitants of Lower Canada constitute, at the present time, the remnant of an old nation lost in the midst of a new people. A foreign population is increasing around them unceasingly and on all sides, which already penetrates among the ancient masters of the country, predominates in their cities, and corrupts their language. This population is identical with that of the United States; it is therefore with truth that I asserted that the British race is not confined within the frontiers of the Union, since it already extends to the Northeast.

To the Northwest nothing is to be met with but a few insignificant Russian settlements; but to the Southwest, Mexico presents a barrier to the Anglo-Americans. Thus, the Spaniards and the Anglo-Americans are, properly speaking, the only two races which divide the possession of the New World. The limits of separation between them have been settled by a treaty; but although the conditions of that treaty are exceedingly favourable to the Anglo-Americans, I do not doubt that they will shortly infringe this arrangement. Vast provinces, extending beyond the frontiers of the Union toward Mexico, are still destitute of inhabitants. The natives of the United States will forestall the rightful occupants of these solitary regions. They will take possession of the soil, and establish social institutions, so that when the legal owner arrives at length, he will find the wilderness under cultivation, and strangers quietly settled in the midst of his inheritance.

The lands of the New World belong to the first occupant, and they are the natural reward of the swiftest pioneer. Even the countries which are already peopled will have some difficulty in securing themselves from this invasion. I have already alluded to what is taking place in the province of Texas. The inhabitants of the United States are perpetually migrating to Texas, where they purchase land; and although they conform to the laws of the country, they are gradually founding the empire of their own language and their own manners. The province of Texas is still part of the Mexican dominions, but it will soon contain no Mexicans; the same thing has occurred whenever the Anglo-Americans have come into contact with populations of a different origin.

It can not be denied that the British race has acquired an amazing preponderance over all the other European races in the New World; and that it is very superior to them in civilization, in industry, and in power. As long as it is only surrounded by desert or thinly peopled countries, as long as it encounters no dense populations upon its route, through which it can not work its way, it will assuredly continue to spread. The lines marked out by treaties will not stop it; but it will everywhere transgress these imaginary barriers.

The geographical position of the British race in the New World is peculiarly favourable to its rapid increase. Above its northern frontiers the icy regions of the Pole extend; and a few degrees below its southern confines lies the burning climate of the Equator. The Anglo-Americans are, therefore, placed in the most temperate and habitable zone of the continent.

It is generally supposed that the prodigious increase of population in the United States is posterior to their Declaration of Independence. But this is an error: the population increased as rapidly under the colonial system as it does at the present day—that is to say, it doubled in about twenty-two years. But this proportion, which is now applied to millions, was then applied to thousands of inhabitants; and the same fact which was scarcely noticeable a century ago is now evident to every observer.

The British subjects in Canada, who are dependent on a king, augment and spread almost as rapidly as the British settlers of the United States, who live under a republican Government. During the War of Independence, which lasted eight years, the population continued to increase without intermission in the same ratio. Although powerful Indian nations allied with the English existed at that time upon the western frontiers, the emigration westward was never checked. While the enemy laid waste the shores of the Atlantic, Kentucky, the western parts of Pennsylvania, and the States of Vermont and of Maine were filling with inhabitants. Nor did the unsettled state of the Constitution, which succeeded the war, prevent the increase of the population, or stop its progress across the wilds. Thus, the difference of laws, the various conditions of peace and war, of order and of anarchy, have exercised no perceptible influence upon the gradual development of the Anglo-Americans. This readily may be understood; for the fact is, that no causes are sufficiently general to exercise a simultaneous influence over the whole of so extensive a territory. One portion of the country always offers a sure retreat from the calamities which afflict another part; and however great may be the evil, the remedy which is at hand is greater still.

It must not, then, be imagined that the impulse of the British race in the New World can be arrested. The dismemberment of the Union, and the hostilities which might ensue, the abolition of republican institutions, and the tyrannical government which might succeed it, may retard this impulse, but they can not prevent it from ultimately fulfilling the destinies to which that race is reserved. No power upon earth can close upon the emigrants that fertile wilderness which offers resources to all industry, and a refuge from all want. Future events, of whatever nature they may be, will not deprive the Americans of their climate or of their inland seas, of their great rivers or of their exuberant soil. Nor will bad laws, revolutions, and anarchy be able to obliterate that love of prosperity and that spirit of enterprise which seem to be the distinctive characteristics of their race, or to extinguish that knowledge which guides them on their way.

Thus, in the midst of the uncertain future, one event at least is sure. At a period which may be said to be near (for we are speaking of the life of a nation), the Anglo-Americans will alone cover the immense space contained between the Polar regions and the Tropics, extending from the coasts of the Atlantic to the shores of the Pacific Ocean. The territory which will probably be occupied by the Anglo-Americans at some future time may be computed to equal three quarters of Europe in extent.[2] The climate of the Union is, upon the whole, preferable to that of Europe, and its natural advantages are not less great; it is therefore evident that its population will at some future time be proportionate to our own. Europe, divided as it is between so many different nations, and torn as it has been by incessant wars and the barbarous manners of the Middle Ages, has notwithstanding attained a population of four hundred and ten inhabitants to the square league. What cause can prevent the United States from having as numerous a population in time?

Many ages must elapse before the divers offsets of the British race in America cease to present the same homogeneous characteristics: and the time can not be foreseen at which a permanent inequality of conditions will be established in the New World. Whatever differences may arise, from peace or from war, from freedom or oppression, from prosperity or want, between the destinies of the different descendants of the great Anglo-American family, they will at least preserve an analogous social condition, and they will hold in common the customs and the opinions to which that social condition has given birth.

In the Middle Ages, the tie of religion was sufficiently powerful to imbue all the different populations of Europe with the same civilization. The British of the New World have a thousand other reciprocal ties; and they live at a time when the tendency to equality is general among mankind. The Middle Ages were a period when everything was broken up; when each people, each province, each city, and each family had a strong tendency to maintain its distinct individuality. At the present time an opposite tendency seems to prevail, and the nations seem to be advancing to unity. Our means of intellectual intercourse unite the most remote parts of the earth; and it is impossible for men to remain strangers to each other, or to be ignorant of the events which are taking place in any corner of the globe. The consequence is that there is less difference, at the present day, between the Europeans and their descendants in the New World than there was between certain towns in the thirteenth century which were only separated by a river. If this tendency to assimilation brings foreign nations closer to each other, it must a fortiori prevent the descendants of the same people from becoming aliens to each other.

The time will therefore come when one hundred and fifty millions of men will be living in North America,[3] equal in condition, the progeny of one race, owing their origin to the same cause, and preserving the same civilization, the same language, the same religion, the same habits, the same manners, and imbued with the same opinions, propagated under the same forms. The rest is uncertain, but this is certain; and it is a fact new to the world—a fact fraught with such portentous consequences as to baffle the efforts even of the imagination.

There are, at the present time, two great nations in the world which seem to tend toward the same end, although they started from different points: I allude to the Russians and the Americans. Both of them have grown up unnoticed; and while the attention of mankind was directed elsewhere, they have suddenly assumed a most prominent place among the nations; and the world learned their existence and their greatness at almost the same time.

All other nations seem to have nearly reached their natural limits, and only to be charged with the maintenance of their power; but these are still in the act of growth; all the others are stopped, or continue to advance with extreme difficulty; these are proceeding with ease and with celerity along a path to which the human eye can assign no term. The American struggles against the natural obstacles which oppose him; the adversaries of the Russian are men; the former combats the wilderness and savage life; the latter, civilization with all its weapons and its arts: the conquests of the one are therefore gained by the ploughshare; those of the other by the sword. The Anglo-American relies upon personal interest to accomplish his ends, and gives free scope to the unguided exertions and common sense of the citizens; the Russian centres all the authority of society in a single arm: the principal instrument of the former is freedom; of the latter servitude. Their starting-point is different, and their courses are not the same; yet each of them seems to be marked out by the will of Heaven to sway the destinies of half the globe.

NOTES

[1] The foremost of these circumstances is, that nations which are accustomed to free institutions and municipal government are better able than any others to found prosperous colonies. The habit of thinking and governing for one's self is indispensable in a new country, where success necessarily depends upon the individual exertions of the settlers.

[2] The United States already extend over a territory equal to one half of Europe. The area of Europe is 500,000 square leagues, and its population 205,000,000 inhabitants.

[3] This would be a population proportionate to that of Europe, taken at a mean rate of 410 inhabitants to the square league.

CHAPTER XXII

THE INFLUENCES OF DEMOCRACY UPON PHILOSOPHY [1]

Philosophical method among the Americans a natural growth—The principal source of belief among democratic nations—Why the Americans display more readiness and more taste for general ideas than their forefathers the English—Why the Americans have never been so eager as the French for general ideas in political matters.

I THINK that in no country in the civilized world is less attention paid to philosophy than in the United States. The Americans have no philosophical school of their own; and they care but little for all the schools into which Europe is divided, the very names of which are scarcely known to them. Nevertheless it is easy to perceive that almost all the inhabitants of the United States conduct their understanding in the same manner, and govern it by the same rules—that is to say, that without ever having taken the trouble to define the rules of a philosophical method, they are in possession of one, common to the whole people. To evade the bondage of system and habit, of family-maxims, class-opinions, and, in some degree, of national prejudices; to accept tradition only as a means of information, and existing facts only as a lesson used in doing otherwise and doing better; to seek the reason of things for one's self, and in one's self alone; to tend to results without being bound to means, and to aim at the substance through the form—such are the principal characteristics of what I shall call the philosophical method of the Americans. But if I go further, and if I seek among these characteristics that which predominates over and includes almost all the rest, I discover that in most of the operations of the mind each American appeals to the individual exercise of his own understanding alone. America is therefore one of the countries in the world where philosophy is least studied, and where the precepts of Descartes are best applied. Nor is this surprising. The Americans do not read the works of Descartes, because their social condition deters them from speculative studies; but they follow his maxims because this very social condition naturally disposes their understanding to adopt them. In the midst of the continual movement which agitates a democratic community the tie which unites one generation to another is relaxed or broken; every man readily loses the trace of the ideas of his forefathers or takes no care about them. Nor can men living in this state of society derive their belief from the opinions of the class to which they belong; for, so to speak, there are no longer any classes, or those which still exist are composed of such mobile elements that their body can never exercise a real control over its members. As to the influence which the intelligence of one man has on that of another, it must necessarily be very limited in a country where the citizens, placed on the footing of a general similitude, are all closely seen by each other; and where, as no signs of incontestable greatness or superiority are perceived in any one of them, they are constantly brought back to their own reason as the most obvious and proximate source of truth. It is not only confidence in this or that man which is then destroyed, but the taste for trusting the ipse dixit of any man whatsoever. Every one shuts himself up in his own breast, and affects from that point to judge the world.

The practice which obtains among the Americans of fixing the standard of their judgment in themselves alone, leads them to other habits of mind. As they perceive that they succeed in resolving without assistance all the little difficulties which their practical life presents, they readily conclude that everything in the world may be explained, and that nothing in it transcends the limits of the understanding. Thus they fall to denying what they can not comprehend; which leaves them but little faith for what-

ever is extraordinary, and an almost insurmountable distaste for whatever is supernatural. As it is on their own
testimony that they are accustomed to rely, they like to
discern the object which engages their attention with extreme clearness; they therefore strip off as much as possible all that covers it, they rid themselves of whatever
separates them from it, they remove whatever conceals it
from sight, in order to view it more closely and in the broad
light of day. This disposition of the mind soon leads them
to contemn forms, which they regard as useless and inconvenient veils placed between them and the truth.

The Americans, then, have not required to extract their
philosophical method from books; they have found it in
themselves. The same thing may be remarked in what
has taken place in Europe. This same method only has
been established and made popular in Europe in proportion as the condition of society has become more equal,
and men have grown more like each other. Let us consider for a moment the connection of the periods in which
this change may be traced. In the sixteenth century the
reformers subjected some of the dogmas of the ancient
faith to the scrutiny of private judgment; but they still
withheld from it the dicussion of all the rest. In the seventeenth century, Bacon in the natural sciences, and Descartes in the study of philosophy in the strict sense of the
term, abolished recognised formulas, destroyed the empire of tradition, and overthrew the authority of the schools.
The philosophers of the eighteenth century, generalizing
at length the same principle, undertook to submit to the
private judgment of each man all the objects of his belief.

Who does not perceive that Luther, Descartes, and
Voltaire employed the same method, and that they differed only in the greater or less use which they professed
should be made of it? Why did the reformers confine
themselves so closely within the circle of religious ideas?
Why did Descartes, choosing only to apply his method to
certain matters, though he had made it fit to be applied to
all, declare that men might judge for themselves in matters

philosophical but not in matters political? How happened it that in the eighteenth century those general applications were all at once drawn from this same method, which Descartes and his predecessors had either not perceived or had rejected? To what, lastly, is the fact to be attributed, that at this period the method we are speaking of suddenly emerged from the schools, to penetrate into society and to become the common standard of intelligence; and that, after it had become popular among the French, it has been ostensibly adopted or secretly followed by all the nations of Europe?

The philosophical method here designated may have been engendered in the sixteenth century—it may have been more accurately defined and more extensively applied in the seventeenth; but neither in the one nor in the other could it be commonly adopted. Political laws, the condition of society, and the habits of mind which are derived from these causes, were as yet opposed to it. It was discovered at a time when men were beginning to equalize and assimilate their conditions. It could only be generally followed in ages when those conditions had at length become nearly equal, and men nearly alike.

The philosophical method of the eighteenth century is then not only French, but it is democratic; and this explains why it was so readily admitted throughout Europe, where it has contributed so powerfully to change the face of society. It is not because the French have changed their former opinions, and altered their former manners, that they have convulsed the world; but because they were the first to generalize and bring to light a philosophical method, by the assistance of which it became easy to attack all that was old, and to open a path to all that was new.

If it be asked why, at the present day, this same method is more rigorously followed and more frequently applied by the French than by the Americans, although the principle of equality be no less complete, and of more ancient date, among the latter people, the fact may be attributed to two circumstances, which it is essential to have clearly understood in the first instance.

It never must be forgotten that religion gave birth to Anglo-American society. In the United States religion is therefore commingled with all the habits of the nation and all the feelings of patriotism; whence it derives a peculiar force. To this powerful reason another of no less intensity may be added: in America religion has, as it were, laid down its own limits. Religious institutions have remained wholly distinct from political institutions, so that former laws have been easily changed while former belief has remained unshaken. Christianity therefore has retained a strong hold on the public mind in America; and, I would more particularly remark, that its sway is not only that of a philosophical doctrine which has been adopted upon inquiry, but of a religion which is believed without discussion. In the United States Christian sects are infinitely diversified and perpetually modified; but Christianity itself is a fact so irresistibly established that no one undertakes either to attack or to defend it. The Americans, having admitted the principal doctrines of the Christian religion without inquiry, are obliged to accept in like manner a great number of moral truths originating in it and connected with it. Hence the activity of individual analysis is restrained within narrow limits, and many of the most important of human opinions are removed from the range of its influence.

The second circumstance to which I have alluded is the following: The social condition and the constitution of the Americans are democratic, but they have not had a democratic revolution. They arrived upon the soil they occupy in nearly the condition in which we see them at the present day; and this is of very considerable importance.

There are no revolutions which do not shake existing belief, enervate authority, and throw doubts over commonly received ideas. The effect of all revolutions is therefore, more or less, to surrender men to their own guidance, and to open to the mind of every man a void and almost unlimited range of speculation. When equality of condition succeeds a protracted conflict between the different classes of which the elder society was composed, envy, hatred, uncharitableness, pride, and exaggerated self-confidence are apt to seize upon the human heart, and plant their sway there for a time. This, independently of equality itself, tends powerfully to divide men—to lead them to mistrust the judgment of others, and to seek the light of truth nowhere but in their own understandings. Every one then attempts to be his own sufficient guide, and makes it his boast to form his own opinions on all subjects. Men are no longer bound together by ideas, but by interests; and it would seem as if human opinions were reduced to a sort of intellectual dust, scattered on every side, unable to collect, unable to cohere.

Thus, that independence of mind which equality supposes to exist, is never so great, nor ever appears so excessive, as at the time when equality is beginning to establish itself, and in the course of that painful labour by which it is established. That sort of intellectual freedom which equality may give ought, therefore, to be very carefully distinguished from the anarchy which revolution brings. Each of these two things must be severally considered in order not to conceive exaggerated hopes or fears of the future.

I believe that the men who will live under the new forms of society will make frequent use of their private judgment; but I am far from thinking that they will often abuse it. This is attributable to a cause of more general application to all democratic countries, and which, in the long run, must needs restrain in them the independence of individual speculation within fixed, and sometimes narrow, limits. I shall proceed to point out this cause.

At different periods dogmatical belief is more or less abundant. It arises in different ways, and it may change its object or its form; but under no circumstances will dogmatical belief cease to exist, or, in other words, men will never cease to entertain some implicit opinions without trying them by actual discussion. If every one undertook to form his own opinions and to seek for truth by isolated paths struck out by himself alone, it is not to be supposed that any considerable number of men would ever unite in any common belief. But obviously without such common belief no society can prosper—say rather no society can subsist; for without ideas held in common there is no common action, and without common action there may still be men, but there is no social body. In order that society should exist, and, a fortiori, that a society should prosper, it is required that all the minds of the citizens should be rallied and held together by certain predominant ideas; and this can not be the case, unless each of them sometimes draws his opinions from the common source, and consents to accept certain matters of belief at the hands of the community.

Now, if I consider man in his isolated capacity, I find that dogmatical belief is not less indispensable to him in order to live alone than it is to enable him to co-operate with his fellow-creatures. If man were forced to demonstrate to himself all the truths of which he makes daily use, his task would never end. He would exhaust his strength in preparatory exercises, without advancing beyond them. As, from the shortness of his life, he has not the time, nor, from the limits of his intelligence, the capacity, to accomplish this, he is reduced to take upon trust a number of facts and opinions which he has not had either the time or the power to verify himself, but which men of greater ability have sought out, or which the world adopts. On this groundwork he raises for himself the structure of his own thoughts; nor is he led to proceed in this manner by choice, so much as he is constrained by the inflexible law of his condition. There is no philosopher of such great parts in the world but that he believes a million of things on the faith of other people, and supposes a great many more truths than he demonstrates. This is not only necessary but desirable. A man who should undertake to inquire into everything for himself could devote to each thing but little time and attention. His task would keep his mind in perpetual unrest, which would prevent him from penetrating to the depth of any truth, or of grappling his mind indissolubly to any conviction. His intellect would be at once independent and powerless. He must, therefore, make his choice from among the various objects of human belief, and he must adopt many opinions without discussion, in order to search the better into that smaller number which he sets apart for investigation. It is true that whoever receives an opinion on the word of another does so far enslave his mind; but it is a salutary servitude which allows him to make a good use of freedom.

A principle of authority must then always occur, under all circumstances, in some part or other of the moral and intellectual world. Its place is variable, but a place it necessarily has. The independence of individual minds may be greater, or it may be less: unbounded it can not be. Thus the question is, not to know whether any intellectual authority exists in the ages of democracy, but simply where it resides and by what standard it is to be measured.

I have shown in another part of the chapter how equality of condition leads men to entertain a sort of instinctive incredulity of the supernatural, and a very lofty and often exaggerated opinion of the human understanding. The men who live at a period of society equality are not, therefore, easily led to place that intellectual authority to which they bow either beyond or above humanity. They commonly seek for the sources of truth in themselves, or in those who are like themselves. This would be enough to prove that at such periods no new religion could be established, and that all schemes for such a purpose would be not only impious but absurd and irrational. It may be foreseen that a democratic people will not easily give credence to divine missions; that they will turn modern prophets to a ready jest; and that they will seek to discover the chief arbiter of their belief within, and not beyond, the limits of their kind.

When the ranks of society are unequal, and men unlike each other in condition, there are some individuals invested with all the power of superior intelligence, learning, and enlightenment, while the multitude is sunk in ignorance and prejudice. Men living at these aristocratic periods are therefore naturally induced to shape their opinions by the superior standard of a person or a class of persons, while they are averse to recognise the infallibility of the mass of the people.

The contrary takes place in ages of equality. The nearer the citizens are drawn to the common level of an equal and similar condition, the less prone does each man become to place implicit faith in a certain man or a certain class of men. But his readiness to believe the multitude increases, and opinion is more than ever mistress of the world. Not only is common opinion the only guide which private judgment retains among a democratic people, but among such a people it possesses a power infinitely beyond what it has elsewhere. At periods of equality men have no faith in one another, by reason of their common resemblance; but this very resemblance gives them almost unbounded confidence in the judgment of the public; for it would not seem probable, as they are all endowed with equal means of judging, but that the greater truth should go with the greater number.

When the inhabitant of a democratic country compares himself individually with all those about him, he feels with pride that he is the equal of any one of them; but when he comes to survey the totality of his fellows, and to place himself in contrast to so huge a body, he is instantly overwhelmed by the sense of his own insignificance and weakness. The same equality which renders him independent of each of his fellow-citizens taken severally exposes him alone and unprotected to the influence of the greater number. The public has therefore among a democratic people a singular power, of which aristocratic nations could never so much as conceive an idea; for it does not persuade to certain opinions, but it enforces them, and infuses them into the faculties by a sort of enormous pressure of the minds of all upon the reason of each.

In the United States the majority undertakes to supply a multitude of ready-made opinions for the use of individuals, who are thus relieved from the necessity of forming opinions of their own. Everybody there adopts great numbers of theories, on philosophy, morals, and politics, without inquiry, upon public trust; and if we look to it very narrowly, it will be perceived that religion herself holds her sway there, much less as a doctrine of revelation than as a commonly received opinion. The fact that the political laws of the Americans are such that the majority rules the community with sovereign sway, materially increases the power which that majority naturally exercises over the mind. For nothing is more customary in man than to recognise superior wisdom in the person of his oppressor. This political omnipotence of the majority in the United States doubtless augments the influence which public opinion would obtain without it over the mind of each member of the community; but the foundations of that influence do not rest upon it. They must be sought for in the principle of equality itself, not in the more or less popular institutions which men living under that condition may give themselves. The intellectual dominion of the greater number would probably be less absolute among a democratic people governed by a king than in the sphere of a pure democracy, but it will always be extremely absolute; and by whatever political laws men are governed in the ages of equality, it may be foreseen that faith in public opinion will become a species of religion there, and the majority its ministering prophet.

Thus intellectual authority will be different, but it will not be diminished; and far from thinking that it will disappear, I augur that it may readily acquire too much preponderance, and confine the action of private judgment within narrower limits than are suited either to the greatness or the happiness of the human race. In the principle of equality I very clearly discern two tendencies; the one leading the mind of every man to untried thoughts, the other inclined to prohibit him from thinking at all. And I perceive how, under the dominion of certain laws, democracy would extinguish that liberty of the mind to which a democratic social condition is favourable; so that, after having broken all the bondage once imposed on it by ranks or by men, the human mind would be closely fettered to the general will of the greatest number.

If the absolute power of the majority were to be substituted by democratic nations for all the different powers which checked or retarded overmuch the energy of individual minds, the evil would only have changed its symptoms. Men would not have found the means of independent life; they would simply have invented (no easy task) a new dress for servitude. There is—and I can not repeat it too often—there is in this matter for profound reflection for those who look on freedom as a holy thing, and who hate not only the despot, but despotism. For myself, when I feel the hand of power lie heavy on my brow, I care but little to know who oppresses me; and I am not the more disposed to pass beneath the yoke because it is held out to me by the arms of a million of men.

The Deity does not regard the human race collectively. He surveys at one glance and severally all the beings of whom mankind is composed, and he discerns in each man the resemblances which assimilate him to all his fellows, and the differences which distinguish him from them. God, therefore, stands in no need of general ideas—that is to say, he is never sensible of the necessity of collecting a considerable number of analogous objects under the same form for greater convenience in thinking. Such is, however, not the case with man. If the human mind were to attempt to examine and pass a judgment on all the individual cases before it, the immensity of detail would soon lead it astray and bewilder its discernment: in this strait, man has recourse to an imperfect but necessary expedient, which at once assists and demonstrates his weakness. Having superficially considered a certain number of objects, and remarked their resemblance, he assigns to them a common name, sets them apart, and proceeds onward.

General ideas are no proof of the strength, but rather of the insufficiency, of the human intellect; for there are in Nature no beings exactly alike, no things precisely identical, nor any rules indiscriminately and alike applicable to several objects at once. The chief merit of general ideas is, that they enable the human mind to pass a rapid judgment on a great many objects at once; but, on the other hand, the notions they convey are never otherwise than incomplete, and they always cause the mind to lose as much in accuracy as it gains in comprehensiveness. As social bodies advance in civilization, they acquire the knowledge of new facts, and they daily lay hold almost unconsciously of some particular truths. The more truths of this kind a man apprehends, the more general ideas is he naturally led to conceive. A multitude of particular facts can not be seen separately, without at last discovering the common tie which connects them. Several individuals lead to the perception of the species; several species to that of the genus. Hence the habit and the taste for general ideas will always be greatest among a people of ancient cultivation and extensive knowledge.

But there are other reasons which impel men to generalize their ideas, or which restrain them from it.

The Americans are much more addicted to the use of general ideas than the English, and entertain a much greater relish for them: this appears very singular at first sight, when it is remembered that the two nations have the same origin, that they lived for centuries under the same laws, and that they still incessantly interchange their opinions and their manners. This contrast becomes much more striking still if we fix our eyes on our own part of the world, and compare together the two most enlightened nations which inhabit it. It would seem as if the mind of the English could only tear itself reluctantly and painfully away from the observation of particular facts, to rise from them to their causes; and that it only generalizes in

spite of itself. Among the French, on the contrary, the
taste for general ideas would seem to have grown to so
ardent a passion that it must be satisfied on every occasion.
I am informed, every morning when I wake, that some
general and eternal law has just been discovered, which I
never heard mentioned before. There is not a mediocre
scribbler who does not try his hand at discovering truths
applicable to a great kingdom, and who is very ill pleased
with himself if he does not succeed in compressing the
human race into the compass of an article. So great a dissimilarity between two very enlightened nations surprises
me. If I again turn my attention to England, and observe
the events which have occurred there in the last half century, I think I may affirm that a taste for general ideas
increases in that country in proportion as its ancient constitution is weakened.

The state of civilization is therefore insufficient by itself
to explain what suggests to the human mind the love of
general ideas, or diverts it from them. When the conditions of men are very unequal, and inequality itself is the
permanent state of society, individual men gradually become so dissimilar that each class assumes the aspect of
a distinct race: only one of these classes is ever in view at
the same instant; and losing sight of that general tie which
binds them all within the vast bosom of mankind, the observation invariably rests not on man, but on certain men.
Those who live in this aristocratic state of society never,
therefore, conceive very general ideas respecting themselves, and that is enough to imbue them with an habitual
distrust of such ideas, and an instinctive aversion to them.

He, on the contrary, who inhabits a democratic country sees around him, on every hand, men differing but
little from each other; he can not turn his mind to any
one portion of mankind without expanding and dilating
his thought till it embraces the whole. All the truths which
are applicable to himself appear to him equally and simi-
larly applicable to each of his fellow-citizens and fellow-
men. Having contracted the habit of generalizing his ideas

in the study which engages him most, and interests him
more than others, he transfers the same habit to all his
pursuits; and thus it is that the craving to discover general laws in everything, to include a great number of objects under the same formula, and to explain a mass of
facts by a single cause, becomes an ardent, and sometimes
an undiscerning, passion in the human mind.

Nothing shows the truth of this proposition more
clearly than the opinions of the ancients respecting their
slaves. The most profound and capacious minds of Rome
and Greece were never able to reach the idea, at once so
general and so simple, of the common likeness of men,
and of the common birthright of each to freedom: they
strove to prove that slavery was in the order of Nature,
and that it would always exist. Nay, more, everything
shows that those of the ancients who had passed from the
servile to the free condition, many of whom have left us
excellent writings, did themselves regard servitude in no
other light.

All the great writers of antiquity belonged to the aristocracy of masters, or at least they saw that aristocracy
established and uncontested before their eyes. Their mind,
after it had expanded itself in several directions, was
barred from further progress in this one; and the advent
of Jesus Christ upon earth was required to teach that all
the members of the human race are by nature equal and
alike.

In the ages of equality all men are independent of each
other, isolated and weak. The movements of the multitude are not permanently guided by the will of any individuals; at such times humanity seems always to advance
of itself. In order, therefore, to explain what is passing
in the world, man is driven to seek for some great causes,
which, acting in the same manner on all our fellow-creatures, thus impel them all involuntarily to pursue the same
track. This again naturally leads the human mind to conceive general ideas, and superinduces a taste for them.

I have already shown in what way the equality of conditions leads every man to investigate truths for himself. It readily may be perceived that a method of this kind must insensibly beget a tendency to general ideas in the human mind. When I repudiate the traditions of rank, profession, and birth; when I escape from the authority of example, to seek out, by the single effort of my reason, the path to be followed, I am inclined to derive the motives of my opinions from human nature itself; which leads me necessarily, and almost unconsciously, to adopt a great number of very general notions.

All that I have here said explains the reasons for which the English display much less readiness and taste for the generalization of ideas than their American progeny, and still less again than their French neighbours; and likewise the reason for which the English of the present day display more of these qualities than their forefathers did. The English have long been a very enlightened and a very aristocratic nation; their enlightened condition urged them constantly to generalize and their aristocratic habits confined them to particularize. Hence arose that philosophy, at once bold and timid, broad and narrow, which has hitherto prevailed in England, and which still obstructs and stagnates in so many minds in that country.

Independently of the causes I have pointed out in what goes before, others may be discerned less apparent, but no less efficacious, which engender among almost every democratic people a taste, and frequently a passion, for general ideas. An accurate distinction must be taken between ideas of this kind. Some are the result of slow, minute, and conscientious labour of the mind, and these extend the sphere of human knowledge; others spring up at once from the first rapid exercise of the wits, and beget none but very superficial and very uncertain notions. Men who live in ages of equality have a great deal of curiosity and very little leisure; their life is so practical, so confused, so excited, so active, that but little time remains to them for thought. Such men are prone to general ideas because they spare them the trouble of studying particulars; they contain, if I may so speak, a great deal in a little compass, and give, in a little time, a great return. If, then, upon a brief and inattentive investigation, a common relation is thought to be detected between certain objects, inquiry is not pushed any further; and without examining in detail how far these different objects differ or agree, they are hastily arranged under one formulary, in order to pass to another subject.

One of the distinguishing characteristics of a democratic period is the taste all men have at such times for easy success and present enjoyment. This occurs in the pursuits of the intellect as well as in all others. Most of those who live at a time of equality are full of an ambition at once aspiring and relaxed: they would fain succeed brilliantly and at once, but they would be dispensed from great efforts to obtain success. These conflicting tendencies lead straight to the research of general ideas, by aid of which they flatter themselves that they can figure very importantly at a small expense, and draw the attention of the public with very little trouble. And I know not whether they be wrong in thinking thus. For their readers are as much averse to investigating anything to the bottom as they can be themselves; and what are generally sought in the productions of the mind are easy pleasure and information without labour.

If aristocratic nations do not make sufficient use of general ideas, and frequently treat them with inconsiderate disdain, it is true, on the other hand, that a democratic people is ever ready to carry ideas of this kind to excess, and to espouse them with injudicious warmth.

I observed that the Americans show a less decided taste for general ideas than the French; this is more especially true in political matters. Although the Americans infuse into their legislation infinitely more general ideas than the English, and although they pay much more attention than the latter people to the adjustment of the practice of affairs to theory, no political bodies in the United States ever have shown so warm an attachment to general ideas

34

as the Constituent Assembly and the Convention in France. At no time has the American people laid hold on ideas of this kind with the passionate energy of the French people in the eighteenth century, or displayed the same blind confidence in the value and absolute truth of any theory. This difference between the Americans and the French originates in several causes, but principally in the following one: The Americans form a democratic people, which has always itself directed public affairs. The French are a democratic people, who, for a long time, could only speculate on the best manner of conducting them. The social condition of France led that people to conceive very general ideas on the subject of government, while its political constitution prevented it from correcting those ideas by experiment, and from gradually detecting their insufficiency; whereas in America the two things constantly balance and correct each other.

It may seem, at first sight, that this is very much opposed to what I have said before, that democratic nations derive their love of theory from the excitement of their active life. A more attentive examination will show that there is nothing contradictory in the proposition. Men living in democratic countries eagerly lay hold of general ideas because they have but little leisure, and because these ideas spare them the trouble of studying particulars. This is true; but it is only to be understood to apply to those matters which are not the necessary and habitual subjects of their thoughts. Mercantile men will take up very eagerly, and without any very close scrutiny, all the general ideas on philosophy, politics, science, or the arts which may be presented to them; but for such as relate to commerce, they will not receive them without inquiry, or adopt them without reserve. The same thing applies to statesmen with regard to general ideas in politics. If, then, there be a subject upon which a democratic people is peculiarly liable to abandon itself, blindly and extravagantly, to general ideas, the best corrective that can be used will be to make that subject a part of the daily practical occupation of that people. The people will then be compelled to enter upon its details, and the details will teach them the weak points of the theory. This remedy may frequently be a painful one, but its effect is certain.

Thus it happens that the democratic institutions which compel every citizen to take a practical part in the government moderate that excessive taste for general theories in politics which the principle of equality suggests.

NOTE

[1] This book was published originally in two parts, the second part beginning with this chapter. De Tocqueville's preface to this part of the work has been included in the Author's Preface, page xliv of this edition.

CHAPTER XXIII

THE INFLUENCES OF DEMOCRACY UPON RELIGION

The manner in which religion in the United States avails itself of democratic tendencies—The progress of Roman Catholicism in the United States—The cause of a leaning to pantheism among democratic nations—The principle of equality suggests to the Americans the idea of the indefinite perfectibility of man.

I HAVE laid it down in a preceding chapter that men can not do without dogmatical belief; and even that it is very much to be desired that such belief should exist among them. I now add that of all the kinds of dogmatical belief the most desirable appears to me to be dogmatical belief in matters of religion; and this is a very clear inference, even from no higher consideration than the interests of this world. There is hardly any human action, however particular a character be assigned to it, which does not originate in some very general idea men have conceived of the Deity, of his relation to mankind, of the nature of their own souls, and of their duties to their fellow-creatures. Nor can anything prevent these ideas from being the common spring from which everything else emanates. Men are therefore immeasurably interested in acquiring fixed ideas of God, of the soul, and of their common duties to their Creator and to their fellow-men; for doubt on these first principles would abandon all their actions to the impulse of chance, and would condemn them to live, to a certain extent, powerless and undisciplined.

This is, then, the subject on which it is most important for each of us to entertain fixed ideas; and, unhappily, it is also the subject on which it is most difficult for each of us, left to himself, to settle his opinions by the sole force of his reason. None but minds singularly free from the ordinary anxieties of life—minds at once penetrating, subtle, and trained by thinking—can, even with the assistance of much time and care, sound the depth of these most necessary truths. And, indeed, we see that these philosophers themselves almost always are enshrouded in uncertainties; that at every step the natural light which illuminates their path grows dimmer and less secure; and that, in spite of all their efforts, they have as yet only discovered a small number of conflicting notions, on which the mind of man has been tossed about for thousands of years, without either laying a firmer grasp on truth, or finding novelty even in its errors. Studies of this nature are far above the average capacity of men; and even if the majority of mankind were capable of such pursuits, it is evident that leisure to cultivate them would still be wanting. Fixed ideas of God and human nature are indispensable to the daily practice of men's lives; but the practice of their lives prevents them from acquiring such ideas.

The difficulty appears to me to be without a parallel. Among the sciences there are some which are useful to the mass of mankind, and which are within its reach; others can only be approached by the few, and are not cultivated by the many, who require nothing beyond their more remote applications: but the daily practice of the science I speak of is indispensable to all, although the study of it is inaccessible to the far greater number.

General ideas respecting God and human nature are therefore the ideas above all others which it is most suitable to withdraw from the habitual action of private judgment, and in which there is most to gain and least to lose by recognising a principle of authority. The first object and one of the principal advantages of religions is to furnish to each of these fundamental questions a solution which is at once clear, precise, intelligible to the mass of mankind, and lasting. There are religions which are very false and very absurd; but it may be affirmed that any religion which remains within the circle I have just traced, without aspiring to go beyond it (as many religions have attempted to do, for the purpose of inclosing on every side the free progress of the human mind), imposes a salutary restraint on the intellect; and it must be admitted that, if it do not save men in another world, such religion is at least very conducive to their happiness and their greatness in this. This is more especially true of men living in free countries. When the religion of a people is destroyed, doubt gets hold of the highest portions of the intellect, and half paralyzes all the rest of its powers. Every man accustoms himself to entertain none but confused and changing notions on the subjects most interesting to his fellow-creatures and himself. His opinions are ill defended and easily abandoned: and, despairing of ever resolving by himself the hardest problems of the destiny of man, he ignobly submits to think no more about them. Such a condition can not but enervate the soul, relax the springs of the will, and prepare a people for servitude. Nor does it only happen, in such a case, that they allow their freedom to be wrested from them; they frequently themselves surrender it. When there is no longer any principle of authority in religion any more than in politics, men are speedily frightened at the aspect of this unbounded independence. The constant agitation of all surrounding things alarms and exhausts them. As everything is at sea in the sphere of the intellect, they determine at least that the mechanism of society should be firm and fixed; and as they can not resume their ancient belief, they assume a master.

For my own part, I doubt whether man can ever support at the same time complete religious independence and entire public freedom. And I am inclined to think that if faith be wanting in him, he must serve; and if he be free, he must believe.

Perhaps, however, this great utility of religions is still more obvious among nations where equality of conditions prevails than among others. It must be acknowledged that equality, which brings great benefits into the world, nevertheless suggests to men (as will be shown hereafter) some very dangerous propensities. It tends to isolate them from each other, to concentrate every man's attention upon himself; and it lays open the soul to an inordinate love of material gratification. The greatest advantage of religion is to inspire diametrically contrary principles. There is no religion which does not place the object of man's desires above and beyond the treasures of earth, and which does not naturally raise his soul to regions far above those of the senses. Nor is there any which does not impose on man some sort of duties to his kind, and thus draws him at times from the contemplation of himself. This occurs in religions the most false and dangerous. Religious nations are therefore naturally strong on the very point on which democratic nations are weak; which shows of what importance it is for men to preserve their religion as their conditions become more equal.

I have neither the right nor the intention of examining the supernatural means which God employs to infuse religious belief into the heart of man. I am at this moment considering religions in a purely human point of view: my object is to inquire by what means they may most easily retain their sway in the democratic ages upon which we are entering. It has been shown that, at times of general cultivation and equality, the human mind does not consent to adopt dogmatical opinions without reluctance, and feels their necessity acutely in spiritual matters only. This proves, in the first place, that at such times religions ought, more cautiously than at any other, to confine themselves within their own precincts; for in seeking to extend their power beyond religious matters, they incur a risk of not being believed at all. The circle within which they seek to bound the human intellect ought therefore to be carefully traced, and beyond its verge the mind should be left in entire freedom to its own guidance. Mohammed professed to derive from Heaven, and he has inserted in the Koran, not only a body of religious doctrines, but political maxims, civil and criminal laws, and theories of science. The Gospel, on the contrary, only speaks of the general relations of men to God and to each other—beyond which it inculcates and imposes no point of faith. This alone, besides a thousand other reasons, would suffice to prove that the former of these religions will never long predominate in cultivated and democratic ages, while the latter is destined to retain its sway at these as at all other periods.

But in continuation of this branch of the subject, I find that in order for religions to maintain their authority, humanly speaking, in democratic ages, they must not only confine themselves strictly within the circle of spiritual matters: their power also depends very much on the nature of the belief they inculcate, on the external forms they assume, and on the obligations they impose. The preceding observation, that equality leads men to very general and very extensive notions, is principally to be understood as applied to the question of religion. Men living in a similar and equal condition in the world readily conceive the idea of the one God, governing every man by the same laws, and granting to every man future happiness on the same conditions. The idea of the unity of mankind constantly leads them back to the idea of the unity of the Creator; while, on the contrary, in a state of society where men are broken up into very unequal ranks, they are apt to devise as many deities as there are nations, castes, classes, or families, and to trace a thousand private roads to Heaven.

It can not be denied that Christianity itself has felt, to a certain extent, the influence which social and political conditions exercise on religious opinions. At the epoch at which the Christian religion appeared upon earth, Providence, by whom the world was doubtless prepared for its coming, had gathered a large portion of the human race, like an immense flock, under the sceptre of the Cæsars. The men of whom this multitude was composed were distinguished by numerous differences; but they had thus much in common, that they all obeyed the same laws, and that every subject was so weak and insignificant in relation to the imperial potentate that all appeared equal when their condition was contrasted with his. This novel and peculiar state of mankind necessarily predisposed men to listen to the general truths which Christianity teaches, and may serve to explain the facility and rapidity with which they then penetrated into the human mind.

The counterpart of this state of things was exhibited after the destruction of the Empire. The Roman World being then, as it were, shattered into a thousand fragments, each nation resumed its pristine individuality. An infinite scale of ranks very soon grew up in the bosom of these nations; the different races were more sharply defined, and each nation was divided by castes into several peoples. In the midst of this common effort, which seemed to be urging human society to the greatest conceivable amount of voluntary subdivision, Christianity did not lose sight of the leading general ideas which it had brought into the world. But it appeared, nevertheless, to lend itself, as much as was possible, to those new tendencies to which the fractional distribution of mankind had given birth. Men continued to worship an only God, the Creator and Preserver of all things; but every people, every city, and, so to speak, every man, thought to obtain some distinct privilege, and win the favour of an especial patron at the foot of the Throne of Grace. Unable to subdivide the Deity, they multiplied and improperly enhanced the importance of the divine agents. The homage due to Saints and Angels became an almost idolatrous worship among the majority of the Christian world; and apprehensions might be entertained for a moment lest the religion of Christ should retrograde toward the superstitions which it had subdued. It seems evident that the more the barriers are removed which separate nation from nation among mankind, and citizen from citizen among a people, the stronger is the bent of the human mind, as if by its own impulse, toward the idea of an only and all-powerful Being, dispensing

equal laws in the same manner to every man. In democratic ages, then, it is more particularly important not to
allow the homage paid to secondary agents to be confounded with the worship due to the Creator alone.

Another truth is no less clear—that religions ought to
assume fewer external observances in democratic periods
than at any others. In speaking of philosophical method
among the Americans, I have shown that nothing is more
repugnant to the human mind in an age of equality than
the idea of subjection to forms. Men living at such times
are impatient of figures; to their eyes symbols appear to
be the puerile artifice which is used to conceal or to set
off truths, which should more naturally be bared to the
light of open day: they are unmoved by ceremonial observances, and they are predisposed to attach a secondary
importance to the details of public worship. Those whose
care it is to regulate the external forms of religion in a
democratic age should pay a close attention to these natural propensities of the human mind, in order not unneces-
sarily to run counter to them. I firmly believe in the
necessity of forms, which fix the human mind in the contemplation of abstract truths, and stimulate its ardour in
the pursuit of them, while they invigorate its powers of
retaining them steadfastly. Nor do I suppose that it is
possible to maintain a religion without external observances; but, on the other hand, I am persuaded that, in
the ages upon which we are entering, it would be peculiarly dangerous to multiply them beyond measure; and
that they ought rather to be limited to as much as is absolutely necessary to perpetuate the doctrine itself, which
is the substance of religions of which the ritual is only the
form.[1] A religion which should become more minute,
more peremptory, and more surcharged with small observances at a time in which men are becoming more equal,
would soon find itself reduced to a band of fanatical zealots
in the midst of an infidel people.

I anticipate the objection, that as all religions have
general and eternal truths for their object, they can not

thus shape themselves to the shifting spirit of every age without forfeiting their claim to certainty in the eyes of mankind. To this I reply again, that the principal opinions which constitute belief, and which theologians call articles of faith, must be very carefully distinguished from the accessories connected with them. Religions are obliged to hold fast to the former, whatever be the peculiar spirit of the age; but they should take good care not to bind themselves in the same manner to the latter at a time when everything is in transition, and when the mind, accustomed to the moving pageant of human affairs, reluctantly endures the attempt to fix it to any given point. The fixity of external and secondary things can only afford a chance of duration when civil society is itself fixed; under any other circumstances I hold it to be perilous.

We shall have occasion to see that, of all the passions which originate in, or are fostered by, equality, there is one which it renders peculiarly intense, and which it infuses at the same time into the heart of every man: I mean the love of well-being. The taste for well-being is the prominent and indelible feature of democratic ages. It may be believed that a religion which should undertake to destroy so deep-seated a passion would meet its own destruction thence in the end; and if it attempted to wean men entirely from the contemplation of the good things of this world, in order to devote their faculties exclusively to the thought of another, it may be foreseen that the soul would at length escape from its grasp, to plunge into the exclusive enjoyment of present and material pleasures. The chief concern of religions is to purify, to regulate, and to restrain the excessive and exclusive taste for well-being which men feel at periods of equality; but they would err in attempting to control it completely or to eradicate it. They will not succeed in curing men of the love of riches: but they may still persuade men to enrich themselves by none but honest means.

This brings me to a final consideration, which com-

prises, as it were, all the others. The more the conditions
of men are equalized and assimilated to each other, the
more important is it for religions, while they carefully abstain from the daily turmoil of secular affairs, not need-
lessly to run counter to the ideas which generally prevail,
and the permanent interests which exist in the mass of
the people. For as public opinion grows to be more and
more evidently the first and most irresistible of existing
powers, the religious principle has no external support
strong enough to enable it long to resist its attacks. This
is not less true of a democratic people, ruled by a despot,
than in a republic. In ages of equality, kings may often
command obedience, but the majority always commands
belief: to the majority, therefore, deference is to be paid
in whatsoever is not contrary to the faith.

I have shown elsewhere how the American clergy
stand aloof from secular affairs. This is the most obvious, but it is not the only, example of their self-restraint.
In America religion is a distinct sphere, in which the
priest is sovereign, but out of which he takes care never
to go. Within its limits he is the master of the mind; beyond them, he leaves men to themselves, and surrenders
them to the independence and instability which belong to
their nature and their age. I have seen no country in
which Christianity is clothed with fewer forms, figures, and
observances than in the United States; or where it presents more distinct, more simple, or more general notions
to the mind. Although the Christians of America are
divided into a multitude of sects, they all look upon their
religion in the same light. This applies to Roman Catholicism as well as to the other forms of belief. There are no
Romish priests who show less taste for the minute individual observances, for extraordinary or peculiar means
of salvation, or who cling more to the spirit, and less to
the letter of the law, than the Roman Catholic priests of
the United States. Nowhere is that doctrine of the Church,
which prohibits the worship reserved to God alone from
being offered to the Saints, more clearly inculcated or

more generally followed. Yet the Roman Catholics of America are very submissive and very sincere.

Another remark is applicable to the clergy of every communion. The American ministers of the Gospel do not attempt to draw or to fix all the thoughts of man upon the life to come; they are willing to surrender a portion of his heart to the cares of the present; seeming to consider the goods of this world as important, although as secondary, objects. If they take no part themselves in productive labour, they are at least interested in its progression, and ready to applaud its results; and while they never cease to point to the other world as the great object of the hopes and fears of the believer, they do not forbid him honestly to court prosperity in this. Far from attempting to show that these things are distinct and contrary to one another, they study rather to find out on what point they are most nearly and closely connected.

All the American clergy know and respect the intellectual supremacy exercised by the majority; they never sustain any but necessary conflicts with it. They take no share in the altercations of parties, but they readily adopt the general opinions of their country and their age; and they allow themselves to be borne away without opposition in the current of feeling and opinion by which everything around them is carried along. They endeavour to amend their contemporaries, but they do not quit fellowship with them. Public opinion is therefore never hostile to them; it rather supports and protects them; and their belief owes its authority at the same time to the strength which is its own, and to that which they borrow from the opinions of the majority.

Thus it is that, by respecting all democratic tendencies not absolutely contrary to herself, and by making use of several of them for her own purposes, Religion sustains an advantageous struggle with that spirit of individual independence which is her most dangerous antagonist.

America is the most democratic country in the world, and it is at the same time (according to reports worthy of belief) the country in which the Roman Catholic religion makes most progress. At first sight this is surprising. Two things must here be accurately distinguished: equality inclines men to wish to form their own opinions; but, on the other hand, it imbues them with the taste and the idea of unity, simplicity, and impartiality in the power which governs society. Men living in democratic ages are therefore very prone to shake off all religious authority; but if they consent to subject themselves to any authority of this kind, they choose at least that it should be single and uniform. Religious powers not radiating from a common centre are naturally repugnant to their minds; and they almost as readily conceive that there should be no religion as that there should be several. At the present time, more than in any preceding one, Roman Catholics are seen to lapse into infidelity, and Protestants to be converted to Roman Catholicism. If the Roman Catholic faith be considered within the pale of the Church, it would seem to be losing ground; without that pale, to be gaining it. Nor is this circumstance difficult of explanation. The men of our days are naturally little disposed to believe; but, as soon as they have any religion, they immediately find in themselves a latent propensity which urges them unconsciously toward Catholicism. Many of the doctrines and the practices of the Romish Church astonish them; but they feel a secret admiration for its discipline, and its great unity attracts them. If Catholicism could at length withdraw itself from the political animosities to which it has given rise, I have hardly any doubt but that the same spirit of the age, which appears to be so opposed to it, would become so favourable as to admit of its great and sudden advancement. One of the most ordinary weaknesses of the human intellect is to seek to reconcile contrary principles, and to purchase peace at the expense of logic. Thus there have ever been, and will ever be, men who, after having submitted some portion of their religious belief to the principle of authority, will seek to exempt several other parts of their faith from its influence, and to keep their minds floating at random between liberty and obedience. But I am inclined to believe that the number of these thinkers will be less in democratic than in other ages; and that our posterity will tend more and more to a single division into two parts —some relinquishing Christianity entirely, and others returning to the bosom of the Church of Rome.

I shall take occasion hereafter to show under what form the preponderating taste of a democratic people for very general ideas manifests itself in politics; but I would point out, at the present stage of my work, its principal effect on philosophy. It can not be denied that pantheism has made great progress in our age. The writings of a part of Europe bear visible marks of it: the Germans introduce it into philosophy, and the French into literature. Most of the works of imagination published in France contain some opinions or some tinge caught from pantheistical doctrines, or they disclose some tendency to such doctrines in their authors. This appears to me not only to proceed from an accidental but from a permanent cause.

When the conditions of society are becoming more equal, and each individual man becomes more like all the rest, more weak and more insignificant, a habit grows up of ceasing to notice the citizens to consider only the people, and of overlooking individuals to think only of their kind. At such times the human mind seeks to embrace a multitude of different objects at once; and it constantly strives to succeed in connecting a variety of consequences with a single cause. The idea of unity so possesses itself of man, and is sought for by him so universally, that if he thinks he has found it, he readily yields himself up to repose in that belief. Nor does he content himself with the discovery that nothing is in the world but a creation and a Creator; still embarrassed by this primary division of things, he seeks to expand and to simplify his conception by including God and the Universe in one great Whole. If there be a philosophical system which teaches that all things material and immaterial, visible and invisible, which the world contains, are only to be considered as the several parts of an immense Being, which alone remains unchanged amid the continual change and ceaseless transformation of all that constitutes it, we may readily infer that such a system, although it destroy the individuality of man—nay, rather because it destroys that individuality —will have secret charms for men living in democracies. All their habits of thought prepare them to conceive it, and predispose them to adopt it. It naturally attracts and fixes their imagination; it fosters the pride, while it soothes the indolence, of their minds. Among the different systems by whose aid Philosophy endeavours to explain the Universe, I believe pantheism to be one of those most fitted to seduce the human mind in democratic ages. Against it all who abide in their attachment to the true greatness of man should struggle and combine.

Equality suggests to the human mind several ideas which would not have originated from any other source, and it modifies almost all those previously entertained. I take as an example the idea of human perfectibility, because it is one of the principal notions that the intellect can conceive, and because it constitutes of itself a great philosophical theory, which is every instant to be traced by its consequences in the practice of human affairs. Although man has many points of resemblance with the brute creation, one characteristic is peculiar to himself— he improves: they are incapable of improvement. Mankind could not fail to discover this difference from its earliest period. The idea of perfectibility is therefore as old as the world; equality did not give birth to it, although it has imparted to it a novel character.

When the citizens of a community are classed according to their rank, their profession, or their birth, and when all men are constrained to follow the career which happens to open before them, every one thinks that the utmost limits of human power are to be discerned in proximity to himself, and none seeks any longer to resist the inevitable law of his destiny. Not, indeed, that an aristocratic people absolutely contests man's faculty of self-improvement, but they do not hold it to be indefinite; amelioration they conceive, but not change: they imagine that the future condition of society may be better, but not essentially different; and while they admit that mankind has made vast strides in improvement, and may still have some to make, they assign to it beforehand certain impassable limits. Thus they do not presume that they have arrived at the supreme good or at absolute truth (what people or what man was ever wild enough to imagine it?), but they cherish a persuasion that they have pretty nearly reached that degree of greatness and knowledge which our imperfect nature admits of; and as nothing moves about them they are willing to fancy that everything is in its fit place. Then it is that the legislator affects to lay down eternal laws; that kings and nations will raise none but imperishable monuments; and that the present generation undertakes to spare generations to come the care of regulating their destinies.

In proportion as castes disappear and the classes of society approximate—as manners, customs, and laws vary, from the tumultuous intercourse of men—as new facts arise —as new truths are brought to light—as ancient opinions are dissipated, and others take their place—the image of an ideal perfection, forever on the wing, presents itself to the human mind. Continual changes are then every instant occurring under the observation of every man: the position of some is rendered worse; and he learns but too well that no people and no individual, how enlightened soever they may be, can lay claim to infallibility—the condition of others is improved; whence he infers that man is endowed with an indefinite faculty of improvement. His reverses teach him that none may hope to have discovered absolute good—his success stimulates him to the never-ending pursuit of it. Thus, forever seeking—forever falling, to rise again—often disappointed, but not discouraged—he tends unceasingly toward that unmeasured greatness so indistinctly visible at the end of the long track

35

which humanity has yet to tread. It can scarcely be believed how many facts naturally flow from the philosophical
theory of the indefinite perfectibility of man, or how strong
an influence it exercises even on men who, living entirely
for the purposes of action and not of thought, seem to
conform their actions to it, without knowing anything
about it. I accost an American sailor, and I inquire why
the ships of his country are built so as to last but for a
short time; he answers without hesitation that the art of
navigation is every day making such rapid progress that
the finest vessel would become almost useless if it lasted
beyond a certain number of years. In these words, which
fall accidentally and on a particular subject from a man
of rude attainments, I recognise the general and systematic
idea upon which a great people directs all its concerns.

Aristocratic nations are naturally too apt to narrow the
scope of human perfectibility; democratic nations to expand it beyond compass.

Note

[1] In all religions there are some ceremonies which are inherent in the
substance of the faith itself, and in these nothing should on any account
be changed. This is especially the case with Roman Catholicism, in
which the doctrine and the form are frequently so closely united as to
form one point of belief.

CHAPTER XXIV

THE INFLUENCES OF DEMOCRACY UPON SCIENCE AND THE ARTS

The example of the Americans does not prove that a democratic people can have no aptitude and no taste for science, literature, or art—Why the Americans are more addicted to practical than to theoretical science—The spirit in which the Americans cultivate the arts—Why the Americans raise some monuments so insignificant, and others so important.

IT must be acknowledged that among few of the civilized nations of our time have the higher sciences made less progress than in the United States; and in few have great artists, fine poets, or celebrated writers been more rare. Many Europeans, struck by this fact, have looked upon it as a natural and inevitable result of equality; and they have supposed that if a democratic state of society and democratic institutions were ever to prevail over the whole earth, the human mind would gradually find its beacon-lights grow dim, and men would relapse into a period of darkness. To reason thus is, I think, to confound several ideas which it is important to divide and to examine separately: it is to mingle, unintentionally, what is democratic with what is only American.

The religion professed by the first emigrants, and bequeathed by them to their descendants, simple in its form of worship, austere and almost harsh in its principles, and hostile to external symbols and to ceremonial pomp, is naturally unfavourable to the fine arts, and only yields a reluctant sufferance to the pleasures of literature. The Americans are a very old and a very enlightened people, who have fallen upon a new and unbounded country, where they may extend themselves at pleasure, and which they may fertilize without difficulty. This state of things is without a parallel in the history of the world. In America, then, every one finds facilities, unknown elsewhere, for making or increasing his fortune. The spirit of gain is always on the stretch, and the human mind, constantly diverted from the pleasures of imagination and the labours of the intellect, is there swayed by no impulse but the pursuit of wealth. Not only are manufacturing and commercial classes to be found in the United States, as they are in all other countries; but, what never occurred elsewhere, the whole community is simultaneously engaged in productive industry and commerce. I am convinced that if the Americans had been alone in the world, with the freedom and the knowledge acquired by their forefathers, and the passions which are their own, they would not have been slow to discover that progress can not long be made in the application of the sciences without cultivating the theory of them; that all the arts are perfected by one another; and, however absorbed they might have been by the pursuit of the principal object of their desires, they would speedily have admitted that it is necessary to turn aside from it occasionally in order the better to attain it in the end.

The taste for the pleasures of the mind is, moreover, so natural to the heart of civilized man that among the polite nations, which are least disposed to give themselves up to these pursuits, a certain number of citizens are always to be found who take part in them. This intellectual craving, when once felt, would very soon have been satisfied. But at the very time when the Americans were naturally inclined to require nothing of science but its special applications to the useful arts and the means of rendering life comfortable, learned and literary Europe was engaged in exploring the common sources of truth, and in improving at the same time all that can minister to the pleasures or satisfy the wants of man. At the head of the enlightened nations of the Old World the inhabitants of the United

States more particularly distinguished one, to which they were closely united by a common origin and by kindred habits. Among this people they found distinguished men of science, artists of skill, writers of eminence, and they were enabled to enjoy the treasures of the intellect without requiring to labour in amassing them. I can not consent to separate America from Europe, in spite of the ocean which intervenes. I consider the people of the United States as that portion of the English people which is commissioned to explore the wilds of the New World; while the rest of the nation, enjoying more leisure and less harassed by the drudgery of life, may devote its energies to thought, and enlarge in all directions the empire of the mind.

The position of the Americans is therefore quite exceptional, and it may be believed that no democratic people will ever be placed in a similar one. Their strictly Puritanical origin—their exclusively commercial habits—even the country they inhabit, which seems to divert their minds from the pursuit of science, literature, and the arts—the proximity of Europe, which allows them to neglect these pursuits without relapsing into barbarism—a thousand special causes, of which I have only been able to point out the most important—have singularly concurred to fix the mind of the American upon purely practical objects. His passions, his wants, his education, and everything about him seem to unite in drawing the native of the United States earthward: his religion alone bids him turn, from time to time, a transient and distracted glance to heaven. Let us cease then to view all democratic nations under the mask of the American people, and let us attempt to survey them at length with their own proper features.

It is possible to conceive a people not subdivided into any castes or scale of ranks; in which the law, recognising no privileges, should divide inherited property into equal shares; but which, at the same time, should be without knowledge and without freedom. Nor is this an empty hypothesis: a despot may find that it is his interest to render his subjects equal and to leave them ignorant, in order more easily to keep them slaves. Not only would a democratic people of this kind show neither aptitude nor taste for science, literature, or art, but it would probably never arrive at the possession of them. The law of descent would of itself provide for the destruction of fortunes at each succeeding generation; and new fortunes would be acquired by none. The poor man, without either knowledge or freedom, would not so much as conceive the idea of raising himself to wealth; and the rich man would allow himself to be degraded to poverty, without a notion of self-defence. Between these two members of the community complete and invincible equality would soon be established.

No one would then have time or taste to devote himself to the pursuits or pleasures of the intellect; but all men would remain paralyzed by a state of common ignorance and equal servitude. When I conceive a democratic society of this kind, I fancy myself in one of those low, close, and gloomy abodes, where the light which breaks in from without soon faints and fades away. A sudden heaviness overpowers me, and I grope through the surrounding darkness, to find the aperture which will restore me to daylight and the air.

But all this is not applicable to men already enlightened who retain their freedom, after having abolished from among them those peculiar and hereditary rights which perpetuated the tenure of property in the hands of certain individuals or certain bodies. When men living in a democratic state of society are enlightened, they readily discover that they are confined and fixed within no limits which constrain them to take up with their present fortune. They all, therefore, conceive the idea of increasing it; if they are free, they all attempt it, but all do not succeed in the same manner. The legislature, it is true, no longer grants privileges, but they are bestowed by Nature. As natural inequality is very great, fortunes become unequal as soon as every man exerts all his faculties to get rich. The law of descent prevents the establishment of wealthy families; but it does not prevent the existence of wealthy individuals. It constantly brings back the members of the community to a common level, from which they as constantly escape: and the inequality of fortunes augments in proportion as knowledge is diffused and liberty increased.

A sect which arose in our time, and was celebrated for its talents and its extravagance, proposed to concentrate all property into the hands of a central power, whose function it should afterward be to parcel it out to individuals, according to their capacity. This would have been a method of escaping from that complete and eternal equality which seems to threaten democratic society. But it would be a simpler and less dangerous remedy to grant no privilege to any, giving to all equal cultivation and equal independence, and leaving every one to determine his own position. Natural inequality will very soon make way for itself, and wealth will spontaneously pass into the hands of the most capable.

Free and democratic communities, then, will always contain a considerable number of people enjoying opulence or competency. The wealthy will not be linked so closely to each other as the members of the former aristocratic class of society: their propensities will be different, and they will scarcely ever enjoy leisure as secure or as complete: but they will be far more numerous than those who belonged to that class of society ever could be. These persons will not be strictly confined to the cares of practical life, and they will still be able, though in different degrees, to indulge in the pursuits and pleasures of the intellect. In those pleasures they will indulge; for if it be true that the human mind leans on one side to the narrow, the practical, and the useful, it naturally rises on the other to the infinite, the spiritual, and the beautiful. Physical wants confine it to the earth; but, as soon as the tie is loosened, it will unbend itself again.

Not only will the number of those who can take an interest in the productions of the mind be enlarged, but the taste for intellectual enjoyment will descend, step by step, even to those who, in aristocratic societies, seem to have neither time nor ability to indulge in them. When hereditary wealth, the privileges of rank, and the prerogatives of birth have ceased to be, and when every man derives his strength from himself alone, it becomes evident that the chief cause of disparity between the fortunes of men is the mind. Whatever tends to invigorate, to extend, or to adorn the mind, instantly rises to great value. The utility of knowledge becomes singularly conspicuous even to the eyes of the multitude: those who have no taste for its charms set store upon its results, and make some efforts to acquire it.

In free and enlightened democratic ages there is nothing to separate men from each other or to retain them in their peculiar sphere; they rise or sink with extreme rapidity. All classes live in perpetual intercourse from their great proximity to each other. They communicate and intermingle every day—they imitate and envy one another: this suggests to the people many ideas, notions, and desires which it never would have entertained if the distinctions of rank had been fixed and society at rest. In such nations the servant never considers himself as an entire stranger to the pleasures and toils of his master, nor the poor man to those of the rich; the rural population assimilates itself to that of the towns, and the provinces to the capital. No one easily allows himself to be reduced to the mere material cares of life; and the humblest artisan casts at times an eager and a furtive glance into the higher regions of the intellect. People do not read with the same notions or in the same manner as they do in an aristocratic community; but the circle of readers is unceasingly expanded, till it includes all the citizens.

As soon as the multitude begins to take an interest in the labours of the mind, it finds out that to excel in some of them is a powerful method of acquiring fame, power, or wealth. The restless ambition which equality begets instantly takes this direction as it does all others. The number of those who cultivate science, letters, and the arts

becomes immense. The intellectual world starts into prodigious activity: every one endeavours to open for himself a path there, and to draw the eyes of the public after
him. Something analogous occurs to what happens in
society in the United States, politically considered. What
is done is often imperfect, but the attempts are innumerable; and, although the results of individual effort are commonly very small, the total amount is always very large.

It is therefore not true to assert that men living in
democratic ages are naturally indifferent to science, literature, and the arts: only it must be acknowledged that they
cultivate them after their own fashion, and bring to the
task their own peculiar qualifications and deficiencies.

If a democratic state of society and democratic institutions do not stop the career of the human mind, they incontestably guide it in one direction in preference to another. Their effects, thus circumscribed, are still exceedingly great; and I trust I may be pardoned if I pause for
a moment to survey them. We had occasion, in speaking of the philosophical method of the American people,
to make several remarks, which must here be turned to
account.

Equality begets in man the desire of judging of everything for himself: it gives him, in all things, a taste for the
tangible and the real, a contempt for tradition and for
forms. These general tendencies are principally discernible in the peculiar subject of this chapter. Those who
cultivate the sciences among a democratic people are
always afraid of losing their way in visionary speculation.
They mistrust systems; they adhere closely to facts and
the study of facts with their own senses. As they do not
easily defer to the mere name of any fellow-man, they are
never inclined to rest upon any man's authority; but, on
the contrary, they are unremitting in their efforts to point
out the weaker points of their neighbours' opinions. Scientific precedents have very little weight with them; they
are never long detained by the subtilty of the schools, nor
ready to accept big words for sterling coin; they penetrate,

as far as they can, into the principal parts of the subject which engages them, and they expound them in the vernacular tongue. Scientific pursuits then follow a freer and a safer course, but a less lofty one.

The mind may, as it appears to me, divide science into three parts. The first comprises the most theoretical principles, and those more abstract notions whose application is either unknown or very remote. The second is composed of those general truths which still belong to pure theory, but lead nevertheless by a straight and short road to practical results. Methods of application and means of execution make up the third. Each of these different portions of science may be separately cultivated, although reason and experience show that none of them can prosper long, if it be absolutely cut off from the other two.

In America the purely practical part of science is admirably understood, and careful attention is paid to the theoretical portion which is immediately requisite to application. On this head the Americans always display a clear, free, original, and inventive power of mind. But scarcely any one in the United States devotes himself to the essentially theoretical and abstract portion of human knowledge. In this respect the Americans carry to excess a tendency which is, I think, discernible, though in a less degree, among all democratic nations.

Nothing is more necessary to the culture of the higher sciences, or of the more elevated departments of science, than meditation; and nothing is less suited to meditation than the structure of democratic society. We do not find there, as among an aristocratic people, one class which clings to a state of repose because it is well off; and another which does not venture to stir because it despairs of improving its condition. Every one is actively in motion: some in quest of power, others of gain. In the midst of this universal tumult—this incessant conflict of jarring interests—this continual stride of men after fortune— where is that calm to be found which is necessary for the deeper combinations of the intellect? How can the mind dwell upon any single point, when everything whirls around it, and man himself is swept and beaten onward by the heady current which rolls all things in its course? But the permanent agitation which subsists in the bosom of a peaceable and established democracy must be distinguished from the tumultuous and revolutionary movements which almost always attend the birth and growth of democratic society. When a violent revolution occurs among a highly civilized people, it can not fail to give a sudden impulse to their feelings and their opinions. This is more particularly true of democratic revolutions, which stir up all the classes of which a people is composed, and beget, at the same time, inordinate ambition in the breast of every member of the community. The French made most surprising advances in the exact sciences at the very time at which they were finishing the destruction of the remains of their former feudal society; yet this sudden fecundity is not to be attributed to democracy, but to the unexampled revolution which attended its growth. What happened at that period was a special incident, and it would be unwise to regard it as the test of a general principle.

Great revolutions are not more common among democratic nations than among others: I am even inclined to believe that they are less so. But there prevails among those populations a small distressing motion—a sort of incessant jostling of men—which annoys and disturbs the mind, without exciting or elevating it. Men who live in democratic communities not only seldom indulge in meditation, but they naturally entertain very little esteem for it. A democratic state of society and democratic institutions plunge the greater part of men into constant active life; and the habits of mind which are suited to an active life are not always suited to a contemplative one. The man of action is frequently obliged to content himself with the best he can get, because he would never accomplish his purpose if he chose to carry every detail to perfection. He has occasion perpetually to rely on ideas which he has not had leisure to search to the bottom; for he is much more frequently aided by the opportunity of an idea than by its strict accuracy; and, in the long-run, he risks less in making use of some false principles than in spending his time in establishing all his principles on the basis of truth. The world is not led by long or learned demonstrations; a rapid glance at particular incidents, the daily study of the fleeting passions of the multitude, the accidents of the time, and the art of turning them to account, decide all its affairs.

In the ages in which active life is the condition of almost every one, men are therefore generally led to attach an excessive value to the rapid bursts and superficial conceptions of the intellect; and, on the other hand, to depreciate below their true standard its slower and deeper labours. This opinion of the public influences the judgment of the men who cultivate the sciences; they are persuaded that they may succeed in those pursuits without meditation, or are deterred from such pursuits as demand it.

There are several methods of studying the sciences. Among a multitude of men you will find a selfish, mercantile, and trading taste for the discoveries of the mind, which must not be confounded with that disinterested passion which is kindled in the heart of the few. A desire to utilize knowledge is one thing; the pure desire to know is another. I do not doubt that in a few minds and far between, an ardent, inexhaustible love of truth springs up, self-supported, and living in ceaseless fruition without ever attaining the satisfaction which it seeks. This ardent love it is—this proud, disinterested love of what is true—that raises men to the abstract sources of truth, to draw their mother-knowledge thence. If Pascal had had nothing in view but some large gain, or even if he had been stimulated by the love of fame alone, I can not conceive that he would ever have been able to rally all the powers of his mind, as he did, for the better discovery of the most hidden things of the Creator. When I see him, as it were, tear his soul from the midst of all the cares of life to devote it wholly to these researches, and, prematurely snapping the links which bind the frame to life, die of old age before forty, I stand amazed, and I perceive that no ordinary cause is at work to produce efforts so extraordinary.

The future will prove whether these passions, at once so rare and so productive, come into being and into growth as easily in the midst of democratic as in aristocratic communities. For myself, I confess that I am slow to believe it. In aristocratic society, the class which gives the tone to opinion, and has the supreme guidance of affairs, being permanently and hereditarily placed above the multitude, naturally conceives a lofty idea of itself and of man. It loves to invent for him noble pleasures, to carve out splendid objects for his ambition. Aristocracies often commit very tyrannical and very inhuman actions; but they rarely entertain grovelling thoughts; and they show a kind of haughty contempt of little pleasures, even while they indulge in them. The effect is greatly to raise the general pitch of society. In aristocratic ages vast ideas are commonly entertained of the dignity, the power, and the greatness of man. These opinions exert their influence on those who cultivate the sciences, as well as on the rest of the community. They facilitate the natural impulse of the mind to the highest regions of thought, and they naturally prepare it to conceive a sublime—nay, almost a divine—love of truth. Men of science at such periods are consequently carried away by theory; and it even happens that they frequently conceive an inconsiderate contempt for the practical part of learning. "Archimedes," says Plutarch, " was of so lofty a spirit that he never condescended to write any treatise on the manner of constructing all these engines of offence and defence. And as he held this science of inventing and putting together engines, and all arts, generally speaking, which tended to any useful end in practice, to be vile, low, and mercenary, he spent his talents and his studious hours in writing of those things only whose beauty and subtilty had in them no admixture of necessity." Such is the aristocratic aim of science; in democratic nations it can not be the same.

The greater part of the men who constitute these nations are extremely eager in the pursuit of actual and physical gratification. As they are always dissatisfied with the position which they occupy, and are always free to leave it, they think of nothing but the means of changing their fortune, or of increasing it. To minds thus predisposed, every new method which leads by a shorter road to wealth, every machine which spares labour, every instrument which diminishes the cost of production, every discovery which facilitates pleasures or augments them, seems to be the grandest effort of the human intellect. It is chiefly from these motives that a democratic people addicts itself to scientific pursuits—that it understands, and that it respects them. In aristocratic ages, science is more particularly called upon to furnish gratification to the mind; in democracies, to the body. You may be sure that the more a nation is democratic, enlightened, and free, the greater will be the number of these interested promoters of scientific genius, and the more will discoveries immediately applicable to productive industry confer gain, fame, and even power on their authors. For in democracies the working class takes a part in public affairs; and public honours, as well as pecuniary remuneration, may be awarded to those who deserve them. In a community thus organized it easily may be conceived that the human mind may be led insensibly to the neglect of theory; and that it is urged, on the contrary, with unparalleled vehemence to the applications of science, or at least to that portion of theoretical science which is necessary to those who make such applications. In vain will some innate propensity raise the mind toward the loftier spheres of the intellect; interest draws it down to the middle zone. There it may develop all its energy and restless activity, there it may engender all its wonders. These very Americans, who have not discovered one of the general laws of mechanics, have introduced into navigation an engine which changes the aspect of the world.

Assuredly I do not contend that the democratic nations

of our time are destined to witness the extinction of the transcendent luminaries of man's intelligence, nor even that no new lights will ever start into existence. At the age at which the world has now arrived, and among so many cultivated nations, perpetually excited by the fever of productive industry, the bonds which connect the different parts of science together can not fail to strike the observation; and the taste for practical science itself, if it be enlightened, ought to lead men not to neglect theory.   In the midst of such numberless attempted applications of so many experiments, repeated every day, it is almost impossible that general laws should not frequently be brought to light; so that great discoveries would be frequent, though great inventors be rare. I believe, moreover, in the high calling of scientific minds. If the democratic principle does not, on the one hand, induce men to cultivate science for its own sake, on the other it enormously increases the number of those who do cultivate it. Nor is it credible that, from among so great a multitude no speculative genius should from time to time arise, inflamed by the love of truth alone. Such a one, we may be sure, would dive into the deepest mysteries of Nature, whatever be the spirit of his country or his age. He requires no assistance in his course—enough that he be not checked in it.

All that I mean to say is this: permanent inequality of conditions leads men to confine themselves to the arrogant and sterile research of abstract truths; while the social condition and the institutions of democracy prepare them to seek the immediate and useful practical results of the sciences. This tendency is natural and inevitable: it is curious to be acquainted with it, and it may be necessary to point it out. If those who are called upon to guide the nations of our time clearly discerned from afar off these new tendencies, which will soon be irresistible, they would understand that, possessing education and freedom, men living in democratic ages can not fail to improve the industrial part of science; and that henceforward all the efforts of the constituted authorities ought to be directed to support the highest branches of learning, and to foster the nobler passion for science itself. In the present age the human mind must be coerced into theoretical studies; it runs of its own accord to practical applications; and, instead of perpetually referring it to the minute examination of secondary effects, it is well to divert it from them sometimes, in order to raise it up to the contemplation of primary causes. Because the civilization of ancient Rome perished in consequence of the invasion of the barbarians, we are perhaps too apt to think that civilization can not perish in any other manner. If the light by which we are guided is ever extinguished, it will dwindle by degrees, and expire of itself. By dint of close adherence to mere applications, principles would be lost sight of; and when the principles were wholly forgotten, the methods derived from them would be ill pursued. New methods could no longer be invented, and men would continue to apply, without intelligence, and without art, scientific processes no longer understood.

When Europeans first arrived in China, three hundred years ago, they found that almost all the arts had reached a certain degree of perfection there; and they were surprised that a people which had attained this point should not have gone beyond it. At a later period they discovered some traces of the higher branches of science which were lost. The nation was absorbed in productive industry: the greater part of its scientific processes had been preserved, but science itself no longer existed there. This served to explain the strangely motionless state in which they found the minds of this people. The Chinese, in following the track of their forefathers, had forgotten the reasons by which the latter had been guided. They still used the formula, without asking for its meaning: they retained the instrument, but they no longer possessed the art of altering or renewing it. The Chinese, then, had lost the power of change; for them to improve was impossible. They were compelled, at all times and in all points, to imitate their predecessors, lest they should stray into utter darkness, by deviating for an instant from the path already laid down for them. The source of human knowledge was all but dry; and though the stream still ran on, it could neither swell its waters nor alter its channel. Notwithstanding this, China had subsisted peaceably for centuries. The invaders who had conquered the country assumed the manners of the inhabitants, and order prevailed there. A sort of physical prosperity was everywhere discernible: revolutions were rare, and war was, so to speak, unknown.

It is then a fallacy to flatter ourselves with the reflection that the barbarians are still far from us; for if there be some nations which allow civilization to be torn from their grasp, there are others who trample it themselves under their feet.

It would be to waste the time of my readers and my own if I strove to demonstrate how the general mediocrity of fortunes, the absence of superfluous wealth, the universal desire of comfort, and the constant efforts by which every one attempts to procure it, make the taste for the useful predominate over the love of the beautiful in the heart of man. Democratic nations, among which all these things exist, will therefore cultivate the arts which serve to render life easy, in preference to those whose object is to adorn it. They will habitually prefer the useful to the beautiful, and they will require that the beautiful should be useful. But I propose to go further; and after having pointed out this first feature, to sketch several others.

It commonly happens that in the ages of privilege the practice of almost all the arts becomes a privilege; and that every profession is a separate walk, upon which it is not allowable for every one to enter. Even when productive industry is free, the fixed character which belongs to aristocratic nations gradually segregates all the persons who practise the same art, till they form a distinct class, always composed of the same families, whose members are all known to each other, and among whom a public opinion of their own and a species of corporate pride soon

36

spring up. In a class or guild of this kind, each artisan has not only his fortune to make, but his reputation to preserve. He is not exclusively swayed by his own interest, or even by that of his customer, but by that of the body to which he belongs; and the interest of that body is, that each artisan should produce the best possible workmanship. In aristocratic ages, the object of the arts is therefore to manufacture as well as possible—not with the greatest despatch, or at the lowest rate.

When, on the contrary, every profession is open to all —when a multitude of persons are constantly embracing and abandoning it—and when its several members are strangers to each other, indifferent, and from their numbers hardly seen among themselves; the social tie is destroyed, and each workman, standing alone, endeavours simply to gain the greatest possible quantity of money at the least possible cost. The will of the customer is then his only limit. But at the same time a corresponding revolution takes place in the customer also. In countries in which riches as well as power are concentrated and retained in the hands of the few, the use of the greater part of this world's goods belongs to a small number of individuals, who are always the same. Necessity, public opinion, or moderate desires exclude all others from the enjoyment of them. As this aristocratic class remains fixed at the pinnacle of greatness on which it stands, without diminution or increase, it is always acted upon by the same wants and affected by them in the same manner. The men of whom it is composed naturally derive from their superior and hereditary position a taste for what is extremely well made and lasting. This affects the general way of thinking of the nation in relation to the arts. It often occurs, among such a people, that even the peasant will rather go without the object he covets than procure them in a state of imperfection. In aristocracies, then, the handicraftsmen work for only a limited number of very fastidious customers: the profit they hope to make depends principally on the perfection of their workmanship.

Such is no longer the case when, all privileges being abolished, ranks are intermingled, and men are forever rising or sinking upon the ladder of society. Among a democratic people a number of citizens always exist whose patrimony is divided and decreasing. They have contracted, under more prosperous circumstances, certain wants, which remain after the means of satisfying such wants are gone; and they are anxiously looking out for some surreptitious method of providing for them. On the other hand, there are always in democracies a large number of men whose fortune is upon the increase, but whose desires grow much faster than their fortunes: and who gloat upon the gifts of wealth in anticipation, long before they have means to command them. Such men are eager to find some short cut to these gratifications, already almost within their reach. From the combination of these two causes the result is, that in democracies there are always a multitude of individuals whose wants are above their means, and who are very willing to take up with imperfect satisfaction rather than abandon the object of their desires.

The artisan readily understands these passions, for he himself partakes in them: in an aristocracy he would seek to sell his workmanship at a high price to the few; he now conceives that the more expeditious way of getting rich is to sell them at a low price to all. But there are only two ways of lowering the price of commodities. The first is to discover some better, shorter, and more ingenious method of producing them: the second is to manufacture a larger quantity of goods, nearly similar, but of less value. Among a democratic population, all the intellectual faculties of the workman are directed to these two objects: he strives to invent methods which may enable him not only to work better, but quicker and cheaper; or, if he can not succeed in that, to diminish the intrinsic qualities of the thing he makes, without rendering it wholly unfit for the use for which it is intended. When none but the wealthy had watches, they were almost all very good ones: few are now made which are worth much, but everybody has one in his pocket. Thus the democratic principle not only tends to direct the human mind to the useful arts, but it induces the artisan to produce with greater rapidity a quantity of imperfect commodities, and the consumer to content himself with these commodities.

Not that in democracies the arts are incapable of producing very commendable works, if such be required. This may occasionally be the case, if customers appear who are ready to pay for time and trouble. In this rivalry of every kind of industry—in the midst of this immense competition and these countless experiments, some excellent workmen are formed who reach the utmost limits of their craft. But they have rarely an opportunity of displaying what they can do; they are scrupulously sparing of their powers; they remain in a state of accomplished mediocrity, which condemns itself, and, though it be very well able to shoot beyond the mark before it, aims only at what it hits. In aristocracies, on the contrary, workmen always do all they can; and when they stop, it is because they have reached the limit of their attainments.

When I arrive in a country where I find some of the finest productions of the arts, I learn from this fact nothing of the social condition or of the political constitution of the country. But if I perceive that the productions of the arts are generally of an inferior quality, very abundant and very cheap, I am convinced that, among the people where this occurs, privilege is on the decline, and that ranks are beginning to intermingle, and will soon be confounded together.

The handicraftsmen of democratic ages endeavour not only to bring their useful productions within the reach of the whole community, but they strive to give to all their commodities attractive qualities which they do not in reality possess. In the confusion of all ranks every one hopes to appear what he is not, and makes great exertions to succeed in this object. This sentiment, indeed, which is but too natural to the heart of man, does not originate in the democratic principle; but that principle applies it to material objects. To mimic virtue is of every age; but the hypocrisy of luxury belongs more particularly to the ages of democracy.

To satisfy these new cravings of human vanity the arts have recourse to every species of imposture: and these devices sometimes go so far as to defeat their own purpose. Imitation diamonds are now made which easily may be mistaken for real ones; as soon as the art of fabricating false diamonds shall have reached so high a degree of perfection that they can not be distinguished from real ones, it is probable that both one and the other will be abandoned, and become mere pebbles again.

This leads me to speak of those arts which are called the fine arts, by way of distinction. I do not believe that it is a necessary effect of a democratic social condition and of democratic institutions to diminish the number of men who cultivate the fine arts; but these causes exert a very powerful influence on the manner in which these arts are cultivated. Many of those who had already contracted a taste for the fine arts are impoverished: on the other hand, many of those who are not yet rich begin to conceive that taste, at least by imitation; and the number of consumers increases, but opulent and fastidious consumers become more scarce. Something analogous to what I have already pointed out in the useful arts then takes place in the fine arts; the productions of artists are more numerous, but the merit of each production is diminished. No longer able to soar to what is great, they cultivate what is pretty and elegant ; and appearance is more attended to than reality. In aristocracies a few great pictures are produced; in democratic countries, a vast number of insignificant ones. In the former, statues are raised of bronze; in the latter, they are modelled in plaster.

When I arrived for the first time at New York, by that part of the Atlantic Ocean which is called the Sound, I was surprised to perceive along the shore, at some distance from the city, a considerable number of little palaces of white marble, several of which were built after the models of ancient architecture. When I went the next day to inspect more closely the building which had particularly attracted my notice, I found that its walls were of white-washed brick, and its columns of painted wood. All the edifices which I had admired the night before were of the same kind.

The social condition and the institutions of democracy impart, moreover, certain peculiar tendencies to all the imitative arts, which it is easy to point out. They frequently withdraw them from the delineation of the soul to fix them exclusively on that of the body: and they substitute the representation of motion and sensation for that of sentiment and thought: in a word, they put the Real in the place of the Ideal. I doubt whether Raphael studied the minutest intracacies of the mechanism of the human body as thoroughly as the draughtsmen of our own time. He did not attach the same importance to rigorous accuracy on this point as they do, because he aspired to surpass Nature. He sought to make of man something which should be superior to man, and to embellish beauty's self. David and his scholars were, on the contrary, as good anatomists as they were good painters. They wonderfully depicted the models which they had before their eyes, but they rarely imagined anything beyond them: they followed Nature with fidelity: while Raphael sought for something better than Nature. They have left us an exact portraiture of man; but he discloses in his works a glimpse of the Divinity. This remark as to the manner of treating a subject is no less applicable to the choice of it. The painters of the Middle Ages generally sought far above themselves, and away from their own time, for mighty subjects, which left to their imagination an unbounded range. Our painters frequently employ their talents in the exact imitation of the details of private life, which they have always before their eyes; and they are forever copying trivial objects, the originals of which are only too abundant in Nature.

I have just observed that in democratic ages monuments of the arts tend to become more numerous and

AN EAST RIVER PALACE.

Photogravure from a photograph.

AN EAST RIVER PALACE.

Photogravure from a photograph.

less important.   I now hasten to point out the exception to this rule.   In a democratic community individuals are very powerless; but the State which represents them all, and contains them all in its grasp, is very powerful.   Nowhere do citizens appear so insignificant as in a democratic nation; nowhere does the nation itself appear greater, or does the mind more easily take in a wide general survey of it.   In democratic communities the imagination is compressed when men consider themselves; it expands indefinitely when they think of the State.   Hence it is that the same men who live on a small scale in narrow dwellings frequently aspire to gigantic splendour in the erection of their public monuments.

The Americans traced out the circuit of an immense city on the site which they intended to make their capital, but which, up to the present time, is hardly more densely peopled than Pontoise, though, according to them, it will one day contain a million inhabitants.   They have already rooted up trees for ten miles round, lest they should interfere with the future citizens of this imaginary metropolis. They have erected a magnificent palace for Congress in the centre of the city, and have given it the pompous name of the Capitol.   The several States of the Union are every day planning and erecting for themselves prodigious undertakings, which would astonish the engineers of the great European nations.   Thus democracy not only leads men to a vast number of inconsiderable productions; it also leads them to raise some monuments on the largest scale: but between these two extremes there is a blank. A few scattered remains of enormous buildings can therefore teach us nothing of the social condition and the institutions of the people by whom they were raised.   I may add, though the remark leads me to step out of my subject, that they do not make us better acquainted with its greatness, its civilization, and its real prosperity.   Whensoever a power of any kind shall be able to make a whole people co-operate in a single undertaking, that power, with a little knowledge and a great deal of time, will succeed in obtaining something enormous from the co-operation of efforts so multiplied. But this does not lead to the conclusion that the people was very happy, very enlightened, or even very strong.

The Spaniards found the city of Mexico full of magnificent temples and vast palaces; but that did not prevent Cortes from conquering the Mexican empire with six hundred foot soldiers and sixteen horses. If the Romans had been better acquainted with the laws of hydraulics, they would not have constructed all the aqueducts which surround the ruins of their cities—they would have made a better use of their power and their wealth. If they had invented the steam-engine, perhaps they would not have extended to the extremities of their empire those long artificial roads which are called Roman roads. These things are at once the splendid memorials of their ignorance and of their greatness. A people which should leave no other vestige of its track than a few leaden pipes in the earth and a few iron rods upon its surface, might have been more the master of Nature than the Romans.

CHAPTER XXV

THE INFLUENCES OF DEMOCRACY UPON LANGUAGE AND LITERATURE

Literary characteristics of democratic ages—The trade of literature—The study of Greek and Latin literature peculiarly useful in democratic communities—The effect of democracy on language—The sources of poetry among democratic nations—The inflated style of American writers and orators—The drama among democratic nations—Characteristics of historians in democratic ages—Parliamentary eloquence in the United States.

WHEN a traveller goes into a bookseller's shop in the United States and examines the American books upon the shelves, the number of works appears extremely great; while that of known authors appears, on the contrary, to be extremely small. He will first meet with a number of elementary treatises, destined to teach the rudiments of human knowledge. Most of these books are written in Europe; the Americans reprint them, adapting them to their own country. Next comes an enormous quantity of religious works, Bibles, sermons, edifying anecdotes, controversial divinity, and reports of charitable societies; lastly, appears the long catalogue of political pamphlets. In America, parties do not write books to combat each others' opinions, but pamphlets which are circulated for a day with incredible rapidity, and then expire. In the midst of all these obscure productions of the human brain are to be found the more remarkable works of that small number of authors whose names are, or ought to be, known to Europeans.

Although America is perhaps in our days the civilized country in which literature is least attended to, a large number of persons are nevertheless to be found there who take an interest in the productions of the mind, and who make them, if not the study of their lives, at least the charm of their leisure hours. But England supplies these readers with the larger portion of the books which they require. Almost all important English books are republished in the United States. The literary genius of Great Britain still darts its rays into the recesses of the forests of the New World. There is hardly a pioneer's hut which does not contain a few odd volumes of Shakespeare. I remember that I read the feudal play of Henry V for the first time in a log-house.

Not only do the Americans constantly draw upon the treasures of English literature, but it may be said with truth that they find the literature of England growing on their own soil. The larger part of that small number of men in the United States who are engaged in the composition of literary works are English in substance, and still more so in form. Thus they transport into the midst of democracy the ideas and literary fashions which are current among the aristocratic nation they have taken for their model. They paint with colours borrowed from foreign manners; and as they hardly ever represent the country they were born in as it really is, they are seldom popular there. The citizens of the United States are themselves so convinced that it is not for them that books are published, that before they can make up their minds upon the merit of one of their authors they generally wait till his fame has been ratified in England, just as in pictures the author of an original is held to be entitled to judge of the merit of a copy. The inhabitants of the United States have then at present, properly speaking, no literature. The only authors whom I acknowledge as American are the journalists. They, indeed, are not great writers, but they speak the language of their countrymen, and make themselves heard by them. Other authors are aliens; they are to the Americans what the imitators of the Greeks and Romans were to us at the revival of learning—an object of curiosity, not of general sympathy. They amuse the mind, but they do not act upon the manners of the people.

I have already said that this state of things is very far from originating in democracy alone, and that the causes of it must be sought for in several peculiar circumstances independent of the democratic principle. If the Americans, retaining the same laws and social condition, had had a different origin, and had been transported into another country, I do not question that they would have had a literature. Even as they now are, I am convinced that they will ultimately have one; but its character will be different from that which marks the American literary productions of our time, and that character will be peculiarly its own. Nor is it impossible to trace this character beforehand.

I suppose an aristocratic people among whom letters are cultivated; the labours of the mind, as well as the affairs of state, are conducted by a ruling class in society. The literary as well as the political career is almost entirely confined to this class, or to those nearest to it in rank. These premises suffice to give me a key to all the rest. When a small number of the same men are engaged at the same time upon the same objects, they easily concert with one another, and agree upon certain leading rules which are to govern them each and all. If the object which attracts the attention of these men is literature, the productions of the mind will soon be subjected by them to precise canons, from which it will no longer be allowable to depart. If these men occupy an hereditary position in the country, they will be naturally inclined, not only to adopt a certain number of fixed rules for themselves, but to follow those which their forefathers laid down for their own guidance; their code will be at once strict and traditional. As they are not necessarily engrossed by the cares of daily life—as they never have been so, any more than their fathers were before them—they have learned to take an interest, for several generations back, in the labours of the mind. They have learned to understand literature as an art, to love it in the end for its own sake, and to feel a scholarlike satisfaction in seeing men conform to its rules. Nor is this all: the men of whom I speak began and will end their lives in easy or in affluent circumstances; hence they naturally have conceived a taste for choice gratifications, and a love of refined and delicate pleasures. Nay more, a kind of indolence of mind and heart, which they frequently contract in the midst of this long and peaceful enjoyment of so much welfare, leads them to put aside, even from their pleasures, whatever might be too startling or too acute. They would rather be amused than intensely excited; they wish to be interested, but not to be carried away.

Now let us fancy a great number of literary performances executed by the men, or for the men, whom I have just described, and we shall readily conceive a style of literature in which everything will be regular and pre-arranged. The slightest work will be carefully touched in its least details; art and labour will be conspicuous in everything; each kind of writing will have rules of its own, from which it will not be allowed to swerve, and which distinguish it from all others. Style will be thought of almost as much importance as thought; and the form will be no less considered than the matter: the diction will be polished, measured, and uniform. The tone of the mind will be always dignified, seldom very animated; and writers will care more to perfect what they produce than to multiply their productions. It will sometimes happen that the members of the literary class, always living among themselves and writing for themselves alone, will lose sight of the rest of the world, which will infect them with a false and laboured style; they will lay down minute literary rules for their exclusive use, which will insensibly lead them to deviate from common sense, and finally to transgress the bounds of Nature. By dint of striving after a mode of parlance different from the vulgar, they will arrive at a sort of aristocratic jargon, which is hardly less remote from pure language than is the coarse dialect of the people.

Such are the natural perils of literature among aristocracies. Every aristocracy which keeps itself entirely aloof
from the people becomes impotent—a fact which is as true
in literature as it is in politics.[1]

Let us now turn the picture and consider the other side
of it; let us transport ourselves into the midst of a democracy, not unprepared by ancient traditions and present culture to partake in the pleasures of the mind. Ranks are
there intermingled and confounded; knowledge and power
are both infinitely subdivided, and, if I may use the expression, scattered on every side. Here, then, is a motley
multitude, whose intellectual wants are to be supplied.
These new votaries of the pleasures of the mind have not
all received the same education; they do not possess the
same degree of culture as their fathers, nor any resemblance
to them—nay, they perpetually differ from themselves, for
they live in a state of incessant change of place, feelings,
and fortunes. The mind of each member of the community
is therefore unattached to that of his fellow-citizens by tradition or by common habits; and they never have had the
power, the inclination, nor the time to concert together.
It is, however, from the bosom of this heterogeneous and
agitated mass that authors spring; and from the same
source their profits and their fame are distributed. I can
understand without difficulty that, under these circumstances, I must expect to meet in the literature of such a
people with but few of those strict conventional rules which
are admitted by readers and by writers in aristocratic ages.
If it should happen that the men of some one period were
agreed upon any such rules, that would prove nothing
for the following period; for among democratic nations
each new generation is a new people. Among such nations, then, literature will not easily be subjected to strict
rules, and it is impossible that any such rules should ever
be permanent.

In democracies it is by no means the case that all the
men who cultivate literature have received a literary education; and most of those who have some tinge of belles-

lettres are either engaged in politics, or in a profession which only allows them to taste occasionally and by stealth the pleasures of the mind. These pleasures, therefore, do not constitute the principal charm of their lives; but they are considered as a transient and necessary recreation amid the serious labours of life. Such men can never acquire a sufficiently intimate knowledge of the art of literature to appreciate its more delicate beauties; and the minor shades of expression must escape them. As the time they can devote to letters is very short, they seek to make the best use of the whole of it. They prefer books which may be easily procured, quickly read, and which require no learned research to be understood. They ask for beauties, self-proffered and easily enjoyed; above all, they must have what is unexpected and new. Accustomed to the struggle, the crosses, and the monotony of practical life, they require rapid emotions, startling passages—truths or errors brilliant enough to rouse them up, and to plunge them at once, as if by violence, into the midst of a subject.

Why should I say more? or who does not understand what is about to follow, before I have expressed it? Taken as a whole, literature in democratic ages can never present, as it does in the periods of aristocracy, an aspect of order, regularity, science, and art; its form will, on the contrary, ordinarily be slighted, sometimes despised. Style will frequently be fantastic, incorrect, overburdened, and loose—almost always vehement and bold. Authors will aim at rapidity of execution, more than at perfection of detail. Small productions will be more common than bulky books; there will be more wit than erudition, more imagination than profundity; and literary performances will bear marks of an untutored and rude vigour of thought—frequently of great variety and singular fecundity. The object of authors will be to astonish rather than to please, and to stir the passions more than to charm the taste. Here and there, indeed, writers will doubtless occur who will choose a different track, and who will, if they are gifted with superior abilities, succeed in finding readers, in spite of their defects or their better qualities; but these exceptions will be rare, and even the authors who shall so depart from the received practice in the main subject of their works, will always relapse into it in some lesser details.

I have just depicted two extreme conditions: the transition by which a nation passes from the former to the latter is not sudden but gradual, and marked with shades of very various intensity. In the passage which conducts a lettered people from the one to the other there is almost always a moment at which the literary genius of democratic nations has its confluence with that of aristocracies, and both seek to establish their joint sway over the human mind. Such epochs are transient, but very brilliant: they are fertile without exuberance, and animated without confusion. The French literature of the eighteenth century may serve as an example.

I should say more than I mean if I were to assert that the literature of a nation is always subordinate to its social condition and its political constitution. I am aware that, independently of these causes, there are several others which confer certain characteristics on literary productions; but these appear to me to be the chief. The relations which exist between the social and political condition of a people and the genius of its authors are always very numerous; whoever knows the one is never completely ignorant of the other.

Democracy not only infuses a taste for letters among the trading classes, but introduces a trading spirit into literature. In aristocracies, readers are fastidious and few in number; in democracies, they are far more numerous and far less difficult to please. The consequence is, that among aristocratic nations no one can hope to succeed without immense exertions, and that these exertions may bestow a great deal of fame, but never can earn much money; while among democratic nations, a writer may flatter himself that he will obtain at a cheap rate a meagre reputation and a large fortune. For this purpose he need not be admired; it is enough that he is liked. The ever-

increasing crowd of readers, and their continual craving
for something new, insure the sale of books which nobody
much esteems.

In democratic periods the public frequently treat authors as kings do their courtiers; they enrich, and they
despise them. What more is needed by the venal souls
which are born in courts, or which are worthy to live there?
Democratic literature is always infested with a tribe of
writers who look upon letters as a mere trade: and for
some few great authors who adorn it you may reckon thousands of idea-mongers.

What was called the People in the most democratic republics of antiquity was very unlike what we designate by
that term. In Athens, all the citizens took part in public
affairs; but there were only twenty thousand citizens to
more than three hundred and fifty thousand inhabitants.
All the rest were slaves, and discharged the greater part
of those duties which belong at the present day to the
lower or even to the middle classes. Athens, then, with
her universal suffrage, was after all merely an aristocratic
republic in which all the nobles had an equal right to the
government. The struggle between the patricians and
plebeians of Rome must be considered in the same light:
it was simply an intestine feud between the elder and
younger branches of the same family. All the citizens belonged, in fact, to the aristocracy, and partook of its character.

It is, moreover, to be remarked, that among the ancients books were always scarce and dear; and that very
great difficulties impeded their publication and circulation.
These circumstances concentrated literary tastes and habits
among a small number of men, who formed a small literary
aristocracy out of the choicer spirits of the great political
aristocracy. Accordingly, nothing goes to prove that literature was ever treated as a trade among the Greeks and
Romans.

These peoples, which not only constituted aristocracies,
but very polished and free nations, of course imparted to

their literary productions the defects and the merits which characterize the literature of aristocratic ages. And, indeed, a very superficial survey of the literary remains of the ancients will suffice to convince us that if those writers were sometimes deficient in variety, or fertility in their subjects, or in boldness, vivacity, or power of generalization in their thoughts, they always displayed exquisite care and skill in their details. Nothing in their works seems to be done hastily or at random: every line is written for the eye of the connoisseur, and is shaped after some conception of ideal beauty. No literature places those fine qualities, in which the writers of democracies are naturally deficient, in bolder relief than that of the ancients; no literature, therefore, ought to be more studied in democratic ages. This study is better suited than any other to combat the literary defects inherent in those ages: as for their more praiseworthy literary qualities, they will spring up of their own accord, without its being necessary to learn to acquire them.

It is important that this point should be clearly understood. A particular study may be useful to the literature of a people, without being appropriate to its social and political wants. If men were to persist in teaching nothing but the literature of the dead languages in a community where every one is habitually led to make vehement exertions to augment or to maintain his fortune, the result would be a very polished, but a very dangerous, race of citizens. For as their social and political condition would give them every day a sense of wants which their education would never teach them to supply, they would perturb the State, in the name of the Greeks and Romans, instead of enriching it by their productive industry.

It is evident that in democratic communities the interest of individuals, as well as the security of the commonwealth, demands that the education of the greater number should be scientific, commercial, and industrial, rather than literary. Greek and Latin should not be taught in all schools; but it is important that those who by their natural disposition or their fortune are destined to cultivate letters or prepared to relish them, should find schools where a complete knowledge of ancient literature may be acquired, and where the true scholar may be formed. A few excellent universities would do more toward the attainment of this object than a vast number of bad grammarschools, where superfluous matters, badly learned, stand in the way of sound instruction in necessary studies.

All who aspire to literary excellence in democratic nations ought frequently to refresh themselves at the springs of ancient literature: there is no more wholesome course for the mind. Not that I hold the literary productions of the ancients to be irreproachable; but I think that they have some especial merits, admirably calculated to counterbalance our peculiar defects. They are a prop on the side on which we are in most danger of falling.

If the reader has rightly understood what I have already said on the subject of literature in general, he will have no difficulty in comprehending that species of influence which a democratic social condition and democratic institutions may exercise over language itself, which is the chief instrument of thought.

American authors may truly be said to live more in England than in their own country; since they constantly study the English writers, and take them every day for their models. But such is not the case with the bulk of the population, which is more immediately subjected to the peculiar causes acting upon the United States. It is not then to the written but to the spoken language that attention must be paid if we would detect the modifications which the idiom of an aristocratic people may undergo when it becomes the language of a democracy.

Englishmen of education, and more competent judges than I can be myself of the nicer shades of expression, have frequently assured me that the language of the educated classes in the United States is notably different from that of the educated classes in Great Britain. They complain not only that the Americans have brought into use a number of new words—the difference and the distance between the two countries might suffice to explain that much—but that these new words are more especially taken from the jargon of parties, the mechanical arts, or the language of trade. They assert, in addition to this, that old English words are often used by the Americans in new acceptations; and lastly, that the inhabitants of the United States frequently intermingle their phraseology in the strangest manner, and sometimes place words together which are always kept apart in the language of the mother-country. These remarks, which were made to me at various times by persons who appeared to be worthy of credit, led me to reflect upon the subject; and my reflections brought me, by theoretical reasoning, to the same point at which my informants had arrived by practical observation.

In aristocracies, language must naturally partake of that state of repose in which everything remains. Few new words are coined, because few new things are made; and even if new things were made, they would be designated by known words, whose meaning has been determined by tradition. If it happens that the human mind bestirs itself at length, or is roused by light breaking in from without, the novel expressions which are introduced are characterized by a degree of learning, intelligence, and philosophy which shows that they do not originate in a democracy. After the fall of Constantinople had turned the tide of science and literature toward the west, the French language was almost immediately invaded by a multitude of new words, which had all Greek or Latin roots. An erudite neologism then sprang up in France which was confined to the educated classes, and which produced no sensible effect, or at least a very gradual one, upon the people. All the nations of Europe successively exhibited the same change. Milton alone introduced more than six hundred words into the English language, almost all derived from the Latin, the Greek, or the Hebrew. The constant agitation which prevails in a democratic community tends unceasingly, on the contrary, to change the character of the language, as it does the aspect of affairs. In the midst of this general stir and competition of minds a great number of new ideas are formed, old ideas are lost, or reappear, or are subdivided into an infinite variety of minor shades. The consequence is, that many words must fall into desuetude, and others must be brought into use.

Democratic nations love change for its own sake; and this is seen in their language as much as in their politics. Even when they do not need to change words, they sometimes feel a wish to transform them. The genius of a democratic people is not only shown by the great number of words they bring into use, but also by the nature of the ideas these new words represent. Among such a people the majority lays down the law in language as well as in everything else; its prevailing spirit is as manifest in that as in other respects. But the majority is more engaged in business than in study—in political and commercial interests than in philosophical speculation or literary pursuits. Most of the words coined or adopted for its use will therefore bear the mark of these habits; they will mainly serve to express the wants of business, the passions of party, or the details of the public administration. In these departments the language will constantly spread, while on the other hand it will gradually lose ground in metaphysics and theology.

As to the source from which democratic nations are wont to derive their new expressions, and the manner in which they go to work to coin them, both may easily be described. Men living in democratic countries know but little of the language which was spoken at Athens and at Rome, and they do not care to dive into the lore of antiquity to find the expression they happen to want. If they have sometimes recourse to learned etymologies, vanity will induce them to search at the roots of the dead languages; but erudition does not naturally furnish them with its resources. The most ignorant, it sometimes happens, will use them most. The eminently democratic desire to get above their own sphere will often lead them to seek to dignify a vulgar profession by a Greek or Latin name. The lower the calling is, and the more remote from learning, the more pompous and erudite is its appellation. Thus the French rope-dancers have transformed themselves into " Acrobates " and " Funambules."

In the absence of knowledge of the dead languages, democratic nations are apt to borrow words from living tongues; for their mutual intercourse becomes perpetual, and the inhabitants of different countries imitate each other the more readily as they grow more like each other every day.

But it is principally upon their own languages that democratic nations attempt to perpetrate innovations. From time to time they resume forgotten expressions in their vocabulary, which they restore to use; or they borrow from some particular class of the community a term peculiar to it, which they introduce with a figurative meaning into the language of daily life. Many expressions which originally belonged to the technical language of a profession or a party are thus drawn into general circulation.

The most common expedient employed by democratic nations to make an innovation in language consists in giving some unwonted meaning to an expression already in use. This method is very simple, prompt, and convenient; no learning is required to use it aright, and ignorance itself rather facilitates the practice; but that practice is most dangerous to the language. When a democratic people doubles the meaning of a word in this way, they sometimes render the signification which it retains as ambiguous as that which it acquires. An author begins by a slight deflection of a known expression from its primitive meaning, and he adapts it, thus modified, as well as he can to his subject. A second writer twists the sense of the expression in another way; a third takes possession of it for another purpose; and as there is no common appeal to the sentence of a permanent tribunal which may definitely settle the signification of the word, it remains in an ambiguous condition. The consequence is that writers hardly ever appear to dwell upon a single thought, but they always seem to point their aim at a knot of ideas, leaving the reader to judge which of them has been hit. This is a deplorable consequence of democracy. I would rather that the language should be made hideous with words imported from the Chinese, the Tartars, or the Hurons, than that the meaning of a word in our own language should become indeterminate. Harmony and uniformity are only secondary beauties in composition; many of these things are conventional, and, strictly speaking, it is possible to forego them; but without clear phraseology there is no good language.

The principle of equality necessarily introduces several other changes into language. In aristocratic ages, when each nation tends to stand aloof from all others and likes to have distinct characteristics of its own, it often happens that several peoples which have a common origin become nevertheless estranged from each other, so that, without ceasing to understand the same language, they no longer all speak it in the same manner. In these ages each nation is divided into a certain number of classes, which see but little of each other, and do not intermingle. Each of these classes contracts, and invariably retains, habits of mind peculiar to itself, and adopts by choice certain words and certain terms, which afterward pass from generation to generation, like their estates. The same idiom then comprises a language of the poor and a language of the rich —a language of the citizen and a language of the nobility —a learned language and a vulgar one. The deeper the divisions, and the more impassable the barriers of society become, the more must this be the case. I would lay a wager that among the castes of India there are amazing variations of language, and that there is almost as much difference between the language of the Pariah and that of the Brahmin as there is in their dress. When, on the contrary, men, being no longer restrained by ranks, meet on terms of constant intercourse—when castes are destroyed, and the classes of society are recruited and intermixed with each other, all the words of a language are mingled. Those which are unsuitable to the greater number perish; the remainder form a common store, whence every one chooses pretty nearly at random. Almost all the different dialects which divided the idioms of European nations are manifestly declining; there is no patois in the New World, and it is disappearing every day from the old countries.

The influence of this revolution in social conditions is as much felt in style as it is in phraseology. Not only does every one use the same words, but a habit springs up of using them without discrimination. The rules which style had set up are almost abolished: the line ceases to be drawn between expressions which seem by their very nature vulgar, and others which appear to be refined. Persons springing from different ranks of society carry the terms and expressions they are accustomed to use with them, into whatever circumstances they may pass; thus the origin of words is lost like the origin of individuals, and there is as much confusion in language as there is in society.

I am aware that in the classification of words there are rules which do not belong to one form of society any more than to another, but which are derived from the nature of things. Some expressions and phrases are vulgar, because the ideas they are meant to express are low in themselves; others are of a higher character, because the objects they are intended to designate are naturally elevated. No intermixture of ranks will ever efface these differences. But the principle of equality can not fail to root out whatever is merely conventional and arbitrary in the forms of thought. Perhaps the necessary classification which I pointed out in the last sentence will always be less respected by a democratic people than by any other, because among such a people there are no men who are permanently disposed by education, culture, and leisure to study the natural laws of language, and who cause those laws to be respected by their own observance of them.

I shall not quit this topic without touching on a feature

of democratic languages, which is perhaps more characteristic of them than any other. It has already been shown that democratic nations have a taste, and sometimes a passion, for general ideas, and that this arises from their peculiar merits and defects. This liking for general ideas is displayed in democratic languages by the continual use of generic terms or abstract expressions, and by the manner in which they are employed. This is the great merit and the great imperfection of these languages. Democratic nations are passionately addicted to generic terms or abstract expressions, because these modes of speech enlarge thought, and assist the operations of the mind by enabling it to include several objects in a small compass. A French democratic writer will be apt to say capacités in the abstract for men of capacity, and without particularizing the objects to which their capacity is applied: he will talk about actualités to designate in one word the things passing before his eyes at the instant; and he will comprehend under the term éventualités whatever may happen in the universe, dating from the moment at which he speaks. Democratic writers are perpetually coining words of this kind, in which they sublimate into further abstraction the abstract terms of the language. Nay, more, to render their mode of speech more succinct, they personify the subject of these abstract terms, and make it act like a real entity. Thus they would say in French, La force des choses veut que les capacités gouvernent.

I can not better illustrate what I mean than by my own example. I have frequently used the word equality in an absolute sense—nay, I have personified equality in several places; thus I have said that equality does such and such things, or refrains from doing others. It may be affirmed that the writers of the age of Louis XIV would not have used these expressions: they would never have thought of using the word equality without applying it to some particular object; and they would rather have renounced the term altogether than have consented to make a living personage of it.

These abstract terms which abound in democratic languages, and which are used on every occasion without attaching them to any particular fact, enlarge and obscure the thoughts they are intended to convey; they render the mode of speech more succinct, and the idea contained in it less clear. But with regard to language, democratic nations prefer obscurity to labour. I know not, indeed, whether this loose style has not some secret charm for those who speak and write among these nations. As the men who live there are frequently left to the efforts of their individual powers of mind, they are almost always a prey to doubt; and as their situation in life is forever changing, they are never held fast to any of their opinions by the certain tenure of their fortunes. Men living in democratic countries are, then, apt to entertain unsettled ideas, and they require loose expressions to convey them. As they never know whether the idea they express to-day will be appropriate to the new position they may occupy to-morrow, they naturally acquire a liking for abstract terms. An abstract term is like a box with a false bottom: you may put in it what ideas you please, and take them out again without being observed.

Among all nations, generic and abstract terms form the basis of language. I do not, therefore, affect to expel these terms from democratic languages; I simply remark that men have an especial tendency, in the ages of democracy, to multiply words of this kind—to take them always by themselves in their most abstract acceptation, and to use them on all occasions, even when the nature of the discourse does not require them.

Various different significations have been given to the word Poetry. It would weary my readers if I were to lead them into a discussion as to which of these definitions ought to be selected: I prefer telling them at once that which I have chosen. In my opinion, Poetry is the search and the delineation of the Ideal. The poet is he who, by suppressing a part of what exists, by adding some imaginary touches to the picture, and by combining certain real circumstances, but which do not, in fact, concurrently happen, completes and extends the work of Nature. Thus the object of poetry is not to represent what is true, but to adorn it, and to present to the mind some loftier imagery. Verse, regarded as the ideal beauty of language, may be eminently poetical; but verse does not, of itself, constitute poetry.

I now proceed to inquire whether, among the actions, the sentiments, and the opinions of democratic nations, there are any which lead to a conception of ideal beauty, and which may for this reason be considered as natural sources of poetry. It must, in the first place, be acknowledged that the taste for ideal beauty, and the pleasure derived from the expression of it, are never so intense or so diffused among a democratic as among an aristocratic people. In aristocratic nations it sometimes happens that the body goes on to act as it were spontaneously, while the higher faculties are bound and burdened by repose. Among these nations the people will very often display poetic tastes, and sometimes allow their fancy to range beyond and above what surrounds them. But in democracies the love of physical gratification, the notion of bettering one's condition, the excitement of competition, the charm of anticipated success, are so many spurs to urge men onward in the active professions they have embraced, without allowing them to deviate for an instant from the track. The main stress of the faculties is to this point. The imagination is not extinct; but its chief function is to devise what may be useful, and to represent what is real.

The principle of equality not only diverts men from the description of ideal beauty—it also diminishes the number of objects to be described. Aristocracy, by maintaining society in a fixed position, is favourable to the solidity and duration of positive religions, as well as to the stability of political institutions. It not only keeps the human mind within a certain sphere of belief, but it predisposes the mind to adopt one faith rather than another. An aristocratic people will always be prone to place intermediate powers between God and man. In this respect it may be said that the aristocratic element is favourable to poetry. When the universe is peopled with supernatural creatures, not palpable to the senses but discovered by the mind, the imagination ranges freely, and poets, finding a thousand subjects to delineate, also find a countless audience to take an interest in their productions. In democratic ages it sometimes happens, on the contrary, that men are as much afloat in matters of belief as they are in their laws. Scepticism, then, draws the imagination of poets back to earth, and confines them to the real and visible world. Even when the principle of equality does not disturb religious belief, it tends to simplify it, and to divert attention from secondary agents, to fix it principally on the Supreme Power. Aristocracy naturally leads the human mind to the contemplation of the past, and fixes it there. Democracy, on the contrary, gives men a sort of instinctive distaste for what is ancient. In this respect aristocracy is far more favourable to poetry; for things commonly grow larger and more obscure as they are more remote; and for this twofold reason they are better suited to the delineation of the ideal.

After having deprived poetry of the past, the principle of equality robs it in part of the present. Among aristocratic nations there are a certain number of privileged personages, whose situation is, as it were, without and above the condition of man; to these, power, wealth, fame, wit, refinement, and distinction in all things appear peculiarly to belong. The crowd never sees them very closely, or does not watch them in minute details; and little is needed to make the description of such men poetical. On the other hand, among the same people, you will meet with classes so ignorant, low, and enslaved that they are no less fit objects for poetry from the excess of their rudeness and wretchedness, than the former are from their greatness and refinement. Besides, as the different classes of which an aristocratic community is composed are widely separated, and imperfectly acquainted with each other, the imagination may always represent them with some addition to, or some subtraction from, what they really are. In democratic communities, where men are all insignificant and very much alike, each man instantly sees all his fellows when he surveys himself. The poets of democratic ages can never, therefore, take any man in particular as the subject of a piece; for an object of slender importance, which is distinctly seen on all sides, will never lend itself to an ideal conception. Thus the principle of equality, in proportion as it has established itself in the world, has dried up most of the old springs of poetry. Let us now attempt to show what new ones it may disclose.

When scepticism had depopulated heaven, and the progress of equality had reduced each individual to smaller and better known proportions, the poets, not yet aware of what they could substitute for the great themes which were departing together with the aristocracy, turned their eyes to inanimate Nature. As they lost sight of gods and heroes, they set themselves to describe streams and mountains. Thence originated, in the last century, that kind of poetry which has been called, by way of distinction, the descriptive. Some have thought that this sort of delineation, embellished with all the physical and inanimate objects which cover the earth, was the kind of poetry peculiar to democratic ages; but I believe this to be an error, and that it only belongs to a period of transition.

I am persuaded that in the end democracy diverts the imagination from all that is external to man, and fixes it on man alone. Democratic nations may amuse themselves for a while with considering the productions of Nature; but they are only excited in reality by a survey of themselves. Here, and here alone, the true sources of poetry among such nations are to be found; and it may be believed that the poets who shall neglect to draw their inspirations hence, will lose all sway over the minds which they would enchant, and will be left in the end with none but unimpassioned spectators of their transports. I have shown how the ideas of progression and of the indefinite perfectibility of the human race belong to democratic ages. Democratic nations care but little for what has been, but they are haunted by visions of what will be; in this direction their unbounded imagination grows and dilates beyond all measure. Here, then, is the wildest range open to the genius of poets, which allows them to remove their performances to a sufficient distance from the eye. Democracy shuts the past against the poet, but opens the future before him. As all the citizens who compose a democratic community are nearly equal and alike, the poet can not dwell upon any one of them; but the nation itself invites the exercise of his powers. The general similitude of individuals, which renders any one of them taken separately an improper subject of poetry, allows poets to include them all in the same imagery, and to take a general survey of the people itself. Democratic nations have a clearer perception than any others of their own aspect; and an aspect so imposing is admirably fitted to the delineation of the ideal.

I readily admit that the Americans have no poets; I can not allow that they have no poetic ideas. In Europe people talk a great deal of the wilds of America, but the Americans themselves never think about them: they are insensible to the wonders of inanimate Nature, and they may be said not to perceive the mighty forests which surround them till they fall beneath the hatchet. Their eyes are fixed upon another sight: the American people views its own march across these wilds—drying swamps, turning the course of rivers, peopling solitudes, and subduing Nature. This magnificent image of themselves does not meet the gaze of the Americans at intervals only; it may be said to haunt every one of them in his least as well as in his most important actions, and to be always flitting before his mind. Nothing conceivable is so petty, so insipid, so crowded with paltry interests, in one word so anti-poetic, as the life of a man in the United States. But among the thoughts which it suggests there is always one which is full of poetry, and that is the hidden nerve which gives vigour to the frame.

In aristocratic ages each people, as well as each individual, is prone to stand separate and aloof from all others. In democratic ages, the extreme fluctuations of men and the impatience of their desires keep them perpetually on the move; so that the inhabitants of different countries intermingle, see, listen to, and borrow from each other's stores. It is then not only the members of the same community who grow more alike; communities are themselves assimilated to one another, and the whole assemblage presents to the eye of the spectator one vast democracy, each citizen of which is a people. This displays the aspect of mankind for the first time in the broadest light. All that belongs to the existence of the human race taken as a whole, to its vicissitudes and to its future, becomes an abundant mine of poetry. The poets who lived in aristocratic ages have been eminently successful in their delineations of certain incidents in the life of a people or a man; but none of them ever ventured to include within his performances the destinies of mankind—a task which poets writing in democratic ages may attempt. At that same time at which every man, raising his eyes above his country, begins at length to discern mankind at large, the Divinity is more and more manifest to the human mind in full and entire majesty. If in democratic ages faith in positive religions be often shaken, and the belief in intermediate agents, by whatever name they are called, be overcast; on the other hand men are disposed to conceive a far broader idea of Providence itself, and its interference in human affairs assumes a new and more imposing appearance to their eyes. Looking at the human race as one great whole, they easily conceive that its destinies are regulated by the same design; and in the actions of every individual they are led to acknowledge a trace of that universal and eternal plan on which God rules our race. This consideration may be taken as another prolific source of poetry which is opened in democratic ages. Democratic poets will always appear trivial and frigid if they seek to invest gods, demons, or angels with corporeal forms, and if they attempt to draw them down from heaven to dispute the supremacy of earth. But if they strive to connect the great events they commemorate with the general providential designs which govern the universe, and, without showing the finger of the Supreme Governor, reveal the thoughts of the Supreme Mind, their works will be admired and understood, for the imagination of their contemporaries takes this direction of its own accord.

It may be foreseen in like manner that poets living in democratic ages will prefer the delineation of passions and ideas to that of persons and achievements. The language, the dress, and the daily actions of men in democracies are repugnant to ideal conceptions. These things are not poetical in themselves; and if it were otherwise, they would cease to be so, because they are too familiar to all those to whom the poet would speak of them. This forces the poet constantly to search below the external surface which is palpable to the senses, in order to read the inner soul: and nothing lends itself more to the delineation of the Ideal than the scrutiny of the hidden depths in the immaterial nature of man. I need not to ramble over earth and sky to discover a wondrous object woven of contrasts, of greatness and littleness infinite, of intense gloom and of amazing brightness—capable at once of exciting pity, admiration, terror, contempt. I find that object in myself. Man springs out of nothing, crosses Time, and disappears forever in the bosom of God; he is seen but for a moment, staggering on the verge of the two abysses, and there he is lost. If man were wholly ignorant of himself, he would have no poetry in him; for it is impossible to describe what the mind does not conceive. If man clearly discerned his own nature, his imagination would remain idle, and would have nothing to add to the picture. But the nature of man is sufficiently disclosed for him to apprehend something of himself; and sufficiently obscure for all the rest to be plunged in thick darkness, in which he gropes forever—and forever in vain—to lay hold on some completer notion of his being.

Among a democratic people poetry will not be fed with legendary lays or the memorials of old traditions. The poet will not attempt to people the universe with supernatural beings in whom his readers and his own fancy have ceased to believe; nor will he present virtues and vices in the mask of frigid personification, which are better received under their own features. All these resources fail him; but Man remains, and the poet needs no more. The destinies of mankind—man himself, taken aloof from his age and his country, and standing in the presence of Nature and of God, with his passions, his doubts, his rare prosperities, and inconceivable wretchedness—will become the chief if not the sole theme of poetry among these nations. Experience may confirm this assertion, if we consider the productions of the greatest poets who have appeared since the world has been turned to democracy. The authors of our age who have so admirably delineated the features of Faust, Childe Harold, Réné, and Jocelyn, did not seek to record the actions of an individual, but to enlarge and to throw light on some of the obscurer recesses of the human heart. Such are the poems of democracy. The principle of equality does not then destroy all the subjects of poetry: it renders them less numerous, but more vast.

I have frequently remarked that the Americans, who generally treat of business in clear, plain language, devoid of all ornament, and so extremely simple as to be often coarse, are apt to become inflated as soon as they attempt a more poetical diction. They then vent their pomposity from one end of a harangue to the other; and to hear them lavish imagery on every occasion, one might fancy that they never spoke of anything with simplicity. The English are more rarely given to a similar failing. The cause of this may be pointed out without much difficulty. In democratic communities each citizen is habitually engaged in the contemplation of a very puny object, namely,

STUMP SPEAKING.

Photogravure from an engraving after a painting by G. C. Bingham.

himself. If he ever raises his looks higher, he then perceives nothing but the immense form of society at large,
or the still more imposing aspect of mankind. His ideas
are all either extremely minute and clear, or extremely
general and vague: what lies between is an open void.
When he has been drawn out of his own sphere, therefore,
he always expects that some amazing object will be offered
to his attention; and it is on these terms alone that he
consents to tear himself for an instant from the petty complicated cares which form the charm and the excitement
of his life. This appears to me sufficiently to explain why
men in democracies, whose concerns are in general so
paltry, call upon their poets for conceptions so vast and
descriptions so unlimited.

The authors, on their part, do not fail to obey a propensity of which they themselves partake; they perpetually
inflate their imaginations, and expanding them beyond
all bounds, they not infrequently abandon the great in
order to reach the gigantic. By these means they hope
to attract the observation of the multitude, and to fix
it easily upon themselves: nor are their hopes disappointed;
for as the multitude seeks for nothing in poetry but subjects of very vast dimensions, it has neither the time to
measure with accuracy the proportions of all the subjects
set before it, nor a taste sufficiently correct to perceive
at once in what respect they are out of proportion. The
author and the public at once vitiate one another.

We have just seen that among democratic nations the
sources of poetry are grand, but not abundant. They are
soon exhausted: and poets, not finding the elements of
the ideal in what is real and true, abandon them entirely
and create monsters. I do not fear that the poetry of
democratic nations will prove too insipid, or that it will
fly too near the ground; I rather apprehend that it will be
forever losing itself in the clouds, and that it will range at
last to purely imaginary regions. I fear that the productions
of democratic poets may often be surcharged with immense and incoherent imagery, with exaggerated descrip-

38

tions and strange creations; and that the fantastic beings of their brain may sometimes make us regret the world of reality.

When the revolution which subverts the social and political state of an aristocratic people begins to penetrate into literature, it generally first manifests itself in the drama, and it always remains conspicuous there. The spectator of a dramatic piece is, to a certain extent, taken by surprise by the impression it conveys. He has no time to refer to his memory, or to consult those more able to judge than himself. It does not occur to him to resist the new literary tendencies which begin to be felt by him; he yields to them before he knows what they are. Authors are very prompt in discovering which way the taste of the public is thus secretly inclined. They shape their productions accordingly; and the literature of the stage, after having served to indicate the approaching literary revolution, speedily completes its accomplishment. If you would judge beforehand of the literature of a people which is lapsing into democracy, study its dramatic productions.

The literature of the stage, moreover, even among aristocratic nations, constitutes the most democratic part of their literature. No kind of literary gratification is so much within the reach of the multitude as that which is derived from theatrical representations. Neither preparation nor study is required to enjoy them: they lay hold on you in the midst of your prejudices and your ignorance. When the yet untutored love of the pleasures of the mind begins to affect a class of the community, it instantly draws them to the stage. The theatres of aristocratic nations have always been filled with spectators not belonging to the aristocracy. At the theatre alone the higher ranks mix with the middle and the lower classes; there alone do the former consent to listen to the opinion of the latter, or at least to allow them to give an opinion at all. At the theatre, men of cultivation and of literary attainments have always had more difficulty than elsewhere in making their taste prevail over that of the people, and in preventing themselves from being carried away by the latter. The pit has frequently made laws for the boxes.

If it be difficult for an aristocracy to prevent the people from getting the upper hand in the theatre, it will readily be understood that the people will be supreme there when democratic principles have crept into the laws and manners—when ranks are intermixed—when minds, as well as fortunes, are brought more nearly together—and when the upper class has lost, with its hereditary wealth, its power, its precedents, and its leisure. The tastes and propensities natural to democratic nations, in respect to literature, will therefore first be discernible in the drama, and it may be foreseen that they will break out there with vehemence. In written productions, the literary canons of aristocracy will be gently, gradually, and, so to speak, legally modified; at the theatre they will be riotously overthrown.

The drama brings out most of the good qualities, and almost all the defects, inherent in democratic literature. Democratic peoples hold erudition very cheap, and care but little for what occurred at Rome and Athens; they want to hear something which concerns themselves, and the delineation of the present age is what they demand.

When the heroes and the manners of antiquity are frequently brought upon the stage, and dramatic authors faithfully observe the rules of antiquated precedent, that is enough to warrant a conclusion that the democratic classes have not yet got the upper hand of the theatres. Racine makes a very humble apology in the preface to the " Britannicus " for having disposed of Junia among the Vestals, who, according to Aulus Gellius, he says, " admitted no one below six years of age nor above ten." We may be sure that he would neither have accused himself of the offence, nor defended himself from censure, if he had written for our contemporaries. A fact of this kind not only illustrates the state of literature at the time when it occurred, but also that of society itself. A democratic stage does not prove that the nation is in a state of democracy, for, as we have just seen, even in aristocracies it may happen that democratic tastes affect the drama; but when the spirit of aristocracy reigns exclusively on the stage, the fact irrefragably demonstrates that the whole of society is aristocratic; and it may be boldly inferred that the same lettered and learned class which sways the dramatic writers commands the people and governs the country.

The refined tastes and the arrogant bearing of an aristocracy will rarely fail to lead it, when it manages the stage, to make a kind of selection in human nature. Some of the conditions of society claim its chief interest; and the scenes which delineate their manners are preferred upon the stage. Certain virtues, and even certain vices, are thought more particularly to deserve to figure there; and they are applauded while all others are excluded. Upon the stage, as well as elsewhere, an aristocratic audience will only meet personages of quality, and share the emotions of kings. The same thing applies to style: an aristocracy is apt to impose upon dramatic authors certain modes of expression which give the key in which everything is to be delivered. By these means the stage frequently comes to delineate only one side of man, or sometimes even to represent what is not to be met with in human nature at all—to rise above Nature and to go beyond it.

In democratic communities the spectators have no such partialities, and they rarely display any such antipathies: they like to see upon the stage that medley of conditions, of feelings, and of opinions, which occurs before their eyes. The drama becomes more striking, more common, and more true. Sometimes, however, those who write for the stage in democracies also transgress the bounds of human nature—but it is on a different side from their predecessors. By seeking to represent in minute detail the little singularities of the moment and the peculiar characteristics of certain personages, they forget to portray the general features of the race.

When the democratic classes rule the stage, they introduce as much license in the manner of treating subjects as in the choice of them. As the love of the drama is, of all literary tastes, that which is most natural to democratic nations, the number of authors and of spectators, as well as of theatrical representations, is constantly increasing among these communities. A multitude composed of elements so different, and scattered in so many different places, can not acknowledge the same rules or submit to the same laws. No concurrence is possible among judges so numerous, who know not when they may meet again; and therefore each pronounces his own sentence on the piece. If the effect of democracy is generally to question the authority of all literary rules and conventions, on the stage it abolishes them altogether, and puts in their place nothing but the whim of each author and of each public.

The drama also displays in an especial manner the truth of what I have said before in speaking more generally of style and art in democratic literature. In reading the criticisms which were occasioned by the dramatic productions of the age of Louis XIV, one is surprised to remark the great stress which the public laid on the probability of the plot, and the importance which was attached to the perfect consistency of the characters, and to their doing nothing which could not be easily explained and understood. The value which was set upon the forms of language at that period, and the paltry strife about words with which dramatic authors were assailed, are no less surprising. It would seem that the men of the age of Louis XIV attached very exaggerated importance to those details, which may be perceived in the study, but which escape attention on the stage. For, after all, the principal object of a dramatic piece is to be performed, and its chief merit is to affect the audience. But the audience and the readers in that age were the same: on quitting the theatre they called up the author for judgment to their own firesides. In democracies, dramatic pieces are listened to, but not read. Most of those who frequent the amusements of the stage do not go there to seek the pleasures of the mind, but the keen emotions of the heart. They do not expect to hear a fine literary work, but to see a play; and provided the author writes the language of his country correctly enough to be understood, and that his characters excite curiosity and awaken sympathy, the audience are satisfied. They ask no more of fiction, and immediately return to real life. Accuracy of style is therefore less required, because the attentive observance of its rules is less perceptible on the stage. As for the probability of the plot, it is incompatible with perpetual novelty, surprise, and rapidity of invention. It is therefore neglected, and the public excuses the neglect. You may be sure that if you succeed in bringing your audience into the presence of something that affects them, they will not care by what road you brought them there; and they will never reproach you for having excited their emotions in spite of dramatic rules.

The Americans very broadly display all the different propensities which I have here described when they go to the theatres; but it must be acknowledged that as yet a very small number of them go to theatres at all. Although play-goers and plays have prodigiously increased in the United States in the last forty years, the population indulges in this kind of amusement with the greatest reserve. This is attributable to peculiar causes, which the reader is already acquainted with, and of which a few words will suffice to remind him. The Puritans who founded the American republics were not only enemies to amusements, but they professed an especial abhorrence for the stage. They considered it as an abominable pastime; and as long as their principles prevailed with undivided sway, scenic performances were wholly unknown among them. These opinions of the first fathers of the colony have left very deep marks on the minds of their descendants. The extreme regularity of habits and the great strictness of manners which are observable in the United States have as yet opposed additional obstacles to the growth of dramatic art. There are no dramatic subjects in a country which has witnessed no great political catastrophes, and in which love invariably leads by a straight and easy road to matrimony. People who spend every day in the week in making money, and the Sunday in going to church, have nothing to invite the Muse of Comedy.

A single fact suffices to show that the stage is not very popular in the United States. The Americans, whose laws allow of the utmost freedom and even license of language in all other respects, have nevertheless subjected their dramatic authors to a sort of censorship. Theatrical performances can only take place by permission of the municipal authorities. This may serve to show how much communities are like individuals; they surrender themselves unscrupulously to their ruling passions, and afterward take the greatest care not to yield too much to the vehemence of tastes which they do not possess.

No portion of literature is connected by closer or more numerous ties with the present condition of society than the drama. The drama of one period can never be suited to the following age, if in the interval an important revolution has changed the manners and the laws of the nation. The great authors of a preceding age may be read; but pieces written for a different public will not be followed. The dramatic authors of the past live only in books. The traditional taste of certain individuals, vanity, fashion, or the genius of an actor may sustain or resuscitate for a time the aristocratic drama among a democracy; but it will speedily fall away of itself—not overthrown, but abandoned.

Historians who write in aristocratic ages are wont to refer all occurrences to the particular will or temper of certain individuals; and they are apt to attribute the most important revolutions to very slight accidents. They trace out the smallest causes with sagacity, and frequently leave the greatest unperceived. Historians who live in democratic ages exhibit precisely opposite characteristics. Most of them attribute hardly any influence to the individual over the destiny of the race, nor to citizens over the fate of a people; but, on the other hand, they assign great general causes to all petty incidents. These contrary tendencies explain each other.

When the historian of aristocratic ages surveys the theatre of the world, he at once perceives a very small number of prominent actors, who manage the whole piece. These great personages, who occupy the front of the stage, arrest the observation, and fix it on themselves; and while the historian is bent on penetrating the secret motives which make them speak and act, the rest escape his memory. The importance of the things which some men are seen to do, gives him an exaggerated estimate of the influence which one man may possess; and naturally leads him to think that, in order to explain the impulses of the multitude, it is necessary to refer them to the particular influence of some one individual.

When, on the contrary, all the citizens are independent of one another, and each of them is individually weak, no one is seen to exert a great, or still less a lasting power, over the community. At first sight, individuals appear to be absolutely devoid of any influence over it; and society would seem to advance alone by the free and voluntary concurrence of all the men who compose it. This naturally prompts the mind to search for that general reason which operates upon so many men's faculties at the same time, and turns them simultaneously in the same direction.

I am very well convinced that even among democratic nations the genius, the vices, or the virtues of certain individuals retard or accelerate the natural current of a people's history: but causes of this secondary and fortuitous nature are infinitely more various, more concealed, more complex, less powerful, and consequently less easy to trace in periods of equality than in ages of aristocracy, when the task of the historian is simply to detach from the mass of general events the particular influences of one man or of a few men. In the former case the historian is soon wearied by the toil; his mind loses itself in this labyrinth; and, in his inability clearly to discern or conspicuously to point out the influence of individuals, he denies their existence. He prefers talking about the characteristics of race, the physical conformation of the country, or the genius of civilization—which abridges his own labours, and satisfies his reader far better at less cost.

M. de Lafayette says somewhere in his " Memoirs " that the exaggerated system of general causes affords surprising consolations to second-rate statesmen. I will add that its effects are not less consolatory to second-rate historians; it can always furnish a few mighty reasons to extricate them from the most difficult part of their work, and it indulges the indolence or incapacity of their minds, while it confers upon them the honours of deep thinking.

For myself, I am of opinion that at all times one great portion of the events of this world are attributable to general facts, and another to special influences. These two kinds of cause are always in operation: their proportion only varies. General facts serve to explain more things in democratic than in aristocratic ages, and fewer things are then assignable to special influences. At periods of aristocracy the reverse takes place: special influences are stronger, general causes weaker—unless, indeed, we consider as a general cause the fact itself of the inequality of conditions, which allows some individuals to baffle the natural tendencies of all the rest. The historians who seek to describe what occurs in democratic societies are right, therefore, in assigning much to general causes, and in devoting their chief attention to discover them; but they are wrong in wholly denying the special influence of individuals, because they can not easily trace or follow it.

The historians who live in democratic ages are not only prone to assign a great cause to every incident, but they are also given to connect incidents together, so as to deduce a system from them. In aristocratic ages, as the attention of historians is constantly drawn to individuals, the connection of events escapes them; or rather, they do not believe in any such connection. To them the clew of history seems every instant crossed and broken by the step of man. In democratic ages, on the contrary, as the historian sees much more of actions than of actors, he may easily establish some kind of sequence and methodical order among the former. Ancient literature, which is so rich in fine historical compositions, does not contain a single great historical system, while the poorest of modern literatures abound with them. It would appear that the ancient historians did not make sufficient use of those general theories which our historical writers are ever ready to carry to excess.

Those who write in democratic ages have another more dangerous tendency. When the traces of individual action upon nations are lost, it often happens that the world goes on to move, though the moving agent is no longer discoverable. As it becomes extremely difficult to discern and to analyze the reasons which, acting separately on the volition of each member of the community, concur in the end to produce movement in the old mass, men are led to believe that this movement is involuntary, and that societies unconsciously obey some superior force ruling over them. But even when the general fact which governs the private volition of all individuals is supposed to be discovered upon the earth, the principle of human free will is not secure. A cause sufficiently extensive to affect millions of men at once, and sufficiently strong to bend them all together in the same direction, may well seem irresistible: having seen that mankind do yield to it, the mind is close upon the inference that mankind can not resist it.

Historians who live in democratic ages, then, not only deny that the few have any power of acting upon the destiny of a people, but they deprive the people themselves of the power of modifying their own condition, and they subject them either to an inflexible Providence, or to some blind necessity. According to them, each nation is indissolubly bound by its position, its origin, its precedents, and its character, to a certain lot which no efforts can ever change. They involve generation in generation, and thus, going back from age to age, and from necessity to necessity, up to the origin of the world, they forge a close and enormous chain, which girds and binds the human race. To their minds it is not enough to show what events have occurred: they would fain show that events could not have occurred otherwise. They take a nation arrived at a certain stage of its history, and they affirm that it could not but follow the track which brought it thither. It is easier to make such an assertion than to show by what means the nation might have adopted a better course.

In reading the historians of aristocratic ages, and especially those of antiquity, it would seem that, to be master of his lot, and to govern his fellow-creatures, man requires only to be master of himself. In perusing the historical volumes which our age has produced, it would seem that man is utterly powerless over himself and over all around him. The historians of antiquity taught how to command: those of our time teach only how to obey; in their writings the author often appears great, but humanity is always diminutive. If this doctrine of necessity, which is so attractive to those who write history in democratic ages, passes from authors to their readers, till it infects the whole mass of the community and gets possession of the public mind, it will soon paralyze the activity of modern society, and reduce Christians to the level of the Turks. I would, moreover, observe that such principles are peculiarly dangerous at the period at which we are arrived. Our contemporaries are but too prone to doubt of the human free will, because each of them feels himself confined on every side by his own weakness; but they are still willing to acknowledge the strength and independence of men united in society. Let not this principle be lost sight of; for the great object in our time is to raise the faculties of men, not to complete their prostration.

Among aristocratic nations all the members of the community are connected with and dependent upon each other; the graduated scale of different ranks acts as a tie, which keeps every one in his proper place and the whole body in subordination. Something of the same kind always occurs in the political assemblies of these nations. Parties naturally range themselves under certain leaders, whom they obey by a sort of instinct, which is only the result of habits contracted elsewhere. They carry the manners of general society into the lesser assemblage.

In democratic countries it often happens that a great number of citizens are tending to the same point; but each one only moves thither, or at least flatters himself that he moves, of his own accord. Accustomed to regulate his doings by personal impulse alone, he does not willingly submit to dictation from without. This taste and habit of independence accompany him into the councils of the nation. If he consents to connect himself with other men in the prosecution of the same purpose, at least he chooses to remain free to contribute to the common success after his own fashion. Hence it is that in democratic countries parties are so impatient of control, and are never manageable except in moments of great public danger. Even then the authority of leaders, which under such circumstances may be able to make men act or speak, hardly ever reaches the extent of making them keep silence.

Among aristocratic nations the members of political assemblies are at the same time members of the aristocracy. Each of them enjoys high established rank in his own right, and the position which he occupies in the assembly is often less important in his eyes than that which he fills in the country. This consoles him for playing no part in the discussion of public affairs, and restrains him from too eagerly attempting to play an insignificant one.

In America, it generally happens that a representative only becomes somebody from his position in the assembly. He is therefore perpetually haunted by a craving to acquire importance there, and he feels a petulant desire to be constantly obtruding his opinions upon the House. His own vanity is not the only stimulant which urges him on in this course, but that of his constituents, and the continual necessity of propitiating them. Among aristocratic nations a member of the legislature is rarely in strict dependence upon his constituents: he is frequently to them a sort of unavoidable representative; sometimes they are themselves strictly dependent upon him; and if at length they reject him, he may easily get elected elsewhere, or, retiring from public life, he may still enjoy the pleasures of splendid idleness. In a democratic country like the United States a representative has hardly ever a lasting hold on the minds of his constituents. However small an electoral body may be, the fluctuations of democracy are constantly changing its aspect; it must, therefore, be courted unceasingly. He is never sure of his supporters, and, if they forsake him, he is left without a resource; for his natural position is not sufficiently elevated for him to be easily known to those not close to him; and, with the complete state of independence prevailing among the people, he can not hope that his friends or the Government will send him down to be returned by an electoral body unacquainted with him. The seeds of his fortune are therefore sown in his own neighbourhood; from that nook of earth he must start to raise himself to the command of a people and to influence the destinies of the world. Thus it is natural that in democratic countries the members of political assemblies think more of their constituents than of their party, while in aristocracies they think more of their party than of their constituents.

But what ought to be said to gratify constituents is not always what ought to be said in order to serve the party to which representatives profess to belong. The general interest of a party frequently demands that members belonging to it should not speak on great questions which they understand imperfectly; that they should speak but little on those minor questions which impede the great ones; lastly, and for the most part, that they should not speak at all. To keep silence is the most useful service that an indifferent spokesman can render to the commonwealth. Constituents, however, do not think so. The population of a district sends a representative to take a part in the government of a country, because they entertain a very lofty notion of his merits. As men appear greater in proportion to the littleness of the objects by which they are surrounded, it may be assumed that the opinion entertained of the delegate will be so much the higher as talents are more rare among his constituents. It will therefore frequently happen that the less constituents have to expect from their representative, the more they will anticipate from him; and, however incompetent he may be, they will not fail to call upon him for signal exertions, corresponding to the rank they have conferred upon him.

Independently of his position as a legislator of the State, electors also regard their representative as the natural patron of the constituency in the legislature; they almost consider him as the proxy of each of his supporters, and they flatter themselves that he will not be less zealous in defence of their private interests than of those of the country. Thus electors are well assured beforehand that the representative of their choice will be an orator; that he will speak often if he can, and that in case he is forced to refrain, he will strive at any rate to compress into his less frequent orations an inquiry into all the great questions of state, combined with a statement of all the petty grievances they have themselves to complain of; so that, though he be not able to come forward frequently, he should on each occasion prove what he is capable of doing; and that, instead of perpetually lavishing his powers, he should occasionally condense them in a small compass, so as to furnish a sort of complete and brilliant epitome of his constituents and of himself. On these terms they will vote for him at the next election. These conditions drive worthy men of humble abilities to despair, who, knowing their own powers, would never voluntarily have come forward. But thus urged on, the representative begins to speak, to the great alarm of his friends; and rushing imprudently into the midst of the most celebrated orators, he perplexes the debate and wearies the House.

All laws which tend to make the representative more dependent on the elector, not only affect the conduct of the legislators, as I have remarked elsewhere, but also their language. They exercise a simultaneous influence on affairs themselves, and on the manner in which affairs are discussed.

There is hardly a member of Congress who can make up his mind to go home without having dispatched at least one speech to his constituents; nor who will endure any interruption until he has introduced into his harangue whatever useful suggestions may be made touching the four-and-twenty States of which the Union is composed, and especially the district which he represents. He therefore presents to the mind of his auditors a succession of great general truths (which he himself only comprehends, and expresses, confusedly), and of petty minutiæ, which he is but too able to discover and to point out. The consequence is that the debates of that great assembly are frequently vague and perplexed, and that they seem rather to drag their slow length along than to advance toward a distinct object. Some such state of things will, I believe, always arise in the public assemblies of democracies.

Propitious circumstances and good laws might succeed in drawing to the legislature of a democratic people men very superior to those who are returned by the Americans to Congress; but nothing will ever prevent the men of slender abilities who sit there from obtruding themselves with complacency, and in all ways, upon the public. The evil does not appear to me to be susceptible of entire cure, because it not only originates in the tactics of that assembly, but in its constitution and in that of the country. The inhabitants of the United States seem themselves to consider the matter in this light; and they show their long experience of parliamentary life not by abstaining from making bad speeches, but by courageously submitting to hear them made. They are resigned to it, as to an evil which they know to be inevitable.

We have shown the petty side of political debates in democratic assemblies—let us now exhibit the more imposing one. The proceedings within the Parliament of England for the last one hundred and fifty years have never occasioned any great sensation out of that country; the opinions and feelings expressed by the speakers have never awakened much sympathy, even among the nations placed nearest to the great arena of British liberty; whereas Europe was excited by the very first debates which took place in the small colonial assemblies of America at the time of the Revolution. This was attributable not only to particular and fortuitous circumstances, but to general and lasting causes. I can conceive nothing more admirable or more powerful than a great orator debating on great questions of state in a democratic assembly. As no particular class is ever represented there by men commissioned to defend its own interests, it is always to the whole nation, and in the name of the whole nation, that the orator speaks. This expands his thoughts, and heightens his power of language. As precedents have there but little weight— as there are no longer any privileges attached to certain property, nor any rights inherent in certain bodies or in certain individuals, the mind must have recourse to general truths derived from human nature to resolve the particular question under discussion. Hence the political debates of a democratic people, however small it may be, have a degree of breadth which frequently renders them attractive to mankind. All men are interested by them, because they treat of man, who is everywhere the same. Among the greatest aristocratic nations, on the contrary, the most general questions are almost always argued on some special grounds derived from the practice of a particular time, or the rights of a particular class; which interest that class alone, or at most the people among whom that class happens to exist. It is owing to this, as much as to the greatness of the French people, and the favourable disposition of the nations who listen to them, that the great effect which the French political debates sometimes produce in the world must be attributed. The orators of France frequently speak to mankind, even when they are addressing their countrymen only.

NOTE

[1] All this is especially true of the aristocratic countries which have been long and peacefully subject to a monarchical government. When liberty prevails in an aristocracy, the higher ranks are constantly obliged to make use of the lower classes; and when they use, they approach them. This frequently introduces something of a democratic spirit into an aristocratic community. There springs up, moreover, in a privileged body, governing with energy and an habitually bold policy, a taste for stir and excitement which must infallibly affect all literary performances.

CHAPTER XXVI

INDIVIDUALISM IN DEMOCRATIC COUNTRIES

Why democratic nations show a more ardent and enduring love of equality than of liberty—Individualism—Individualism stronger at the close of a democratic revolution than at other periods—That the Americans combat the effects of individualism by free institutions.

THE first and most intense passion that is engendered by the equality of conditions is, I need hardly say, the love of that same equality. My readers will therefore not be surprised that I speak of it before all others. Everybody has remarked that in our time, and especially in France, this passion for equality is every day gaining ground in the human heart. It has been said a hundred times that our contemporaries are far more ardently and tenaciously attached to equality than to freedom; but as I do not find that the causes of the fact have been sufficiently analyzed, I shall endeavour to point them out.

It is possible to imagine an extreme point at which freedom and equality would meet and be confounded together. Let us suppose that all the members of the community take a part in the government, and that each one of them has an equal right to take a part in it. As none is different from his fellows, none can exercise a tyrannical power: men will be perfectly free, because they will all be entirely equal; and they will all be perfectly equal, because they will be entirely free. To this ideal state democratic nations tend. Such is the completest form that equality can assume upon earth; but there are a thousand others which, without being equally perfect, are not less cherished by those nations.

The principle of equality may be established in civil society without prevailing in the political world. Equal rights may exist of indulging in the same pleasures, of entering the same professions, of frequenting the same places—in a word, of living in the same manner and seeking wealth by the same means, although all men do not take an equal share in the government. A kind of equality may even be established in the political world, though there should be no political freedom there. A man may be the equal of all his countrymen save one, who is the master of all without distinction, and who selects equally from among them all the agents of his power. Several other combinations might be easily imagined, by which very great equality would be united to institutions more or less free, or even to institutions wholly without freedom. Although men can not become absolutely equal unless they be entirely free, and consequently equality, pushed to its farthest extent, may be confounded with freedom, yet there is good reason for distinguishing the one from the other. The taste which men have for liberty, and that which they feel for equality, are, in fact, two different things; and I am not afraid to add that, among democratic nations, they are two unequal things.

Upon close inspection, it will be seen that there is in every age some peculiar and preponderating fact with which all others are connected; this fact almost always gives birth to some pregnant idea or some ruling passion, that attracts to itself, and bears away in its course, all the feelings and opinions of the time: it is like a great stream, toward which each of the surrounding rivulets seems to flow. Freedom has appeared in the world at different times and under various forms; it has not been exclusively bound to any social condition, and it is not confined to democracies. Freedom can not, therefore, form the distinguishing characteristic of democratic ages. The peculiar and preponderating fact which marks those ages as its own is the equality of conditions; the ruling passion of men in those periods is the love of this equality.

Ask not what singular charm the men of democratic ages find in being equal, or what special reasons they may have for clinging so tenaciously to equality rather than to the other advantages which society holds out to them: equality is the distinguishing characteristic of the age they live in; that, of itself, is enough to explain that they prefer it to all the rest.

But independently of this reason there are several others, that will at all times habitually lead men to prefer equality to freedom. If a people could ever succeed in destroying, or even in diminishing, the equality which prevails in its own body, this could only be accomplished by long and laborious efforts. Its social condition must be modified, its laws abolished, its opinions superseded, its habits changed, its manners corrupted. But political liberty is more easily lost; to neglect to hold it fast is to allow it to escape. Men therefore not only cling to equality because it is dear to them; they also adhere to it because they think it will last forever.

That political freedom may compromise in its excesses the tranquility, the property, the lives of individuals, is obvious to the narrowest and most unthinking minds. But, on the contrary, none but attentive and clear-sighted men perceive the perils with which equality threatens us, and they commonly avoid pointing them out. They know that the calamities they apprehend are remote, and flatter themselves that they will only fall upon future generations, for which the present generation takes but little thought. The evils which freedom sometimes brings with it are immediate; they are apparent to all, and all are more or less affected by them. The evils which extreme equality may produce are slowly disclosed; they creep gradually into the social frame; they are only seen at intervals, and at the moment at which they become most violent habit already causes them to be no longer felt. The advantages which freedom brings are only shown by length of time; and it is always easy to mistake the cause in which they originate. The advantages of equality are instantaneous, and they may be traced constantly from their source. Political liberty bestows exalted pleasures, from time to time, upon a certain number of citizens. Equality every day confers a number of small enjoyments on every man. The charms of equality are felt every instant, and are within the reach of all; the noblest hearts are not insensible to them, and the most vulgar souls exult in them. The passion which equality engenders must therefore be at once strong and general. Men can not enjoy political liberty unpurchased by some sacrifices, and they never obtain it without great exertions. But the pleasures of equality are self-proffered: each of the petty incidents of life seems to occasion them, and in order to taste them nothing is required but to live.

Democratic nations are at all times fond of equality, but there are certain epochs at which the passion they entertain for it swells to the height of fury. This occurs at the moment when the old social system, long menaced, completes its own destruction after a last intestine struggle, and when the barriers of rank are at length thrown down. At such times men pounce upon equality as their booty, and they cling to it as to some precious treasure which they fear to lose. The passion for equality penetrates on every side into men's hearts, expands there, and fills them entirely. Tell them not that by this blind surrender of themselves to an exclusive passion they risk their dearest interests: they are deaf. Show them not freedom escaping from their grasp, while they are looking another way: they are blind—or rather, they can discern but one sole object to be desired in the universe.

What I have said is applicable to all democratic nations: what I am about to say concerns the French alone. Among most modern nations, and especially among all those of the continent of Europe, the taste and the idea of freedom only began to exist and to extend itself at the time when social conditions were tending to equality, and as a consequence of that very equality. Absolute kings were the most efficient levellers of ranks among their subjects. Among these nations equality preceded freedom: equality was therefore a fact of some standing when freedom was still a novelty: the one had already created customs, opinions, and laws belonging to it, when the other, alone and for the first time, came into actual existence. Thus the latter was still only an affair of opinion and of taste, while the former had already crept into the habits of the people, possessed itself of their manners, and given a particular turn to the smallest actions of their lives. Can it be wondered that the men of our own time prefer the one to the other?

I think that democratic communities have a natural taste for freedom: left to themselves, they will seek it, cherish it, and view any privation of it with regret. But for equality, their passion is ardent, insatiable, incessant, invincible: they call for equality in freedom; and if they can not obtain that, they still call for equality in slavery. They will endure poverty, servitude, barbarism—but they will not endure aristocracy. This is true at all times, and especially true in our own. All men and all powers seeking to cope with this irresistible passion will be overthrown and destroyed by it. In our age, freedom can not be established without it, and despotism itself can not reign without its support.

I have shown how it is that in ages of equality every man seeks for his opinions within himself: I am now about to show how it is that, in the same ages, all his feelings are turned toward himself alone. Individualism is a novel expression, to which a novel idea has given birth. Our fathers were only acquainted with egotism. Egotism is a passionate and exaggerated love of self, which leads a man to connect everything with his own person, and to prefer himself to everything in the world. Individualism is a mature and calm feeling, which disposes each member of the community to sever himself from the mass of his fellow-creatures; and to draw apart with his family and his friends; so that, after he has thus formed a little circle of his own, he willingly leaves society at large to itself. Egotism originates in blind instinct: individualism proceeds from erroneous judgment more than from depraved feelings; it originates as much in the deficiencies of the mind as in the perversity of the heart. Egotism blights the germ of all virtue; individualism, at first, only saps the virtues of public life; but, in the long run, it attacks and destroys all others, and is at length absorbed in downright egotism. Egotism is a vice as old as the world, which does not belong to one form of society more than to another: individualism is of democratic origin, and it threatens to spread in the same ratio as the equality of conditions.

Among aristocratic nations, as families remain for centuries in the same condition, often on the same spot, all generations become, as it were, contemporaneous. A man almost always knows his forefathers, and respects them: he thinks he already sees his remote descendants, and he loves them. He willingly imposes duties on himself toward the former and the latter; and he will frequently sacrifice his personal gratifications to those who went before and to those who will come after him. Aristocratic institutions have, moreover, the effect of closely binding every man to several of his fellow-citizens. As the classes of an aristocratic people are strongly marked and permanent, each of them is regarded by its own members as a sort of lesser country, more tangible and more cherished than the country at large. As in aristocratic communities all the citizens occupy fixed positions, one above the other, the result is that each of them always sees a man above himself whose patronage is necessary to him, and below himself another man whose co-operation he may claim. Men living in aristocratic ages are therefore almost always closely attached to something placed out of their own sphere, and they are often disposed to forget themselves. It is true that in those ages the notion of human fellowship is faint, and that men seldom think of sacrificing themselves for mankind; but they often sacrifice themselves for other men. In democratic ages, on the contrary, when the duties of each individual to the race are much more clear, devoted service to any one man becomes more rare; the bond of human affection is extended, but it is relaxed.

Among democratic nations new families are constantly springing up, others are constantly falling away, and all that remain change their condition; the woof of time is every instant broken, and the track of generations effaced. Those who went before are soon forgotten; of those who will come after no one has any idea: the interest of man is confined to those in close propinquity to himself. As each class approximates to other classes, and intermingles with them, its members become indifferent and as strangers to one another. Aristocracy had made a chain of all the members of the community, from the peasant to the king: democracy breaks that chain, and severs every link of it. As social conditions become more equal, the number of persons increases who, although they are neither rich enough nor powerful enough to exercise any great influence over their fellow-creatures, have nevertheless acquired or retained sufficient education and fortune to satisfy their own wants. They owe nothing to any man, they expect nothing from any man; they acquire the habit of always considering themselves as standing alone, and they are apt to imagine that their whole destiny is in their own hands. Thus not only does democracy make every man forget his ancestors, but it hides his descendants, and separates his contemporaries from him; it throws him back forever upon himself alone, and threatens in the end to confine him entirely within the solitude of his own heart.

The period when the construction of democratic society upon the ruins of an aristocracy has just been completed, is especially that at which this separation of men from one another, and the egotism resulting from it, most forcibly strike the observation. Democratic communities not only contain a large number of independent citizens, but they are filled constantly with men who, having entered but yesterday upon their independent condition, are intoxicated with their new power. They entertain a presumptuous confidence in their strength, and as they do not suppose that they can henceforward ever have occasion to claim the assistance of their fellow-creatures, they do not scruple to show that they care for nobody but themselves.

An aristocracy seldom yields without a protracted struggle, in the course of which implacable animosities are kindled between the different classes of society. These passions survive the victory, and traces of them may be observed in the midst of the democratic confusion which ensues. Those members of the community who were at the top of the late gradations of rank can not immediately forget their former greatness; they will long regard themselves as aliens in the midst of the newly composed society. They look upon all those whom this state of society has made their equals as oppressors, whose destiny can excite no sympathy; they have lost sight of their former equals, and feel no longer bound by a common interest to their fate: each of them, standing aloof, thinks that he is reduced to care for himself alone. Those, on the contrary, who were formerly at the foot of the social scale, and who have been brought up to the common level by a sudden revolution, can not enjoy their newly acquired independence without secret uneasiness; and if they meet with some of their former superiors on the same footing as themselves, they stand aloof from them with an expression of triumph and of fear. It is, then, commonly at the outset of democratic society that citizens are most disposed to live apart. Democracy leads men not to draw near to their fellow-creatures; but democratic revolutions lead them to shun each other, and perpetuate in a state of equality the animosities which the state of inequality engendered. The great advantage of the Americans is that they have arrived at a state of democracy without having to endure a democratic revolution; and that they are born equal, instead of becoming so.

Despotism, which is of a very timorous nature, is never more secure of continuance than when it can keep men asunder; and all its influence is commonly exerted for that purpose. No vice of the human heart is so acceptable to it as egotism: a despot easily forgives his subjects for not loving him, provided they do not love each other. He does not ask them to assist him in governing the state; it is enough that they do not aspire to govern it themselves. He stigmatizes as turbulent and unruly spirits those who would combine their exertions to promote the prosperity of the community, and, perverting the natural meaning of words, he applauds as good citizens those who have no sympathy for any but themselves. Thus the vices that despotism engenders are precisely those that equality fosters. These two things mutually and perniciously complete and assist each other. Equality places men side by side, unconnected by any common tie; despotism raises barriers to keep them asunder; the former predisposes them not to consider their fellow-creatures, the latter makes general indifference a sort of public virtue.

Despotism, then, which is at all times dangerous, is more particularly to be feared in democratic ages. It is easy to see that in those same ages men stand most in need of freedom. When the members of a community are forced to attend to public affairs, they are necessarily drawn from the circle of their own interests, and snatched at times from self-observation. As soon as a man begins to treat of public affairs in public, he begins to perceive that he is not so independent of his fellow-men as he had at first imagined, and that, in order to obtain their support, he must often lend them his co-operation.

When the public is supreme, there is no man who does not feel the value of public good-will, or who does not endeavour to court it by drawing to himself the esteem and affection of those among whom he is to live. Many of the passions which congeal and keep asunder human hearts are then obliged to retire and hide below the surface. Pride must be dissembled; disdain dares not break out; egotism fears its own self. Under a free government, as most public offices are elective, the men whose elevated minds or aspiring hopes are too closely circumscribed in private life, constantly feel that they can not do without the population which surrounds them. Men learn at such times to think of their fellow-men from ambitious motives; and they frequently find it, in a manner, their interest to forget themselves.

I may here be met by an objection derived from electioneering intrigues, the meannesses of candidates, and the calumnies of their opponents. These are opportunities for animosity which occur the oftener the more frequent elections become. Such evils are doubtless great, but they are transient; whereas the benefits which attend them remain. The desire of being elected may lead some men for a time to violent hostility; but this same desire leads all men in the long-run mutually to support each other; and if it happens that an election accidentally severs two friends, the electoral system brings a multitude of citizens permanently together, who would always have remained unknown to each other. Freedom engenders private animosities, but despotism gives birth to general indifference.

The Americans have combated by free institutions the tendency of equality to keep men asunder, and they have subdued it. The legislators of America did not suppose that a general representation of the whole nation would suffice to ward off a disorder at once so natural to the frame of democratic society, and so fatal: they also thought that it would be well to infuse political life into each portion of the territory, in order to multiply to an infinite extent opportunities of acting in concert for all the members of the community, and to make them constantly feel their mutual dependence on each other. The plan was a wise one. The general affairs of a country only engage the attention of leading politicians, who assemble from time to time in the same places; and as they often lose sight of each other afterward, no lasting ties are established between them. But if the object be to have the local affairs of a district conducted by the men who reside there, the same persons are always in contact, and they are, in a manner, forced to be acquainted, and to adapt themselves to one another.

It is difficult to draw a man out of his own circle to interest him in the destiny of the state, because he does not clearly understand what influence the destiny of the state can have upon his own lot. But if it be proposed to make a road across the end of his estate, he will see at a glance that there is a connection between this small public affair and his greatest private affairs; and he will discover, without its being shown to him, the close tie which unites private to general interest. Thus, far more may be done by intrusting to the citizens the administration of minor affairs than by surrendering to them the control of important ones, toward interesting them in the public welfare, and convincing them that they constantly stand in need one of the other in order to provide for it. A brilliant achievement may win for you the favour of a people at one stroke; but to earn the love and respect of the population which surrounds you, a long succession of little services rendered and of obscure good deeds—a constant habit of kindness, and an established reputation for disinterestedness—will be required. Local freedom, then, which leads a great number of citizens to value the affection of their neighbours and of their kindred, perpetually brings men together, and forces them to help one another, in spite of the propensities which sever them.

In the United States the more opulent citizens take great care not to stand aloof from the people; on the contrary, they constantly keep on easy terms with the lower classes: they listen to them, they speak to them every day. They know that the rich in democracies always stand in need of the poor; and that in democratic ages you attach a poor man to you more by your manner than by benefits conferred. The magnitude of such benefits, which sets off the difference of conditions, causes a secret irritation to those who reap advantage from them; but the charm of simplicity of manners is almost irresistible: their affability carries men away, and even their want of polish is not always displeasing. This truth does not take root at once in the minds of the rich. They generally resist it as long as the democratic revolution lasts, and they do not acknowledge it immediately after that revolution is accomplished. They are very ready to do good to the people, but they still choose to keep them at arm's length; they think that is sufficient, but they are mistaken. They might spend fortunes thus without warming the hearts of the population around them—that population does not ask them for the sacrifice of their money, but of their pride.

It would seem as if every imagination in the United States were upon the stretch to invent means of increasing the wealth and satisfying the wants of the public. The best-informed inhabitants of each district constantly use their information to discover new truths which may augment the general prosperity; and if they have made any such discoveries, they eagerly surrender them to the mass of the people.

When the vices and weaknesses, frequently exhibited by those who govern in America, are closely examined, the prosperity of the people occasions—but improperly occasions—surprise. Elected magistrates do not make the American democracy flourish; it flourishes because the magistrates are elective.

It would be unjust to suppose that the patriotism and the zeal that every American displays for the welfare of his fellow-citizens are wholly insincere. Although private interest directs the greater part of human actions in the United States as well as elsewhere, it does not regulate them all. I must say that I have often seen Americans make great and real sacrifices to the public welfare; and I have remarked a hundred instances in which they hardly ever failed to lend faithful support to each other. The free institutions which the inhabitants of the United States possess, and the political rights of which they make so much use, remind every citizen, and in a thousand ways, that he lives in society. They every instant impress upon his mind the notion that it is the duty, as well as the interest of men, to make themselves useful to their fellow-creatures; and as he sees no particular ground of animosity to them, since he is never either their master or their slave, his heart readily leans to the side of kindness. Men attend to the interests of the public, first by necessity, afterward by choice: what was intentional becomes an instinct; and by dint of working for the good of one's fellow-citizens, the habit and the taste for serving them is at length acquired.

Many people in France consider equality of conditions as one evil, and political freedom as a second. When they are obliged to yield to the former, they strive at least to escape from the latter. But I contend that in order to combat the evils which equality may produce, there is only one effectual remedy—namely, political freedom.

CHAPTER XXVII

PUBLIC ASSOCIATIONS

*The use that the Americans make of public associations in civil life—
The relation between public associations and the newspapers—Connection of civil and political associations.*

I DO not propose to speak of those political associations
—by the aid of which men endeavour to defend themselves against the despotic influence of a majority—
or against the aggressions of regal power. That subject
I have already treated. If each citizen did not learn, in
proportion as he individually becomes more feeble, and
consequently more incapable of preserving his freedom
single-handed, to combine with his fellow-citizens for the
purpose of defending it, it is clear that tyranny would un-
avoidably increase together with equality.

Only those associations that are formed in civil life,
without reference to political objects, are here adverted
to. The political associations that exist in the United
States are only a single feature in the midst of the immense assemblage of associations in that country. Americans of all ages, all conditions, and all dispositions, constantly form associations. They have not only commercial
and manufacturing companies, in which all take part, but
associations of a thousand other kinds—religious, moral,
serious, futile, extensive or restricted, enormous or diminutive. The Americans make associations to give entertain-
ments, to found establishments for education, to build inns,
to construct churches, to diffuse books, to send mission-
aries to the antipodes; and in this manner they found hos-
pitals, prisons, and schools. If it be proposed to advance

some truth, or to foster some feeling by the encouragement of a great example, they form a society. Wherever, at the head of some new undertaking, you see the Government in France, or a man of rank in England, in the United States you will be sure to find an association. I met with several kinds of associations in America, of which I confess I had no previous notion; and I have often admired the extreme skill with which the inhabitants of the United States succeed in proposing a common object to the exertions of a great many men, and in getting them voluntarily to pursue it. I have since travelled over England, whence the Americans have taken some of their laws and many of their customs; and it seemed to me that the principle of association was by no means so constantly or so adroitly used in that country. The English often perform great things singly; whereas the Americans form associations for the smallest undertakings. It is evident that the former people consider association as a powerful means of action, but the latter seem to regard it as the only means they have of acting.

Thus the most democratic country on the face of the earth is that in which men have in our time carried to the highest perfection the art of pursuing in common the object of their common desires, and have applied this new science to the greatest number of purposes. Is this the result of accident? or is there in reality any necessary connection between the principle of association and that of equality? Aristocratic communities always contain, among a multitude of persons who by themselves are powerless, a small number of powerful and wealthy citizens, each of whom can achieve great undertakings single-handed. In aristocratic societies men do not need to combine in order to act, because they are strongly held together. Every wealthy and powerful citizen constitutes the head of a permanent and compulsory association, composed of all those who are dependent upon him, or whom he makes subservient to the execution of his designs. Among democratic nations, on the contrary, all the citizens are inde-

pendent and feeble; they can do hardly anything by themselves, and none of them can oblige his fellow-men to lend
him their assistance. They all, therefore, fall into a state
of incapacity, if they do not learn voluntarily to help each
other. If men living in democratic countries had no right
and no inclination to associate for political purposes, their
independence would be in great jeopardy; but they might
long preserve their wealth and their cultivation: whereas
if they never acquired the habit of forming associations in
ordinary life, civilization itself would be endangered. A
people among whom individuals should lose the power of
achieving great things single-handed, without acquiring
the means of producing them by united exertions, would
soon relapse into barbarism.

Unhappily, the same social condition that renders associations so necessary to democratic nations renders their
formation more difficult among those nations than among
all others. When several members of an aristocracy agree
to combine, they easily succeed in doing so; as each of
them brings great strength to the partnership, the number of its members may be very limited; and when the
members of an association are limited in number, they
may easily become mutually acquainted, understand each
other, and establish fixed regulations. The same opportunities do not occur among democratic nations, where the
associated members must always be very numerous for
their association to have any power.

I am aware that many of my countrymen are not in
the least embarrassed by this difficulty. They contend that
the more enfeebled and incompetent the citizens become,
the more able and active the Government ought to be
rendered, in order that society at large may execute what
individuals can no longer accomplish. They believe this
answers the whole difficulty, but I think they are mistaken.
A government might perform the part of some of the
largest American companies; and several States, members
of the Union, have already attempted it; but what political
power could ever carry on the vast multitude of lesser

40

undertakings that the American citizens perform every day, with the assistance of the principle of association? It is easy to foresee that the time is drawing near when man will be less and less able to produce, of himself alone, the commonest necessaries of life. The task of the governing power will therefore perpetually increase, and its very efforts will extend it every day. The more it stands in the place of associations, the more will individuals, losing the notion of combining together, require its assistance: these are causes and effects that unceasingly engender each other. Will the administration of the country ultimately assume the management of all the manufactures, which no single citizen is able to carry on? And if a time at length arrives, when, in consequence of the extreme subdivision of landed property, the soil is split into an infinite number of parcels, so that it can only be cultivated by companies of husbandmen, will it be necessary that the head of the government should leave the helm of state to follow the plough? The morals and the intelligence of a democratic people would be as much endangered as its business and manufactures if the government ever wholly usurped the place of private companies.

Feelings and opinions are recruited, the heart is enlarged, and the human mind is developed by no other means than by the reciprocal influence of men upon each other. I have shown that these influences are almost null in democratic countries; they must therefore be artificially created, and this can only be accomplished by associations.

When the members of an aristocratic community adopt a new opinion, or conceive a new sentiment, they give it a station, as it were, beside themselves, upon the lofty platform where they stand; and opinions or sentiments so conspicuous to the eyes of the multitude are easily introduced into the minds or hearts of all around. In democratic countries the governing power alone is naturally in a condition to act in this manner; but it is easy to see that its action is always inadequate, and often dangerous. A government can no more be competent to keep alive and to renew the circulation of opinions and feelings among a great people than to manage all the speculations of productive industry. No sooner does a government attempt to go beyond its political sphere and to enter upon this new track, than it exercises, even unintentionally, an insupportable tyranny; for a government can only dictate strict rules, the opinions which it favours are rigidly enforced, and it is never easy to discriminate between its advice and its commands. Worse still will be the case if the government really believes itself interested in preventing all circulation of ideas; it will then stand motionless, and oppressed by the heaviness of voluntary torpor. Governments, therefore, should not be the only active powers: associations ought, in democratic nations, to stand in lieu of those powerful private individuals whom the equality of conditions has swept away.

As soon as several of the inhabitants of the United States have taken up an opinion or a feeling that they wish to promote in the world, they look out for mutual assistance; and as soon as they have found each other out, they combine. From that moment they are no longer isolated men, but a power seen from afar, whose actions serve for an example, and whose language is listened to. The first time I heard in the United States that a hundred thousand men had bound themselves publicly to abstain from spirituous liquors, it appeared to me more like a joke than a serious engagement; and I did not at once perceive why these temperate citizens could not content themselves with drinking water by their own firesides. I at last understood that three hundred thousand Americans, alarmed by the progress of drunkenness around them, had made up their minds to patronize temperance. They acted just in the same way as a man of high rank who should dress very plainly, in order to inspire the humbler orders with a contempt of luxury. It is probable that if these hundred thousand men had lived in France, each of them would singly have memorialized the government to watch the public-houses all over the kingdom.

Nothing, in my opinion, is more deserving of our attention than the intellectual and moral associations of America. The political and industrial associations of that country strike us forcibly; but the others elude our observation, or if we discover them, we understand them imperfectly, because we have hardly ever seen anything of the kind. It must, however, be acknowledged that they are as necessary to the American people as the former, and perhaps more so. In democratic countries the science of association is the mother of science; the progress of all the rest depends upon the progress it has made. Among the laws that rule human societies there is one that seems to be more precise and clear than all others. If men are to remain civilized, or to become so, the art of associating together must grow and improve in the same ratio in which the equality of conditions is increased.

When men are no longer united among themselves by firm and lasting ties, it is impossible to obtain the co-operation of any great number of them, unless you can persuade every man whose concurrence you require that his private interest obliges him voluntarily to unite his exertions to the exertions of all the rest. This can only be habitually and conveniently effected by means of a newspaper; nothing but a newspaper can drop the same thought into a thousand minds at the same moment. A newspaper is an adviser who does not require to be sought, but who comes of his own accord, and talks to you briefly every day of the common weal, without distracting you from your private affairs.

Newspapers, therefore, become more necessary in proportion as men become more equal, and individualism more to be feared. To suppose that they only serve to protect freedom would be to diminish their importance: they maintain civilization. I shall not deny that in democratic countries newspapers frequently lead the citizens to launch together in very ill-digested schemes; but if there were no newspapers there would be no common activity. The evil which they produce is therefore much less than that which they cure.

The effect of a newspaper is not only to suggest the same purpose to a great number of persons, but also to furnish means for executing in common the designs that they may have singly conceived. The principal citizens who inhabit an aristocratic country discern each other from afar; and if they wish to unite their forces, they move toward each other, drawing a multitude of men after them. It frequently happens, on the contrary, in democratic countries, that a great number of men who wish or who want to combine can not accomplish it, because as they are very insignificant and lost amid the crowd, they can not see, and know not where to find, one another. A newspaper then takes up the notion or the feeling that had occurred simultaneously, but singly, to each of them. All are then immediately guided toward this beacon; and these wandering minds, which had long sought each other in darkness, at length meet and unite.

The newspaper brought them together, and the newspaper is still necessary to keep them united. In order that an association among a democratic people should have any power, it must be a numerous body. The persons of whom it is composed are therefore scattered over a wide extent, and each of them is detained in the place of his domicile by the narrowness of his income, or by the small unremitting exertions by which he earns it. Means then must be found to converse every day without seeing each other, and to take steps in common without having met. Thus hardly any democratic association can do without newspapers. There is consequently a necessary connection between public associations and newspapers: newspapers make associations, and associations make newspapers; and if it has been correctly advanced that associations will increase in number as the conditions of men become more equal, it is not less certain that the number of newspapers increases in proportion to that of associations. Thus it is in America that we find at the same time the greatest number of associations, and the greatest number of newspapers.

This connection between the number of newspapers and that of associations leads us to the discovery of a further connection between the state of the periodical press and the form of the administration in a country; and shows that the number of newspapers must diminish or increase among a democratic people, in proportion as its administration is more or less centralized. For among democratic nations the exercise of local powers can not be intrusted to the principal members of the community as in aristocracies. Those powers must either be abolished, or placed in the hands of very large numbers of men, who then, in fact, constitute an association permanently established by law for the purpose of administering the affairs of a certain extent of territory; and they require a journal, to bring to them every day, in the midst of their own minor concerns, some intelligence of the state of their public weal. The more numerous local powers are, the greater is the number of men in whom they are vested by law; and as this want is hourly felt, the more profusely do newspapers abound.

The extraordinary subdivision of administrative power has much more to do with the enormous number of American newspapers than the great political freedom of the country and the absolute liberty of the press. If all the inhabitants of the Union had the suffrage—but a suffrage which should only extend to the choice of their legislators in Congress—they would require but few newspapers, because they would only have to act together on a few very important but very rare occasions. But within the pale of the great association of the nation, lesser associations have been established by law in every country, every city, and, indeed, in every village, for the purposes of local administration. The laws of the country thus compel every American to co-operate every day of his life with some of his fellow-citizens for a common purpose, and each one of them requires a newspaper to inform him what all the others are doing.

I am of opinion that a democratic people,[1] without any national representative assemblies, but with a great number of small local powers, would have in the end more newspapers than another people governed by a centralized administration and an elective legislation. What best explains to me the enormous circulation of the daily press in the United States, is that among the Americans I find the utmost national freedom combined with local freedom of every kind. There is a prevailing opinion in France and England that the circulation of newspapers would be indefinitely increased by removing the taxes which have been laid upon the press. This is a very exaggerated estimate of the effects of such a reform. Newspapers increase in numbers, not according to their cheapness, but according to the more or less frequent want that a great number of men may feel for intercommunication and combination.

In like manner I should attribute the increasing influence of the daily press to causes more general than those by which it is commonly explained. A newspaper can only subsist on the condition of publishing sentiments or principles common to a large number of men. A newspaper, therefore, always represents an association that is composed of its habitual readers. This association may be more or less defined, more or less restricted, more or less numerous; but the fact that the newspaper keeps alive, is a proof that at least the germ of such an association exists in the minds of its readers.

This leads me to a last reflection, with which I shall conclude this topic. The more equal the conditions of men become, and the less strong men individually are, the more easily do they give way to the current of the multitude, and the more difficult is it for them to adhere by themselves to an opinion that the multitude discard. A newspaper represents an association; it may be said to address each of its readers in the name of all the others, and to exert its influence over them in proportion to their individual weakness. The power of the newspaper press must therefore increase as the social conditions of men become more equal.

There is only one country on the face of the earth where the citizens enjoy unlimited freedom of association for political purposes. This same country is the only one in the world where the continual exercise of the right of association has been introduced into civil life, and where all the advantages that civilization can confer are procured by means of it. In all the countries where political associations are prohibited, civil associations are rare. It is hardly probable that this is the result of accident; but the inference should rather be that there is a natural, and perhaps a necessary, connection between these two kinds of associations. Certain men happen to have a common interest in some concern—either a commercial undertaking is to be managed, or some speculation in manufactures to be tried; they meet, they combine, and thus by degrees they become familiar with the principle of association. The greater is the multiplicity of small affairs, the more do men, even without knowing it, acquire facility in prosecuting great undertakings in common. Civil associations, therefore, facilitate political association: but, on the other hand, political association singularly strengthens and improves associations for civil purposes. In civil life every man may, strictly speaking, fancy that he can provide for his own wants; in politics, he can fancy no such thing. When a people, then, have any knowledge of public life, the notion of association, and the wish to coalesce, present themselves every day to the minds of the whole community: whatever natural repugnance may restrain men from acting in concert, they will always be ready to combine for the sake of a party. Thus political life makes the love and practice of association more general; it imparts a desire of union, and teaches the means of combination to numbers of men who would have always lived apart.

Politics not only give birth to numerous associations, but to associations of great extent. In civil life it seldom happens that any one interest draws a very large number of men to act in concert; much skill is required to bring such an interest into existence: but in politics opportunities present themselves every day. Now it is solely in great associations that the general value of the principle of association is displayed. Citizens who are individually powerless do not very clearly anticipate the strength which they may acquire by uniting together; it must be shown to them in order to be understood. Hence it is often easier to collect a multitude for a public purpose than a few persons; a thousand citizens do not see what interest they have in combining together—ten thousand will be perfectly aware of it. In politics men combine for great undertakings; and the use they make of the principle of association in important affairs practically teaches them that it is their interest to help each other in those of less moment. A political association draws a number of individuals at the same time out of their own circle; however they may be naturally kept asunder by age, mind, and fortune, it places them nearer together and brings them into contact. Once met, they can always meet again.

Men can embark in few civil partnerships without risking a portion of their possessions; this is the case with all manufacturing and trading companies. When men are as yet but little versed in the art of association, and are unacquainted with its principal rules, they are afraid, when first they combine in this manner, of buying their experience dear. They therefore prefer depriving themselves of a powerful instrument of success to running the risks which attend the use of it. They are, however, less reluctant to join political associations, which appear to them to be without danger, because they adventure no money in them. But they can not belong to these associations for any length of time without finding out how order is maintained among a large number of men, and by what contrivance they are made to advance, harmoniously and methodically, to the same object. Thus they learn to surrender their own will to that of all the rest, and to make their own exertions subordinate to the common impulse—things which it is not less necessary to know in civil than in political associations. Political associations may therefore be considered as large free schools, where all the members of the community go to learn the general theory of association.

But even if political association did not directly contribute to the progress of civil association, to destroy the former would be to impair the latter. When citizens can only meet in public for certain purposes, they regard such meetings as a strange proceeding of rare occurrence, and they rarely think at all about it. When they are allowed to meet freely for all purposes, they ultimately look upon public association as the universal, or in a manner the sole means, which men can employ to accomplish the different purposes they may have in view. Every new want instantly revives the notion. The art of association then becomes, as I have said before, the mother of action, studied and applied by all.

When some kinds of associations are prohibited and others allowed, it is difficult to distinguish the former from the latter beforehand. In this state of doubt men abstain from them altogether, and a sort of public opinion passes current, that tends to cause any association whatsoever to be regarded as a bold and almost an illicit enterprise.[2]

It is therefore chimerical to suppose that the spirit of association, when it is repressed on some one point, will nevertheless display the same vigour on all others; and that if men be allowed to prosecute certain undertakings in common, that is quite enough for them eagerly to set about them. When the members of a community are allowed and accustomed to combine for all purposes, they will combine as readily for the lesser as for the more important ones; but if they are only allowed to combine for small affairs, they will be neither inclined nor able to effect it. It is in vain that you will leave them entirely free to prosecute their business on joint-stock account: they will hardly care to avail themselves of the rights you have granted to them; and, after having exhausted your strength in vain efforts to put down prohibited associations, you will be surprised that you can not persuade men to form the associations you encourage.

I do not say that there can be no civil associations in a country where political association is prohibited; for men can never live in society without embarking in some common undertakings: but I maintain that in such a country civil associations will always be few in number, feebly planned, unskilfully managed, that they will never form any vast designs, or that they will fail in the execution of them.

This naturally leads me to think that freedom of association in political matters is not so dangerous to public tranquility as is supposed; and that possibly, after having agitated society for some time, it may strengthen the State in the end. In democratic countries political associations are, so to speak, the only powerful persons who aspire to rule the State. Accordingly, the governments of our time look upon associations of this kind just as sovereigns in the Middle Ages regarded the great vassals of the crown: they entertain a sort of instinctive abhorrence of them, and they combat them on all occasions. They bear, on the contrary, a natural good-will to civil associations, because they readily discover that, instead of directing the minds of the community to public affairs, these institutions serve to divert them from such reflections; and that, by engaging them more and more in the pursuit of objects that can not be attained without public tranquility, they deter them from revolutions. But these governments do not attend to the fact that political associations tend amazingly to multiply and facilitate those of a civil character, and that in avoiding a dangerous evil they deprive themselves of an efficacious remedy.

When you see the Americans freely and constantly forming associations for the purpose of promoting some political principle, of raising one man to the head of affairs, or of wresting power from another, you have some difficulty in understanding that men so independent do not constantly fall into the abuse of freedom. If, on the other hand, you survey the infinite number of trading companies which are in operation in the United States, and perceive that the Americans are on every side unceasingly engaged in the execution of important and difficult plans, which the slightest revolution would throw into confusion, you will readily comprehend why people so well employed are by no means tempted to perturb the State, nor to destroy that public tranquility by which they all profit.

Is it enough to observe these things separately, or should we not discover the hidden tie which connects them? In their political associations, the Americans of all conditions, minds, and ages, daily acquire a general taste for association, and grow accustomed to the use of it. There they meet together in large numbers, they converse, they listen to each other, and they are mutually stimulated to all sorts of undertakings. They afterward transfer to civil life the notions they have thus acquired, and make them subservient to a thousand purposes. Thus it is by the enjoyment of a dangerous freedom that the Americans learn the art of rendering the dangers of freedom less formidable.

If a certain moment in the existence of a nation be selected, it is easy to prove that political associations perturb the State, and paralyze productive industry; but take the whole life of a people, and it may perhaps be easy to demonstrate that freedom of association in political matters is favourable to the prosperity and even to the tranquility of the community.

I said in the former part of this work: " The unrestrained liberty of political association can not be entirely assimilated to the liberty of the press. The one is at the same time less necessary and more dangerous than the other. A nation may confine it within certain limits without ceasing to be mistress of itself; and it may sometimes be obliged to do so in order to maintain its own authority." And further on I added: " It can not be denied that the unrestrained liberty of association for political purposes is the last degree of liberty which a people is fit for. If it does not throw them into anarchy, it perpetually brings them, as it were, to the verge of it." Thus I do not think that a nation is always at liberty to invest its citizens with an absolute right of association for political purposes; and I doubt whether, in any country or in any age, it be wise to set no limits to freedom of association. A certain nation, it is said, could not maintain tranquility in the community, cause the laws to be respected, or establish a lasting government, if the right of association were not confined within narrow limits. These blessings are doubtless invaluable, and I can imagine that, to acquire or to preserve them, a nation may impose upon itself severe temporary restrictions: but still it is well that the nation should know at what price these blessings are purchased. I can understand that it may be advisable to cut off a man's arm in order to save his life; but it would be ridiculous to assert that he will be as dexterous as he was before he lost it.

NOTES

[1] The administration of an aristocratic people may be the reverse of centralized, and yet the want of newspapers be little felt, because local powers are then vested in a very small number of men, who either act apart, or can easily meet and come to an understanding.

[2] This is more especially true when the executive government has a discretionary power of allowing or prohibiting associations. When certain associations are simply prohibited by law, and the courts of justice have to punish infringements of that law, the evil is far less considerable. Then every citizen knows beforehand pretty nearly what he has to expect. He abstains from prohibited associations and embarks in those which are legally sanctioned. It is by these restrictions that all free nations have always admitted that the right of association might be limited. But if the legislature should invest a man with a power of ascertaining beforehand which associations are dangerous and which are useful, and should authorize him to destroy all associations in the bud or allow them to be formed, as nobody would be able to foresee in what cases associations might be established and in what cases they would be put down, the spirit of association would be entirely paralyzed. The former of these laws would only assail certain associations; the latter would apply to society itself, and inflict an injury upon it. I can conceive that a regular government may have recourse to the former, but I do not concede that any government has the right of enacting the latter.

CHAPTER XXVIII

THE PRINCIPLE OF INTEREST RIGHTLY UNDERSTOOD

The Americans combat individualism by the principle of interest rightly understood—The Americans apply the principle of interest rightly understood to religious matters.

WHEN the world was managed by a few rich and powerful individuals, these persons loved to entertain a lofty idea of the duties of man. They were fond of professing that it is praiseworthy to forget one's self, and that good should be done without hope of reward, as it is by the Deity himself. Such were the standard opinions of that time in morals. I doubt whether men were more virtuous in aristocratic ages than in others; but they were incessantly talking of the beauties of virtue, and its utility was only studied in secret. But since the imagination takes less lofty flights and every man's thoughts are centred in himself, moralists are alarmed by this idea of self-sacrifice, and they no longer venture to present it to the human mind. They therefore content themselves with inquiring whether the personal advantage of each member of the community does not consist in working for the good of all; and when they have hit upon some point on which private interest and public interest meet and amalgamate, they are eager to bring it into notice. Observations of this kind are gradually multiplied: what was only a single remark becomes a general principle; and it is held as a truth that man serves himself in serving his fellow-creatures, and that his private interest is to do good.

I have already shown, in several parts of this work, by

what means the inhabitants of the United States almost always manage to combine their own advantage with that of their fellow-citizens: my present purpose is to point out the general rule which enables them to do so.   In the United States hardly anybody talks of the beauty of virtue; but they maintain that virtue is useful, and prove it every day.   The American moralists do not profess that men ought to sacrifice themselves for their fellow-creatures because it is noble to make such sacrifices; but they boldly aver that such sacrifices are as necessary to him who imposes them upon himself as to him for whose sake they are made.   They have found out that in their country and their age man is brought home to himself by an irresistible force; and losing all hope of stopping that force, they turn all their thoughts to the direction of it.   They therefore do not deny that every man may follow his own interest; but they endeavour to prove that it is the interest of every man to be virtuous.   I shall not here enter into the reasons they allege, which would divert me from my subject: suffice it to say that they have convinced their fellow-countrymen.

Montaigne said long ago, " Were I not to follow the straight road for its straightness, I should follow it for having found by experience that in the end it is commonly the happiest and most useful track."   The doctrine of interest rightly understood is not then new, but among the Americans of our time it finds universal acceptance: it has become popular there; you may trace it at the bottom of all their actions, you will remark it in all they say. It is as often to be met with on the lips of the poor man as of the rich.   In Europe the principle of interest is much grosser than it is in America, but at the same time it is less common, and especially it is less avowed; among us men still constantly feign great abnegation which they no longer feel.   The Americans, on the contrary, are fond of explaining almost all the actions of their lives by the principle of interest rightly understood; they show with complacency how an enlightened regard for themselves constantly prompts them to assist each other, and inclines them willingly to sacrifice a portion of their time and property to the welfare of the State.   In this respect I think they frequently fail to do themselves justice; for in the United States, as well as elsewhere, people are sometimes seen to give way to those disinterested and spontaneous impulses which are natural to man; but the Americans seldom allow that they yield to emotions of this kind; they are more anxious to do honour to their philosophy than to themselves.

I might here pause, without attempting to pass a judgment on what I have described.   The extreme difficulty of the subject would be my excuse, but I shall not avail myself of it; and I had rather that my readers, clearly perceiving my object, should refuse to follow me than that I should leave them in suspense.   The principle of interest rightly understood is not a lofty one, but it is clear and sure.   It does not aim at mighty objects, but it attains without excessive exertion all those at which it aims.   As it lies within the reach of all capacities, every one can without difficulty apprehend and retain it.   By its admirable conformity to human weaknesses, it easily obtains great dominion; nor is that dominion precarious, since the principle checks one personal interest by another, and uses, to direct the passions, the very same instrument which excites them.   The principle of interest rightly understood produces no great acts of self-sacrifice, but it suggests daily small acts of self-denial.   By itself it can not suffice to make a man virtuous, but it disciplines a number of citizens in habits of regularity, temperance, moderation, foresight, self-command; and, if it does not lead men straight to virtue by the will, it gradually draws them in that direction by their habits.   If the principle of interest rightly understood were to sway the whole moral world, extraordinary virtues would doubtless be more rare; but I think that gross depravity would then also be less common.   The principle of interest rightly understood perhaps prevents some men from rising far above the level of mankind; but a great number of other men, who were falling far below it, are caught and restrained by it. Observe some few individuals, they are lowered by it; survey mankind, it is raised. I am not afraid to say that the principle of interest, rightly understood, appears to me the best suited of all philosophical theories to the wants of the men of our time, and that I regard it as their chief remaining security against themselves. Toward it, therefore, the minds of the moralists of our age should turn; even should they judge it to be incomplete, it must nevertheless be adopted as necessary.

I do not think upon the whole that there is more egotism among us than in America; the only difference is, that there it is enlightened—here it is not. Every American will sacrifice a portion of his private interests to preserve the rest; we would fain preserve the whole, and oftentimes the whole is lost. Everybody I see about me seems bent on teaching his contemporaries, by precept and example, that what is useful is never wrong. Will nobody undertake to make them understand how what is right may be useful? No power upon earth can prevent the increasing equality of conditions from inclining the human mind to seek out what is useful, or from leading every member of the community to be wrapped up in himself. It must therefore be expected that personal interest will become more than ever the principal, if not the sole, spring of men's actions; but it remains to be seen how each man will understand his personal interest. If the members of a community, as they become more equal, become more ignorant and coarse, it is difficult to foresee to what pitch of stupid excesses their egotism may lead them; and no one can foretell into what disgrace and wretchedness they would plunge themselves, lest they should have to sacrifice something of their own well-being to the prosperity of their fellow-creatures. I do not think that the system of interest, as it is professed in America, is, in all its parts, self-evident; but it contains a great number of truths so evident that men, if they are but educated, can not fail to

41

see them. Educate, then, at any rate; for the age of implicit self-sacrifice and instinctive virtues is already flitting far away from us, and the time is fast approaching when freedom, public peace, and social order itself will not be able to exist without education.

If the principle of interest rightly understood had nothing but the present world in view, it would be very insufficient; for there are many sacrifices which can only find their recompense in another; and whatever ingenuity may be put forth to demonstrate the utility of virtue, it will never be an easy task to make that man live aright who has no thoughts of dying. It is therefore necessary to ascertain whether the principle of interest rightly understood is easily compatible with religious belief. The philosophers who inculcate this system of morals tell men that to be happy in this life they must watch their own passions and steadily control their excess; that lasting happiness can only be secured by renouncing a thousand transient gratifications; and that a man must perpetually triumph over himself in order to secure his own advantage. The founders of almost all religions have held the same language. The track they point out to man is the same, only that the goal is more remote; instead of placing in this world the reward of the sacrifices they impose, they transport it to another. Nevertheless I can not believe that all those who practise virtue from religious motives are only actuated by the hope of a recompense. I have known zealous Christians who constantly forgot themselves, to work with greater ardour for the happiness of their fellow-men; and I have heard them declare that all they did was only to earn the blessings of a future state. I can not but think that they deceive themselves: I respect them too much to believe them.

Christianity, indeed, teaches that a man must prefer his neighbour to himself in order to gain eternal life; but Christianity also teaches that men ought to benefit their fellow-creatures for the love of God. A sublime expression! Man, searching by his intellect into the Divine conception, and seeing that order is the purpose of God, freely combines to prosecute the great design; and while he sacrifices his personal interests to this consummate order of all created things, expects no other recompense than the pleasure of contemplating it. I do not believe that interest is the sole motive of religious men: but I believe that interest is the principal means which religions themselves employ to govern men, and I do not question that this way they strike into the multitude and become popular. It is not easy clearly to perceive why the principle of interest rightly understood should keep aloof from religious opinions; and it seems to me more easy to show why it should draw men to them. Let it be supposed that, in order to obtain happiness in this world, a man combats his instinct on all occasions and deliberately calculates every action of his life; that, instead of yielding blindly to the impetuosity of first desires, he has learned the art of resisting them, and that he has accustomed himself to sacrifice without an effort the pleasure of a moment to the lasting interest of his whole life. If such a man believes in the religion which he professes, it will cost him but little to submit to the restrictions it may impose. Reason herself counsels him to obey, and habit has prepared him to endure them. If he should have conceived any doubts as to the object of his hopes, still he will not easily allow himself to be stopped by them; and he will decide that it is wise to risk some of the advantages of this world in order to preserve his rights to the great inheritance promised him in another. "To be mistaken in believing that the Christian religion is true," says Pascal, "is no great loss to any one; but how dreadful to be mistaken in believing it to be false!"

The Americans do not affect a brutal indifference to a future state; they affect no puerile pride in despising perils which they hope to escape from. They therefore profess their religion without shame and without weakness; but there generally is, even in their zeal, something so indescribably tranquil, methodical, and deliberate that it would seem as if the head, far more than the heart, brought them to the foot of the altar. The Americans not only follow their religion from interest, but they often place in this world the interest which makes them follow it. In the middle ages the clergy spoke of nothing but a future state; they hardly cared to prove that a sincere Christian may be a happy man here below. But the American preachers are constantly referring to the earth; and it is only with great difficulty that they can divert their attention from it. To touch their congregations, they always show them how favourable religious opinions are to freedom and public tranquility; and it is often difficult to ascertain from their discourses whether the principal object of religion is to procure eternal felicity in the other world or prosperity in this.

CHAPTER XXIX

THE DESIRE FOR WEALTH AND FOR PHYSICAL PROSPERITY

The taste for physical well-being in America—Peculiar effects of the love of physical gratifications in democratic ages—Causes of fanatical enthusiasm in some Americans—Causes of the restless spirit of the Americans in the midst of their prosperity—Taste for physical gratifications united in America to love of freedom and attention to public affairs—That religious belief sometimes turns the thoughts of the Americans to immaterial pleasures—That excessive care of worldly welfare may impair that welfare—That in times marked by equality of conditions and sceptical opinions, it is important to remove to a distance the objects of human actions.

IN America the passion for physical well-being is not always exclusive, but it is general; and if all do not feel it in the same manner, yet it is felt by all. Carefully to satisfy all, even the least wants of the body, and to provide the little conveniences of life, is uppermost in every mind. Something of an analogous character is more and more apparent in Europe. Among the causes that produce these similar consequences in both hemispheres, several are so connected with my subject as to deserve notice.

When riches are hereditarily fixed in families, there are a great number of men who enjoy the comforts of life without feeling an exclusive taste for those comforts. The heart of man is not so much caught by the undisturbed possession of anything valuable as by the desire, as yet imperfectly satisfied, of possessing it, and by the incessant dread of losing it. In aristocratic communities, the wealthy, never having experienced a condition different from their own, entertain no fear of changing it; the

615

existence of such conditions hardly occurs to them. The comforts of life are not to them the end of life, but simply a way of living; they regard them as existence itself— enjoyed, but scarcely thought of. As the natural and instinctive taste which all men feel for being well off is thus satisfied without trouble and without apprehension, their faculties are turned elsewhere, and cling to more arduous and more lofty undertakings, which excite and engross their minds. Hence it is that, in the midst of physical gratifications, the members of an aristocracy often display a haughty contempt of these very enjoyments, and exhibit singular powers of endurance under the privation of them. All the revolutions which have ever shaken or destroyed aristocracies, have shown how easily men accustomed to superfluous luxuries can do without the necessaries of life; whereas men who have toiled to acquire a competency can hardly live after they have lost it.

If I turn my observation from the upper to the lower classes, I find analogous effects produced by opposite causes. Among a nation where aristocracy predominates in society, and keeps it stationary, the people in the end get as much accustomed to poverty as the rich to their opulence. The latter bestow no anxiety on their physical comforts, because they enjoy them without an effort; the former do not think of things which they despair of obtaining, and which they hardly know enough of to desire them. In communities of this kind, the imagination of the poor is driven to seek another world; the miseries of real life inclose it around, but it escapes from their control, and flies to seek its pleasures far beyond. When, on the contrary, the distinctions of ranks are confounded together and privileges are destroyed—when hereditary property is subdivided, and education and freedom widely diffused, the desire of acquiring the comforts of the world haunts the imagination of the poor, and the dread of losing them that of the rich. Many scanty fortunes spring up; those who possess them have a sufficient share of physical gratifications to conceive a taste for these pleasures—not enough to satisfy it. They never procure them without exertion, and they never indulge in them without apprehension. They are, therefore, always straining to pursue or to retain gratifications so delightful, so imperfect, so fugitive.

If I were to inquire what passion is most natural to men who are stimulated and circumscribed by the obscurity of their birth or the mediocrity of their fortune, I could discover none more peculiarly appropriate to their condition than this love of physical prosperity. The passion for physical comforts is essentially a passion of the middle classes: with those classes it grows and spreads, with them it preponderates. From them it mounts into the higher orders of society, and descends into the mass of the people. I never met in America with any citizen so poor as not to cast a glance of hope and envy on the enjoyments of the rich, or whose imagination did not possess itself by anticipation of those good things which fate still obstinately withheld from him. On the other hand, I never perceived among the wealthier inhabitants of the United States that proud contempt of physical gratifications which is sometimes to be met with even in the most opulent and dissolute aristocracies. Most of these wealthy persons were once poor: they have felt the sting of want; they were long a prey to adverse fortunes; and now that the victory is won, the passions which accompanied the contest have survived it: their minds are, as it were, intoxicated by the small enjoyments which they have pursued for forty years. Not but that in the United States, as elsewhere, there are a certain number of wealthy persons who, having come into their property by inheritance, possess, without exertion, an opulence they have not earned. But even these men are not less devotedly attached to the pleasures of material life. The love of well-being is now become the predominant taste of the nation; the great current of man's passions runs in that channel, and sweeps everything along in its course.

It may be supposed, from what has just been said, that

the love of physical gratifications must constantly urge the Americans to irregularities in morals, disturb the peace of families, and threaten the security of society at large. Such is not the case: the passion for physical gratifications produces in democracies effects very different from those that it occasions in aristocratic nations. It sometimes happens that, wearied with public affairs and sated with opulence, amid the ruin of religious belief and the decline of the State, the heart of an aristocracy may by degrees be seduced to the pursuit of sensual enjoyments only. At other times the power of the monarch or the weakness of the people, without stripping the nobility of their fortunes, compels them to stand aloof from the administration of affairs, and while the road to mighty enterprise is closed, abandons them to the inquietude of their own desires; they then fall back heavily upon themselves, and seek in the pleasures of the body oblivion of their former greatness. When the members of an aristocratic body are thus exclusively devoted to the pursuit of physical gratifications, they commonly concentrate in that direction all the energy which they derive from their long experience of power. Such men are not satisfied with the pursuit of comfort; they require sumptuous depravity and splendid corruption. The worship they pay the senses is a gorgeous one; and they seem to vie with each other in the art of degrading their own natures. The stronger, the more famous, and the more free an aristocracy has been, the more depraved will it then become; and however brilliant may have been the lustre of its virtues, I dare predict that they will always be surpassed by the splendour of its vices.

The taste for physical gratifications leads a democratic people into no such excesses. The love of well-being is there displayed as a tenacious, exclusive, universal passion; but its range is confined. To build enormous palaces, to conquer or to mimic Nature, to ransack the world in order to gratify the passions of a man, is not thought of: but to add a few roods of land to your field, to plant

an orchard, to enlarge a dwelling, to be always making
life more comfortable and convenient, to avoid trouble,
and to satisfy the smallest wants without effort and almost
without cost. These are small objects, but the soul clings
to them; it dwells upon them closely and day by day, till
they at last shut out the rest of the world, and sometimes
intervene between itself and Heaven.

This, it may be said, can only be applicable to those
members of the community who are in humble circumstances; wealthier individuals will display tastes akin to
those which belonged to them in aristocratic ages. I contest the proposition: in point of physical gratifications, the
most opulent members of a democracy will not display
tastes very different from those of the people; whether it
be that, springing from the people, they really share those
tastes, or that they esteem it a duty to submit to them.
In democratic society the sensuality of the public has taken
a moderate and tranquil course, to which all are bound
to conform: it is as difficult to depart from the common
rule by one's vices as by one's virtues. Rich men who
live amid democratic nations are therefore more intent
on providing for their smallest wants than for their extraordinary enjoyments; they gratify a number of petty
desires, without indulging in any great irregularities of
passion: thus they are more apt to become enervated than
debauched.

The especial taste that the men of democratic ages
entertain for physical enjoyments is not naturally opposed
to the principles of public order; nay, it often stands in
need of order that it may be gratified. Nor is it adverse
to regularity of morals, for good morals contribute to public tranquility and are favourable to industry. It may
even be frequently combined with a species of religious
morality: men wish to be as well off as they can in this
world, without foregoing their chance of another. Some
physical gratifications can not be indulged in without
crime; from such they strictly abstain. The enjoyment
of others is sanctioned by religion and morality; to these

the heart, the imagination, and life itself are unreservedly given up; till, in snatching at these lesser gifts, men lose sight of those more precious possessions which constitute the glory and the greatness of mankind. The reproach I address to the principle of equality is not that it leads men away in the pursuit of forbidden enjoyments, but that it absorbs them wholly in quest of those which are allowed. By these means, a kind of virtuous materialism may ultimately be established in the world, which would not corrupt, but enervate the soul, and noiselessly unbend its springs of action.

Although the desire of acquiring the good things of this world is the prevailing passion of the American people, certain momentary outbreaks occur, when their souls seem suddenly to burst the bonds of matter by which they are restrained, and to soar impetuously toward Heaven. In all the States of the Union, but especially in the half-peopled country of the Far West, wandering preachers may be met with who hawk about the word of God from place to place. Whole families—old men, women, and children—cross rough passes and untrodden wilds, coming from a great distance to join a camp-meeting, where they totally forget for several days and nights, in listening to these discourses, the cares of business and even the most urgent wants of the body. Here and there, in the midst of American society, you meet with men, full of a fanatical and almost wild enthusiasm, which hardly exists in Europe. From time to time strange sects arise, that endeavour to strike out extraordinary paths to eternal happiness. Religious insanity is very common in the United States.

Nor ought these facts to surprise us. It was not man who implanted in himself the taste for what is infinite and the love of what is immortal: these lofty instincts are not the offspring of his capricious will; their steadfast foundation is fixed in human nature, and they exist in spite of his efforts. He may cross and distort them—destroy them he can not. The soul has wants that must be satisfied;

and whatever pains be taken to divert it from itself, it soon grows weary, restless, and disquieted amid the enjoyments of sense. If ever the faculties of the great majority of mankind were exclusively bent upon the pursuit of material objects, it might be anticipated that an amazing reaction would take place in the souls of some men. They would drift at large in the world of spirits, for fear of remaining shackled by the close bondage of the body.

It is not then wonderful if, in the midst of a community whose thoughts tend earthward, a small number of individuals are to be found who turn their looks to Heaven. I should be surprised if mysticism did not soon make some advance among a people solely engaged in promoting its own worldly welfare. It is said that the deserts of the Thebaid were peopled by the persecutions of the Emperors and the massacres of the Circus; I should rather say that it was by the luxuries of Rome and the Epicurean philosophy of Greece. If their social condition, their present circumstances, and their laws did not confine the minds of the Americans so closely to the pursuit of worldly welfare, it is probable that they would display more reserve and more experience whenever their attention is turned to things immaterial, and that they would check themselves without difficulty. But they feel imprisoned within bounds which they will apparently never be allowed to pass. As soon as they have passed these bounds, their minds know not where to fix themselves, and they often rush unrestrained beyond the range of common sense.

In certain remote corners of the Old World you may still sometimes stumble upon a small district which seems to have been forgotten amid the general tumult, and to have remained stationary while everything around it was in motion. The inhabitants are for the most part extremely ignorant and poor; they take no part in the business of the country, and they are frequently oppressed by the government; yet their countenances are generally placid, and their spirits light. In America I saw the freest and most enlightened men placed in the happiest circumstances that the world affords: it seemed to me as if a cloud habitually hung upon their brow, and I thought them serious and almost sad even in their pleasures. The chief reason of this contrast is that the former do not think of the ills they endure—the latter are forever brooding over advantages they do not possess. It is strange to see with what feverish ardour the Americans pursue their own welfare; and to watch the vague dread that constantly torments them lest they should not have chosen the shortest path which may lead to it. A native of the United States clings to this world's goods as if he were certain never to die; and he is so hasty in grasping at all within his reach that one would suppose he was constantly afraid of not living long enough to enjoy them. He clutches everything, he holds nothing fast, but soon loosens his grasp to pursue fresh gratifications.

In the United States a man builds a house to spend his latter years in it, and he sells it before the roof is on: he plants a garden, and lets it just as the trees are coming into bearing: he brings a field into tillage, and leaves other men to gather the crops: he embraces a profession, and gives it up: he settles in a place, which he soon afterward leaves, to carry his changeable longings elsewhere. If his private affairs leave him any leisure, he instantly plunges into the vortex of politics; and if at the end of a year of unremitting labour he finds he has a few days' vacation, his eager curiosity whirls him over the vast extent of the United States, and he will travel fifteen hundred miles in a few days to shake off his happiness. Death at length overtakes him, but it is before he is weary of his bootless chase of that complete felicity which is forever on the wing.

At first sight there is something surprising in this strange unrest of so many happy men, restless in the midst of abundance. The spectacle itself is, however, as old as the world; the novelty is to see a whole people furnish an exemplification of it. Their taste for physical gratifications must be regarded as the original source of that secret inquietude that the actions of the Americans betray, and of that inconstancy of which they afford fresh examples every day. He who has set his heart exclusively upon the pursuit of worldly welfare is always in a hurry, for he has but a limited time at his disposal to reach it, to grasp it, and to enjoy it. The recollection of the brevity of life is a constant spur to him. Besides the good things which he possesses, he every instant fancies a thousand others which death will prevent him from trying if he does not try them soon. This thought fills him with anxiety, fear, and regret, and keeps his mind in ceaseless trepidation, which leads him perpetually to change his plans and his abode. If in addition to the taste for physical well-being a social condition be superadded, in which the laws and customs make no condition permanent, here is a great additional stimulant to this restlessness of temper. Men will then be seen continually to change their track, for fear of missing the shortest cut to happiness. It may readily be conceived that if men, passionately bent upon physical gratifications, desire eagerly, they are also easily discouraged: as their ultimate object is to enjoy, the means to reach that object must be prompt and easy, or the trouble of acquiring the gratification would be greater than the gratification itself. Their prevailing frame of mind, then, is at once ardent and relaxed, violent and enervated. Death is often less dreaded than perseverance in continuous efforts to one end.

The equality of conditions leads by a still straighter road to several of the effects which I have here described. When all the privileges of birth and fortune are abolished, when all professions are accessible to all, and a man's own energies may place him at the top of any one of them, an easy and unbounded career seems open to his ambition, and he will readily persuade himself that he is born to no vulgar destinies. But this is an erroneous notion, which is corrected by daily experience. The same equality which allows every citizen to conceive these lofty hopes renders all the citizens less able to realize them: it circumscribes their powers on every side, while it gives freer scope to their desires. Not only are they themselves powerless, but they are met at every step by immense obstacles, which they did not at first perceive. They have swept away the privileges of some of their fellow-creatures which stood in their way, but they have opened the door to universal competition: the barrier has changed its shape rather than its position. When men are nearly alike, and all follow the same track, it is very difficult for any one individual to walk quick and cleave a way through the dense throng which surrounds and presses him. This constant strife between the propensities springing from the equality of conditions and the means it supplies to satisfy them harasses and wearies the mind.

It is possible to conceive men arrived at a degree of freedom which should completely content them; they would then enjoy their independence without anxiety and without impatience. But men will never establish any equality with which they can be contented. Whatever efforts a people may make, they will never succeed in reducing all the conditions of society to a perfect level; and even if they unhappily attained that absolute and complete depression, the inequality of minds would still remain, which, coming directly from the hand of God, will forever escape the laws of man. However democratic, then, the social state and the political constitution of a people may be, it is certain that every member of the community will always find out several points about him that command his own position; and we may foresee that his looks will be doggedly fixed in that direction. When inequality of conditions is the common law of society, the most marked inequalities do not strike the eye: when everything is nearly on the same level, the slightest are marked enough to hurt it. Hence the desire of equality always becomes more insatiable in proportion as equality is more complete.

Among democratic nations men easily attain a certain equality of conditions: they can never attain the equality they desire. It perpetually retires from before them, yet without hiding itself from their sight, and in retiring draws them on. At every moment they think they are about to grasp it; it escapes at every moment from their hold. They are near enough to see its charms, but too far off to enjoy them; and before they have fully tasted its delights they die. To these causes must be attributed that strange melancholy that oftentimes will haunt the inhabitants of democratic countries in the midst of their abundance, and that disgust at life that sometimes seizes upon them in the midst of calm and easy circumstances. Complaints are made in France that the number of suicides increases; in America suicide is rare, but insanity is said to be more common than anywhere else. These are all different symptoms of the same disease. The Americans do not put an end to their lives, however disquieted they may be, because their religion forbids it; and among them materialism may be said hardly to exist, notwithstanding the general passion for physical gratification. The will resists—reason frequently gives way.

In democratic ages enjoyments are more intense than in the ages of aristocracy, and especially the number of those who partake in them is larger: but, on the other hand, it must be admitted that man's hopes and his desires are oftener blasted, the soul is more stricken and perturbed, and care itself more keen.

When a democratic state turns to absolute monarchy, the activity that was before directed to public and to private affairs is all at once centred upon the latter: the immediate consequence is, for some time, great physical prosperity; but this impulse soon slackens, and the amount of productive industry is checked. I know not if a single trading or manufacturing people can be cited, from the Tyrians down to the Florentines and the English, who were not a free people also. There is therefore a close bond and necessary relation between these two elements—freedom and productive industry. This proposition is generally true of all nations, but especially of democratic nations. I have already shown that men who live in ages of equality continually require to form associations in order to procure the things they covet; and, on the other hand, I have shown how great political freedom improves and diffuses the art of association. Freedom, in these ages, is therefore especially favourable to the production of wealth; nor is it difficult to perceive that despotism is especially adverse to the same result. The nature of despotic power in democratic ages is not to be fierce or cruel, but minute and meddling. Despotism of this kind, though it does not trample on humanity, is directly opposed to the genius of commerce and the pursuits of industry.

Thus the men of democratic ages require to be free in order more readily to procure those physical enjoyments for which they are always longing. It sometimes happens, however, that the excessive taste they conceive for these same enjoyments abandons them to the first master who appears. The passion for worldly welfare then defeats itself, and, without perceiving it, throws the object of their desires to a greater distance.

There is, indeed, a most dangerous passage in the history of a democratic people. When the taste for physical gratifications among such a people has grown more rapidly than their education and their experience of free institutions, the time will come when men are carried away, and lose all self-restraint, at the sight of the new possessions they are about to lay hold upon. In their intense and exclusive anxiety to make a fortune, they lose sight of the close connection that exists between the private fortune of each of them and the prosperity of all. It is not necessary to do violence to such a people in order to strip them of the rights they enjoy; they themselves willingly loosen their hold. The discharge of political duties appears to them to be a troublesome annoyance, that diverts them from their occupations and business. If they be required to elect representatives, to support the Government by personal service, to meet on public business, they have no time—they can not waste their precious time

in useless engagements: such idle amusements are unsuited to serious men who are engaged with the more important interests of life. These people think they are
following the principle of self-interest, but the idea they
entertain of that principle is a very rude one; and the
better to look after what they call their business, they
neglect their chief business, which is to remain their own
masters.

As the citizens who work do not care to attend to public business, and as the class which might devote its leisure
to these duties has ceased to exist, the place of the Government is, as it were, unfilled. If at that critical moment
some able and ambitious man grasps the supreme power,
he will find the road to every kind of usurpation open before him. If he does but attend for some time to the material prosperity of the country, no more will be demanded
of him. Above all, he must insure public tranquility: men
who are possessed by the passion of physical gratification
generally find out that the turmoil of freedom disturbs their
welfare before they discover how freedom itself serves to
promote it. If the slightest rumour of public commotion
intrudes into the petty pleasures of private life, they are
aroused and alarmed by it. The fear of anarchy perpetually haunts them, and they are always ready to fling away
their freedom at the first disturbance.

I readily admit that public tranquility is a great good;
but at the same time I can not forget that all nations have
been enslaved by being kept in good order. Certainly it
is not to be inferred that nations ought to despise public
tranquility; but that state ought not to content them. A
nation that asks nothing of its government but the maintenance of order is already a slave at heart—the slave of
its own well-being, awaiting but the hand that will bind
it. By such a nation the despotism of faction is not less
to be dreaded than the despotism of an individual. When
the bulk of the community is engrossed by private concerns, the smallest parties need not despair of getting the
upper hand in public affairs. At such times it is not rare

42

to see upon the great stage of the world, as we see at our theatres, a multitude represented by a few players, who alone speak in the name of an absent or inattentive crowd: they alone are in action while all are stationary; they regulate everything by their own caprice; they change the laws, and tyrannize at will over the manners of the country; and then men wonder to see into how small a number of weak and worthless hands a great people may fall.

Hitherto the Americans have fortunately escaped all the perils that I have just pointed out; and in this respect they are really deserving of admiration. Perhaps there is no country in the world where fewer idle men are to be met with than in America, or where all who work are more eager to promote their own welfare. But if the passion of the Americans for physical gratifications is vehement, at least it is not indiscriminating; and reason, though unable to restrain it, still directs its course. An American attends to his private concerns as if he were alone in the world, and the next minute he gives himself up to the common weal as if he had forgotten them. At one time he seems animated by the most selfish cupidity, at another by the most lively patriotism. The human heart can not be thus divided. The inhabitants of the United States alternately display so strong and so similar a passion for their own welfare and for their freedom that it may be supposed that these passions are united and mingled in some part of their character. And indeed the Americans believe their freedom to be the best instrument and surest safeguard of their welfare: they are attached to the one by the other. They by no means think that they are not called upon to take a part in the public weal; they believe, on the contrary, that their chief business is to secure for themselves a government which will allow them to acquire the things they covet, and which will not debar them from the peaceful enjoyment of those possessions which they have acquired.

In the United States, on the seventh day of every week, the trading and working life of the nation seems suspended; all noises cease; a deep tranquility, say rather the solemn calm of meditation, succeeds the turmoil of the week, and the soul resumes possession and contemplation of itself. Upon this day the marts of traffic are deserted; every member of the community, accompanied by his children, goes to church, where he listens to strange language which would seem unsuited to his ear. He is told of the countless evils caused by pride and covetousness: he is reminded of the necessity of checking his desires, of the finer pleasures that belong to virtue alone, and of the true happiness that attends it. On his return home, he does not turn to the ledgers of his calling, but he opens the book of Holy Scripture; there he meets with sublime or affecting descriptions of the greatness and goodness of the Creator, of the infinite magnificence of the handiwork of God, of the lofty destinies of man, of his duties, and of his immortal privileges. Thus it is that the American at times steals an hour from himself; and laying aside for a while the petty passions which agitate his life, and the ephemeral interests which engross it, he strays at once into an ideal world, where all is great, eternal, and pure.

I have endeavoured to point out in another part of this work the causes to which the maintenance of the political institutions of the Americans is attributable; and religion appeared to be one of the most prominent among them. I am now treating of the Americans in an individual capacity, and I again observe that religion is not less useful to each citizen than to the whole State. The Americans show, by their practice, that they feel the high necessity of imparting morality to democratic communities by means of religion. What they think of themselves in this respect is a truth of which every democratic nation ought to be thoroughly persuaded.

I do not doubt that the social and political constitutions of a people predispose them to adopt a certain belief and certain tastes, which afterward flourish without difficulty among them; while the same causes may divert a people from certain opinions and propensities, without any voluntary effort, and, as it were, without any distinct consciousness, on their part. The whole art of the legislator is correctly to discern beforehand these natural inclinations of communities of men, in order to know whether they should be assisted, or whether it may not be necessary to check them. For the duties incumbent on the legislator differ at different times; the goal toward which the human race ought ever to be tending is alone stationary; the means of reaching it are perpetually to be varied.

If I had been born in an aristocratic age, in the midst of a nation where the hereditary wealth of some, and the irremediable penury of others, should equally divert men from the idea of bettering their condition, and hold the soul as it were in a state of torpor fixed on the contemplation of another world, I should then wish that it were possible for me to rouse that people to a sense of their wants; I should seek to discover more rapid and more easy means for satisfying the fresh desires which I might have awakened; and, directing the most strenuous efforts of the human mind to physical pursuits, I should endeavour to stimulate it to promote the well-being of man. If it happened that some men were immoderately incited to the pursuit of riches, and displayed an excessive liking for physical gratifications, I should not be alarmed; these peculiar symptoms would soon be absorbed in the general aspect of the people.

The attention of the legislators of democracies is called to other cares. Give democratic nations education and freedom, and leave them alone. They will soon learn to draw from this world all the benefits that it can afford; they will improve each of the useful arts, and will day by day render life more comfortable, more convenient, and more easy. Their social condition naturally urges them in this direction; I do not fear that they will slacken their course.

But while man takes delight in this honest and lawful pursuit of his well-being, it is to be apprehended that he may in the end lose the use of his sublimest faculties; and that while he is busied in improving all around him, he may at length degrade himself. Here, and here only, does the peril lie. It should therefore be the unceasing object of the legislators of democracies, and of all the virtuous and enlightened men who live there, to raise the souls of their fellow-citizens, and keep them lifted up toward Heaven. It is necessary that all who feel an interest in the future destinies of democratic society should unite, and that all should make joint and continual efforts to diffuse the love of the infinite, a sense of greatness, and a love of pleasures not of earth. If among the opinions of a democratic people any of those pernicious theories exist that tend to inculcate that all perishes with the body, let men by whom such theories are professed be marked as the natural foes of such a people.

The Materialists are offensive to me in many respects; their doctrines I hold to be pernicious, and I am disgusted at their arrogance. If their system could be of any utility to man, it would seem to be by giving him a modest opinion of himself. But these reasoners show that it is not so; and when they think they have said enough to establish that they are brutes, they show themselves as proud as if they had demonstrated that they are gods. Materialism is, among all nations, a dangerous disease of the human mind; but it is more especially to be dreaded among a democratic people, because it readily amalgamates with that vice which is most familiar to the heart under such circumstances. Democracy encourages a taste for physical gratification: this taste, if it becomes excessive, soon disposes men to believe that all is matter only; and materialism, in turn, hurries them back with mad impatience to these same delights: such is the fatal circle within which democratic nations are driven round. It were well that they should see the danger and hold back.

Most religions are only general, simple, and practical means of teaching men the doctrine of the immortality of the soul. That is the greatest benefit that a democratic people derives from its belief, and hence belief is more necessary to such a people than to all others. When, therefore, any religion has struck its roots deep into a democracy, beware lest you disturb them; but rather watch it carefully, as the most precious bequest of aristocratic ages. Seek not to supersede the old religious opinions of men by new ones; lest in the passage from one faith to another, the soul being left for a while stripped of all belief, the love of physical gratifications should grow upon it and fill it wholly.

The doctrine of metempsychosis is assuredly not more rational than that of materialism; nevertheless if it were absolutely necessary that a democracy should choose one of the two, I should not hesitate to decide that the community would run less risk of being brutalized by believing that the soul of man will pass into the carcass of a hog than by believing that the soul of man is nothing at all. The belief in a supersensual and immortal principle, united for a time to matter, is so indispensable to man's greatness that its effects are striking even when it is not united to the doctrine of future reward and punishment; and when it holds no more than that after death the Divine principle contained in man is absorbed in the Deity, or transferred to animate the frame of some other creature. Men holding so imperfect a belief will still consider the body as the secondary and inferior portion of their nature, and they will despise it even while they yield to its influence; whereas they have a natural esteem and secret admiration for the immaterial part of man, even though they sometimes refuse to submit to its dominion. That is enough to give a lofty cast to their opinions and their tastes, and to bid them tend with no interested motive, and as it were by impulse, to pure feelings and elevated thoughts.

It is not certain that Socrates and his followers had very fixed opinions as to what would befall man hereafter; but the sole point of belief on which they were determined—that the soul has nothing in common with the body, and survives it—was enough to give the Platonic philosophy that sublime aspiration by which it is distinguished. It is clear from the works of Plato that many philosophical writers, his predecessors or contemporaries, professed materialism. These writers have not reached us, or have reached us in mere fragments. The same thing has happened in almost all ages; the greater part of the most famous minds in literature adhere to the doctrines of a supersensual philosophy. The instinct and the taste of the human race maintain those doctrines; they save them oftentimes in spite of men themselves, and raise the names of their defenders above the tide of time. It must not, then, be supposed that at any period or under any political condition the passion for physical gratifications, and the opinions which are superinduced by that passion, can ever content a whole people. The heart of man is of a larger mould: it can at once comprise a taste for the possessions of earth and the love of those of heaven: at times it may seem to cling devotedly to the one, but it will never be long without thinking of the other.

If it be easy to see that it is more particularly important in democratic ages that spiritual opinions should prevail, it is not easy to say by what means those who govern democratic nations may make them predominate. I am no believer in the prosperity, any more than in the durability, of official philosophies; and as to state religions, I have always held that if they be sometimes of momentary service to the interests of political power, they always, sooner or later, become fatal to the church. Nor do I think with those who assert, that to raise religion in the eyes of the people, and to make them do honour to her spiritual doctrines, it is desirable indirectly to give her ministers a political influence which the laws deny them. I am so much alive to the almost inevitable dangers which beset religious belief whenever the clergy take part in public affairs, and I am so convinced that Christianity must be maintained at any cost in the bosom of modern democracies, that I would rather shut up the priesthood within the sanctuary than allow them to step beyond it.

What means, then, remain in the hands of constituted authorities to bring men back to spiritual opinions, or to hold them fast to the religion by which those opinions are suggested? My answer will do me harm in the eyes of politicians. I believe that the sole effectual means which governments can employ in order to have the doctrine of the immortality of the soul duly respected, is ever to act as if they believed in it themselves; and I think that it is only by scrupulous conformity to religious morality in great affairs that they can hope to teach the community at large to know, to love, and to observe it in the lesser concerns of life.

There is a closer tie than is commonly supposed between the improvement of the soul and the amelioration of what belongs to the body. Man may leave these two things apart, and consider each of them alternately; but he can not sever them entirely without at last losing sight of one and of the other. The beasts have the same senses as ourselves, and very nearly the same appetites. We have no sensual passions which are not common to our race and theirs, and which are not to be found, at least in the germ, in a dog as well as in a man. Whence is it, then, that the animals can only provide for their first and lowest wants, whereas we can infinitely vary and endlessly increase our enjoyments?

We are superior to the beasts in this, that we use our souls to find out those material benefits to which they are only led by instinct. In man, the angel teaches the brute the art of contenting its desires. It is because man is capable of rising above the things of the body, and of contemning life itself, of which the beasts have not the least notion, that he can multiply these same things of the body to a degree that inferior races are equally unable to conceive. Whatever elevates, enlarges, and expands the soul, renders it more capable of succeeding in those very undertakings which concern it not. Whatever, on the other hand, enervates or lowers it, weakens it for all purposes, the chiefest, as well as the least, and threatens to render it almost equally impotent for the one and for the other. Hence the soul must remain great and strong, though it were only to devote its strength and greatness from time to time to the service of the body. If men were ever to content themselves with material objects, it is probable that they would lose by degrees the art of producing them; and they would enjoy them in the end, like the brutes, without discernment and without improvement.

In the ages of faith the final end of life is placed beyond life. The men of those ages therefore naturally, and in a manner involuntarily, accustom themselves to fix their gaze for a long course of years on some immovable object, toward which they are constantly tending; and they learn by insensible degrees to repress a multitude of petty passing desires, in order to be the better able to content that great and lasting desire which possesses them. When these same men engage in the affairs of this world, the same habits may be traced in their conduct. They are apt to set up some general and certain aim and end to their actions here below, toward which all their efforts are directed: they do not turn from day to day to chase some novel object of desire, but they have settled designs which they are never weary of pursuing. This explains why religious nations have so often achieved such lasting results: for while they were thinking only of the other world, they had found out the great secret of success in this. Religions give men a general habit of conducting themselves with a view to futurity: in this respect they are not less useful to happiness in this life than to felicity hereafter; and this is one of their chief political characteristics.

But in proportion as the light of faith grows dim, the range of man's sight is circumscribed, as if the end and aim of human actions appeared every day to be more within his reach. When men have once allowed themselves to think no more of what is to befall them after life, they readily lapse into that complete and brutal indifference to futurity, which is but too conformable to some propensities of mankind. As soon as they have lost the habit of placing their chief hopes upon remote events, they naturally seek to gratify without delay their smallest desires; and no sooner do they despair of living forever than they are disposed to act as if they were to exist but for a single day. In sceptical ages it is always, therefore, to be feared that men may perpetually give way to their daily casual desires; and that, wholly renouncing whatever can not be acquired without protracted effort, they may establish nothing great, permanent, and calm.

If the social condition of a people, under these circumstances, becomes democratic, the danger which I here point out is thereby increased. When every one is constantly striving to change his position—when an immense field for competition is thrown open to all—when wealth is amassed or dissipated in the shortest possible space of time amid the turmoil of democracy, visions of sudden and easy fortunes—of great possessions easily won and lost—of chance, under all its forms—haunt the mind. The instability of society itself fosters the natural instability of man's desires. In the midst of these perpetual fluctuations of his lot, the present grows upon his mind, until it conceals futurity from his sight, and his looks go no further than the morrow.

In those countries in which unhappily irreligion and democracy coexist, the most important duty of philosophers and of those in power is to be always striving to place the objects of human actions far beyond man's immediate range. Circumscribed by the character of his country and his age, the moralist must learn to vindicate his principles in that position. He must constantly endeavour to show his contemporaries that, even in the midst of the perpetual commotion around them, it is easier than they think to conceive and to execute protracted undertakings. He must teach them that, although the aspect of mankind may have changed, the methods by which men may provide for their prosperity in this world are still the same;

and that among democratic nations, as well as elsewhere, it is only by resisting a thousand petty selfish passions of the hour that the general and unquenchable passion for happiness can be satisfied.

The task of those in power is not less clearly marked out. At all times it is important that those who govern nations should act with a view to the future: but this is even more necessary in democratic and sceptical ages than in any others. By acting thus, the leading men of democracies not only make public affairs prosperous, but they also teach private individuals, by their example, the art of managing private concerns. Above all, they must strive as much as possible to banish chance from the sphere of politics. The sudden and undeserved promotion of a courtier produces only a transient impression in an aristocratic country, because the aggregate institutions and opinions of the nation habitually compel men to advance slowly in tracks which they can not get out of. But nothing is more pernicious than similar instances of favour exhibited to the eyes of a democratic people: they give the last impulse to the public mind in a direction where everything hurries it onward. At times of scepticism and equality more especially, the favour of the people or of the prince, which chance may confer or chance withhold, ought never to stand in lieu of attainments or services. It is desirable that every advancement should there appear to be the result of some effort; so that no greatness should be of too easy acquirement, and that ambition should be obliged to fix its gaze long upon an object before it is gratified. Governments must apply themselves to restore to men that love of the future with which religion and the state of society no longer inspire them; and, without saying so, they must practically teach the community day by day that wealth, fame, and power are the rewards of labour—that great success stands at the utmost range of long desires, and that nothing lasting is obtained but what is obtained by toil. When men have accustomed themselves to foresee from afar what is likely to befall them in the world and to feed upon hopes, they can hardly confine their minds within the precise circumference of life, and they are ready to break the boundary and cast their looks beyond. I do not doubt that, by training the members of a community to think of their future condition in this world they would be gradually and unconsciously brought nearer to religious convictions. Thus the means which allow men up to a certain point to go without religion, are perhaps, after all, the only means we still possess for bringing mankind back by a long and roundabout path to a state of faith.

CHAPTER XXX

OCCUPATIONS AND BUSINESS CALLINGS

That among the Americans all honest callings are honourable—That almost all the Americans follow industrial callings—That aristocracy may be engendered by manufactures.

AMONG a democratic people, where there is no hereditary wealth, every man works to earn a living, or has worked, or is born of parents who have worked. The notion of labour is therefore presented to the mind on every side as the necessary, natural, and honest condition of human existence. Not only is labour not dishonourable among such a people, but it is held in honour: the prejudice is not against it, but in its favour. In the United States a wealthy man thinks that he owes it to public opinion to devote his leisure to some kind of industrial or commercial pursuit, or to public business. He would think himself in bad repute if he employed his life solely in living. It is for the purpose of escaping this obligation to work that so many rich Americans come to Europe, where they find some scattered remains of aristocratic society, among which idleness is still held in honour.

Equality of conditions not only ennobles the notion of labour in men's estimation, but it raises the notion of labour as a source of profit. In aristocracies it is not exactly labour that is despised, but labour with a view to profit. Labour is honorific in itself, when it is undertaken at the sole bidding of ambition or of virtue. Yet in aristocratic society it constantly happens that he who works for honour is not insensible to the attractions of profit.

But these two desires only intermingle in the innermost depths of his soul: he carefully hides from every eye the point at which they join; he would fain conceal it from himself. In aristocratic countries there are few public officers who do not affect to serve their country without interested motives. Their salary is an incident of which they think but little, and of which they always affect not to think at all. Thus the notion of profit is kept distinct from that of labour; however they may be united in point of fact, they are not thought of together.

In democratic communities these two notions are, on the contrary, always palpably united. As the desire of well-being is universal—as fortunes are slender or fluctuating—as every one wants either to increase his own resources, or to provide fresh ones for his progeny, men clearly see that it is profit which, if not wholly at least partially, leads them to work. Even those who are principally actuated by the love of fame are necessarily made familiar with the thought that they are not exclusively actuated by that motive; and they discover that the desire of getting a living is mingled in their minds with the desire of making life illustrious.

As soon as, on the one hand, labour is held by the whole community to be an honourable necessity of man's condition, and, on the other, as soon as labour is always ostensibly performed, wholly or in part, for the purpose of earning remuneration, the immense interval which separated different callings in aristocratic societies disappears. If all are not alike, all at least have one feature in common. No profession exists in which men do not work for money; and the remuneration which is common to them all gives them all an air of resemblance. This serves to explain the opinions which the Americans entertain with respect to different callings. In America no one is degraded because he works, for every one about him works also; nor is any one humiliated by the notion of receiving pay, for the President of the United States also works for pay. He is paid for commanding, other men for obeying orders. In the United States professions are more or less laborious, more or less profitable; but they are never either high or low: every honest calling is honourable.

Agriculture is, perhaps, of all the useful arts that which improves most slowly among democratic nations. Frequently, indeed, it would seem to be stationary, because other arts are making rapid strides toward perfection. On the other hand, almost all the tastes and habits which the equality of condition engenders naturally lead men to commercial and industrial occupations.

Suppose an active, enlightened, and free man, enjoying a competency, but full of desires: he is too poor to live in idleness; he is rich enough to feel himself protected from the immediate fear of want, and he thinks how he can better his condition. This man has conceived a taste for physical gratifications, which thousands of his fellow-men indulge in around him; he has himself begun to enjoy these pleasures, and he is eager to increase his means of satisfying these tastes more completely. But life is slipping away, time is urgent—to what is he to turn? The cultivation of the ground promises an almost certain result to his exertions, but a slow one; men are not enriched by it without patience and toil. Agriculture is therefore only suited to those who have already large superfluous wealth, or to those whose penury bids them only seek a bare subsistence. The choice of such a man as we have supposed is soon made; he sells his plot of ground, leaves his dwelling, and embarks in some hazardous but lucrative calling. Democratic communities abound in men of this kind; and in proportion as the equality of conditions becomes greater, their multitude increases. Thus democracy not only swells the number of working-men, but it leads men to prefer one kind of labour to another; and while it diverts them from agriculture, it encourages their taste for commerce and manufactures.[1]

This spirit may be observed even among the richest members of the community. In democratic countries, however opulent a man is supposed to be, he is almost always discontented with his fortune, because he finds that he is less rich than his father was, and he fears that his sons will be less rich than himself. Most rich men in democracies are therefore constantly haunted by the desire of obtaining wealth, and they naturally turn their attention to trade and manufactures, which appear to offer the readiest and most powerful means of success. In this respect they share the instincts of the poor, without feeling the same necessities; say rather, they feel the most imperious of all necessities, that of not sinking in the world.

In aristocracies the rich are at the same time those who govern. The attention which they unceasingly devote to important public affairs diverts them from the lesser cares which trade and manufactures demand. If the will of an individual happens nevertheless to turn his attention to business, the will of the body to which he belongs will immediately debar him from pursuing it; for however men may declaim against the rule of numbers, they can not wholly escape their sway; and even among those aristocratic bodies which most obstinately refuse to acknowledge the rights of the majority of the nation, a private majority is formed which governs the rest.[2]

In democratic countries, where money does not lead those who possess it to political power, but often removes them from it, the rich do not know how to spend their leisure. They are driven into active life by the inquietude and the greatness of their desires, by the extent of their resources, and by the taste for what is extraordinary, which is almost always felt by those who rise, by whatsoever means, above the crowd. Trade is the only road open to them. In democracies nothing is greater or more brilliant than commerce: it attracts the attention of the public, and fills the imagination of the multitude; all energetic passions are directed toward it. Neither their own prejudices, nor those of anybody else, can prevent the rich from devoting themselves to it. The wealthy members of democracies never form a body which has manners and regulations of its own; the opinions peculiar to their class do not restrain them, and the common opinions of their country urge them on. Moreover, as all the large fortunes which are to be met with in a democratic community are of commercial growth, many generations must succeed each other before their possessors can have entirely laid aside their habits of business.

Circumscribed within the narrow space which politics leave them, rich men in democracies eagerly embark in commercial enterprise: there they can extend and employ their natural advantages; and indeed it is even by the boldness and the magnitude of their industrial speculations that we may measure the slight esteem in which productive industry would have been held by them if they had been born amid an aristocracy.

A similar observation is likewise applicable to all men living in democracies, whether they be poor or rich. Those who live in the midst of democratic fluctuations have always before their eyes the phantom of chance; and they end by liking all undertakings in which chance plays a part. They are, therefore, all led to engage in commerce, not only for the sake of the profit it holds out to them, but for the love of the constant excitement occasioned by that pursuit.

The United States of America have only been emancipated for half a century [in 1840] from the state of colonial dependence in which they stood to Great Britain; the number of large fortunes there is small, and capital is still scarce. Yet no people in the world has made such rapid progress in trade and manufactures as the Americans: they constitute at the present day the second maritime nation in the world; and although their manufactures have to struggle with almost insurmountable natural impediments, they are not prevented from making great and daily advances. In the United States the greatest undertakings and speculations are executed without difficulty, because the whole population is engaged in productive industry, and because the poorest as well as the most opulent members of the commonwealth are ready to combine

43

their efforts for these purposes. The consequence is, that a stranger is constantly amazed by the immense public works executed by a nation which contains, so to speak, no rich men. The Americans arrived but as yesterday on the territory which they inhabit, and they have already changed the whole order of Nature for their own advantage. They have joined the Hudson to the Mississippi, and made the Atlantic Ocean communicate with the Gulf of Mexico, across a continent of more than five hundred leagues in extent which separates the two seas. The longest railroads which have been constructed up to the present time are in America. But what most astonishes me in the United States is not so much the marvellous grandeur of some undertakings, as the innumerable multitude of small ones. Almost all the farmers of the United States combine some trade with agriculture; most of them make agriculture itself a trade. It seldom happens that an American farmer settles for good upon the land which he occupies: especially in the districts of the far West he brings land into tillage in order to sell it again, and not to farm it: he builds a farmhouse on the speculation that, as the state of the country will soon be changed by the increase of population, a good price will be gotten for it. Every year a swarm of the inhabitants of the North arrive in the Southern States, and settle in the parts where the cotton-plant and the sugar-cane grow. These men cultivate the soil in order to make it produce in a few years enough to enrich them; and they already look forward to the time when they may return home to enjoy the competency thus acquired. Thus the Americans carry their business-like qualities into agriculture; and their trading passions are displayed in that as in their other pursuits.

The Americans make immense progress in productive industry, because they all devote themselves to it at once; and for this same reason they are exposed to very unexpected and formidable embarrassments. As they are all engaged in commerce, their commercial affairs are affected by such various and complex causes that it is impossible to foresee what difficulties may arise. As they are all more or less engaged in productive industry, at the least shock given to business all private fortunes are put in jeopardy at the same time, and the State is shaken. I believe that the return of these commercial panics is an endemic disease of the democratic nations of our age. It may be rendered less dangerous, but it can not be cured; because it does not originate in accidental circumstances, but in the temperament of these nations.

I have shown that democracy is favourable to the growth of manufactures, and that it increases without limit the numbers of the manufacturing classes: we shall now see by what side-road manufacturers may possibly in their turn bring men back to aristocracy. It is acknowledged that when a workman is engaged every day upon the same detail, the whole commodity is produced with greater ease, promptitude, and economy. It is likewise acknowledged that the cost of the production of manufactured goods is diminished by the extent of the establishment in which they are made, and by the amount of capital employed or of credit. These truths had long been imperfectly discerned, but in our time they have been demonstrated. They have been already applied to many very important kinds of manufactures, and the humblest will gradually be governed by them. I know of nothing in politics which deserves to fix the attention of the legislator more closely than these two new axioms of the science of manufactures.

When a workman is unceasingly and exclusively engaged in the fabrication of one thing, he ultimately does his work with singular dexterity; but at the same time he loses the general faculty of applying his mind to the direction of the work. He every day becomes more adroit and less industrious; so that it may be said of him that in proportion as the workman improves the man is degraded. What can be expected of a man who has spent twenty years of his life in making heads for pins? and to what can that mighty human intelligence, which has so often stirred the world, be applied in him, except it be to investigate the best method of making pins' heads? When a work-man has spent a considerable portion of his existence in this manner, his thoughts are forever set upon the object of his daily toil; his body has contracted certain fixed habits, which it can never shake off: in a word, he no longer belongs to himself, but to the calling which he has chosen. It is in vain that laws and manners have been at the pains to level all barriers around such a man, and to open to him on every side a thousand different paths to fortune; a theory of manufactures more powerful than manners and laws binds him to a craft, and frequently to a spot, which he can not leave: it assigns to him a certain place in society, beyond which he can not go: in the midst of universal movement it has rendered him stationary.

In proportion as the principle of the division of labour is more extensively applied, the workman becomes more weak, more narrow-minded, and more dependent. The art advances, the artisan recedes. On the other hand, in proportion as it becomes more manifest that the produc-tions of manufactures are by so much the cheaper and better as the manufacture is larger and the amount of capi-tal employed more considerable, wealthy and educated men come forward to embark in manufactures which were here-tofore abandoned to poor or ignorant handicraftsmen. The magnitude of the efforts required, and the importance of the results to be obtained, attract them. Thus at the very time at which the science of manufactures lowers the class of workmen, it raises the class of masters.

Whereas the workman concentrates his faculties more and more upon the study of a single detail, the master surveys a more extensive whole, and the mind of the latter is enlarged in proportion as that of the former is nar-rowed. In a short time the one will require nothing but physical strength without intelligence; the other stands in need of science, and almost of genius, to insure success. This man resembles more and more the administrator of a vast empire—that man, a brute. The master and the workman have then here no similarity, and their differences increase every day. They are only connected as the two rings at the extremities of a long chain. Each of them fills the station which is made for him, and out of which he does not get: the one is continually, closely, and necessarily dependent upon the other, and seems as much born to obey as that other is to command. What is this but aristocracy?

As the conditions of men constituting the nation become more and more equal, the demand for manufactured commodities becomes more general and more extensive; and the cheapness which places these objects within the reach of slender fortunes becomes a great element of success. Hence there are every day more men of great opulence and education who devote their wealth and knowledge to manufactures; and who seek, by opening large establishments, and by a strict division of labour, to meet the fresh demands which are made on all sides. Thus, in proportion as the mass of the nation turns to democracy, that particular class which is engaged in manufactures becomes more aristocratic. Men grow more alike in the one —more unlike in the other; and inequality increases in the less numerous class in the same ratio in which it decreases in the community. Hence it would appear, on searching to the bottom, that aristocracy should naturally spring out of the bosom of democracy.

But this kind of aristocracy by no means resembles those kinds that preceded it. It will be observed at once that, as it applies exclusively to manufactures and to some manufacturing calling, it is a monstrous exception in the general aspect of society. The small aristocratic societies which are formed by some manufacturers in the midst of the immense democracy of our age, contain, like the great aristocratic societies of former ages, some men who are very opulent, and a multitude who are wretchedly poor. The poor have few means of escaping from their condition and becoming rich; but the rich are constantly becoming poor, or they give up business when they have realized a fortune. Thus the elements of which the class of the poor is composed are fixed; but the elements of which the class of the rich is composed are not so. To say the truth, though there are rich men, the class of rich men does not exist; for these rich individuals have no feelings or purposes in common, no mutual traditions or mutual hopes; there are therefore members, but no body.

Not only are the rich not compactly united among themselves, but there is no real bond between them and the poor. Their relative position is not a permanent one; they are constantly drawn together or separated by their interests. The workman is generally dependent on the master, but not on any particular master; these two men meet in the factory, but know not each other elsewhere; and while they come into contact on one point, they stand very wide apart on all others. The manufacturer asks nothing of the workman but his labour; the workman expects nothing from him but his wages. The one contracts no obligation to protect, nor the other to defend; and they are not permanently connected either by habit or by duty. The aristocracy created by business rarely settles in the midst of the manufacturing population which it directs: the object is not to govern that population, but to use it. An aristocracy thus constituted can have no great hold upon those whom it employs; and even if it succeed in retaining them at one moment, they escape the next: it knows not how to will, and it can not act. The territorial aristocracy of former ages was either bound by law, or thought itself bound by usage, to come to the relief of its serving-men, and to succour their distresses. But the manufacturing aristocracy of our age first impoverishes and debases the men who serve it, and then abandons them to be supported by the charity of the public. This is a natural consequence of what has been said before. Between the workmen and the master there are frequent relations, but no real partnership.

I am of opinion, upon the whole, that the manufacturing aristocracy which is growing up under our eyes is one of the harshest which ever existed in the world; but at the same time it is one of the most confined and least dangerous. Nevertheless, the friends of democracy should keep their eyes anxiously fixed in this direction; for if ever a permanent inequality of conditions and aristocracy again penetrate into the world, it may be predicted that this is the channel by which they will enter.

NOTES

[1] It has often been remarked that manufacturers and mercantile men are inordinately addicted to physical gratifications, and this has been attributed to commerce and manufactures ; but that is, I apprehend, to take the effect for the cause. The taste for physical gratifications is not imparted to men by commerce or manufactures, but it is rather this taste which leads men to embark in commerce and manufactures, as a means by which they hope to satisfy themselves more promptly and more completely. All the causes which make the love of worldly welfare predominate in the heart of man are favourable to the growth of commerce and manufactures. Equality of conditions is one of those causes ; it encourages trade, not directly by giving men a taste for business, but indirectly by strengthening and expanding in their minds a taste for prosperity.

[2] Some aristocracies have devoted themselves to commerce, and have cultivated manufactures with success. The history of the world might furnish several conspicuous examples. But, generally speaking, it may be affirmed that the aristocratic principle is not favourable to trade and manufactures. Moneyed aristocracies are the only exception to the rule. Among such aristocracies there are hardly any desires which do not require wealth to satisfy them ; the love of riches becomes, so to speak, the high road of human passions, which is crossed by or connected with all lesser tracks. The love of money and the thirst for that distinction which attaches to power are then so closely intermixed in the same souls that it becomes difficult to discover whether men grow covetous from ambition, or whether they are ambitious from covetousness. This is the case in England, where men seek to get rich in order to arrive at distinction, and seek distinctions as a manifestation of their wealth. The mind is then seized by both ends, and hurried into trade and manufactures, which are the shortest roads that lead to opulence. This, however, strikes me as an exceptional and transitory circumstance. When wealth is become the only symbol of aristocracy, it is very difficult for the wealthy to maintain sole possession of political power. The aristocracy of birth and pure Democracy are at the two extremes of the social and political state of nations : between them moneyed aristocracy finds its place. The latter approximates to the aristocracy of birth by conferring great privileges on a small number of persons ; it so far belongs to the democratic element, that these privileges may be successively acquired by all. It frequently forms a natural transition between these two conditions of society, and it is difficult to say whether it closes the reign of aristocratic institutions, or whether it already opens the new era of democracy.

CHAPTER XXXI

INFLUENCE OF DEMOCRACY ON MANNERS

That manners are softened as social conditions become more equal—That democracy renders the habitual intercourse of the Americans simple and easy—Why the Americans show so little sensitiveness in their own country, and are so sensitive in Europe—Consequences.

WE perceive that for several ages social conditions have tended to equality, and we discover that in the course of the same period the manners of society have been softened. Are these two things merely contemporaneous, or does any secret link exist between them, so that the one can not go on without making the other advance? Several causes may concur to render the manners of a people less rude; but, of all these causes, the most powerful appears to me to be the equality of conditions. Equality of conditions and growing civility in manners are then, in my eyes, not only contemporaneous occurrences, but correlative facts. When the fabulists seek to interest us in the actions of beasts, they invest them with human notions and passions; the poets who sing of spirits and angels do the same: there is no wretchedness so deep, nor any happiness so pure, as to fill the human mind and touch the heart, unless we are ourselves held up to our own eyes under other features.

This is strictly applicable to the subject upon which we are at present engaged. When all men are irrevocably marshalled in an aristocratic community, according to their professions, their property, and their birth, the members of each class, considering themselves as children of the same family, cherish a constant and lively sympathy toward each other, which can never be felt in an equal degree by the citizens of a democracy. But the same feeling does not exist between the several classes toward each other. Among an aristocratic people each caste has its own opinions, feelings, rights, manners, and modes of living. Thus the men of whom each caste is composed do not resemble the mass of their fellow-citizens; they do not think or feel in the same manner, and they scarcely believe that they belong to the same human race. They can not, therefore, thoroughly understand what others feel, nor judge of others by themselves. Yet they are sometimes eager to lend each other mutual aid; but this is not contrary to my previous observation. These aristocratic institutions, which made the beings of one and the same race so different, nevertheless bound them to each other by close political ties. Although the serf had no natural interest in the fate of nobles, he did not the less think himself obliged to devote his person to the service of that noble who happened to be his lord: and although the noble held himself to be of a different nature from that of his serfs, he nevertheless held that his duty and his honour constrained him to defend, at the risk of his own life, those who dwelt upon his domains.

It is evident that these mutual obligations did not originate in the law of Nature, but in the law of society; and that the claim of social duty was more stringent than that of mere humanity. These services were not supposed to be due from man to man, but to the vassal or to the lord. Feudal institutions awakened a lively sympathy for the sufferings of certain men, but none at all for the miseries of mankind. They infused generosity rather than mildness into the manners of the time, and although they prompted men to great acts of self-devotion, they engendered no real sympathies; for real sympathies can only exist between those who are alike; and in aristocratic ages men acknowledge none but the members of their own caste to be like themselves.

When the chroniclers of the Middle Ages, who all

belonged to the aristocracy by birth or education, relate
the tragical end of a noble, their grief flows apace; whereas they tell you at a breath, and without wincing, of massacres and tortures inflicted on the common sort of people.
Not that these writers felt habitual hatred or systematic
disdain for the people; war between the several classes of
the community was not yet declared. They were impelled
by an instinct rather than by a passion; as they had formed
no clear notion of a poor man's sufferings, they cared but
little for his fate. The same feelings animated the lower
orders whenever the feudal tie was broken. The same ages
which witnessed so many heroic acts of self-devotion on
the part of vassals for their lords were stained with atro-
cious barbarities, exercised from time to time by the lower
classes on the higher. It must not be supposed that this
mutual insensibility arose solely from the absence of public
order and education; for traces of it are to be found in the
following centuries, which became tranquil and enlightened while they remained aristocratic. In 1675 the lower
classes in Brittany revolted at the imposition of a new tax.
These disturbances were put down with unexampled
atrocity. Observe the language in which Madame de
Sévigné, a witness of these horrors, relates them to her
daughter:

"AUX ROCHERS, *30 Octobre, 1675.*

"Mon Dieu, ma fille, que votre lettre d'Aix est plai-
sante! Au moins relisez vos lettres avant que de les en-
voyer; laissez-vous surprendre à leur agrément, et con-
solez-vous par ce plaisir de la peine que vous avez d'en
tant écrire. Vous avez donc baisé toute la Provence? il
n'y aurait pas satisfaction à baiser toute la Bretagne, à
moins qu'on n'aimât à sentir le vin. . . . Voulez-vous
savoir des nouvelles de Rennes? On à fait une taxe de
cent mille écus sur le bourgeois; et si on ne trouve point
cette somme dans vingt-quatre heures, elle sera doublée
et exigible par les soldats. On a chassé et banni toute une
grande rue, et défendu de les recueillir sous peine de la
vie; de sorte qu'on voyait tous ces misérables, vieillards,

femmes accouchées, enfans, errer en pleurs au sortir de cette ville sans savoir où aller. On roua avant-hier un violon, qui avait commencé la danse et la pillerie du papier timbré; il a été écartelé après sa mort, et ses quatre quartiers exposés aux quatre coins de la ville. On a pris soixante bourgeois, et on commence demain les punitions. Cette province est un bel exemple pour les autres, et surtout de respecter les gouverneurs et les gouvernantes, et de ne point jeter de pierres dans leur jardin.[1]

"Madame de Tarente était hier dans ces bois par un temps enchanté: il n'est question ni de chambre ni de collation; elle entre par la barrière et s'en retourne de même. . . ."

In another letter she adds:

"Vous me parlez bien plaisamment de nos misères; nous ne sommes plus si roués; un en huit jours, pour entretenir la justice. Il est vrai que la penderie me paraît maintenant un refraîchissement. J'ai une tout autre idée de la justice, depuis que je suis en ce pays. Vos galériens me paraissent une société d'honnêtes gens qui se sont retirés du monde pour mener une vie douce."

It would be a mistake to suppose that Madame de Sévigné, who wrote these lines, was a selfish or cruel person; she was passionately attached to her children, and very ready to sympathize in the sorrows of her friends; nay, her letters show that she treated her vassals and serv- ants with kindness and indulgence. But Madame de Sévigné had no clear notion of suffering in any one who was not a person of quality.

In our time the harshest man writing to the most insensible person of his acquaintance would not venture wantonly to indulge in the cruel jocularity which I have quoted; and even if his own manners allowed him to do so, the manners of society at large would forbid it. Whence does this arise? Have we more sensibility than our forefathers? I know not that we have; but I am sure that our insensibility is extended to a far greater range of objects. When all the ranks of a community are nearly equal, as all men think and feel in nearly the same manner, each of them may judge in a moment of the sensations of all the others: he casts a rapid glance upon himself, and that is enough. There is no wretchedness into which he can not readily enter, and a secret instinct reveals to him its extent. It signifies not that strangers or foes be the sufferers; imagination puts him in their place: something like a personal feeling is mingled with his pity, and makes himself suffer while the body of his fellow-creature is in torture. In democratic ages men rarely sacrifice themselves for one another; but they display general compassion for the members of the human race. They inflict no useless ills; and they are happy to relieve the griefs of others, when they can do so without much hurting themselves ; they are not disinterested, but they are humane.

Although the Americans have in a manner reduced egotism to a social and philosophical theory, they are nevertheless extremely open to compassion. In no country is criminal justice administered with more mildness than in the United States. While the English seem disposed carefully to retain the bloody traces of the dark ages in their penal legislation, the Americans have almost expunged capital punishment from their codes. North America is, I think, the only one country upon earth in which the life of no one citizen has been taken for a political offence in the course of the last fifty years. The circumstance which conclusively shows that this singular mildness of the Americans arises chiefly from their social condition, is the manner in which they treat their slaves. Perhaps there is not, upon the whole, a single European colony in the New World in which the physical condition of the blacks is less severe than in the United States; yet the slaves still endure horrid sufferings there, and are constantly exposed to barbarous punishments. It is easy to perceive that the lot of these unhappy beings inspires their masters with but little compassion, and that they look upon slavery, not only as an institution which is profitable to them, but as an evil which does not affect them. Thus the same man who is full of humanity toward his fellow-creatures when they are at the same time his equals, becomes insensible to their afflictions as soon as that equality ceases. His mildness should, therefore, be attributed to the equality of conditions, rather than to civilization and education.

What I have here remarked of individuals is to a certain extent applicable to nations. When each nation has its distinct opinions, belief, laws, and customs, it looks upon itself as the whole of mankind, and is moved by no sorrows but its own. Should war break out between two nations animated by this feeling, it is sure to be waged with great cruelty. At the time of their highest culture, the Romans slaughtered the generals of their enemies, after having dragged them in triumph behind a car; and they flung their prisoners to the beasts of the Circus for the amusement of the people. Cicero, who declaimed so vehemently at the notion of crucifying a Roman citizen, had not a word to say against these horrible abuses of victory. It is evident that in his eyes a barbarian did not belong to the same human race as a Roman. On the contrary, in proportion as nations become more like each other, they become reciprocally more compassionate, and the law of nations is mitigated.

Democracy does not attach men strongly to each other; but it places their habitual intercourse upon an easier footing. If two Englishmen chance to meet at the Antipodes, where they are surrounded by strangers whose language and manners are almost unknown to them, they will first stare at each other with much curiosity and a kind of secret uneasiness; they will then turn away, or, if one accosts the other, they will take care only to converse with a constrained and absent air upon very unimportant subjects. Yet there is no enmity between these men; they have never seen each other before, and each believes the other to be a respectable person. Why, then, should they stand so cautiously apart? We must go back to England to learn the reason.

When it is birth alone, independent of wealth, which classes men in society, every one knows exactly what his own position is upon the social scale; he does not seek to rise, he does not fear to sink. In a community thus organized, men of different castes communicate very little with each other; but if accident brings them together, they are ready to converse without hoping or fearing to lose their own position. Their intercourse is not upon a footing of equality, but it is not constrained. When moneyed aristocracy succeeds to aristocracy of birth, the case is altered. The privileges of some are still extremely great, but the possibility of acquiring those privileges is open to all: whence it follows that those who possess them are constantly haunted by the apprehension of losing them, or of other men's sharing them; those who do not yet enjoy them long to possess them at any cost, or, if they fail, to appear at least to possess them—which is not impossible. As the social importance of men is no longer ostensibly and permanently fixed by blood, and is infinitely varied by wealth, ranks still exist, but it is not easy clearly to distinguish at a glance those who respectively belong to them. Secret hostilities then arise in the community; one set of men endeavour by innumerable artifices to penetrate, or to appear to penetrate, among those who are above them; another set are constantly in arms against these usurpers of their rights; or rather the same individual does both at once, and while he seeks to raise himself into a higher circle, he is always on the defensive against the intrusion of those below him.

Such is the condition of England at the present time; and I am of opinion that the peculiarity before adverted to is principally to be attributed to this cause. An aristocratic pride is still extremely great among the English, and as the limits of aristocracy are ill defined, everybody lives in constant dread lest advantage should be taken of his familiarity. Unable to judge at once of the social position of those he meets, an Englishman prudently avoids all contact with them. Men are afraid lest some slight service rendered should draw them into an unsuitable acquaintance; they dread civilities, and they avoid the obtrusive gratitude of a stranger quite as much as his hatred. Many people attribute these singular anti-social propensities, and the reserved and taciturn bearing of the English, to purely physical causes. I may admit that there is something of it in their race, but much more of it is attributable to their social condition, as is proved by the contrast of the Americans.

In America, where the privileges of birth never existed, and where riches confer no peculiar rights on their possessors, men unacquainted with each other are very ready to frequent the same places, and find neither peril nor advantage in the free interchange of their thoughts. If they meet by accident, they neither seek nor avoid intercourse; their manner is therefore natural, frank, and open: it is easy to see that they hardly expect or apprehend anything from each other, and that they do not care to display, any more than to conceal, their position in the world. If their demeanour is often cold and serious, it is never haughty or constrained; and if they do not converse, it is because they are not in a humour to talk, not because they think it their interest to be silent. In a foreign country two Americans are at once friends, simply because they are Americans. They are repulsed by no prejudice; they are attracted by their common country. For two Englishmen the same blood is not enough; they must be brought together by the same rank. The Americans remark this unsociable mood of the English as much as the French do, and they are not less astonished by it. Yet the Americans are connected with England by their origin, their religion, their language, and partially by their manners: they only differ in their social condition. It may therefore be inferred that the reserve of the English proceeds from the constitution of their country much more than from that of its inhabitants.

The temper of the Americans is vindictive, like that of all serious and reflecting nations. They hardly ever forget an offence, but it is not easy to offend them; and their resentment is as slow to kindle as it is to abate. In aristocratic communities where a small number of persons manage everything, the outward intercourse of men is subject to settled conventional rules. Every one then thinks he knows exactly what marks of respect or of condescension he ought to display, and none are presumed to be ignorant of the science of etiquette. These usages of the first class in society afterward serve as a model to all the others; besides which each of the latter lays down a code of its own, to which all its members are bound to conform. Thus the rules of politeness form a complex system of legislation, which it is difficult to be perfectly master of, but from which it is dangerous for any one to deviate; so that men are constantly exposed involuntarily to inflict or to receive bitter affronts. But as the distinctions of rank are obliterated, as men differing in education and in birth meet and mingle in the same places of resort, it is almost impossible to agree upon the rules of good breeding. As its laws are uncertain, to disobey them is not a crime, even in the eyes of those who know what they are; men attach more importance to intentions than to forms, and they grow less civil, but at the same time less quarrelsome. There are many little attentions which an American does not care about; he thinks they are not due to him, or he presumes that they are not known to be due: he therefore either does not perceive a rudeness or he forgives it; his manners become less courteous, and his character more plain and masculine.

The mutual indulgence which the Americans display, and the manly confidence with which they treat each other, also result from another deeper and more general cause, which I have already adverted to in the preceding chapter. In the United States the distinctions of rank in civil society are slight, in political society they are null; an American, therefore, does not think himself bound to pay particular attentions to any of his fellow-citizens, nor does he require such attentions from them toward himself. As he does not see that it is his interest eagerly to seek the company of any of his countrymen, he is slow to fancy that his own company is declined: despising no one on account of his station, he does not imagine that any one can despise him for that cause; and until he has clearly perceived an insult, he does not suppose that an affront was intended. The social condition of the Americans naturally accustoms them not to take offence in small matters; and, on the other hand, the democratic freedom which they enjoy transfuses this same mildness of temper into the character of the nation. The political institutions of the United States constantly bring citizens of all ranks into contact, and compel them to pursue great undertakings in concert. People thus engaged have scarcely time to attend to the details of etiquette, and they are, besides, too strongly interested in living harmoniously for them to stick at such things. They therefore soon acquire a habit of considering the feelings and opinions of those whom they meet more than their manners, and they do not allow themselves to be annoyed by trifles.

I have often remarked in the United States that it is not easy to make a man understand that his presence may be dispensed with; hints will not always suffice to shake him off. I contradict an American at every word he says, to show him that his conversation bores me; he instantly labours with fresh pertinacity to convince me; I preserve a dogged silence, and he thinks I am meditating deeply on the truths which he is uttering; at last I rush from his company, and he supposes that some urgent business hurries me elsewhere. This man will never understand that he wearies me to extinction unless I tell him so: and the only way to get rid of him is to make him my enemy for life.

It appears surprising at first sight that the same man

44

transported to Europe suddenly becomes so sensitive and captious, that I often find it as difficult to avoid offending him here as it was to put him out of countenance. These two opposite effects proceed from the same cause. Democratic institutions generally give men a lofty notion of their country and of themselves. An American leaves his country with a heart swollen with pride; on arriving in Europe he at once finds out that we are not so engrossed by the United States and the great people which inhabits them as he had supposed, and this begins to annoy him. He has been informed that the conditions of society are not equal in our part of the globe, and he observes that among the nations of Europe the traces of rank are not wholly obliterated; that wealth and birth still retain some indeterminate privileges, which force themselves upon his notice while they elude definition. He is, therefore, profoundly ignorant of the place which he ought to occupy in this half-ruined scale of classes, which are sufficiently distinct to hate and despise each other, yet sufficiently alike for him to be always confounding them. He is afraid of ranging himself too high—still more is he afraid of being ranged too low; this twofold peril keeps his mind constantly on the stretch, and embarrasses all he says and does. He learns from tradition that in Europe ceremonial observances were infinitely varied according to different ranks; this recollection of former times completes his perplexity, and he is the more afraid of not obtaining those marks of respect which are due to him, as he does not exactly know in what they consist. He is like a man surrounded by traps: society is not a recreation for him, but a serious toil: he weighs your least actions, interrogates your looks, and scrutinizes all you say, lest there should be some hidden allusion to affront him. I doubt whether there was ever a provincial man of quality so punctilious in breeding as he is: he endeavours to attend to the slightest rules of etiquette, and does not allow one of them to be waived toward himself: he is full of scruples and at the same time of pretensions; he wishes to do enough, but fears to do too much; and as he does not very well know the limits of the one or of the other, he keeps up a haughty and embarrassed air of reserve.

But this is not all: here is yet another double of the human heart. An American is forever talking of the admirable equality which prevails in the United States: aloud he makes it the boast of his country, but in secret he deplores it for himself; and he aspires to show that, for his part, he is an exception to the general state of things which he vaunts. There is hardly an American to be met with who does not claim some remote kindred with the first founders of the colonies; and as for the scions of the noble families of England, America seemed to me to be covered with them. When an opulent American arrives in Europe, his first care is to surround himself with all the luxuries of wealth: he is so afraid of being taken for the plain citizen of a democracy that he adopts a hundred distorted ways of bringing some new instance of his wealth before you every day. His house will be in the most fashionable part of the town: he will always be surrounded by a host of servants. I have heard an American complain that in the best houses of Paris the society was rather mixed; the taste which prevails there was not pure enough for him; and he ventured to hint that, in his opinion, there was a want of elegance of manner; he could not accustom himself to see wit concealed under such unpretending forms.

These contrasts ought not to surprise us. If the vestiges of former aristocratic distinctions were not so completely effaced in the United States, the Americans would be less simple and less tolerant in their own country— they would require less, and be less fond of borrowed manners in ours.

When men feel a natural compassion for their mutual sufferings—when they are brought together by easy and frequent intercourse, and no sensitive feelings keep them asunder, it may readily be supposed that they will lend assistance to one another whenever it is needed. When an American asks for the co-operation of his fellow-citizens it is seldom refused, and I have often seen it afforded spontaneously and with great good-will. If an accident happens on the highway, everybody hastens to help the sufferer; if some great and sudden calamity befalls a family, the purses of a thousand strangers are at once willingly opened, and small but numerous donations pour in to relieve their distress. It often happens among the most civilized nations of the globe that a poor wretch is as friendless in the midst of a crowd as the savage in his wilds: this is hardly ever the case in the United States. The Americans, who are always cold and often coarse in their manners, seldom show insensibility; and if they do not proffer services eagerly, yet they do not refuse to render them.

All this is not in contradiction to what I have said before on the subject of individualism. The two things are so far from combating each other that I can see how they agree. Equality of conditions, while it makes men feel their independence, shows them their own weakness: they are free, but exposed to a thousand accidents; and experience soon teaches them that, although they do not habitually require the assistance of others, a time almost always comes when they can not do without it. We constantly see in Europe that men of the same profession are ever ready to assist each other; they are all exposed to the same ills, and that is enough to teach them to seek mutual preservatives, however hard-hearted and selfish they may otherwise be. When one of them falls into danger, from which the others may save him by a slight transient sacrifice or a sudden effort, they do not fail to make the attempt. Not that they are deeply interested in his fate; for if, by chance, their exertions are unavailing, they immediately forget the object of them, and return to their own business; but a sort of tacit and almost involuntary agreement has been passed between them, by which each one owes to the others a temporary support which he may claim for himself in turn. Extend to a people the remark here applied to a class, and you will understand my meaning. A similar covenant exists, in fact, between all the citizens of a democracy: they all feel themselves subject to the same weakness and the same dangers; and their interest, as well as their sympathy, makes it a rule with them to lend each other mutual assistance when required. The more equal social conditions become, the more do men display this reciprocal disposition to oblige each other. In democracies no great benefits are conferred, but good offices are constantly rendered: a man seldom displays self-devotion, but all men are ready to be of service to one another.

NOTE

[1] To feel the point of this joke the reader should recollect that Madame de Grignan was Gouvernante de Provence.

CHAPTER XXXII

INFLUENCE OF DEMOCRACY UPON SOCIAL AND DOMESTIC RELATIONS

How democracy affects the relation of masters and servants—That democratic institutions and manners tend to raise rents and shorten the terms of leases—Influence of democracy on wages—Influence of democracy on kindred—Education of young women in the United States—The young woman in the character of a wife—That the equality of conditions contributes to the maintenance of good morals in America—How the Americans understand the equality of the sexes —That the principle of equality naturally divides the Americans into a number of small private circles—Some reflections on American manners.

A N American who had travelled for a long time in Europe once said to me: "The English treat their servants with a stiffness and imperiousness of manner which surprise us; but, on the other hand, the French sometimes treat their attendants with a degree of familiarity or of politeness which we can not conceive. It looks as if they were afraid to give orders: the posture of the superior and the inferior is ill maintained." The remark was a just one, and I have often made it myself. I have always considered England as the country in the world where, in our time, the bond of domestic service is drawn most tightly, and France as the country where it is most relaxed. Nowhere have I seen masters stand so high or so low as in these two countries. Between these two extremes the Americans are to be placed. Such is the fact as it appears upon the surface of things: to discover the causes of that fact, it is necessary to search the matter thoroughly.

No communities have ever yet existed in which social conditions have been so equal that there were neither rich nor poor, and consequently neither masters nor servants. Democracy does not prevent the existence of these two classes, but it changes their dispositions and modifies their mutual relations. Among aristocratic nations servants form a distinct class, not more variously composed than that of masters. A settled order is soon established; in the former as well as in the latter class a scale is formed, with numerous distinctions or marked gradations of rank, and generations succeed each other thus without any change of position. These two communities are superposed one above the other, always distinct, but regulated by analogous principles. This aristocratic constitution does not exert a less powerful influence on the notions and manners of servants than on those of masters; and, although the effects are different, the same cause may easily be traced. Both classes constitute small communities in the heart of the nation, and certain permanent notions of right and wrong are ultimately engendered among them. The different acts of human life are viewed by one particular and unchanging light. In the society of servants, as in that of masters, men exercise a great influence over each other: they acknowledge settled rules, and in the absence of law they are guided by a sort of public opinion: their habits are settled, and their conduct is placed under a certain control.

These men, whose destiny is to obey, certainly do not understand fame, virtue, honesty, and honour in the same manner as their masters; but they have a pride, a virtue, and an honesty pertaining to their condition; and they have a notion, if I may use the expression, of a sort of servile honour.[1] Because a class is mean, it must not be supposed that all who belong to it are mean-hearted; to think so would be a great mistake. However lowly it may be, he who is foremost there, and who has no notion of quitting it, occupies an aristocratic position which inspires him with lofty feelings, pride, and self-respect, that fit him for the higher virtues and actions above the common. Among aristocratic nations it was by no means rare to find men of noble and vigorous minds in the service of the great, who felt not the servitude they bore, and who submitted to the will of their masters without any fear of their displeasure. But this was hardly ever the case among the inferior ranks of domestic servants. It may be imagined that he who occupies the lowest stage of the order of menials stands very low indeed. The French created a word on purpose to designate the servants of the aristocracy—they called them "lackeys." This word lackey served as the strongest expression, when all others were exhausted, to designate human meanness. Under the old French monarchy, to denote by a single expression a low-spirited, contemptible fellow, it was usual to say that he had the soul of a lackey; the term was enough to convey all that was intended.

The permanent inequality of conditions not only gives servants certain peculiar virtues and vices, but it places them in a peculiar relation with respect to their masters. Among aristocratic nations the poor man is familiarized from his childhood with the notion of being commanded: to whichever side he turns his eyes the graduated structure of society and the aspect of obedience meet his view. Hence in those countries the master readily obtains prompt, complete, respectful, and easy obedience from his servants, because they revere in him not only their master but the class of masters. He weighs down their will by the whole weight of the aristocracy. He orders their actions—to a certain extent he even directs their thoughts. In aristocracies the master often exercises, even without being aware of it, an amazing sway over the opinions, the habits, and the manners of those who obey him, and his influence extends even further than his authority.

In aristocratic communities there are not only hereditary families of servants as well as of masters, but the same families of servants adhere for several generations to the same families of masters (like two parallel lines which neither meet nor separate); and this considerably modifies the mutual relations of these two classes of persons. Thus, although in aristocratic society the master and servant have no natural resemblance—although, on the contrary, they are placed at an immense distance on the scale of human beings by their fortune, education, and opinions— yet time ultimately binds them together. They are con- nected by a long series of common reminiscences, and however different they may be, they grow alike; while in democracies, where they are naturally almost alike, they always remain strangers to each other. Among an aris- tocratic people the master gets to look upon his servants as an inferior and secondary part of himself, and he often takes an interest in their lot by a last stretch of egotism.

Servants, on their part, are not averse to regard them- selves in the same light; and they sometimes identify them- selves with the person of the master, so that they become an appendage to him in their own eyes as well as in his. In aristocracies a servant fills a subordinate position which he can not get out of; above him is another man, hold- ing a superior rank which he can not lose. On one side are obscurity, poverty, obedience for life; on the other, and also for life, fame, wealth, and command. The two conditions are always distinct and always in propinquity; the tie that connects them is as lasting as they are them- selves. In this predicament the servant ultimately detaches his notion of interest from his own person; he deserts him- self as it were, or rather he transports himself into the character of his master, and thus assumes an imaginary personality. He complacently invests himself with the wealth of those who command him; he shares their fame, exalts himself by their rank, and feeds his mind with bor- rowed greatness, to which he attaches more importance than those who fully and really possess it. There is some- thing touching, and at the same time ridiculous, in this strange confusion of two different states of being. These passions of masters, when they pass into the souls of me- nials, assume the natural dimensions of the place they occupy—they are contracted and lowered. What was pride in the former becomes puerile vanity and paltry ostentation in the latter. The servants of a great man are commonly most punctilious as to the marks of respect due to him, and they attach more importance to his slightest privileges than he does himself. In France a few of these old servants of the aristocracy are still to be met with here and there; they have survived their race, which will soon disappear with them altogether. In the United States I never saw any one at all like them. The Americans are not only unacquainted with the kind of man, but it is hardly possible to make them understand that such ever existed. It is scarcely less difficult for them to conceive it than for us to form a correct notion of what a slave was among the Romans, or a serf in the Middle Ages. All these men were, in fact, though in different degrees, results of the same cause: they are all retiring from our sight, and disappearing in the obscurity of the past, together with the social condition to which they owed their origin.

Equality of conditions turns servants and masters into new beings, and places them in new relative positions. When social conditions are nearly equal, men are constantly changing their situations in life: there is still a class of menials and a class of masters, but these classes are not always composed of the same individuals, still less of the same families; and those who command are not more secure of perpetuity than those who obey. As servants do not form a separate people, they have no habits, prejudices, or manners peculiar to themselves; they are not remarkable for any particular turn of mind or moods of feeling. They know no vices or virtues of their condition, but they partake of the education, the opinions, the feelings, the virtues and the vices of their contemporaries; and they are honest men or scoundrels in the same way as their masters are. The conditions of servants are not less equal than those of masters. As no marked ranks or fixed subordination are to be found among them, they will not display either the meanness or the greatness which characterize the aristocracy of menials as well as all other aristocracies. I never saw a man in the United States who reminded me of that class of confidential servants of which we still retain a reminiscence in Europe, neither did I ever meet with such a thing as a lackey: all traces of the one and of the other have disappeared.

In democracies servants are not only equal among themselves, but it may be said that they are in some sort the equals of their masters. This requires explanation in order to be rightly understood. At any moment a servant may become a master, and he aspires to rise to that condition: the servant is therefore not a different man from the master. Why, then, has the former a right to command, and what compels the latter to obey?—the free and temporary consent of both their wills. Neither of them is by nature inferior to the other; they only become so for a time by covenant. Within the terms of this covenant, the one is a servant, the other a master; beyond it they are two citizens of the commonwealth—two men. I beg the reader particularly to observe that this is not only the notion which servants themselves entertain of their own condition; domestic service is looked upon by masters in the same light; and the precise limits of authority and obedience are as clearly settled in the mind of the one as in that of the other.

When the greater part of the community have long attained a condition nearly alike, and when equality is an old and acknowledged fact, the public mind, which is never affected by exceptions, assigns certain general limits to the value of man, above or below which no man can long remain placed. It is in vain that wealth and poverty, authority and obedience, accidentally interpose great distances between two men; public opinion, founded upon the usual order of things, draws them to a common level, and creates a species of imaginary equality between them, in spite of the real inequality of their conditions. This all-powerful opinion penetrates at length even into the hearts of those whose interest might arm them to resist it; it affects their judgment while it subdues their will. In their inmost convictions the master and the servant no longer perceive any deep-seated difference between them, and they neither hope nor fear to meet with any such at any time. They are, therefore, neither subject to disdain nor to anger, and they discern in each other neither humility nor pride. The master holds the contract of service to be the only source of his power, and the servant regards it as the only cause of his obedience. They do not quarrel about their reciprocal situations, but each knows his own and keeps it.

In the French army the common soldier is taken from nearly the same classes as the officer, and may hold the same commissions; out of the ranks he considers himself entirely equal to his military superiors, and in point of fact he is so; but when under arms he does not hesitate to obey, and his obedience is not the less prompt, precise, and ready for being voluntary and defined. This example may give a notion of what takes place between masters and servants in democratic communities.

It would be preposterous to suppose that those warm and deep-seated affections, which are sometimes kindled in the domestic service of aristocracy, will ever spring up between these two men, or that they will exhibit strong instances of self-sacrifice. In aristocracies masters and servants live apart, and frequently their only intercourse is through a third person; yet they commonly stand firmly by one another. In democratic countries the master and the servant are close together; they are in daily personal contact, but their minds do not intermingle; they have common occupations, hardly ever common interests. Among such a people the servant always considers himself as a sojourner in the dwelling of his masters. He knew nothing of their forefathers—he will see nothing of their descendants—he has nothing lasting to expect from their hand. Why, then, should he confound his life with theirs, and whence should so strange a surrender of himself proceed? The reciprocal position of the two men is changed —their mutual relations must be so too.

I would fain illustrate all these reflections by the example of the Americans; but for this purpose the distinctions of persons and places must be accurately traced. In the South of the Union, slavery exists; all that I have just said is consequently inapplicable there. In the North, the majority of servants are either freed-men or the children of freed-men; these persons occupy a contested position in the public estimation; by the laws they are brought up to the level of their masters—by the manners of the country they are obstinately detruded from it. They do not themselves clearly know their proper place, and they are almost always either insolent or craven. But in the Northern States, especially in New England, there are a certain number of whites, who agree, for wages, to yield a temporary obedience to the will of their fellow-citizens. I have heard that these servants commonly perform the duties of their situation with punctuality and intelligence; and that without thinking themselves naturally inferior to the person who orders them, they submit without reluctance to obey him. They appear to me to carry into service some of those manly habits which independence and equality engender. Having once selected a hard way of life, they do not seek to escape from it by indirect means; and they have sufficient respect for themselves not to refuse to their masters that obedience which they have freely promised. On their part, masters require nothing of their servants but the faithful and rigorous performance of the covenant: they do not ask for marks of respect, they do not claim their love or devoted attachment; it is enough that, as servants, they are exact and honest. It would not then be true to assert that, in democratic society, the relation of servants and masters is disorganized: it is organized on another footing; the rule is different, but there is a rule.

It is not my purpose to inquire whether the new state of things which I have just described is inferior to that which preceded it, or simply different. Enough for me that it is fixed and determined: for what is most important to meet with among men is not any given ordering, but order. But what shall I say of those sad and troubled times at which equality is established in the midst of the tumult of revolution—when democracy, after having been introduced into the state of society, still struggles with difficulty against the prejudices and manners of the country? The laws, and partially public opinion, already declare that no natural or permanent inferiority exists between the servant and the master. But this new belief has not yet reached the innermost convictions of the latter, or rather his heart rejects it; in the secret persuasion of his mind the master thinks that he belongs to a peculiar and superior race; he dares not say so, but he shudders while he allows himself to be dragged to the same level. His authority over his servants becomes timid and at the same time harsh: he has already ceased to entertain for them the feelings of patronizing kindness which long uncontested power always engenders, and he is surprised that, being changed himself, his servant changes also. He wants his attendants to form regular and permanent habits, in a condition of domestic service which is only temporary: he requires that they should appear contented with and proud of a servile condition, which they will one day shake off—that they should sacrifice themselves to a man who can neither protect nor ruin them—and, in short, that they should contract an indissoluble engagement to a being like themselves, and one who will last no longer than they will.

Among aristocratic nations it often happens that the condition of domestic service does not degrade the character of those who enter upon it, because they neither know nor imagine any other; and the amazing inequality which is manifest between them and their master appears to be the necessary and unavoidable consequence of some hidden law of Providence. In democracies the condition of domestic service does not degrade the character of those who enter upon it, because it is freely chosen, and adopted for a time only; because it is not stigmatized by public opinion, and creates no permanent inequality between the servant and the master.   But while the transition from one social condition to another is going on, there is almost always a time when men's minds fluctuate between the aristocratic notion of subjection and the democratic notion of obedience.   Obedience then loses its moral importance in the eyes of him who obeys; he no longer considers it as a species of divine obligation, and he does not yet view it under its purely human aspect; it has to him no character of sanctity or of justice, and he submits to it as to a degrading but profitable condition.   At that moment a confused and imperfect phantom of equality haunts the minds of servants; they do not at once perceive whether the equality to which they are entitled is to be found within or without the pale of domestic service; and they rebel in their hearts against a subordination to which they have subjected themselves, and from which they derive actual profit.   They consent to serve, and they blush to obey; they like the advantages of service, but not the master; or rather, they are not sure that they ought not themselves to be masters, and they are inclined to consider him who orders them as an unjust usurper of their own rights.   Then it is that the dwelling of every citizen offers a spectacle somewhat analogous to the gloomy aspect of political society.   A secret and intestine warfare is going on there between powers, ever rivals and suspicious of one another: the master is ill-natured and weak, the servant ill-natured and intractable; the one constantly attempts to evade by unfair restrictions his obligation to protect and to remunerate—the other his obligation to obey.   The reins of domestic government dangle between them, to be snatched at by one or the other.   The lines which divide authority from oppression, liberty from license, and right from might, are to their eyes so jumbled together and confused that no one knows exactly what he is, or what he may be, or what he ought to be.   Such a condition is not democracy, but revolution.

What has been said of servants and masters is applicable, to a certain extent, to land-owners and farming tenants; but this subject deserves to be considered by itself. In America there are, properly speaking, no tenant farmers; every man owns the ground he tills. It must be admitted that democratic laws tend greatly to increase the number of land-owners, and to diminish that of farming tenants. Yet what takes place in the United States is much less attributable to the institutions of the country than to the country itself. In America land is cheap, and any one may easily become a land-owner; its returns are small, and its produce can not well be divided between a land-owner and a farmer. America, therefore, stands alone in this as well as in many other respects, and it would be a mistake to take it as an example.

I believe that in democratic as well as in aristocratic countries there will be land-owners and tenants, but the connection existing between them will be of a different kind. In aristocracies the hire of a farm is paid to the landlord, not only in rent, but in respect, regard, and duty; in democracies the whole is paid in cash. When estates are divided and passed from hand to hand, and the permanent connection which existed between families and the soil is dissolved, the land-owner and the tenant are only casually brought into contact. They meet for a moment to settle the conditions of the agreement, and then lose sight of each other; they are two strangers brought together by a common interest, and who keenly talk over a matter of business, the sole object of which is to make money.

In proportion as property is subdivided and wealth distributed over the country, the community is filled with people whose former opulence is declining, and with others whose fortunes are of recent growth and whose wants increase more rapidly than their resources. For all such persons the smallest pecuniary profit is a matter of importance, and none of them feel disposed to waive any of their claims, or to lose any portion of their income. As ranks are intermingled, and as very large as well as very scanty fortunes become more rare, every day brings the social condition of the land-owner nearer to that of the farmer; the one has not naturally any uncontested superiority over the other; between two men who are equal, and not at ease in their circumstances, the contract of hire is exclusively an affair of money. A man whose estate extends over a whole district, and who owns a hundred farms, is well aware of the importance of gaining at the same time the affections of some thousands of men; this object appears to call for his exertions, and to attain it he will readily make considerable sacrifices. But he who owns a hundred acres is insensible to similar considerations, and he cares but little to win the private regard of his tenant.

An aristocracy does not expire like a man in a single day; the aristocratic principle is slowly undermined in men's opinion before it is attacked in their laws. Long before open war is declared against it, the tie which had hitherto united the higher classes to the lower may be seen to be gradually relaxed. Indifference and contempt are betrayed by one class, jealousy and hatred by the others; the intercourse between rich and poor becomes less frequent and less kind, and rents are raised. This is not the consequence of a democratic revolution, but its certain harbinger; for an aristocracy which has lost the affections of the people, once and forever, is like a tree dead at the root, which is the more easily torn up by the winds the higher its branches have spread.

In the course of the last fifty years the rents of farms have amazingly increased, not only in France, but throughout the greater part of Europe. The remarkable improvements which have taken place in agriculture and manufactures within the same period do not suffice in my opinion to explain this fact; recourse must be had to another cause more powerful and more concealed. I believe that cause is to be found in the democratic institutions which several European nations have adopted, and in the democratic passions which more or less agitate all the rest. I

45

have frequently heard great English land-owners congratulate themselves that, at the present day, they derive a much larger income from their estates than their fathers did. They have perhaps good reason to be glad; but most assuredly they know not what they are glad of. They think they are making a clear gain, when it is in reality only an exchange; their influence is what they are parting with for cash; and what they gain in money will ere long be lost in power.

There is yet another sign by which it is easy to know that a great democratic revolution is going on or approaching. In the middle ages almost all lands were leased for lives, or for very long terms; the domestic economy of that period shows that leases for ninety-nine years were more frequent then than leases for twelve years are now. Men then believed that families were immortal; men's conditions seemed settled forever, and the whole of society appeared to be so fixed that it was not supposed that anything would ever be stirred or shaken in its structure. In ages of equality, the human mind takes a different bent; the prevailing notion is that nothing abides, and man is haunted by the thought of mutability. Under this impression the land-owner and the tenant himself are instinctively averse to protracted terms of obligation; they are afraid of being tied up to-morrow by the contract which benefits them to-day. They have vague anticipations of some sudden and unforeseen change in their conditions; they mistrust themselves; they fear lest their taste should change, and lest they should lament that they can not rid themselves of what they coveted; nor are such fears unfounded, for in democratic ages that which is most fluctuating amid the fluctuation of all around is the heart of man.

Most of the remarks which I have already made in speaking of servants and masters may be applied to masters and workmen. As the gradations of the social scale come to be less observed, while the great sink the humble rise, and as poverty as well as opulence ceases to be hereditary, the distance, both in reality and in opinion, which

heretofore separated the workman from the master is lessened every day.   The workman conceives a more lofty
opinion of his rights, of his future, of himself; he is filled
with new ambition and with new desires, he is harassed
by new wants.   Every instant he views with longing eyes
the profits of his employer; and in order to share them,
he strives to dispose of his labour at a higher rate, and
he generally succeeds at length in the attempt.   In democratic countries, as well as elsewhere, most of the branches
of productive industry are carried on at a small cost by
men little removed by their wealth or education above
the level of those whom they employ.   These manufacturing speculators are extremely numerous; their interests
differ; they can not, therefore, easily concert or combine
their exertions.   On the other hand, the workmen have
almost always some sure resources, which enable them to
refuse to work when they can not get what they conceive
to be the fair price of their labour.   In the constant struggle for wages which is going on between these two classes,
their strength is divided, and success alternates from one
to the other.   It is even probable that in the end the interest of the working class must prevail; for the high
wages which they have already obtained make them every
day less dependent on their masters; and as they grow
more independent, they have greater facilities for obtaining a further increase of wages.

I shall take for example that branch of productive industry which is still at the present day the most generally
followed in France, and in almost all the countries of the
world—I mean the cultivation of the soil.   In France most
of those who labour for hire in agriculture are themselves
owners of certain plots of ground, which just enable them
to subsist without working for any one else.   When these
labourers come to offer their services to a neighbouring
land-owner or farmer, if he refuses them a certain rate of
wages, they retire to their own small property and await
another opportunity.

I think that, upon the whole, it may be asserted that

a slow and gradual rise of wages is one of the general laws of democratic communities. In proportion as social conditions become more equal, wages rise; and as wages are higher, social conditions become more equal. But a great and gloomy exception occurs in our own time. I have shown in a preceding chapter that aristocracy, expelled from political society, has taken refuge in certain departments of productive industry, and has established its sway there under another form; this powerfully affects the rate of wages. As a large capital is required to embark in the great manufacturing speculations to which I allude, the number of persons who enter upon them is exceedingly limited: as their number is small, they can easily concert together, and fix the rate of wages as they please. Their workmen, on the contrary, are exceedingly numerous, and the number of them is always increasing; for, from time to time, an extraordinary run of business takes place, during which wages are inordinately high, and they attract the surrounding population to the factories. But, when once men have embraced that line of life, we have already seen that they can not quit it again, because they soon contract habits of body and mind which unfit them for any other sort of toil. These men have generally but little education and industry, with but few resources; they stand, therefore, almost at the mercy of the master. When competition, or other fortuitous circumstances, lessen his profits, he can reduce the wages of his workmen almost at pleasure, and make from them what he loses by the chances of business. Should the workmen strike, the master, who is a rich man, can very well wait without being ruined until necessity brings them back to him; but they must work day by day or they die, for their only property is in their hands. They have long been impoverished by oppression, and the poorer they become the more easily may they be oppressed: they can never escape from this fatal circle of cause and consequence. It is not then surprising that wages, after having sometimes suddenly risen, are permanently lowered in this branch of industry; whereas in other callings the price of labour, which generally increases but little, is nevertheless constantly augmented.

This state of dependence and wretchedness, in which a part of the manufacturing population of our time lives, forms an exception to the general rule, contrary to the state of all the rest of the community; but, for this very reason, no circumstance is more important or more deserving of the especial consideration of the legislator; for when the whole of society is in motion, it is difficult to keep any one class stationary; and when the greater number of men are opening new paths to fortune, it is no less difficult to make the few support in peace their wants and their desires.

I have just examined the changes which the equality of conditions produces in the mutual relations of the several members of the community among democratic nations, and among the Americans in particular. I would now go deeper, and inquire into the closer ties of kindred: my object here is not to seek for new truths, but to show in what manner facts already known are connected with my subject.

It has been universally remarked that in our time the several members of a family stand upon an entirely new footing toward each other; that the distance which formerly separated a father from his sons has been lessened; and that paternal authority, if not destroyed, is at least impaired. Something analogous to this, but even more striking, may be observed in the United States. In America the family, in the Roman and aristocratic signification of the word, does not exist. All that remains of it are a few vestiges in the first years of childhood, when the father exercises, without opposition, that absolute domestic authority which the feebleness of his children renders necessary, and which their interest, as well as his own incontestable superiority, warrants. But as soon as the young American approaches manhood, the ties of filial obedience are relaxed day by day: master of his thoughts, he is soon master of his conduct. In America there is, strictly speaking, no adolescence: at the close of boyhood the man appears, and begins to trace out his own path. It would be an error to suppose that this is preceded by a domestic struggle, in which the son has obtained by a sort of moral violence the liberty that his father refused him. The same habits, the same principles which impel the one to assert his independence, predispose the other to consider the use of that independence as an incontestable right. The former does not exhibit any of those rancorous or irregular passions which disturb men long after they have shaken off an established authority; the latter feels none of that bitter and angry regret which is apt to survive a by-gone power. The father foresees the limits of his authority long beforehand, and when the time arrives he surrenders it without a struggle: the son looks forward to the exact period at which he will be his own master; and he enters upon his freedom without precipitation and without effort, as a possession which is his own and which no one seeks to wrest from him.[2]

It may perhaps not be without utility to show how these changes which take place in family relations are closely connected with the social and political revolution which is approaching its consummation under our own observation. There are certain great social principles which a people either introduces everywhere or tolerates nowhere. In countries which are aristocratically constituted with all the gradations of rank, the Government never makes a direct appeal to the mass of the governed: as men are united together, it is enough to lead the foremost; the rest will follow. This is equally applicable to the family, as to all aristocracies which have a head. Among aristocratic nations, social institutions recognise, in truth, no one in the family but the father; children are received by society at his hands; society governs him, he governs them. Thus the parent has not only a natural right, but he acquires a political right, to command them: he is the author and the support of his family; but he is also its constituted ruler. In democracies, where the government picks out every individual singly from the mass, to make him subservient to the general laws of the community, no such intermediate person is required: a father is there, in the eye of the law, only a member of the community, older and richer than his sons.

When most of the conditions of life are extremely unequal, and the inequality of these conditions is permanent, the notion of a superior grows upon the imaginations of men: if the law invested him with no privileges, custom and public opinion would concede them. When, on the contrary, men differ but little from each other, and do not always remain in dissimilar conditions of life, the general notion of a superior becomes weaker and less distinct: it is vain for legislation to strive to place him who obeys very much beneath him who commands; the manners of the time bring the two men nearer to one another, and draw them daily toward the same level. Although the legislation of an aristocratic people should grant no peculiar privileges to the heads of families, I shall not be the less convinced that their power is more respected and more extensive than in a democracy; for I know that, whatsoever the laws may be, superiors always appear higher and inferiors lower in aristocracies than among democratic nations.

When men live more for the remembrance of what has been than for the care of what is, and when they are more given to attend to what their ancestors thought than to think themselves, the father is the natural and necessary tie between the past and the present—the link by which the ends of these two chains are connected. In aristocracies, then, the father is not only the civil head of the family, but the oracle of its traditions, the expounder of its customs, the arbiter of its manners. He is listened to with deference, he is addressed with respect, and the love which is felt for him is always tempered with fear. When the condition of society becomes democratic, and men adopt as their general principle that it is good and lawful to judge of all things for one's self, using former points of belief not as a rule of faith but simply as a means of information, the power which the opinions of a father exercise over those of his sons diminishes as well as his legal power.

Perhaps the subdivision of estates which democracy brings with it contributes more than anything else to change the relations existing between a father and his children. When the property of the father of a family is scanty, his son and himself constantly live in the same place, and share the same occupations: habit and necessity bring them together, and force them to hold constant communication: the inevitable consequence is a sort of familiar intimacy, which renders authority less absolute, and which can ill be reconciled with the external forms of respect. Now in democratic countries the class of those who are possessed of small fortunes is precisely that which gives strength to the notions, and a particular direction to the manners, of the community. That class makes its opinions preponderate as universally as its will, and even those who are most inclined to resist its commands are carried away in the end by its example. I have known eager opponents of democracy who allowed their children to address them with perfect colloquial equality.

Thus, at the same time that the power of aristocracy is declining, the austere, the conventional, and the legal part of parental authority vanishes, and a species of equality prevails around the domestic hearth. I know not, upon the whole, whether society loses by the change, but I am inclined to believe that man individually is a gainer by it. I think that, in proportion as manners and laws become more democratic, the relation of father and son becomes more intimate and more affectionate; rules and authority are less talked of; confidence and tenderness are oftentimes increased, and it would seem that the natural bond is drawn closer in proportion as the social bond is loosened. In a democratic family the father exercises no other power than that with which men love to invest the affection and the experience of age; his orders would perhaps be disobeyed, but his advice is for the most part authoritative. Though he be not hedged in with ceremonial respect, his sons at least accost him with confidence; no settled form of speech is appropriated to the mode of addressing him, but they speak to him constantly, and are ready to consult him day by day; the master and the constituted ruler have vanished—the father remains.   Nothing more is needed, in order to judge of the difference between the two states of society in this respect, than to peruse the family correspondence of aristocratic ages.   The style is always correct, ceremonious, stiff, and so cold that the natural warmth of the heart can hardly be felt in the language.   The language, on the contrary, addressed by a son to his father in democratic countries is always marked by mingled freedom, familiarity, and affection, which at once show that new relations have sprung up in the bosom of the family.

A similar revolution takes place in the mutual relations of children.   In aristocratic families, as well as in aristocratic society, every place is marked out beforehand. Not only does the father occupy a separate rank, in which he enjoys extensive privileges, but even the children are not equal among themselves.   The age and sex of each irrevocably determine his rank, and secure to him certain privileges: most of these distinctions are abolished or diminished by democracy.   In aristocratic families the eldest son, inheriting the greater part of the property, and almost all the rights of the family, becomes the chief, and, to a certain extent, the master, of his brothers.   Greatness and power are for him—for them, mediocrity and dependence.   Nevertheless, it would be wrong to suppose that, among aristocratic nations, the privileges of the eldest son are advantageous to himself alone, or that they excite nothing but envy and hatred in those around him.   The eldest son commonly endeavours to procure wealth and power for his brothers, because the general splendour of the house is reflected back on him who represents it; the younger sons seek to back the elder brother in all his undertakings, because the greatness and power of the head of the family better enable him to provide for all its branches. The different members of an aristocratic family are therefore very closely bound together; their interests are connected, their minds agree, but their hearts are seldom in harmony.

Democracy also binds brothers to each other, but by very different means. Under democratic laws all the children are perfectly equal, and consequently independent: nothing brings them forcibly together, but nothing keeps them apart; and as they have the same origin, as they are trained under the same roof, as they are treated with the same care, and as no peculiar privilege distinguishes or divides them, the affectionate and youthful intimacy of early years easily springs up between them. Scarcely any opportunities occur to break the tie thus formed at the outset of life; for their brotherhood brings them daily together, without embarrassing them. It is not, then, by interest, but by common associations and by the free sympathy of opinion and of taste, that democracy unites brothers to each other. It divides their inheritance, but it allows their hearts and minds to mingle together. Such is the charm of these democratic manners, that even the partisans of aristocracy are caught by it; and after having experienced it for some time, they are by no means tempted to revert to the respectful and frigid observances of aristocratic families. They would be glad to retain the domestic habits of democracy if they might throw off its social conditions and its laws; but these elements are indissolubly united, and it is impossible to enjoy the former without enduring the latter.

The remarks I have made on filial love and fraternal affection are applicable to all the passions which emanate spontaneously from human nature itself. If a certain mode of thought or feeling is the result of some peculiar condition of life, when that condition is altered nothing whatever remains of the thought or feeling. Thus a law may bind two members of the community very closely to one another; but that law being abolished, they stand asunder. Nothing was more strict than the tie which united the vassal to the lord under the feudal system: at the present day the two men know not each other; the fear, the gratitude, and the affection which formerly connected them have vanished, and not a vestige of the tie remains. Such, however, is not the case with those feelings which are natural to mankind. Whenever a law attempts to tutor these feelings in any particular manner, it seldom fails to weaken them; by attempting to add to their intensity, it robs them of some of their elements, for they are never stronger than when left to themselves.

Democracy, which destroys or obscures almost all the old conventional rules of society, and which prevents men from readily assenting to new ones, entirely effaces most of the feelings to which these conventional rules have given rise; but it only modifies some others, and frequently imparts to them a degree of energy and sweetness unknown before. Perhaps it is not impossible to condense into a single proposition the whole meaning of this chapter, and of several others that preceded it. Democracy loosens social ties, but it draws the ties of Nature more tight; it brings kindred more closely together, while it places the various members of the community more widely apart.

No free communities ever existed without morals; and, as I observed in the former part of this work, morals are the work of woman. Consequently, whatever affects the condition of women, their habits, and their opinions, has great political importance in my eyes. Among almost all Protestant nations young women are far more the mistresses of their own actions than they are in Catholic countries. This independence is still greater in Protestant countries like England, which have retained or acquired the right of self-government; the spirit of freedom is then infused into the domestic circle by political habits and by religious opinions. In the United States the doctrines of Protestantism are combined with great political freedom and a most democratic state of society; and nowhere are young women surrendered so early or so completely to their own guidance. Long before an American girl arrives at the age of marriage, her emancipation from maternal control begins: she has scarcely ceased to be a child when she already thinks for herself, speaks with freedom, and acts on her own impulse. The great scene of the world is constantly open to her view: far from seeking concealment, it is every day disclosed to her more completely, and she is taught to survey it with a firm and calm gaze. Thus the vices and dangers of society are early revealed to her; as she sees them clearly, she views them without illusions, and braves them without fear; for she is full of reliance on her own strength, and her reliance seems to be shared by all who are about her. An American girl scarcely ever displays that virginal bloom in the midst of young desires, or that innocent and ingenuous grace which usually attend the European woman in the transition from girlhood to youth. It is rarely that an American woman at any age displays childish timidity or ignorance. Like the young women of Europe, she seeks to please, but she knows precisely the cost of pleasing. If she does not abandon herself to evil, at least she knows that it exists; and she is remarkable rather for purity of manners than for chastity of mind. I have been frequently surprised, and almost frightened, at the singular address and happy boldness with which young women in America contrive to manage their thoughts and their language amid all the difficulties of stimulating conversation; a philosopher would have stumbled at every step along the narrow path which they trod without accidents and without effort. It is easy, indeed, to perceive that, even amid the independence of early youth, an American woman is always mistress of herself: she indulges in all permitted pleasures, without yielding herself up to any of them; and her reason never allows the reins of self-guidance to drop, though it often seems to hold them loosely.

In France, where remnants of every age are still so strangely mingled in the opinions and tastes of the people, women commonly receive a reserved, retired, and almost conventional education, as they did in aristocratic times; and then they are suddenly abandoned, without a guide and without assistance, in the midst of all the irregularities inseparable from democratic society. The Americans are more consistent. They have found out that in a democracy the independence of individuals can not fail to be very great, youth premature, tastes ill-restrained, customs fleeting, public opinion often unsettled and powerless, paternal authority weak, and marital authority contested. Under these circumstances, believing that they had little chance of repressing in woman the most vehement passions of the human heart, they held that the surer way was to teach her the art of combating those passions for herself. As they could not prevent her virtue from being exposed to frequent danger, they determined that she should know how best to defend it; and more reliance was placed on the free vigour of her will than on safeguards which have been shaken or overthrown. Instead, then, of inculcating mistrust of herself, they constantly seek to enhance their confidence in her own strength of character. As it is neither possible nor desirable to keep a young woman in perpetual or complete ignorance, they hasten to give her a precocious knowledge on all subjects. Far from hiding the corruptions of the world from her, they prefer that she should see them at once and train herself to shun them; and they hold it of more importance to protect her conduct than to be overscrupulous of her innocence.

Although the Americans are a very religious people, they do not rely on religion alone to defend the virtue of woman; they seek to arm her reason also. In this they have followed the same method as in several other respects; they first make the most vigorous efforts to bring individual independence to exercise a proper control over itself, and they do not call in the aid of religion until they have reached the utmost limits of human strength. I am aware that an education of this kind is not without danger; I am sensible that it tends to invigorate the judgment at the expense of the imagination, and to make cold and vir-

tuous women instead of affectionate wives and agreeable
companions to man. Society may be more tranquil and
better regulated, but domestic life has often fewer charms.
These, however, are secondary evils, which may be braved
for the sake of higher interests. At the stage at which
we are now arrived the time for choosing is no longer
within our control; a democratic education is indispensable
to protect women from the dangers with which democratic
institutions and manners surround them.

In America the independence of woman is irrecoverably
lost in the bonds of matrimony: if an unmarried woman
is less constrained there than elsewhere, a wife is subjected
to stricter obligations. The former makes her father's
house an abode of freedom and of pleasure; the latter lives
in the home of her husband as if it were a cloister. Yet
these two different conditions of life are perhaps not so
contrary as may be supposed, and it is natural that the
American women should pass through the one to arrive
at the other.

Religious peoples and trading nations entertain peculiarly serious notions of marriage: the former consider the
regularity of woman's life as the best pledge and most certain sign of the purity of her morals; the latter regard it
as the highest security for the order and prosperity of the
household. The Americans are at the same time a puritanical people and a commercial nation: their religious
opinions, as well as their trading habits, consequently lead
them to require much abnegation on the part of woman,
and a constant sacrifice of her pleasures to her duties which
is seldom demanded of her in Europe. Thus in the United
States the inexorable opinion of the public carefully circumscribes woman within the narrow circle of domestic
interests and duties, and forbids her to step beyond it.

Upon her entrance into the world a young American
woman finds these notions firmly established; she sees the
rules which are derived from them; she is not slow to perceive that she can not depart for an instant from the established usages of her contemporaries without putting in

jeopardy her peace of mind, her honour, nay, even her social existence; and she finds the energy required for such an act of submission in the firmness of her understanding and in the virile habits which her education has given her. It may be said that she has learned by the use of her independence to surrender it without a struggle and without a murmur when the time comes for making the sacrifice. But no American woman falls into the toils of matrimony as into a snare held out to her simplicity and ignorance. She has been taught beforehand what is expected of her, and voluntarily and freely does she enter upon this engagement. She supports her new condition with courage, because she chose it. As in America paternal discipline is very relaxed and the conjugal tie very strict, a young woman does not contract the latter without considerable circumspection and apprehension. Precocious marriages are rare. Thus American women do not marry until their understandings are exercised and ripened; whereas in other countries most women generally only begin to exercise and to ripen their understandings after marriage.

I by no means suppose, however, that the great change which takes place in all the habits of women in the United States, as soon as they are married, ought solely to be attributed to the constraint of public opinion: it is frequently imposed upon themselves by the sole effort of their own will. When the time for choosing a husband is arrived, that cold and stern reasoning power which has been educated and invigorated by the free observation of the world, teaches an American woman that a spirit of levity and independence in the bonds of marriage is a constant subject of annoyance, not of pleasure; it tells her that the amusements of the girl can not become the recreations of the wife, and that the sources of a married woman's happiness are in the home of her husband. As she clearly discerns beforehand the only road which can lead to domestic happiness, she enters upon it at once, and follows it to the end without seeking to turn back.

The same strength of purpose which the young wives

of America display, in bending themselves at once and without repining to the austere duties of their new condition, is no less manifest in all the great trials of their lives. In no country in the world are private fortunes more precarious than in the United States. It is not uncommon for the same man, in the course of his life, to rise and sink again through all the grades which lead from opulence to poverty. American women support these vicissitudes with calm and unquenchable energy: it would seem that their desires contract, as easily as they expand, with their fortunes.[3]

The greater part of the adventurers who migrate every year to people the Western wilds, belong, as I observed in the former part of this work, to the old Anglo-American race of the Northern States. Many of these men, who rush so boldly onward in pursuit of wealth, were already in the enjoyment of a competency in their own part of the country. They take their wives along with them, and make them share the countless perils and privations which always attend the commencement of these expeditions. I have often met, even on the verge of the wilderness, with young women who, after having been brought up amid all the comforts of the large towns of New England, had passed, almost without any intermediate stage, from the wealthy abode of their parents to a comfortless hovel in a forest. Fever, solitude, and a tedious life had not broken the springs of their courage. Their features were impaired and faded, but their looks were firm: they appeared to be at once sad and resolute. I do not doubt that these young American women had amassed, in the education of their early years, that inward strength which they displayed under these circumstances. The early culture of the girl may still, therefore, be traced, in the United States, under the aspect of marriage: her part is changed, her habits are different, but her character is the same.

Some philosophers and historians have said, or have hinted, that the strictness of female morality was increased or diminished simply by the distance of a country from

the equator. This solution of the difficulty was an easy
one; and nothing was required but a globe and a pair of
compasses to settle in an instant one of the most difficult
problems in the condition of mankind. But I am not aware
that this principle of the materialists is supported by facts.
The same nations have been chaste or dissolute at different periods of their history; the strictness or the laxity of
their morals depended, therefore, on some variable cause,
not only on the natural qualities of their country, which
were invariable. I do not deny that in certain climates
the passions which are occasioned by the mutual attraction of the sexes are peculiarly intense; but I am of opinion that this natural intensity may always be excited or
restrained by the condition of society and by political institutions.

Although the travellers who have visited North America differ on a great number of points, they all agree in
remarking that morals are far more strict there than elsewhere. It is evident that on this point the Americans are
very superior to their progenitors the English. A superficial glance at the two nations will establish the fact. In
England, as in all other countries of Europe, public malice
is constantly attacking the frailties of women. Philosophers and statesmen are heard to deplore that morals are
not sufficiently strict, and the literary productions of the
country constantly lead one to suppose so. In America
all books, novels not excepted, suppose women to be
chaste, and no one thinks of relating affairs of gallantry.
No doubt this great regularity of American morals originates partly in the country, in the race of the people, and
in their religion: but all these causes, which operate elsewhere, do not suffice to account for it; recourse must be
had to some special reason. This reason appears to me
to be the principle of equality and the institutions derived
from it. Equality of conditions does not of itself engender
regularity of morals, but it unquestionably facilitates and
increases it.[4]

Among aristocratic nations birth and fortune frequently
46

make two such different beings of man and woman that they can never be united to each other. Their passions draw them together, but the condition of society, and the notions suggested by it, prevent them from contracting a permanent and ostensible tie. The necessary consequence is a great number of transient and clandestine connections. Nature secretly avenges herself for the constraint imposed upon her by the laws of man. This is not so much the case when the equality of conditions has swept away all the imaginary, or the real, barriers which separated man from woman. No girl then believes that she can not become the wife of the man who loves her; and this renders all breaches of morality before marriage very uncommon: for, whatever be the credulity of the passions, a woman will hardly be able to persuade herself that she is beloved when her lover is perfectly free to marry her and does not.

The same cause operates, though more indirectly, on married life. Nothing better serves to justify an illicit passion, either to the minds of those who have conceived it or to the world which looks on, than compulsory or accidental marriages.[5] In a country in which a woman is always free to exercise her power of choosing, and in which education has prepared her to choose rightly, public opinion is inexorable to her faults. The rigour of the Americans arises in part from this cause. They consider marriage as a covenant which is often onerous, but every condition of which the parties are strictly bound to fulfil, because they knew all those conditions beforehand, and were perfectly free not to have contracted them.

The very circumstances which render matrimonial fidelity more obligatory also render it more easy. In aristocratic countries the object of marriage is rather to unite property than persons; hence the husband is sometimes at school and the wife at nurse when they are betrothed. It can not be wondered at if the conjugal tie which holds the fortunes of the pair united allows their hearts to rove; this is the natural result of the nature of the contract. When, on the contrary, a man always chooses a wife for himself, without any external coercion or even guidance, it is generally a conformity of tastes and opinions which brings a man and a woman together, and this same conformity keeps and fixes them in close habits of intimacy.

Our forefathers had conceived a very strange notion on the subject of marriage: as they had remarked that the small number of love-matches which occurred in their time almost always turned out ill, they resolutely inferred that it was exceedingly dangerous to listen to the dictates of the heart on the subject. Accident appeared to them to be a better guide than choice. Yet it was not very difficult to perceive that the examples which they witnessed did, in fact, prove nothing at all. For, in the first place, if democratic nations leave a woman at liberty to choose her husband, they take care to give her mind sufficient knowledge, and her will sufficient strength, to make so important a choice: whereas the young women who, among aristocratic nations, furtively elope from the authority of their parents to throw themselves of their own accord into the arms of men whom they have had neither time to know, nor ability to judge of, are totally without those securities. It is not surprising that they make a bad use of their freedom of action the first time they avail themselves of it; nor that they fall into such cruel mistakes, when, not having received a democratic education, they choose to marry in conformity to democratic customs. But this is not all. When a man and woman are bent upon marriage in spite of the differences of an aristocratic state of society, the difficulties to be overcome are enormous. Having broken or relaxed the bonds of filial obedience, they have then to emancipate themselves by a final effort from the sway of custom and the tyranny of opinion; and when at length they have succeeded in this arduous task, they stand estranged from their natural friends and kinsmen: the prejudice they have crossed separates them from all, and places them in a situation which soon breaks their courage and sours their hearts. If, then, a couple married in this manner are first unhappy and afterward criminal, it ought not to be attributed to the freedom of their choice, but rather to their living in a community in which this freedom of choice is not admitted.

Moreover, it should not be forgotten that the same effort which makes a man violently shake off a prevailing error, commonly impels him beyond the bounds of reason; that, to dare to declare war, in however just a cause, against the opinion of one's age and country, a violent and adventurous spirit is required, and that men of this character seldom arrive at happiness or virtue, whatever be the path they follow. And this, it may be observed by the way, is the reason why, in the most necessary and righteous revolutions, it is so rare to meet with virtuous or moderate revolutionary characters. There is, then, no just ground for surprise if a man, who in an age of aristocracy chooses to consult nothing but his own opinion and his own taste in the choice of a wife, soon finds that infractions of morality and domestic wretchedness invade his household: but when this same line of action is in the natural and ordinary course of things, when it is sanctioned by parental authority and backed by public opinion, it can not be doubted that the internal peace of families will be increased by it, and conjugal fidelity more rigidly observed.

Almost all men in democracies are engaged in public or professional life; and, on the other hand, the limited extent of common incomes obliges a wife to confine herself to the house, in order to watch in person and very closely over the details of domestic economy. All these distinct and compulsory occupations are so many natural barriers, which, by keeping the two sexes asunder, render the solicitations of the one less frequent and less ardent— the resistance of the other more easy.

Not, indeed, that the equality of conditions can ever succeed in making men chaste, but it may impart a less dangerous character to their breaches of morality. As no one has, then, either sufficient time or opportunity to assail a virtue armed in self-defence, there will be at the

same time a great number of courtesans and a great number of virtuous women. This state of things causes la-
mentable cases of individual hardship, but it does not prevent the body of society from being strong and alert: it
does not destroy family ties, or enervate the morals of the
nation. Society is endangered not by the great profligacy
of a few, but by laxity of morals among all. In the eyes
of a legislator, prostitution is less to be dreaded than intrigue.

The tumultuous and constantly harassed life which
equality makes men lead, not only distracts them from
the passion of love, by denying them time to indulge in
it, but it diverts them from it by another more secret but
more certain road. All men who live in democratic ages
more or less contract the ways of thinking of the manufacturing and trading classes; their minds take a serious,
deliberate, and positive turn; they are apt to relinquish
the ideal, in order to pursue some visible and proximate
object, which appears to be the natural and necessary aim
of their desires. Thus the principle of equality does not
destroy the imagination, but lowers its flight to the level
of the earth. No men are less addicted to reverie than
the citizens of a democracy; and few of them are ever
known to give way to those idle and solitary meditations
which commonly precede and produce the great emotions
of the heart. It is true they attach great importance to
procuring for themselves that sort of deep, regular, and
quiet affection which constitutes the charm and safeguard
of life, but they are not apt to run after those violent
and capricious sources of excitement which disturb and
abridge it.

I am aware that all this is only applicable in its full
extent to America, and can not at present be extended to
Europe. In the course of the last half century, while laws
and customs have impelled several European nations with
unexampled force toward democracy, we have not had occasion to observe that the relations of man and woman
have become more orderly or more chaste. In some places

the very reverse may be detected: some classes are more strict—the general morality of the people appears to be more lax. I do not hesitate to make the remark, for I am as little disposed to flatter my contemporaries as to malign them. This fact must distress, but it ought not to surprise us. The propitious influence which a democratic state of society may exercise upon orderly habits is one of those tendencies which can only be discovered after a time. If the equality of conditions is favourable to purity of morals, the social commotion by which conditions are rendered equal is adverse to it. In the last fifty years, during which France has been undergoing this transformation, that country has rarely had freedom, always disturbance. Amid this universal confusion of notions and this general stir of opinions—amid this incoherent mixture of the just and the unjust, of truth and falsehood, of right and might—public virtue has become doubtful, and private morality wavering. But all revolutions, whatever may have been their object or their agents, have at first produced similar consequences; even those which have in the end drawn the bonds of morality more tightly began by loosening them. The violations of morality which the French frequently witness do not appear to me to have a permanent character; and this is already betokened by some curious signs of the times.

Nothing is more wretchedly corrupt than an aristocracy which retains its wealth when it has lost its power, and which still enjoys a vast deal of leisure after it is reduced to mere vulgar pastimes. The energetic passions and great conceptions which animated it heretofore, leave it then; and nothing remains to it but a host of petty consuming vices, which cling about it like worms upon a carcass. No one denies that the French aristocracy of the last century was extremely dissolute; whereas established habits and ancient belief still preserved some respect for morality among the other classes of society. Nor will it be contested that at the present day the remnants of that same aristocracy exhibit a certain severity of morals; while laxity of morals appears to have spread among the middle and lower ranks. So that the same families which were most profligate fifty years ago are nowadays the most exemplary, and democracy seems only to have strengthened the morality of the aristocratic classes. The French Revolution, by dividing the fortunes of the nobility, by forcing them to attend assiduously to their affairs and to their families, by making them live under the same roof with their children, and, in short, by giving a more rational and serious turn to their minds, has imparted to them, almost without their being aware of it, a reverence for religious belief, a love of order, of tranquil pleasures, of domestic endearments, and of comfort; whereas the rest of the nation, which had naturally these same tastes, was carried away into excesses by the effort which was required to overthrow the laws and political habits of the country. The old French aristocracy has undergone the consequences of the revolution, but it neither felt the revolutionary passions, nor shared in the anarchical excitement which produced that crisis; it may easily be conceived that this aristocracy feels the salutary influence of the revolution in its manners before those who achieve it. It may, therefore, be said, though at first it seems paradoxical, that, at the present day, the most anti-democratic classes of the nation principally exhibit the kind of morality which may reasonably be anticipated from democracy. I can not but think that when we shall have obtained all the effects of this democratic revolution, after having got rid of the tumult it has caused, the observations which are now only applicable to the few will gradually become true of the whole community.

I have shown how democracy destroys or modifies the different inequalities which originate in society; but is this all? or does it not ultimately affect that great inequality of man and woman which has seemed, up to the present day, to be eternally based in human nature? I believe that the social changes which bring nearer to the same level the father and son, the master and servant, and superiors and inferiors generally speaking, will raise woman and make her more and more the equal of man. But here, more than ever, I feel the necessity of making myself clearly understood; for there is no subject on which the coarse and lawless fancies of our age have taken a freer range.

There are people in Europe who, confounding together the different characteristics of the sexes, would make of man and woman beings not only equal but alike. They would give to both the same functions, impose on both the same duties, and grant to both the same rights; they would mix them in all things—their occupations, their pleasures, their business. It may readily be conceived that by thus attempting to make one sex equal to the other, both are degraded; and from so preposterous a medley of the works of Nature nothing could ever result but weak men and disorderly women.

It is not thus that the Americans understand that species of democratic equality which may be established between the sexes. They admit that as Nature has appointed such wide differences between the physical and moral constitution of man and woman, her manifest design was to give a distinct employment to their various faculties; and they hold that improvement does not consist in making beings so dissimilar do pretty nearly the same things, but in getting each of them to fulfil their respective tasks in the best possible manner. The Americans have applied to the sexes the great principle of political economy which governs the manufactures of our age, by carefully dividing the duties of man from those of woman, in order that the great work of society may be the better carried on.

In no country has such constant care been taken as in America to trace two clearly distinct lines of action for the two sexes, and to make them keep pace one with the other, but in two pathways which are always different. American women never manage the outward concerns of the family, or conduct a business, or take a part in political life; nor are they, on the other hand, ever compelled to perform the rough labour of the fields, or to make any of those laborious exertions which demand the exertion of physical strength. No families are so poor as to form an exception to this rule. If, on the one hand, an American woman can not escape from the quiet circle of domestic employments, on the other hand she is never forced to go beyond it. Hence it is that the women of America, who often exhibit a masculine strength of understanding and a manly energy, generally preserve great delicacy of personal appearance and always retain the manners of women, although they sometimes show that they have the hearts and minds of men.

Nor have the Americans ever supposed that one consequence of democratic principles is the subversion of marital power, or the confusion of the natural authorities in families. They hold that every association must have a head in order to accomplish its object, and that the natural head of the conjugal association is man. They do not, therefore, deny him the right of directing his partner; and they maintain, that in the smaller association of husband and wife, as well as in the great social community, the object of democracy is to regulate and legalize the powers which are necessary, not to subvert all power. This opinion is not peculiar to one sex, and contested by the other: I never observed that the women of America consider conjugal authority as a fortunate usurpation of their rights, nor that they thought themselves degraded by submitting to it. It appeared to me, on the contrary, that they attach a sort of pride to the voluntary surrender of their own will, and make it their boast to bend themselves to the yoke, not to shake it off. Such at least is the feeling expressed by the most virtuous of their sex; the others are silent; and in the United States it is not the practice for a guilty wife to clamour for the rights of women, while she is trampling on her holiest duties.

It has often been remarked that in Europe a certain degree of contempt lurks even in the flattery which men

lavish upon women: although a European frequently affects to be the slave of woman, it may be seen that he never
sincerely thinks her his equal. In the United States men
seldom compliment women, but they daily show how much
they esteem them. They constantly display an entire confidence in the understanding of a wife, and a profound
respect for her freedom; they have decided that her mind
is just as fitted as that of a man to discover the plain truth,
and her heart as firm to embrace it; and they have never
sought to place her virtue, any more than his, under the
shelter of prejudice, ignorance, and fear. It would seem
that in Europe, where man so easily submits to the despotic sway of women, they are nevertheless curtailed of
some of the greatest qualities of the human species, and
considered as seductive but imperfect beings; and (what
may well provoke astonishment) women ultimately look
upon themselves in the same light, and almost consider it
as a privilege that they are entitled to show themselves
futile, feeble, and timid. The women of America claim no
such privileges.

Again, it may be said that in our morals we have reserved strange immunities to man; so that there is, as it
were, one virtue for his use, and another for the guidance
of his partner; and that, according to the opinion of the
public, the very same act may be punished alternately as
a crime or only as a fault. The Americans know not this
iniquitous division of duties and rights; among them the
seducer is as much dishonoured as his victim. It is true
that the Americans rarely lavish upon women those eager
attentions which are commonly paid them in Europe; but
their conduct to women always implies that they suppose
them to be virtuous and refined; and such is the respect
entertained for the moral freedom of the sex, that in the
presence of a woman the most guarded language is used,
lest her ear should be offended by an expression. In
America a young unmarried woman may, alone and without fear, undertake a long journey.

The legislators of the United States, who have miti-

gated almost all the penalties of criminal law, still make
rape a capital offence, and no crime is visited with more
inexorable severity by public opinion. This may be accounted for; as the Americans can conceive nothing more
precious than a woman's honour, and nothing which ought
so much to be respected as her independence, they hold
that no punishment is too severe for the man who deprives
her of them against her will. In France, where the same
offence is visited with far milder penalties, it is frequently
difficult to get a verdict from a jury against the prisoner.
Is this a consequence of contempt of decency or contempt
of women? I can not but believe that it is a contempt of
one and of the other.

Thus the Americans do not think that man and woman
have either the duty or the right to perform the same
offices, but they show an equal regard for both their respective parts; and though their lot is different, they consider both of them as being of equal value. They do not
give to the courage of woman the same form or the same
direction as to that of man; but they never doubt her courage: and if they hold that man and his partner ought not
always to exercise their intellect and understanding in the
same manner, they at least believe the understanding of
the one to be as sound as that of the other, and her intellect to be as clear. Thus, then, while they have allowed
the social inferiority of woman to subsist, they have done
all they could to raise her morally and intellectually to the
level of man; and in this respect they appear to me to
have excellently understood the true principle of democratic improvement. As for myself, I do not hesitate to
avow that, although the women of the United States are
confined within the narrow circle of domestic life, and their
situation is in some respects one of extreme dependence,
I have nowhere seen woman occupying a loftier position;
and if I were asked, now that I am drawing to the close
of this work, in which I have spoken of so many important things done by the Americans, to what the singular
prosperity and growing strength of that people ought

mainly to be attributed, I should reply—to the superiority of their women.

It may probably be supposed that the final consequence and necessary effect of democratic institutions is to confound together all the members of the community in private as well as in public life, and to compel them all to live in common; but this would be to ascribe a very coarse and oppressive form to the equality which originates in democracy. No state of society or laws can render men so much alike, but that education, fortune, and tastes will interpose some differences between them; and, though different men may sometimes find it to their interest to combine for the same purposes, they will never make it their pleasure. They will, therefore, always tend to evade the provisions of legislation, whatever they may be; and departing in some one respect from the circle within which they were to be bounded, they will set up, close by the great political community, small private circles, united together by the similitude of their conditions, habits, and manners.

In the United States the citizens have no sort of preeminence over each other; they owe each other no mutual obedience or respect; they all meet for the administration of justice, for the government of the State, and in general to treat of the affairs which concern their common welfare; but I never heard that attempts have been made to bring them all to follow the same diversions, or to amuse themselves promiscuously in the same places of recreation. The Americans, who mingle so readily in their political assemblies and courts of justice, are wont, on the contrary, carefully to separate into small distinct circles, in order to indulge by themselves in the enjoyments of private life. Each of them is willing to acknowledge all his fellow-citizens as his equals, but he will only receive a very limited number of them among his friends or his guests. This appears to me to be very natural. In proportion as the circle of public society is extended, it may be anticipated that the sphere of private intercourse will be contracted; far from

supposing that the members of modern society will ultimately live in common, I am afraid that they may end by
forming nothing but small coteries.

Among aristocratic nations the different classes are
like vast chambers, out of which it is impossible to get,
into which it is impossible to enter. These classes have no
communication with each other, but within their pale men
necessarily live in daily contact; even though they would
not naturally suit, the general conformity of a similar condition brings them nearer together. But when neither law
nor custom professes to establish frequent and habitual
relations between certain men, their intercourse originates
in the accidental analogy of opinions and tastes; hence
private society is infinitely varied. In democracies, where
the members of the community never differ much from
each other, and naturally stand in such propinquity that
they may all at any time be confounded in one general
mass, numerous artificial and arbitrary distinctions spring
up, by means of which every man hopes to keep himself
aloof, lest he should be carried away in the crowd against
his will. This can never fail to be the case; for human
institutions may be changed, but not man: whatever
may be the general endeavour of a community to render its members equal and alike, the personal pride
of individuals will always seek to rise above the line,
and to form somewhere an inequality to their own advantage.

In aristocracies men are separated from each other by
lofty stationary barriers; in democracies they are divided
by a number of small and almost invisible threads, which
are constantly broken or moved from place to place. Thus,
whatever may be the progress of equality, in democratic
nations a great number of small private communities will
always be formed within the general pale of political society; but none of them will bear any resemblance in its
manners to the highest class in aristocracies.

Nothing seems at first sight less important than the
outward form of human actions, yet there is nothing upon

which men set more store: they grow used to everything except to living in a society which has not their own manners. The influence of the social and political state of a country upon manners is therefore deserving of serious examination. Manners are, generally, the product of the very basis of the character of a people, but they are also sometimes the result of an arbitrary convention between certain men; thus they are at once natural and acquired. When certain men perceive that they are the foremost persons in society, without contestation and without effort—when they are constantly engaged on large objects, leaving the more minute details to others—and when they live in the enjoyment of wealth which they did not amass and which they do not fear to lose, it may be supposed that they feel a kind of haughty disdain of the petty interests and practical cares of life, and that their thoughts assume a natural greatness, which their language and their manners denote. In democratic countries manners are generally devoid of dignity, because private life is there extremely petty in its character; and they are frequently low, because the mind has few opportunities of rising above the engrossing cares of domestic interests. True dignity in manners consists in always taking one's proper station, neither too high nor too low; and this is as much within the reach of a peasant as of a prince. In democracies all stations appear doubtful; hence it is that the manners of democracies, though often full of arrogance, are commonly wanting in dignity, and, moreover, they are never either well disciplined or accomplished.

The men who live in democracies are too fluctuating for a certain number of them ever to succeed in laying down a code of good breeding, and in forcing people to follow it. Every man, therefore, behaves after his own fashion, and there is always a certain incoherence in the manners of such times, because they are moulded upon the feelings and notions of each individual, rather than upon an ideal model proposed for general imitation. This, however, is much more perceptible at the time when an aristocracy has just been overthrown than after it has long been destroyed. New political institutions and new social elements then bring to the same places of resort, and frequently compel to live in common, men whose education and habits are still amazingly dissimilar, and this renders the motley composition of society peculiarly visible. The existence of a former strict code of good breeding is still remembered, but what it contained or where it is to be found is already forgotten. Men have lost the common law of manners, and they have not yet made up their minds to do without it; but every one endeavours to make to himself some sort of arbitrary and variable rule, from the remnant of former usages; so that manners have neither the regularity and the dignity which they often display among aristocratic nations, nor the simplicity and freedom which they sometimes assume in democracies; they are at once constrained and without constraint.

This, however, is not the normal state of things. When the equality of conditions is long established and complete, as all men entertain nearly the same notions and do nearly the same things, they do not require to agree or to copy from one another in order to speak or act in the same manner: their manners are constantly characterized by a number of lesser diversities, but not by any great differences. They are never perfectly alike, because they do not copy from the same pattern; they are never very unlike, because their social condition is the same. At first sight a traveller would observe that the manners of all the Americans are exactly similar; it is only upon close examination that the peculiarities in which they differ may be detected.

The English make game of the manners of the Americans; but it is singular that most of the writers who have drawn these ludicrous delineations belonged themselves to the middle classes in England, to whom the same delineations are exceedingly applicable: so that these pitiless censors for the most part furnish an example of the very thing they blame in the United States; they do not perceive that they are deriding themselves, to the great amusement of the aristocracy of their own country.

Nothing is more prejudicial to democracy than its outward forms of behaviour; many men would willingly endure its vices, who can not support its manners. I can not, however, admit that there is nothing commendable in the manners of a democratic people. Among aristocratic nations, all who live within reach of the first class in society commonly strain to be like it, which gives rise to ridiculous and insipid imitations. As a democratic people does not possess any models of high breeding, at least it escapes the daily necessity of seeing wretched copies of them. In democracies manners are never so refined as among aristocratic nations, but, on the other hand, they are never so coarse. Neither the coarse oaths of the populace, nor the elegant and choice expressions of the nobility, are to be heard there: the manners of such a people are often vulgar, but they are neither brutal nor mean. I have already observed that in democracies no such thing as a regular code of good breeding can be laid down; this has some inconveniences and some advantages. In aristocracies the rules of propriety impose the same demeanour on every one; they make all the members of the same class appear alike, in spite of their private inclinations; they adorn and they conceal the natural man. Among a democratic people manners are neither so tutored nor so uniform, but they are frequently more sincere. They form, as it were, a light and loosely-woven veil, through which the real feelings and private opinions of each individual are easily discernible. The form and the substance of human actions often, therefore, stand in closer relation; and if the great picture of human life be less embellished, it is more true. Thus it may be said, in one sense, that the effect of democracy is not exactly to give men any particular manners, but to prevent them from having manners at all.

The feelings, the passions, the virtues, and the vices of an aristocracy may sometimes reappear in a democracy, but not its manners; they are lost, and vanish forever, as soon as the democratic revolution is completed. It would seem that nothing is more lasting than the manners of an aristocratic class, for they are preserved by that class for some time after it has lost its wealth and its power— nor so fleeting, for no sooner have they disappeared than not a trace of them is to be found; and it is scarcely possible to say what they have been as soon as they have ceased to be. A change in the state of society works this miracle, and a few generations suffice to consummate it. The principal characteristics of aristocracy are handed down by history after an aristocracy is destroyed, but the light and exquisite touches of manners are effaced from men's memories almost immediately after its fall. Men can no longer conceive what these manners were when they have ceased to witness them; they are gone, and their departure was unseen, unfelt; for in order to feel that refined enjoyment which is derived from choice and distinguished manners, habit and education must have prepared the heart, and the taste for them is lost almost as easily as the practice of them. Thus not only a democratic people can not have aristocratic manners, but they neither comprehend nor desire them; and as they never have thought of them, it is to their minds as if such things had never been. Too much importance should not be attached to this loss, but it may well be regretted.

I am aware that it has not infrequently happened that the same men have had very high-bred manners and very low-born feelings: the interior of courts has sufficiently shown what imposing externals may conceal the meanest hearts. But though the manners of aristocracy did not constitute virtue, they sometimes embellish virtue itself. It was no ordinary sight to see a numerous and powerful class of men, whose every outward action seemed constantly to be dictated by a natural elevation of thought and feeling, by delicacy and regularity of taste, and by urbanity of manners. Those manners threw a pleasing illusory charm over human nature; and though the picture was

47

often a false one, it could not be viewed without a noble satisfaction.

NOTES

[1] If the principal opinions by which men are guided are examined closely and in detail, the analogy appears still more striking, and one is surprised to find among them, just as much as among the haughtiest scions of a feudal race, pride of birth, respect for their ancestry and their descendants, disdain of their inferiors, a dread of contact, a taste for etiquette, precedents, and antiquity.

[2] The Americans, however, have not yet thought fit to strip the parent, as has been done in France, of one of the chief elements of parental authority, by depriving him of the power of disposing of his property at his death. In the United States there are no restrictions on the powers of a testator. In this respect, as in almost all others, it is easy to perceive that if the political legislation of the Americans is much more democratic than that of the French, the civil legislation of the latter is infinitely more democratic than that of the former. This may easily be accounted for. The civil legislation of France was the work of a man who saw that it was his interest to satisfy the democratic passions of his contemporaries in all that was not directly and immediately hostile to his own power. He was willing to allow some popular principles to regulate the distribution of property and the government of families, provided they were not to be introduced into the administration of public affairs. While the torrent of democracy overwhelmed the civil laws of the country, he hoped to find an easy shelter behind its political institutions. This policy was at once both adroit and selfish ; but a compromise of this kind could not last ; for in the end political institutions never fail to become the image and expression of civil society ; and in this sense it may be said that nothing is more political in a nation than its civil legislation.

[3] See Appendix, S.

[4] See Appendix, T.

[5] The literature of Europe sufficiently corroborates this remark. When a European author wishes to depict in a work of imagination any of those great catastrophes in matrimony which so frequently occur among us, he takes care to bespeak the compassion of the reader by bringing before him ill-assorted or compulsory marriages. Although habitual tolerance has long since relaxed our morals, an author could hardly succeed in interesting us in the misfortunes of his characters if he did not first palliate their faults. This artifice seldom fails : the daily scenes we witness prepare us long beforehand to be indulgent. But American writers could never render these palliations probable to their readers ; their customs and laws are opposed to it ; and as they despair of rendering levity of conduct pleasing, they cease to depict it. This is one of the causes to which must be attributed the small number of novels published in the United States.

CHAPTER XXXIII

INFLUENCE OF DEMOCRACY UPON PUBLIC RELATIONS

The gravity of the Americans, and why it does not prevent them from often committing inconsiderate actions—Why the national vanity of the Americans is more restless and captious than that of the English —That the aspect of society in the United States is at once excited and monotonous—Honour[1] in the United States and in democratic communities—Why so many ambitious men and so little lofty ambition are to be found in the United States—The trade of place-hunting in certain democratic countries.

MEN who live in democratic countries do not value the simple, turbulent, or coarse diversions in which the people indulge in aristocratic communities: such diversions are thought by them to be puerile or insipid. Nor have they a greater inclination for the intellectual and refined amusements of the aristocratic classes. They want something productive and substantial in their pleasures; they want to mix actual fruition with their joy. In aristocratic communities the people readily give themselves up to bursts of tumultuous and boisterous gaiety, which shake off at once the recollection of their privations: the natives of democracies are not fond of being thus violently broken in upon, and they never lose sight of their own selves without regret. They prefer to these frivolous delights those more serious and silent amusements which are like business, and which do not drive business wholly from their minds. An American, instead of going in a leisure hour to dance merrily at some place of public resort, as the fellows of his calling continue to do throughout the greater part of Europe, shuts himself up at home to drink. He thus enjoys two pleasures: he can go on thinking of his business, and he can get drunk decently by his own fireside.   .

I thought that the English constituted the most serious nation on the face of the earth, but I have since seen the Americans and have changed my opinion. I do not mean to say that temperament has not a great deal to do with the character of the inhabitants of the United States, but I think that their political institutions are a still more influential cause. I believe the seriousness of the Americans arises partly from their pride. In democratic countries even poor men entertain a lofty notion of their personal importance: they look upon themselves with complacency, and are apt to suppose that others are looking at them too. With this disposition they watch their language and their actions with care, and do not lay themselves open so as to betray their deficiencies; to preserve their dignity they think it necessary to retain their gravity.

But I detect another more deep-seated and powerful cause which instinctively produces among the Americans this astonishing gravity. Under a despotism communities give way at times to bursts of vehement joy; but they are generally gloomy and moody, because they are afraid. Under absolute monarchies tempered by the customs and manners of the country, their spirits are often cheerful and even, because as they have some freedom and a good deal of security, they are exempted from the most important cares of life; but all free peoples are serious, because their minds are habitually absorbed by the contemplation of some dangerous or difficult purpose. This is more especially the case among those free nations which form democratic communities. Then there are in all classes a very large number of men constantly occupied with the serious affairs of the government; and those whose thoughts are not engaged in the direction of the commonwealth are wholly engrossed by the acquisition of a private fortune. Among such a people a serious demeanour ceases to be peculiar to certain men, and becomes a habit of the nation.

We are told of small democracies in the days of antiquity, in which the citizens met upon the public places with garlands of roses, and spent almost all their time in dancing and theatrical amusements. I do not believe in such republics any more than in that of Plato; or, if the things we read of really happened, I do not hesitate to affirm that these supposed democracies were composed of very different elements from ours, and that they had nothing in common with the latter except their name. But it must not be supposed that, in the midst of all their toils, the people who live in democracies think themselves to be pitied; the contrary is remarked to be the case. No men are fonder of their own condition. Life would have no relish for them if they were delivered from the anxieties which harass them, and they show more attachment to their cares than aristocratic nations to their pleasures.

I am next led to inquire how it is that these same democratic nations, which are so serious, sometimes act in so inconsiderate a manner. The Americans, who almost always preserve a staid demeanour and a frigid air, nevertheless frequently allow themselves to be borne away, far beyond the bounds of reason, by a sudden passion or a hasty opinion, and they sometimes gravely commit strange absurdities. This contrast ought not to surprise us. There is one sort of ignorance which originates in extreme publicity. In despotic states men know not how to act, because they are told nothing; in democratic nations they often act at random, because nothing is to be left untold. The former do not know—the latter forget; and the chief features of each picture are lost to them in a bewilderment of details.

It is astonishing what imprudent language a public man may sometimes use in free countries, and especially in democratic states, without being compromised; whereas in absolute monarchies a few words dropped by accident are enough to unmask him forever, and ruin him without hope of redemption. This is explained by what goes before. When a man speaks in the midst of a great crowd, many of his words are not heard, or are forthwith obliterated from the memories of those who hear them; but amid the silence of a mute and motionless throng the slightest whisper strikes the ear.

In democracies men are never stationary; a thousand chances waft them to and fro, and their life is always the sport of unforeseen or (so to speak) extemporaneous circumstances. Thus they are often obliged to do things which they have imperfectly learned, to say things they imperfectly understand, and to devote themselves to work for which they are unprepared by long apprenticeship. In aristocracies every man has one sole object which he unceasingly pursues, but among democratic nations the existence of man is more complex; the same mind will almost always embrace several objects at the same time, and these objects are frequently wholly foreign to each other: as it can not know them all well, the mind is readily satisfied with imperfect notions of each.

When the inhabitant of democracies is not urged by his wants, he is so at least by his desires; for of all the possessions which he sees around him, none are wholly beyond his reach. He therefore does everything in a hurry, he is always satisfied with "pretty well," and never pauses more than an instant to consider what he has been doing. His curiosity is at once insatiable and cheaply satisfied; for he cares more to know a great deal quickly than to know anything well: he has no time and but little taste to search things to the bottom.

Thus, then, democratic peoples are grave, because their social and political condition constantly leads them to engage in serious occupations; and they act inconsiderately, because they give but little time and attention to each of these occupations. The habit of inattention must be considered as the greatest bane of the democratic character.

All free nations are vainglorious, but national pride is not displayed by all in the same manner. The Americans in their intercourse with strangers appear impatient of the smallest censure and insatiable of praise. The most slender eulogium is acceptable to them; the most exalted seldom contents them; they unceasingly harass you to extort praise, and if you resist their entreaties they fall to praising themselves. It would seem as if, doubting their own merit, they wished to have it constantly exhibited before their eyes. Their vanity is not only greedy, but restless and jealous; it will grant nothing, while it demands everything, but is ready to beg and to quarrel at the same time. If I say to an American that the country he lives in is a fine one, " Ay," he replies, " there is not its fellow in the world." If I applaud the freedom which its inhabitants enjoy, he answers, " Freedom is a fine thing, but few nations are worthy to enjoy it." If I remark the purity of morals which distinguishes the United States, " I can imagine," says he, " that a stranger, who has been struck by the corruption of all other nations, is astonished at the difference." At length I leave him to the contemplation of himself; but he returns to the charge, and does not desist till he has got me to repeat all I had just been saying. It is impossible to conceive a more troublesome or more garrulous patriotism; it wearies even those who are disposed to respect it.[2]

Such is not the case with the English. An Englishman calmly enjoys the real or imaginary advantages which in his opinion his country possesses. If he grants nothing to other nations, neither does he solicit anything for his own. The censure of foreigners does not affect him, and their praise hardly flatters him; his position with regard to the rest of the world is one of disdainful and ignorant reserve: his pride requires no sustenance, it nourishes itself. It is remarkable that two nations, so recently sprung from the same stock, should be so opposite to one another in their manner of feeling and conversing.

In aristocratic countries the great possess immense privileges, upon which their pride rests, without seeking to rely upon the lesser advantages which accrue to them. As these privileges came to them by inheritance, they regard them in some sort as a portion of themselves, or at least as a natural right inherent in their own persons.

714   DEMOCRACY IN AMERICA

They therefore entertain a calm sense of their superiority; they do not dream of vaunting privileges which every one perceives and no one contests, and these things are not sufficiently new to them to be made topics of conversation. They stand unmoved in their solitary greatness, well assured that they are seen of all the world without any effort to show themselves off, and that no one will attempt to drive them from that position. When an aristocracy carries on the public affairs, its national pride naturally assumes this reserved, indifferent, and haughty form, which is imitated by all the other classes of the nation.

When, on the contrary, social conditions differ but little, the slightest privileges are of some importance; as every man sees around himself a million of people enjoying precisely similar or analogous advantages, his pride becomes craving and jealous, he clings to mere trifles, and doggedly defends them. In democracies, as the conditions of life are very fluctuating, men have almost always recently acquired the advantages which they possess; the consequence is that they feel extreme pleasure in exhibiting them, to show others and convince themselves that they really enjoy them. As at any instance these same advantages may be lost, their possessors are constantly on the alert, and make a point of showing that they still retain them. Men living in democracies love their country just as they love themselves, and they transfer the habits of their private vanity to their vanity as a nation. The restless and insatiable vanity of a democratic people originates so entirely in the equality and precariousness of social conditions, that the members of the haughtiest nobility display the very same passion in those lesser portions of their existence in which there is anything fluctuating or contested. An aristocratic class always differs greatly from the other classes of the nation, by the extent and perpetuity of its privileges; but it often happens that the only differences between the members who belong to it consist in small transient advantages, which may any day be lost or acquired.

The members of a powerful aristocracy, collected in a capital or a court, have been known to contest with virulence those frivolous privileges which depend on the caprice of fashion or the will of their master. These persons then displayed toward each other precisely the same puerile jealousies which animate the men of democracies, the same eagerness to snatch the smallest advantages which their equals contested, and the same desire to parade ostentatiously those of which they were in possession. If national pride ever entered into the minds of courtiers, I do not question that they would display it in the same manner as the members of a democratic community.

It would seem that nothing can be more adapted to stimulate and to feed curiosity than the aspect of the United States. Fortunes, opinions, and laws are there in ceaseless variation: it is as if immutable Nature herself were mutable, such are the changes worked upon her by the hand of man. Yet in the end the sight of this excited community becomes monotonous, and after having watched the moving pageant for a time the spectator is tired of it. Among aristocratic nations every man is pretty nearly stationary in his own sphere; but men are astonishingly unlike each other—their passions, their notions, their habits, and their tastes are essentially different: nothing changes, but everything differs. In democracies, on the contrary, all men are alike and do things pretty nearly alike. It is true that they are subject to great and frequent vicissitudes; but as the same events of good or adverse fortune are continually recurring, the name of the actors only is changed, the piece is always the same. The aspect of American society is animated, because men and things are always changing; but it is monotonous, because all these changes are alike.

Men living in democratic ages have many passions, but most of their passions either end in the love of riches or proceed from it. The cause of this is, not that their souls are narrower, but that the importance of money is really greater at such times. When all the members of a community are independent of or indifferent to each other, the co-operation of each of them can only be obtained by paying for it: this infinitely multiplies the purposes to which wealth may be applied, and increases its value. When the reverence that belonged to what is old has vanished, birth, condition, and profession no longer distinguish men, or scarcely distinguish them at all: hardly anything but money remains to create strongly marked differences between them, and to raise some of them above the common level. The distinction originating in wealth is increased by the disappearance and diminution of all other distinctions. Among aristocratic nations money only reaches to a few points on the vast circle of man's desires—in democracies it seems to lead to all. The love of wealth is therefore to be traced, either as a principal or an accessory motive, at the bottom of all that the Americans do: this gives to all their passions a sort of family likeness, and soon renders the survey of them exceedingly wearisome. This perpetual recurrence of the same passion is monotonous; the peculiar methods by which this passion seeks its own gratification are no less so.

In an orderly and constituted democracy like the United States, where men can not enrich themselves by war, by public office, or by political confiscation, the love of wealth mainly drives them into business and manufactures. Although these pursuits often bring about great commotions and disasters, they can not prosper without strictly regular habits and a long routine of petty uniform acts. The stronger the passion is, the more regular are these habits, and the more uniform are these acts. It may be said that it is the vehemence of their desires which makes the Americans so methodical; it perturbs their minds, but it disciplines their lives.

The remark I here apply to America may indeed be addressed to almost all our contemporaries. Variety is disappearing from the human race; the same ways of acting, thinking, and feeling are to be met with all over the world. This is not only because nations work more upon each other, and are more faithful in their mutual imitation; but as the men of each country relinquish more and more the peculiar opinions and feelings of a caste, a profession, or a family, they simultaneously arrive at something nearer to the constitution of man, which is everywhere the same. Thus they become more alike, even without having imitated each other. Like travellers scattered about some large wood, which is intersected by paths converging to one point, if all of them keep their eyes fixed upon that point and advance toward it, they insensibly draw nearer together—though they seek not, though they see not, though they know not each other; and they will be surprised at length to find themselves all collected on the same spot. All the nations which take, not any particular man, but man himself, as the object of their researches and their imitations, are tending in the end to a similar state of society, like these travellers converging to the central plot of the forest.

It would seem that men employ two very distinct methods in the public estimation of the actions of their fellow-men; at one time they judge them by those simple notions of right and wrong which are diffused all over the world; at another they refer their decision to a few very special notions which belong exclusively to some particular age and country. It often happens that these two rules differ; they sometimes conflict: but they are never either entirely identified or entirely annulled by one another. Honour,[1] at the periods of its greatest power, sways the will more than the belief of men; and even while they yield without hesitation and without a murmur to its dictates, they feel notwithstanding, by a dim but mighty instinct, the existence of a more general, more ancient, and more holy law, which they sometimes disobey although they cease not to acknowledge it. Some actions have been held to be at the same time virtuous and dishonourable—a refusal to fight a duel is a case in point.

I think these peculiarities may be otherwise explained than by the mere caprices of certain individuals and nations, as has hitherto been the customary mode of reasoning on the subject. Mankind is subject to general and lasting wants that have engendered moral laws, to the neglect of which men have ever and in all places attached the notion of censure and shame: to infringe them was to do ill—to do well was to conform to them. Within the bosom of this vast association of the human race, lesser associations have been formed which are called nations; and amid these nations further subdivisions have assumed the names of classes or castes. Each of these associations forms, as it were, a separate species of the human race; and though it has no essential difference from the mass of mankind, to a certain extent it stands apart and has certain wants peculiar to itself. To these special wants must be attributed the modifications which affect in various degrees and in different countries the mode of considering human actions, and the estimate which ought to be formed of them. It is the general and permanent interest of mankind that men should not kill each other: but it may happen to be the peculiar and temporary interest of a people or a class to justify, or even to honour, homicide.

Honour is simply that peculiar rule, founded upon a peculiar state of society, by the application of which a people or a class allot praise or blame. Nothing is more unproductive to the mind than an abstract idea; I therefore hasten to call in the aid of facts and examples to illustrate my meaning.

I select the most extraordinary kind of honour which was ever known in the world, and that which we are best acquainted with—viz., aristocratic honour springing out of feudal society. I shall explain it by means of the principle already laid down, and I shall explain the principle by means of the illustration. I am not here led to inquire when and how the aristocracy of the Middle Ages came into existence, why it was so deeply severed from the remainder of the nation, or what founded and consolidated its power. I take its existence as an established fact, and

I am endeavouring to account for the peculiar view which it took of the greater part of human actions. The first thing that strikes me is, that in the feudal world actions were not always praised or blamed with reference to their intrinsic worth, but that they were sometimes appreciated exclusively with reference to the person who was the actor or the object of them, which is repugnant to the general conscience of mankind. Thus some of the actions which were indifferent on the part of a man in humble life, dishonoured a noble; others changed their whole character according as the person aggrieved by them belonged or did not belong to the aristocracy. When these different notions first arose, the nobility formed a distinct body amid the people, which it commanded from the inaccessible heights where it was ensconced. To maintain this peculiar position, which constituted its strength, it not only required political privileges, but it required a standard of right and wrong for its own especial use. That some particular virtue or vice belonged to the nobility rather than to the humble classes—that certain actions were guiltless when they affected the villain, which were criminal when they touched the noble—these were often arbitrary matters; but that honour or shame should be attached to a man's actions according to his condition, was a result of the internal constitution of an aristocratic community. This has been actually the case in all the countries which have had an aristocracy; as long as a trace of the principle remains, these peculiarities will still exist; to debauch a woman of colour scarcely injures the reputation of an American—to marry her dishonours him.

In some cases feudal honour enjoined revenge, and stigmatized the forgiveness of insults; in others it imperiously commanded men to conquer their own passions, and imposed forgetfulness of self. It did not make humanity or kindness its law, but it extolled generosity; it set more store on liberality than on benevolence; it allowed men to enrich themselves by gambling or by war, but not by labour; it preferred great crimes to small earnings; cupidity was less distasteful to it than avarice; violence it often sanctioned, but cunning and treachery it invariably reprobated as contemptible. These fantastical notions did not proceed exclusively from the caprices of those who entertained them. A class which has succeeded in placing itself at the head of and above all others, and which makes perpetual exertions to maintain this lofty position, must especially honour those virtues which are conspicuous for their dignity and splendour, and which may be easily combined with pride and the love of power. Such men would not hesitate to invert the natural order of the conscience in order to give those virtues precedence before all others. It may even be conceived that some of the more bold and brilliant vices would readily be set above the quiet unpretending virtues. The very existence of such a class in society renders these things unavoidable.

The nobles of the Middle Ages placed military courage foremost among virtues, and in lieu of many of them. This was again a peculiar opinion which arose necessarily from the peculiarity of the state of society. Feudal aristocracy existed by war and for war; its power had been founded by arms, and by arms that power was maintained; it therefore required nothing more than military courage, and that quality was naturally exalted above all others; whatever denoted it, even at the expense of reason and humanity, was therefore approved and frequently enjoined by the manners of the time. Such was the main principle; the caprice of man was only to be traced in minuter details. That a man should regard a tap on the cheek as an unbearable insult, and should be obliged to kill in single combat the person who struck him thus lightly, is an arbitrary rule; but that a noble could not tranquilly receive an insult, and was dishonoured if he allowed himself to take a blow without fighting, were direct consequences of the fundamental principles and the wants of a military aristocracy.

Thus it was true to a certain extent to assert that the laws of honour were capricious; but these caprices of honour were always confined within certain necessary limits. The peculiar rule, which was called honour by our fore-fathers, is so far from being an arbitrary law in my eyes, that I would readily engage to ascribe its most incoherent and fantastical injunctions to a small number of fixed and invariable wants inherent in feudal society.

If I were to trace the notion of feudal honour into the domain of politics, I should not find it more difficult to explain its dictates. The state of society and the political institutions of the Middle Ages were such that the supreme power of the nation never governed the community directly. That power did not exist in the eyes of the people: every man looked up to a certain individual whom he was bound to obey; by that intermediate personage he was connected with all the others. Thus in feudal society the whole system of the commonwealth rested upon the sentiment of fidelity to the person of the lord: to destroy that sentiment was to open the sluices of anarchy. Fidelity to a political superior was, moreover, a sentiment of which all the members of the aristocracy had constant opportunities of estimating the importance; for every one of them was a vassal as well as a lord, and had to command as well as to obey. To remain faithful to the lord, to sacrifice one's self for him if called upon, to share his good or evil fortunes, to stand by him in his undertakings whatever they might be—such were the first injunctions of feudal honour in relation to the political institutions of those times. The treachery of a vassal was branded with extraordinary severity by public opinion, and a name of peculiar infamy was invented for the offence which was called felony.

On the contrary, few traces are to be found in the Middle Ages of the passion which constituted the life of the nations of antiquity—I mean patriotism—the word itself is not of very ancient date in the language.[3] Feudal institutions concealed the country at large from men's sight, and rendered the love of it less necessary. The nation was forgotten in the passions which attached men to persons. Hence it was no part of the strict law of feudal honour to remain faithful to one's country. Not, indeed, that the love of their country did not exist in the hearts of our forefathers; but it constituted a dim and feeble instinct, which has grown more clear and strong in proportion as aristocratic classes have been abolished, and the supreme power of the nation centralized. This may be clearly seen from the contrary judgments which European nations have passed upon the various events of their histories, according to the generations by which such judgments have been formed. The circumstance which most dishonoured the Constable de Bourbon in the eyes of his contemporaries was that he bore arms against his king: that which most dishonours him in our eyes, is that he made war against his country; we brand him as deeply as our forefathers did, but for different reasons.

I have chosen the honour of feudal times by way of illustration of my meaning, because its characteristics are more distinctly marked and more familiar to us than those of any other period; but I might have taken an example elsewhere, and I should have reached the same conclusion by a different road. Although we are less perfectly acquainted with the Romans than with our own ancestors, yet we know that certain peculiar notions of glory and disgrace obtained among them, which were not solely derived from the general principles of right and wrong. Many human actions were judged differently, according as they affected a Roman citizen or a stranger, a freeman or a slave; certain vices were blazoned abroad, certain virtues were extolled above all others. " In that age," says Plutarch in the life of Coriolanus, " martial prowess was more honoured and prized in Rome than all the other virtues, insomuch that it was called virtus, the name of virtue itself, by applying the name of the kind to this particular species; so that virtue in Latin was as much as to say valour." Can any one fail to recognise the peculiar want of that singular community which was formed for the conquest of the world?

Any nation would furnish us with similar ground of

observation; for, as I have already remarked, whenever men collect together as a distinct community, the notion of honour instantly grows up among them; that is to say, a system of opinions peculiar to themselves as to what is blamable or commendable; and these peculiar rules always originate in the special habits and special interests of the community. This is applicable to a certain extent to democratic communities as well as to others, as we shall now proceed to prove by the example of the Americans.[4] Some loose notions of the old aristocratic honour of Europe are still to be found scattered among the opinions of the Americans; but these traditional opinions are few in number, they have but little root in the country, and but little power. They are like a religion which has still some temples left standing, though men have ceased to believe in it. But amid these half-obliterated notions of exotic honour some new opinions have sprung up, which constitute what may be termed in our days American honour. I have shown how the Americans are constantly driven to engage in commerce and industry. Their origin, their social condition, their political institutions, and even the spot they inhabit, urge them irresistibly in this direction. Their present condition is, then, that of an almost exclusively manufacturing and commercial association, placed in the midst of a new and boundless country, which their principal object is to explore for purposes of profit. This is the characteristic which most peculiarly distinguishes the American people from all others at the present time. All those quiet virtues which tend to give a regular movement to the community, and to encourage business, will therefore be held in peculiar honour by that people, and to neglect those virtues will be to incur public contempt. All the more turbulent virtues, which often dazzle, but more frequently disturb society, will on the contrary occupy a subordinate rank in the estimation of this same people: they may be neglected without forfeiting the esteem of the community—to acquire them would perhaps be to run a risk of losing it.

48

The Americans make a no less arbitrary classification of men's vices. There are certain propensities which appear censurable to the general reason and the universal conscience of mankind, but which happen to agree with the peculiar and temporary wants of the American community: these propensities are lightly reproved, sometimes even encouraged; for instance, the love of wealth and the secondary propensities connected with it may be more particularly cited. To clear, to till, and to transform the vast uninhabited continent which is his domain, the American requires the daily support of an energetic passion; that passion can only be the love of wealth; the passion for wealth is therefore not reprobated in America, and, provided it does not go beyond the bounds assigned to it for public security, it is held in honour. The American lauds as a noble and praiseworthy ambition what our own forefathers in the Middle Ages stigmatized as servile cupidity, just as he treats as a blind and barbarous frenzy that ardour of conquest and martial temper which bore them to battle. In the United States fortunes are lost and regained without difficulty; the country is boundless, and its resources inexhaustible. The people have all the wants and cravings of a growing creature; and whatever be their efforts, they are always surrounded by more than they can appropriate. It is not the ruin of a few individuals which may be soon repaired, but the inactivity and sloth of the community at large which would be fatal to such a people. Boldness of enterprise is the foremost cause of its rapid progress, its strength, and its greatness. Commercial business is there like a vast lottery, by which a small number of men continually lose, but the State is always a gainer; such a people ought, therefore, to encourage and do honour to boldness in commercial speculations. But any bold speculation risks the fortune of the speculator and of all those who put their trust in him. The Americans, who make a virtue of commercial temerity, have no right in any case to brand with disgrace those who practise it. Hence arises the strange indulgence which is shown to bankrupts in the United States; their honour does not suffer by such an accident. In this respect the Americans differ, not only from the nations of Europe, but from all the commercial nations of our time, and accordingly they resemble none of them in their position or their wants.

In America all those vices which tend to impair the purity of morals, and to destroy the conjugal tie, are treated with a degree of severity which is unknown in the rest of the world. At first sight this seems strangely at variance with the tolerance shown there on other subjects, and one is surprised to meet with a morality so relaxed and so austere among the self-same people. But these things are less incoherent than they seem to be. Public opinion in the United States very gently represses that love of wealth which promotes the commercial greatness and the prosperity of the nation, and it especially condemns that laxity of morals which diverts the human mind from the pursuit of well-being, and disturbs the internal order of domestic life which is so necessary to success in business. To earn the esteem of their countrymen, the Americans are therefore constrained to adapt themselves to orderly habits—and it may be said in this sense that they make it a matter of honour to live chastely.

On one point American honour accords with the notions of honour acknowledged in Europe; it places courage as the highest virtue, and treats it as the greatest of the moral necessities of man; but the notion of courage itself assumes a different aspect. In the United States martial valour is but little prized; the courage which is best known and most esteemed is that which emboldens men to brave the dangers of the ocean, in order to arrive earlier in port—to support the privations of the wilderness without complaint, and solitude more cruel than privations—the courage which renders them almost insensible to the loss of a fortune laboriously acquired, and instantly prompts to fresh exertions to make another. Courage of this kind is peculiarly necessary to the maintenance and prosperity of the American communities, and it is held by them in peculiar honour and estimation; to betray a want of it is to incur certain disgrace.

I have yet another characteristic point which may serve to place the idea of this chapter in stronger relief. In a democratic society like that of the United States, where fortunes are scanty and insecure, everybody works, and work opens a way to everything: this has changed the point of honour quite round, and has turned it against idleness. I have sometimes met in America with young men of wealth, personally disinclined to all laborious exertion, but who had been compelled to embrace a profession. Their disposition and their fortune allowed them to remain without employment; public opinion forbade it, too imperiously to be disobeyed. In the European countries, on the contrary, where aristocracy is still struggling with the flood which overwhelms it, I have often seen men, constantly spurred on by their wants and desires, remain in idleness, in order not to lose the esteem of their equals; and I have known them to submit to ennui and privation rather than to work. No one can fail to perceive that these opposite obligations are two different rules of conduct, both nevertheless originating in the notion of honour.

What our forefathers designated as honour absolutely was in reality only one of its forms; they gave a generic name to what was only a species. Honour, therefore, is to be found in democratic as well as in aristocratic ages, but it will not be difficult to show that it assumes a different aspect in the former. Not only are its injunctions different, but we shall shortly see that they are less numerous, less precise, and that its dictates are less rigorously obeyed. The position of a caste is always much more peculiar than that of a people. Nothing is so much out of the way of the world as a small community invariably composed of the same families (as was, for instance, the aristocracy of the Middle Ages), whose object is to concentrate and to retain, exclusively and hereditarily, education, wealth, and power among its own members. But the more out of the way the position of a community happens to be, the more

numerous are its special wants, and the more extensive
are its notions of honour corresponding to those wants.
The rules of honour will therefore always be less numerous among a people not divided into castes than among
any other. If ever any nations are constituted in which
it may even be difficult to find any peculiar classes of society, the notion of honour will be confined to a small number of precepts, which will be more and more in accordance
with the moral laws adopted by the mass of mankind.
Thus the laws of honour will be less peculiar and less multifarious among a democratic people than in an aristocracy.
They will also be more obscure; and this is a necessary
consequence of what goes before; for as the distinguishing marks of honour are less numerous and less peculiar,
it must often be difficult to distinguish them. To this
other reasons may be added. Among the aristocratic nations of the Middle Ages, generation succeeded generation
in vain; each family was like a never-dying, ever-station-
ary man, and the state of opinions was hardly more changeable than that of conditions. Every one then had always
the same objects before his eyes, which he contemplated
from the same point; his eyes gradually detected the smallest details, and his discernment could not fail to become
in the end clear and accurate. Thus not only had the men
of feudal times very extraordinary opinions in matters of
honour, but each of those opinions was present to their
minds under a clear and precise form.

This can never be the case in America, where all men
are in constant motion; and where society, transformed
daily by its own operations, changes its opinions together
with its wants. In such a country men have glimpses of
the rules of honour, but they have seldom time to fix attention upon them.

But even if society were motionless, it would still be
difficult to determine the meaning which ought to be attached to the word honour. In the Middle Ages, as each
class had its own honour, the same opinions was never
received at the same time by a large number of men; and

this rendered it possible to give it a determined and accurate form, which was the more easy, as all those by whom it was received, having a perfectly identical and most peculiar position, were naturally disposed to agree upon the points of a law which was made for themselves alone. Thus the code of honour became a complete and detailed system, in which everything was anticipated and provided for beforehand, and a fixed and always palpable standard was applied to human actions. Among a democratic nation, like the Americans, in which ranks are identified, and the whole of society forms one single mass, composed of elements which are all analogous though not entirely similar, it is impossible ever to agree beforehand on what shall or shall not be allowed by the laws of honour. Among that people, indeed, some national wants do exist which give rise to opinions common to the whole nation on points of honour; but these opinions never occur at the same time, in the same manner, or with the same intensity to the minds of the whole community; the law of honour exists, but it has no organs to promulgate it.

The confusion is far greater still in a democratic country like France, where the different classes of which the former fabric of society was composed, being brought together but not yet mingled, import day by day into each other's circles various and sometimes conflicting notions of honour—where every man, at his own will and pleasure, forsakes one portion of his forefathers' creed, and retains another; so that, amid so many arbitrary measures, no common rule can ever be established, and it is almost impossible to predict which actions will be held in honour and which will be thought disgraceful. Such times are wretched, but they are of short duration.

As honour, among democratic nations, is imperfectly defined, its influence is of course less powerful; for it is difficult to apply with certainty and firmness a law which is not distinctly known. Public opinion, the natural and supreme interpreter of the laws of honour, not clearly discerning to which side censure or approval ought to lean, can only pronounce a hesitating judgment. Sometimes the opinion of the public may contradict itself; more frequently it does not act, and lets things pass.

The weakness of the sense of honour in democracies also arises from several other causes. In aristocratic countries, the same notions of honour are always entertained by only a few persons, always limited in number, often separated from the rest of their fellow-citizens. Honour is easily mingled and identified in their minds with the idea of all that distinguishes their own position; it appears to them as the chief characteristic of their own rank; they apply its different rules with all the warmth of personal interest, and they feel (if I may use the expression) a passion for complying with its dictates. This truth is extremely obvious in the old black-letter law books on the subject of trial by battel. The nobles, in their disputes, were bound to use the lance and sword; whereas the villains used only sticks among themselves, " inasmuch as," to use the words of the old books, " villains have no honour." This did not mean, as it may be imagined at the present day, that these people were contemptible; but simply that their actions were not to be judged by the same rules which were applied to the actions of the aristocracy.

It is surprising, at first sight, that when the sense of honour is most predominant, its injunctions are usually most strange; so that the further it is removed from common reason the better it is obeyed; whence it has sometimes been inferred that the laws of honour were strengthened by their own extravagance. The two things, indeed, originate from the same source, but the one is not derived from the other. Honour becomes fantastical in proportion to the peculiarity of the wants which it denotes, and the paucity of the men by whom those wants are felt; and it is because it denotes wants of this kind that its influence is great. Thus the notion of honour is not the stronger for being fantastical, but it is fantastical and strong from the self-same cause.

Further, among aristocratic nations each rank is different, but all ranks are fixed; every man occupies a place in his own sphere which he can not relinquish, and he lives there amid other men who are bound by the same ties. Among these nations no man can either hope or fear to escape being seen; no man is placed so low but that he has a stage of his own, and none can avoid censure or applause by his obscurity. In democratic states, on the contrary, where all the members of the community are mingled in the same crowd and in constant agitation, public opinion has no hold on men; they disappear at every instant, and elude its power. Consequently the dictates of honour will be there less imperious and less stringent; for honour acts solely for the public eye—differing in this respect from mere virtue, which lives upon itself contented with its own approval.

If the reader has distinctly apprehended all that goes before, he will understand that there is a close and necessary relation between the inequality of social conditions and what has here been styled honour—a relation which, if I am not mistaken, had not before been clearly pointed out. I shall therefore make one more attempt to illustrate it satisfactorily. Suppose a nation stands apart from the rest of mankind, independently of certain general wants inherent in the human race, it will also have wants and interests peculiar to itself: certain opinions of censure or approbation forthwith arise in the community, which are peculiar to itself, and which are styled honour by the members of that community. Now suppose that in this same nation a caste arises, which, in its turn, stands apart from all the other classes, and contracts certain peculiar wants, which give rise in their turn to special opinions. The honour of this caste, composed of a medley of the peculiar notions of the nation, and the still more peculiar notions of the caste, will be as remote as it is possible to conceive from the simple and general opinions of men.

Having reached this extreme point of the argument, I now return. When ranks are commingled and privileges abolished, the men of whom a nation is composed being once more equal and alike, their interests and wants become identical, and all the peculiar notions which each caste styled honour successively disappear: the notion of honour no longer proceeds from any other source than the wants peculiar to the nation at large, and it denotes the individual character of that nation to the world. Lastly, if it be allowable to suppose that all the races of mankind should be commingled, and that all the peoples of earth should ultimately come to have the same interests, the same wants, undistinguished from each other by any characteristic peculiarities, no conventional value whatever would then be attached to men's actions; they would all be regarded by all in the same light; the general necessities of mankind, revealed by conscience to every man, would become the common standard. The simple and general notions of right and wrong only would then be recognised in the world, to which, by a natural and necessary tie, the idea of censure or approbation would be attached. Thus, to comprise all my meaning in a single proposition, the dissimilarities and inequalities of men gave rise to the notion of honour; that notion is weakened in proportion as these differences are obliterated, and with them it would disappear.

The first thing which strikes a traveller in the United States is the innumerable multitude of those who seek to throw off their original condition; and the second is the rarity of lofty ambition to be observed in the midst of the universally ambitious stir of society. No Americans are devoid of a yearning desire to rise; but hardly any appear to entertain hopes of great magnitude, or to drive at very lofty aims. All are constantly seeking to acquire property, power, and reputation—few contemplate these things upon a great scale; and this is the more surprising, as nothing is to be discerned in the manners or laws of America to limit desire, or to prevent it from spreading its impulses in every direction. It seems difficult to attribute this singular state of things to the equality of social conditions; for at the instant when that same equality was established in France, the flight of ambition became unbounded. Nevertheless, I think that the principal cause which may be assigned to this fact is to be found in the social condition and democratic manners of the Americans.

All revolutions enlarge the ambition of men: this proposition is more peculiarly true of those revolutions which overthrow an aristocracy. When the former barriers which kept back the multitude from fame and power are suddenly thrown down, a violent and universal rise takes place toward that eminence so long coveted and at length to be enjoyed. In this first burst of triumph nothing seems impossible to any one: not only are desires boundless, but the power of satisfying them seems almost boundless too. Amid the general and sudden renewal of laws and customs, in this vast confusion of all men and all ordinances, the various members of the community rise and sink again with excessive rapidity; and power passes so quickly from hand to hand that none need despair of catching it in turn. It must be recollected, moreover, that the people who destroy an aristocracy have lived under its laws; they have witnessed its splendour, and they have unconsciously imbibed the feelings and notions which it entertained. Thus at the moment when an aristocracy is dissolved, its spirit still pervades the mass of the community, and its tendencies are retained long after it has been defeated. Ambition is therefore always extremely great as long as a democratic revolution lasts, and it will remain so for some time after the revolution is consummated. The reminiscence of the extraordinary events which men have witnessed is not obliterated from their memory in a day. The passions which a revolution has roused do not disappear at its close. A sense of instability remains in the midst of re-established order: a notion of easy success survives the strange vicissitudes which gave it birth; desires still remain extremely enlarged, when the means of satisfying them are diminished day by day. The taste for large fortunes subsists, though large fortunes are rare: and on every side we trace the ravages of inordinate and hapless ambition kindled in hearts which they consume in secret and in vain.

At length, however, the last vestiges of the struggle are effaced; the remains of aristocracy completely disappear; the great events by which its fall was attended are forgotten; peace succeeds to war, and the sway of order is restored in the new realm; desires are again adapted to the means by which they may be fulfilled; the wants, the opinions, and the feelings of men cohere once more; the level of the community is permanently determined, and democratic society established. A democratic nation, arrived at this permanent and regular state of things, will present a very different spectacle from that which we have just described; and we may readily conclude that, if ambition becomes great while the conditions of society are growing equal, it loses that quality when they have grown so. As wealth is subdivided and knowledge diffused, no one is entirely destitute of education or of property; the privileges and disqualifications of caste being abolished, and men having shattered the bonds which held them fixed, the notion of advancement suggests itself to every mind, the desire to rise swells in every heart, and all men want to mount above their station: ambition is the universal feeling.

But if the equality of conditions gives some resources to all the members of the community, it also prevents any of them from having resources of great extent, which necessarily circumscribes their desires within somewhat narrow limits. Thus among democratic nations ambition is ardent and continual, but its aim is not habitually lofty; and life is generally spent in eagerly coveting small objects which are within reach. What chiefly diverts the men of democracies from lofty ambition is not the scantiness of their fortunes, but the vehemence of the exertions they daily make to improve them. They strain their faculties to the utmost to achieve paltry results, and this can not fail speedily to limit their discernment and to circumscribe their powers. They might be much poorer and still be greater.

The small number of opulent citizens who are to be found amid a democracy do not constitute an exception to this rule. A man who raises himself by degrees to wealth and power, contracts, in the course of this protracted labour, habits of prudence and restraint which he can not afterward shake off. A man can not enlarge his mind as he would his house. The same observation is applicable to the sons of such a man; they are born, it is true, in a lofty position, but their parents were humble; they have grown up amid feelings and notions which they can not afterward easily get rid of; and it may be presumed that they will inherit the propensities of their father as well as his wealth. It may happen, on the contrary, that the poorest scion of a powerful aristocracy may display vast ambition, because the traditional opinions of his race and the general spirit of his order still buoy him up for some time above his fortune.

Another thing which prevents the men of democratic periods from easily indulging in the pursuit of lofty objects is the lapse of time which they foresee must take place before they can be ready to approach them. "It is a great advantage," says Pascal, "to be a man of quality, since it brings one man as forward at eighteen or twenty as another man would be at fifty, which is a clear gain of thirty years." Those thirty years are commonly wanting to the ambitious characters of democracies. The principle of equality, which allows every man to arrive at everything, prevents all men from rapid advancement.

In a democratic society, as well as elsewhere, there are only a certain number of great fortunes to be made; and as the paths which lead to them are indiscriminately open to all, the progress of all must necessarily be slackened. As the candidates appear to be nearly alike, and as it is difficult to make a selection without infringing the principle of equality, which is the supreme law of democratic societies, the first idea which suggests itself is to make them all advance at the same rate and submit to the same probation. Thus in proportion as men become more alike, and the principle of equality is more peaceably and deeply infused into the institutions and manners of the country, the rules of advancement become more inflexible, advancement itself slower, the difficulty of arriving quickly at a certain height far greater. From hatred of privilege and from the embarrassment of choosing, all men are at last constrained, whatever may be their standard, to pass the same ordeal; all are indiscriminately subjected to a multitude of petty preliminary exercises, in which their youth is wasted and their imagination quenched, so that they despair of ever fully attaining what is held out to them; and when at length they are in a condition to perform any extraordinary acts, the taste for such things has forsaken them.

In China, where the equality of conditions is exceedingly great and very ancient, no man passes from one public office to another without undergoing a probationary trial. This probation occurs afresh at every stage of his career; and the notion is now so rooted in the manners of the people that I remember to have read a Chinese novel, in which the hero, after numberless crosses, succeeds at length in touching the heart of his mistress by taking honours. A lofty ambition breathes with difficulty in such an atmosphere.

The remark I apply to politics extends to everything; equality everywhere produces the same effects; where the laws of a country do not regulate and retard the advancement of men by positive enactment, competition attains the same end. In a well-established democratic community great and rapid elevation is therefore rare; it forms an exception to the common rule; and it is the singularity of such occurrences that makes men forget how rarely they happen. Men living in democracies ultimately discover these things; they find out at last that the laws of their country open a boundless field of action before them, but that no one can hope to hasten across it. Between them and the final object of their desires, they perceive a multitude of small intermediate impediments, which must be slowly surmounted: this prospect wearies and discourages their ambition at once. They therefore give up hopes so doubtful and remote, to search nearer to themselves for less lofty and more easy enjoyments. Their horizon is not bounded by the laws but narrowed by themselves.

I have remarked that lofty ambitions are more rare in the ages of democracy than in times of aristocracy: I may add that when, in spite of these natural obstacles, they do spring into existence, their character is different. In aristocracies the career of ambition is often wide, but its boundaries are determined. In democracies ambition commonly ranges in a narrower field, but if once it gets beyond that, hardly any limits can be assigned to it. As men are individually weak—as they live asunder, and in constant motion—as precedents are of little authority and laws but of short duration, resistance to novelty is languid, and the fabric of society never appears perfectly erect or firmly consolidated. So that, when once an ambitious man has the power in his grasp, there is nothing he may not dare; and when it is gone from him, he meditates the overthrow of the State to regain it. This gives to great political ambition a character of revolutionary violence, which it seldom exhibits to an equal degree in aristocratic communities. The common aspect of democratic nations will present a great number of small and very rational objects of ambition, from among which a few ill-controlled desires of a larger growth will at intervals break out: but no such a thing as ambition conceived and contrived on a vast scale is to be met with there.

I have shown elsewhere by what secret influence the principle of equality makes the passion for physical gratifications and the exclusive love of the present predominate in the human heart: these different propensities mingle with the sentiment of ambition, and tinge it, as it were, with their hues. I believe that ambitious men in democracies are less engrossed than any others with the interests and the judgment of posterity; the present moment alone engages and absorbs them. They are more apt to complete a number of undertakings with rapidity than to raise lasting monuments of their achievements; and they care much more for success than for fame. What they most ask of men is obedience—what they most covet is empire. Their manners have in almost all cases remained below the height of their station; the consequence is that they frequently carry very low tastes into their extraordinary fortunes, and that they seem to have acquired the supreme power only to minister to their coarse or paltry pleasures.

I think that in our time it is very necessary to cleanse, to regulate, and to adapt the feeling of ambition, but that it would be extremely dangerous to seek to impoverish and to repress it over-much. We should attempt to lay down certain extreme limits, which it should never be allowed to outstep; but its range within those established limits should not be too much checked. I confess that I apprehend much less for democratic society from the boldness than from the mediocrity of desires. What appears to me most to be dreaded is that, in the midst of the small incessant occupations of private life, ambition should lose its vigour and its greatness—that the passions of man should abate, but at the same time be lowered, so that the march of society should every day become more tranquil and less aspiring. I think then that the leaders of modern society would be wrong to seek to lull the community by a state of too uniform and too peaceful happiness; and that it is well to expose it from time to time to matters of difficulty and danger, in order to raise ambition and to give it a field of action. Moralists are constantly complaining that the ruling vice of the present time is pride. This is true in one sense, for indeed no one thinks that he is not better than his neighbour, or consents to obey his superior; but it is extremely false in another; for the same man who can not endure subordination or equality has so contemptible an opinion of himself that he thinks he is only born to indulge in vulgar pleasures. He willingly takes up with low desires, without daring to embark in lofty enterprises, of which he scarcely dreams. Thus, far from thinking that humility ought to be preached to our contemporaries, I would have endeavours made to give them a more enlarged idea of themselves and of their kind. Humility is unwholesome to them; what they most want is, in my opinion, pride. I would willingly exchange several of our small virtues for this one vice.

In the United States as soon as a man has acquired some education and pecuniary resources, he either endeavours to get rich by commerce or industry, or he buys land in the bush and turns pioneer. All that he asks of the State is not to be disturbed in his toil, and to be secure of his earnings. Among the greater part of European nations, when a man begins to feel his strength and to extend his desires, the first thing that occurs to him is to get some public employment. These opposite effects, originating in the same cause, deserve our passing notice.

When public employments are few in number, ill-paid and precarious, while the different lines of business are numerous and lucrative, it is to business, and not to official duties, that the new and eager desires engendered by the principle of equality turn from every side. But if, while the ranks of society are becoming more equal, the education of the people remains incomplete, or their spirit the reverse of bold—if commerce and industry, checked in their growth, afford only slow and arduous means of making a fortune—the various members of the community, despairing of ameliorating their own condition, rush to the head of the State and demand its assistance. To relieve their own necessities at the cost of the public treasury appears to them to be the easiest and most open, if not the only, way they have to rise above a condition which no longer contents them; place-hunting becomes the most generally followed of all trades. This must especially be the case in those great centralized monarchies in which the number of paid offices is immense, and the tenure of them tolerably secure, so that no one despairs of obtaining a place, and of enjoying it as undisturbedly as an hereditary fortune.

I shall not remark that the universal and inordinate desire for place is a great social evil; that it destroys the spirit of independence in the citizen, and diffuses a venal and servile humour throughout the frame of society; that it stifles the manlier virtues: nor shall I be at the pains to demonstrate that this kind of traffic only creates an unproductive activity, which agitates the country without adding to its resources: all these things are obvious. But I would observe that a government which encourages this tendency risks its own tranquility, and places its very existence in great jeopardy. I am aware that at a time like our own, when the love and respect which formerly clung to authority are seen gradually to decline, it may appear necessary to those in power to lay a closer hold on every man by his own interest, and it may seem convenient to use his own passions to keep him in order and in silence; but this can not be so long, and what may appear to be a source of strength for a certain time will assuredly become in the end a great cause of embarrassment and weakness.

Among democratic nations, as well as elsewhere, the number of official appointments has in the end some limits; but among those nations, the number of aspirants is unlimited; it perpetually increases, with a gradual and irresistible rise in proportion as social conditions become more equal, and is only checked by the limits of the population. Thus, when public employments afford the only outlet for ambition, the government necessarily meets with a permanent opposition at last; for it is tasked to satisfy with limited means unlimited desires. It is very certain that of all people in the world the most difficult to restrain and to manage are a people of solicitants. Whatever endeavours are made by rulers, such a people can never be contented; and it is always to be apprehended that they will ultimately overturn the constitution of the country, and change the aspect of the State, for the sole purpose of making a clearance of places. The sovereigns of the present age, who strive to fix upon themselves alone all those novel desires which are aroused by equality, and to satisfy them, will repent in the end, if I am not mistaken, that they ever embarked in this policy: they will one day discover that they have hazarded their own power, by making it so necessary; and that the more safe and honest course would have been to teach their subjects the art of providing for themselves.

NOTES

[1] The word Honour is not always used in the same sense either in French or English. 1. It first signifies the dignity, glory, or reverence which a man receives from his kind; and in this sense a man is said to acquire honour. 2. Honour signifies the aggregate of those rules by the assistance of which this dignity, glory, or reverence is obtained. Thus we say that a man has always strictly obeyed the laws of honour; or a man has violated his honour.—The word is here used in the latter sense.

[2] See Appendix, U.

[3] Even the word patrie was not used by the French writers until the sixteenth century.

[4] I speak here of the Americans inhabiting those States where slavery does not exist; they alone can be said to present a complete picture of democratic society.

CHAPTER XXXIV

WARFARE AND REVOLUTIONS AMONG DEMOCRATIC PEOPLES

Why great revolutions will become more rare—Why democratic nations are naturally desirous of peace, and democratic armies of war—The most warlike and most revolutionary class in democratic armies—Causes that render democratic armies weaker than other armies at the outset of a campaign, and more formidable in protracted warfare—Of discipline in democratic armies—Considerations on war in democratic communities.

A PEOPLE which has existed for centuries under a system of castes and classes can only arrive at a democratic state of society by passing through a long series of more or less critical transformations, accomplished by violent efforts, and after numerous vicissitudes; in the course of which, property, opinions, and power are rapidly transferred from one hand to another. Even after this great revolution is consummated, the revolutionary habits engendered by it may long be traced, and it will be followed by deep commotion. As all this takes place at the very time at which social conditions are becoming more equal, it is inferred that some concealed relation and secret tie exists between the principle of equality itself and revolution, insomuch that the one can not exist without giving rise to the other.

On this point reasoning may seem to lead to the same result as experience. Among a people whose ranks are nearly equal, no ostensible bond connects men together, or keeps them settled in their station. None of them have either a permanent right or power to command—none are forced by their condition to obey; but every man, finding himself possessed of some education and some resources, may choose his own path and proceed apart from all his fellow-men. The same causes which make the members of the community independent of each other, continually impel them to new and restless desires, and constantly spur them onward. It therefore seems natural that, in a democratic community, men, things, and opinions should be forever changing their form and place, and that democratic ages should be times of rapid and incessant transformation.

But is this really the case? does the equality of social conditions habitually and permanently lead men to revolution? does that state of society contain some perturbing principle which prevents the community from ever subsiding into calm, and disposes the citizens to alter incessantly their laws, their principles, and their manners? I do not believe it; and as the subject is important, I beg for the reader's close attention. Almost all the revolutions which have changed the aspect of nations have been made to consolidate or to destroy social inequality. Remove the secondary causes which have produced the great convulsions of the world, and you will almost always find the principle of inequality at the bottom. Either the poor have attempted to plunder the rich, or the rich to enslave the poor. If, then, a state of society can ever be founded in which every man shall have something to keep, and little to take from others, much will have been done for the peace of the world. I am aware that among a great democratic people there will always be some members of the community in great poverty, and others in great opulence; but the poor, instead of forming the immense majority of the nation, as is always the case in aristocratic communities, are comparatively few in number, and the laws do not bind them together by the ties of irremediable and hereditary penury. The wealthy, on their side, are scarce and powerless; they have no privileges which attract public observation; even their wealth, as it is no longer incorporated and bound up with the soil, is impalpable, and as it were invisible. As there is no longer a race of poor men, so there is no longer a race of rich men; the latter spring up daily from the multitude, and relapse into it again. Hence they do not form a distinct class, which may be easily marked out and plundered; and, moreover, as they are connected with the mass of their fellow-citizens by a thousand secret ties, the people can not assail them without inflicting an injury upon itself. Between these two extremes of democratic communities stand an innumerable multitude of men almost alike, who, without being exactly either rich or poor, are possessed of sufficient property to desire the maintenance of order, yet not enough to excite envy. Such men are the natural enemies of violent commotions: their stillness keeps all beneath them and above them still, and secures the balance of the fabric of society. Not, indeed, that even these men are contented with what they have got, or that they feel a natural abhorrence for a revolution in which they might share the spoil without sharing the calamity; on the contrary, they desire, with unexampled ardour, to get rich, but the difficulty is to know from whom riches can be taken. The same state of society which constantly prompts desires, restrains these desires within necessary limits: it gives men more liberty of changing and less interest in change.

Not only are the men of democracies not naturally desirous of revolutions, but they are afraid of them. All revolutions more or less threaten the tenure of property: but most of those who live in democratic countries are possessed of property—not only are they possessed of property, but they live in the condition of men who set the greatest store upon their property. If we attentively consider each of the classes of which society is composed, it is easy to see that the passions engendered by property are keenest and most tenacious among the middle classes. The poor often care but little for what they possess, because they suffer much more from the want of what they have not than they enjoy the little they have. The rich have many other passions besides that of riches to satisfy; and, besides, the long and arduous enjoyment of a great fortune sometimes makes them in the end insensible to its charms. But the men who have a competency, alike removed from opulence and from penury, attach an enormous value to their possessions. As they are still almost within the reach of poverty, they see its privations near at hand, and dread them; between poverty and themselves there is nothing but a scanty fortune, upon which they immediately fix their apprehensions and their hopes. Every day increases the interest they take in it, by the constant cares which it occasions; and they are the more attached to it by their continual exertions to increase the amount. The notion of surrendering the smallest part of it is insupportable to them, and they consider its total loss as the worst of misfortunes. Now these eager and apprehensive men of small property constitute the class which is constantly increased by the equality of conditions. Hence, in democratic communities, the majority of the people do not clearly see what they have to gain by a revolution, but they continually and in a thousand ways feel that they might lose by one.

I have shown in another part of this work that the equality of conditions naturally urges men to embark in commercial and industrial pursuits, and that it tends to increase and to distribute real property: I have also pointed out the means by which it inspires every man with an eager and constant desire to increase his welfare. Nothing is more opposed to revolutionary passions than these things. It may happen that the final result of a revolution is favourable to commerce and manufactures; but its first consequence will almost always be the ruin of manufactures and mercantile men, because it must always change at once the general principles of consumption, and temporarily upset the existing proportion between supply and demand. I know of nothing more opposite to revolutionary manners than commercial manners. Commerce is naturally adverse to all the violent passions; it loves to temporize, takes delight in compromise, and studiously avoids irritation. It is patient, insinuating, flexible, and never has recourse to extreme measures until obliged by the most absolute necessity. Commerce renders men independent of each other, gives them a lofty notion of their personal importance, leads them to seek to conduct their own affairs, and teaches how to conduct them well; it therefore prepares men for freedom, but preserves them from revolutions. In a revolution the owners of personal property have more to fear than all others; for on the one hand their property is often easy to seize, and on the other it may totally disappear at any moment—a subject of alarm to which the owners of real property are less exposed, since, although they may lose the income of their estates, they may hope to preserve the land itself through the greatest vicissitudes. Hence the former are much more alarmed at the symptoms of revolutionary commotion than the latter. Thus nations are less disposed to make revolutions in proportion as personal property is augmented and distributed among them, and as the number of those possessing it increases. Moreover, whatever profession men may embrace, and whatever species of property they may possess, one characteristic is common to them all. No one is fully contented with his present fortune—all are perpetually striving in a thousand ways to improve it. Consider any one of them at any period of his life, and he will be found engaged with some new project for the purpose of increasing what he has; talk not to him of the interests and the rights of mankind, this small domestic concern absorbs for the time all his thoughts, and inclines him to defer political excitement to some other season. This not only prevents men from making revolutions, but deters men from desiring them. Violent political passions have but little hold on those who have devoted all their faculties to the pursuit of their well-being. The ardour which they display in small matters calms their zeal for momentous undertakings.

From time to time, indeed, enterprising and ambitious men will arise in democratic communities, whose unbounded aspirations can not be contented by following the beaten track. Such men like revolutions and hail their approach; but they have great difficulty in bringing them about, unless unwonted events come to their assistance. No man can struggle with advantage against the spirit of his age and country; and, however powerful he may be supposed to be, he will find it difficult to make his contemporaries share in feelings and opinions which are repugnant to all their feelings and desires.

It is a mistake to believe that, when once the equality of conditions has become the old and uncontested state of society, and has imparted its characteristics to the manners of a nation, men will easily allow themselves to be thrust into perilous risks by an imprudent leader or a bold innovator. Not, indeed, that they will resist him openly, by well-contrived schemes, or even by a premeditated plan of resistance. They will not struggle energetically against him, sometimes they will even applaud him—but they do not follow him. To his vehemence they secretly oppose their inertia—to his revolutionary tendencies their conservative interests—their homely tastes to his adventurous passions—their good sense to the flights of his genius —to his poetry their prose. With immense exertion he raises them for an instant, but they speedily escape from him, and fall back, as it were, by their own weight. He strains himself to rouse the indifferent and distracted multitude, and finds at last that he is reduced to impotence, not because he is conquered, but because he is alone.

I do not assert that men living in democratic communities are naturally stationary; I think, on the contrary, that a perpetual stir prevails in the bosom of those societies, and that rest is unknown there; but I think that men bestir themselves within certain limits beyond which they hardly ever go. They are forever varying, altering, and restoring secondary matters; but they carefully abstain from touching what is fundamental. They love change, but they dread revolutions. Although the Americans are constantly modifying or abrogating some of their laws, they by no means display revolutionary passions. It may be easily seen, from the promptitude with which they check and calm themselves when public excitement begins to grow alarming, and at the very moment when passions seem most roused, that they dread a revolution as the worst of misfortunes, and that every one of them is inwardly resolved to make great sacrifices to avoid such a catastrophe. In no country in the world is the love of property more active and more anxious than in the United States; nowhere does the majority display less inclination for those principles which threaten to alter, in whatever manner, the laws of property. I have often remarked that theories which are of a revolutionary nature, since they can not be put in practice without a complete and sometimes a sudden change in the state of property and persons, are much less favourably viewed in the United States than in the great monarchical countries of Europe: if some men profess them, the bulk of the people reject them with instinctive abhorrence. I do not hesitate to say that most of the maxims commonly called democratic in France would be proscribed by the democracy of the United States. This may easily be understood; in America men have the opinions and passions of democracy, in Europe we have still the passions and opinions of revolution. If ever America undergoes great revolutions, they will be brought about by the presence of the black race on the soil of the United States—that is to say, they will owe their origin, not to the equality, but to the inequality, of conditions.

When social conditions are equal, every man is apt to live apart, centred in himself and forgetful of the public. If the rulers of democratic nations were either to neglect to correct this fatal tendency, or to encourage it from a notion that it weans men from political passions and thus wards off revolutions, they might eventually produce the evil they seek to avoid, and a time might come when the inordinate passions of a few men, aided by the unintelligent selfishness or the pusillanimity of the greater number, would ultimately compel society to pass through strange vicissitudes. In democratic communities revolutions are seldom desired except by a minority; but a minority may sometimes effect them. I do not assert that democratic nations are secure from revolutions; I merely say that the state of society in those nations does not lead to revolutions, but rather wards them off. A democratic people left to itself will not easily embark in great hazards; it is only led to revolutions unawares; it may sometimes undergo them, but it does not make them; and I will add that, when such a people has been allowed to acquire sufficient knowledge and experience, it will not suffer them to be made. I am well aware that in this respect public institutions may themselves do much; they may encourage or repress the tendencies which originate in the state of society. I therefore do not maintain, I repeat, that a people is secure from revolutions simply because conditions are equal in the community; but I think that, whatever the institutions of such a people may be, great revolutions will always be far less violent and less frequent than is supposed; and I can easily discern a state of polity which, when combined with the principle of equality, would render society more stationary than it has ever been in our western part of the world.

The observations I have here made on events may also be applied in part to opinions. Two things are surprising in the United States—the mutability of the greater part of human actions, and the singular stability of certain principles. Men are in constant motion; the mind of man appears almost unmoved. When once an opinion has spread over the country and struck root there, it would seem that no power on earth is strong enough to eradicate it. In the United States, general principles in religion, philosophy, morality, and even politics, do not vary, or at least are only modified by a hidden and often an imperceptible process: even the grossest prejudices are obliterated with incredible slowness, amid the continual friction of men and things.

I hear it said that it is in the nature and the habits of democracies to be constantly changing their opinions and feelings. This may be true of small democratic nations, like those of the ancient world, in which the whole community could be assembled in a public place and then excited at will by an orator. But I saw nothing of the kind among the great democratic people which dwells upon the opposite shores of the Atlantic Ocean. What struck me in the United States was the difficulty of shaking the majority in an opinion once conceived, or of drawing it off from a leader once adopted. Neither speaking nor writing can accomplish it; nothing but experience will avail, and even experience must be repeated. This is surprising at first sight, but a more attentive investigation explains the fact. I do not think that it is as easy as is supposed to uproot the prejudices of a democratic people —to change its belief—to supersede principles once established, by new principles in religion, politics, and morals —in a word, to make great and frequent changes in men's minds. Not that the human mind is there at rest—it is in constant agitation; but it is engaged in infinitely varying the consequences of known principles, and in seeking for new consequences, rather than in seeking for new principles. Its motion is one of rapid circumvolution, rather than of straightforward impulse by rapid and direct effort; it extends its orbit by small continual and hasty movements, but it does not suddenly alter its position.

Men who are equal in rights, in education, in fortune, or, to comprise all in one word, in their social condition, have necessarily wants, habits, and tastes which are hardly dissimilar. As they look at objects under the same aspect, their minds naturally tend to analogous conclusions; and, though each of them may deviate from his contemporaries and form opinions of his own, they will involuntarily and unconsciously concur in a certain number of received opinions. The more attentively I consider the effects of equality upon the mind, the more am I persuaded that the intellectual anarchy which we witness about us is not, as many men suppose, the natural state of democratic nations. I think it is rather to be regarded as an accident peculiar to their youth, and that it only breaks out at that period of transition when men have already snapped the former ties which bound them together, but are still amazingly different in origin, education, and manners; so that, having retained opinions, propensities, and tastes of great diversity, nothing any longer prevents men from avowing them openly. The leading opinions of men become similar in proportion as their conditions assimilate; such appears to me to be the general and permanent law—the rest is casual and transient.

I believe that it will rarely happen to any man among a democratic community, suddenly to frame a system of notions very remote from that which his contemporaries have adopted; and if some such innovator appeared, I apprehend that he would have great difficulty in finding listeners, still more in finding believers. When the conditions of men are almost equal, they do not easily allow themselves to be persuaded by each other. As they all live in close intercourse, as they have learned the same things together, and as they lead the same life, they are not naturally disposed to take one of themselves for a guide, and to follow him implicitly. Men seldom take the opinion of their equal, or of a man like themselves, upon trust. Not only is confidence in the superior attainments of certain individuals weakened among democratic nations, as I have elsewhere remarked, but the general notion of the intellectual superiority which any man whatsoever may acquire in relation to the rest of the community is soon overshadowed. As men grow more like each other, the doctrine of the equality of the intellect gradually infuses itself into their opinions; and it becomes more difficult for any innovator to acquire or to exert much influence over the minds of a people. In such communities sudden intellectual revolutions will therefore be rare; for, if we read aright the history of the world, we shall find that great and rapid changes in human opinions have been produced far less by the force of reasoning than by the authority of a name. Observe, too, that as the men who

live in democratic societies are not connected with each
other by any tie, each of them must be convinced individually; while in aristocratic society it is enough to convince a few—the rest follow. If Luther had lived in an
age of equality, and had not had princes and potentates
for his audience, he would perhaps have found it more
difficult to change the aspect of Europe. Not, indeed, that
the men of democracies are naturally strongly persuaded of
the certainty of their opinions, or are unwavering in belief;
they frequently entertain doubts which no one, in their
eyes, can remove. It sometimes happens at such times
that the human mind would willingly change its position;
but as nothing urges or guides it forward, it oscillates to
and fro without progressive motion.[1]

Even when the reliance of a democratic people has been
won, it is still no easy matter to gain their attention. It
is extremely difficult to obtain a hearing from men living
in democracies, unless it be to speak to them of themselves.
They do not attend to the things said to them, because they
are always fully engrossed with the things they are doing.
For indeed few men are idle in democratic nations; life is
passed in the midst of noise and excitement, and men are
so engaged in acting that little time remains to them for
thinking. I would especially remark that they are not
only employed, but that they are passionately devoted to
their employments. They are always in action, and each
of their actions absorbs their faculties: the zeal which they
display in business puts out the enthusiasm they might
otherwise entertain for ideas. I think that it is extremely
difficult to excite the enthusiasm of a democratic people
for any theory which has not a palpable, direct, and immediate connection with the daily occupations of life:
therefore they will not easily forsake their old opinions;
for it is enthusiasm which flings the minds of men out of
the beaten track, and effects the great revolutions of the
intellect as well as the great revolutions of the political
world. Thus democratic nations have neither time nor
taste to go in search of novel opinions. Even when those

they possess become doubtful, they still retain them, because it would take too much time and inquiry to change them—they retain them, not as certain, but as established.

There are yet other and more cogent reasons that prevent any great change from being easily effected in the principles of a democratic people. I have already adverted to them at the commencement of this part of my work. If the influence of individuals is weak and hardly perceptible among such a people, the power exercised by the mass upon the mind of each individual is extremely great—I have already shown for what reasons. I would now observe that it is wrong to suppose that this depends solely upon the form of government, and that the majority would lose its intellectual supremacy if it were to lose its political power. In aristocracies men have often much greatness and strength of their own: when they find themselves at variance with the greater number of their fellow-countrymen, they withdraw to their own circle, where they support and console themselves. Such is not the case in a democratic country; there public favour seems as necessary as the air we breathe, and to live at variance with the multitude is, as it were, not to live. The multitude requires no laws to coerce those who think not like itself: public disapprobation is enough; a sense of their loneliness and impotence overtakes them and drives them to despair.

Whenever social conditions are equal, public opinion presses with enormous weight upon the mind of each individual; it surrounds, directs, and oppresses him; and this arises from the very constitution of society, much more than from its political laws. As men grow more alike, each man feels himself weaker in regard to all the rest; as he discerns nothing by which he is considerably raised above them, or distinguished from them, he mistrusts himself as soon as they assail him. Not only does he mistrust his strength, but he even doubts of his right; and he is very near acknowledging that he is in the wrong, when the greater number of his countrymen assert that he is so.

The majority do not need to constrain him—they convince him. In whatever way, then, the powers of a democratic community may be organized and balanced, it will always be extremely difficult to believe what the bulk of the people reject, or to profess what they condemn.

This circumstance is extraordinarily favourable to the stability of opinions. When an opinion has taken root among a democratic people, and established itself in the minds of the bulk of the community, it afterward subsists by itself and is maintained without effort, because no one attacks it. Those who at first rejected it as false, ultimately receive it as the general impression; and those who still dispute it in their hearts, conceal their dissent; they are careful not to engage in a dangerous and useless conflict. It is true that when the majority of a democratic people change their opinions they may suddenly and arbitrarily effect strange revolutions in men's minds; but their opinions do not change without much difficulty, and it is almost as difficult to show that they are changed.

Time, events, or the unaided individual action of the mind, will sometimes undermine or destroy an opinion, without any outward sign of the change. It has not been openly assailed, no conspiracy has been formed to make war on it, but its followers one by one noiselessly secede —day by day a few of them abandon it, until at last it is only professed by a minority. In this state it will still continue to prevail. As its enemies remain mute, or only interchange their thoughts by stealth, they are themselves unaware for a long period that a great revolution has actually been effected; and in this state of uncertainty they take no steps—they observe each other and are silent. The majority have ceased to believe what they believed before; but they still affect to believe, and this empty phantom of public opinion is strong enough to chill innovators, and to keep them silent and at a respectful distance. We live at a time which has witnessed the most rapid changes of opinion in the minds of men; nevertheless it may be that the leading opinions of society will ere long be more settled than they have been for several centuries in our history: that time is not yet come, but it may perhaps be approaching. As I examine more closely the natural wants and tendencies of democratic nations, I grow persuaded that if ever social equality is generally and permanently established in the world, great intellectual and political revolutions will become more difficult and less frequent than is supposed. Because the men of democracies appear always excited, uncertain, eager, changeable in their wills and in their positions, it is imagined that they are suddenly to abrogate their laws, to adopt new opinions, and to assume new manners. But if the principle of equality predisposes men to change, it also suggests to them certain interests and tastes which can not be satisfied without a settled order of things; equality urges them on, but at the same time it holds them back; it spurs them, but fastens them to earth—it kindles their desires, but limits their powers. This, however, is not perceived at first; the passions which tend to sever the citizens of a democracy are obvious enough; but the hidden force which restrains and unites them is not discernible at a glance.

Amid the ruins which surround me, shall I dare to say that revolutions are not what I most fear for coming generations? If men continue to shut themselves more closely within the narrow circle of domestic interests and to live upon that kind of excitement, it is to be apprehended that they may ultimately become inaccessible to those great and powerful public emotions which perturb nations—but which enlarge them and recruit them. When property becomes so fluctuating, and the love of property so restless and so ardent, I can not but fear that men may arrive at such a state as to regard every new theory as a peril, every innovation as an irksome toil, every social improvement as a stepping-stone to revolution, and so refuse to move altogether for fear of being moved too far. I dread, and I confess it, lest they should at last so entirely give way to a cowardly love of present enjoyment, as to lose sight of the interests of their future selves and of those

of their descendants; and to prefer to glide along the easy
current of life, rather than to make, when it is necessary,
a strong and sudden effort to a higher purpose. It is believed by some that modern society will be ever changing
its aspect; for myself, I fear that it will ultimately be too
invariably fixed in the same institutions, the same prejudices, the same manners, so that mankind will be stopped
and circumscribed; that the mind will swing backward
and forward forever, without begetting fresh ideas; that
man will waste his strength in bootless and solitary trifling;
and, though in continual motion, that humanity will cease
to advance.

The same interests, the same fears, the same passions
which deter democratic nations from revolutions, deter
them also from war; the spirit of military glory and the
spirit of revolution are weakened at the same time and
by the same causes. The ever-increasing numbers of men
of property—lovers of peace, the growth of personal wealth
which war so rapidly consumes, the mildness of manners,
the gentleness of heart, those tendencies to pity which are
engendered by the equality of conditions, that coolness of
understanding which renders men comparatively insensible
to the violent and poetical excitement of arms—all these
causes concur to quench the military spirit. I think it may
be admitted as a general and constant rule that, among
civilized nations, the warlike passions will become more
rare and less intense in proportion as social conditions
shall be more equal. War is nevertheless an occurrence
to which all nations are subject, democratic nations as well
as others. Whatever taste they may have for peace, they
must hold themselves in readiness to repel aggression, or,
in other words, they must have an army.

Fortune, which has conferred so many peculiar benefits upon the inhabitants of the United States, has placed
them in the midst of a wilderness, where they have, so to
speak, no neighbours: a few thousand soldiers are sufficient for their wants; but this is peculiar to America, not
to democracy. The equality of conditions, and the man-

ners as well as the institutions resulting from it, do not
exempt a democratic people from the necessity of standing armies, and their armies always exercise a powerful
influence over their fate. It is therefore of singular importance to inquire what are the natural propensities of
the men of whom these armies are composed.

Among aristocratic nations, especially among those in
which birth is the only source of rank, the same inequality
exists in the army as in the nation; the officer is noble,
the soldier is a serf; the one is naturally called upon to
command, the other to obey. In aristocratic armies, the
private soldier's ambition is therefore circumscribed within
very narrow limits. Nor has the ambition of the officer
an unlimited range. An aristocratic body not only forms
a part of the scale of ranks in the nation, but it contains a
scale of ranks within itself: the members of whom it is
composed are placed one above another, in a particular
and unvarying manner. Thus one man is born to the
command of a regiment, another to that of a company;
when once they have reached the utmost object of their
hopes, they stop of their own accord, and remain contented with their lot. There is, besides, a strong cause,
which, in aristocracies, weakens the officer's desire of promotion. Among aristocratic nations, an officer, independently of his rank in the army, also occupies an elevated
rank in society; the former is almost always in his eyes
only an appendage to the latter. A nobleman who embraces the profession of arms follows it less from motives
of ambition than from a sense of the duties imposed on
him by his birth. He enters the army in order to find
an honourable employment for the idle years of his youth,
and to be able to bring back to his home and his peers
some honourable recollections of military life; but his principal object is not to obtain by that profession either property, distinction, or power, for he possesses these advantages in his own right, and enjoys them without leaving
his home.

In democratic armies all the soldiers may become officers, which makes the desire of promotion general, and immeasurably extends the bounds of military ambition. The officer, on his part, sees nothing which naturally and necessarily stops him at one grade more than at another; and each grade has immense importance in his eyes, because his rank in society almost always depends on his rank in the army. Among democratic nations it often happens that an officer has no property but his pay, and no distinction but that of military honours: consequently as often as his duties change, his fortune changes, and he becomes, as it were, a new man. What was only an appendage to his position in aristocratic armies has thus become the main point, the basis of his whole condition. Under the old French monarchy officers were always called by their titles of nobility; they are now always called by the title of their military rank. This little change in the forms of language suffices to show that a great revolution has taken place in the constitution of society and in that of the army. In democratic armies the desire of advancement is almost universal: it is ardent, tenacious, perpetual; it is strengthened by all other desires, and only extinguished with life itself. But it is easy to see that, of all armies in the world, those in which advancement must be slowest in time of peace are the armies of democratic countries. As the number of commissions is naturally limited, while the number of competitors is almost unlimited, and as the strict law of equality is over all alike, none can make rapid progress—many can make no progress at all. Thus the desire of advancement is greater, and the opportunities of advancement fewer, there than elsewhere. All the ambitious spirits of a democratic army are consequently ardently desirous of war, because war makes vacancies, and warrants the violation of that law of seniority which is the sole privilege natural to democracy.

We thus arrive at this singular consequence, that of all armies those most ardently desirous of war are democratic armies, and of all nations those most fond of peace are democratic nations: and, what makes these facts still more extraordinary, is that these contrary effects are produced at the same time by the principle of equality.

All the members of the community, being alike, constantly harbour the wish, and discover the possibility, of changing their condition and improving their welfare: this makes them fond of peace, which is favourable to industry, and allows every man to pursue his own little undertakings to their completion. On the other hand, this same equality makes soldiers dream of fields of battle, by increasing the value of military honours in the eyes of those who follow the profession of arms, and by rendering those honours accessible to all. In either case the inquietude of the heart is the same, the taste for enjoyment as insatiable, the ambition of success as great—the means of gratifying it are alone different.

These opposite tendencies of the nation and the army expose democratic communities to great dangers. When a military spirit forsakes a people, the profession of arms immediately ceases to be held in honour, and military men fall to the lowest rank of the public servants: they are little esteemed, and no longer understood. The reverse of what takes place in aristocratic ages then occurs; the men who enter the army are no longer those of the highest, but of the lowest rank. Military ambition is only indulged in when no other is possible. Hence arises a circle of cause and consequence from which it is difficult to escape: the best part of the nation shuns the military profession because that profession is not honoured, and the profession is not honoured because the best part of the nation has ceased to follow it. It is then no matter of surprise that democratic armies are often restless, ill-tempered, and dissatisfied with their lot, although their physical condition is commonly far better and their discipline less strict than in other countries. The soldier feels that he occupies an inferior position, and his wounded pride either stimulates his taste for hostilities which would render his services necessary, or gives him a turn for revolutions, during which he may hope to win by force of arms the political influence and personal importance now denied him. The composition of democratic armies makes this last-mentioned danger much to be feared. In democratic communities almost every man has some property to preserve; but democratic armies are generally led by men without property, most of whom have little to lose in civil broils. The bulk of the nation is naturally much more afraid of revolutions than in the ages of aristocracy, but the leaders of the army much less so.

Moreover, as among democratic nations (to repeat what I have just remarked) the wealthiest, the best educated, and the most able men seldom adopt the military profession, the army, taken collectively, eventually forms a small nation by itself, where the mind is less enlarged, and habits are more rude than in the nation at large. Now, this small uncivilized nation has arms in its possession, and alone knows how to use them: for, indeed, the pacific temper of the community increases the danger to which a democratic people is exposed from the military and turbulent spirit of the army. Nothing is so dangerous as an army amid an unwarlike nation; the excessive love of the whole community for quiet continually puts its constitution at the mercy of the soldiery.

It may, therefore, be asserted, generally speaking, that if democratic nations are naturally prone to peace from their interests and their propensities, they are constantly drawn to war and revolutions by their armies. Military revolutions, which are scarcely ever to be apprehended in aristocracies, are always to be dreaded among democratic nations. These perils must be reckoned among the most formidable which beset their future fate, and the attention of statesmen should be sedulously applied to find a remedy for the evil.

When a nation perceives that it is inwardly affected by the restless ambition of its army, the first thought which occurs is to give this inconvenient ambition an object by going to war. I speak no ill of war: war almost always enlarges the mind of a people, and raises their character.

In some cases it is the only check to the excessive growth of certain propensities which naturally spring out of the equality of conditions, and it must be considered as a necessary corrective to certain inveterate diseases to which democratic communities are liable. War has great advantages, but we must not flatter ourselves that it can diminish the danger I have just pointed out. That peril is only suspended by it, to return more fiercely when the war is over; for armies are much more impatient of peace after having tasted military exploits. War could only be a remedy for a people which should always be athirst for military glory. I foresee that all the military rulers who may rise up in great democratic nations will find it easier to conquer with their armies than to make their armies live at peace after conquest. There are two things which a democratic people will always find very difficult—to begin a war, and to end it.

Again, if war has some peculiar advantages for democratic nations, on the other hand it exposes them to certain dangers which aristocracies have no cause to dread to an equal extent. I shall only point out two of these. Although war gratifies the army, it embarrasses and often exasperates that countless multitude of men whose minor passions every day require peace in order to be satisfied. Thus there is some risk of its causing, under another form, the disturbance it is intended to prevent. No protracted war can fail to endanger the freedom of a democratic country. Not, indeed, that after every victory it is to be apprehended that the victorious generals will possess themselves by force of the supreme power, after the manner of Sylla and Cæsar: the danger is of another kind. War does not always give over democratic communities to military government, but it must invariably and immeasurably increase the powers of civil government; it must almost compulsorily concentrate the direction of all men and the management of all things in the hands of the administration. If it lead not to despotism by sudden violence, it prepares men for it more gently by their habits. All those who seek

WAR NEWS.

Photogravure from a painting by Richard Caton Woodville in the
Metropolitan Museum of Art, New York City.

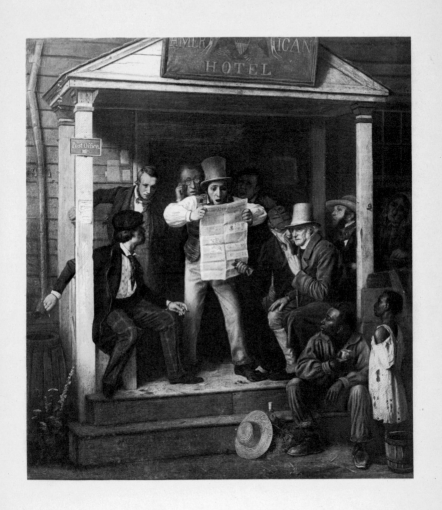

to destroy the liberties of a democratic nation ought to know that war is the surest and the shortest means to accomplish it. This is the first axiom of the science.

One remedy, which appears to be obvious when the ambition of soldiers and officers becomes the subject of alarm, is to augment the number of commissions to be distributed by increasing the army. This affords temporary relief, but it plunges the country into deeper difficulties at some future period. To increase the army may produce a lasting effect in an aristocratic community, because military ambition is there confined to one class of men, and the ambition of each individual stops, as it were, at a certain limit; so that it may be possible to satisfy all who feel its influence. But nothing is gained by increasing the army among a democratic people, because the number of aspirants always rises in exactly the same ratio as the army itself. Those whose claims have been satisfied by the creation of new commissions are instantly succeeded by a fresh multitude beyond all power of satisfaction; and even those who were but now satisfied soon begin to crave more advancement; for the same excitement prevails in the ranks of the army as in the civil classes of democratic society, and what men want is not to reach a certain grade, but to have constant promotion. Though these wants may not be very vast, they are perpetually recurring. Thus a democratic nation, by augmenting its army, only allays for a time the ambition of the military profession, which soon becomes even more formidable, because the number of those who feel it is increased. I am of opinion that a restless and turbulent spirit is an evil inherent in the very constitution of democratic armies, and beyond hope of cure. The legislators of democracies must not expect to devise any military organization capable by its influence of calming and restraining the military profession: their efforts would exhaust their powers before the object is attained.

The remedy for the vices of the army is not to be found in the army itself, but in the country. Democratic nations are naturally afraid of disturbance and of despotism; the object is to turn these natural instincts into well-digested, deliberate, and lasting tastes. When men have at last learned to make a peaceful and profitable use of freedom, and have felt its blessing—when they have conceived a manly love of order, and have freely submitted themselves to discipline—these same men, if they follow the profession of arms, bring into it, unconsciously and almost against their will, these same habits and manners. The general spirit of the nation being infused into the spirit peculiar to the army, tempers the opinions and desires engendered by military life, or represses them by the mighty force of public opinion. Teach but the citizens to be educated, orderly, firm, and free, the soldiers will be disciplined and obedient. Any law which, in repressing the turbulent spirit of the army, should tend to diminish the spirit of freedom in the nation, and to overshadow the notion of law and right, would defeat its object: it would do much more to favour, than to defeat, the establishment of military tyranny.

After all, and in spite of all precautions, a large army amid a democratic people will always be a source of great danger; the most effectual means of diminishing that danger would be to reduce the army, but this is a remedy which all nations have it not in their power to use.

It is a part of the essence of a democratic army to be very numerous in proportion to the people to which it belongs, as I shall hereafter show. On the other hand, men living in democratic times seldom choose a military life. Democratic nations are therefore soon led to give up the system of voluntary recruiting for that of compulsory enlistment. The necessity of their social condition compels them to resort to the latter means, and it may easily be foreseen that they will all eventually adopt it. When military service is compulsory, the burden is indiscriminately and equally borne by the whole community. This is another necessary consequence of the social condition of these nations, and of their notions. The government may do almost whatever it pleases, provided it appeals to the whole community at once: it is the unequal distribution of the weight, not the weight itself, which commonly occasions resistance. But as military service is common to all the citizens, the evident consequence is that each of them remains but for a few years on active duty. Thus it is in the nature of things that the soldier in democracies only passes through the army, while among most aristocratic nations the military profession is one which the soldier adopts, or which is imposed upon him, for life.

This has important consequences. Among the soldiers of a democratic army, some acquire a taste for military life, but the majority being enlisted against their will, and ever ready to go back to their homes, do not consider themselves as seriously engaged in the military profession, and are always thinking of quitting it. Such men do not contract the wants, and only half partake in the passions, which that mode of life engenders. They adapt themselves to their military duties, but their minds are still attached to the interests and the duties which engaged them in civil life. They do not, therefore, imbibe the spirit of the army —or rather, they infuse the spirit of the community at large into the army, and retain it there. Among democratic nations the private soldiers remain most like civilians: upon them the habits of the nation have the firmest hold, and public opinion most influence. It is by the instrumentality of the private soldiers especially that it may be possible to infuse into a democratic army the love of freedom and the respect of rights, if these principles have once been successfully inculcated on the people at large. The reverse happens among aristocratic nations, where the soldiery have eventually nothing in common with their fellow-citizens, and where they live among them as strangers, and often as enemies. In aristocratic armies the officers are the conservative element, because the officers alone have retained a strict connection with civil society, and never forego their purpose of resuming their place in it sooner or later: in democratic armies the private soldiers stand in this position, and from the same cause.

It often happens, on the contrary, that in these same democratic armies the officers contract tastes and wants wholly distinct from those of the nation—a fact which may be thus accounted for : Among democratic nations, the man who becomes an officer severs all the ties which bound him to civil life; he leaves it forever; he has no interest to resume it. His true country is the army, since he owes all he has to the rank he has attained in it; he therefore follows the fortunes of the army, rises or sinks with it, and henceforward directs all his hopes to that quarter only. As the wants of an officer are distinct from those of the country, he may perhaps ardently desire war, or labour to bring about a revolution at the very moment when the nation is most desirous of stability and peace. There are, nevertheless, some causes which allay this restless and war-like spirit. Though ambition is universal and continual among democratic nations, we have seen that it is seldom great. A man who, being born in the lower classes of the community, has risen from the ranks to be an officer, has already taken a prodigious step. He has gained a footing in a sphere above that which he filled in civil life, and he has acquired rights which most democratic nations will ever consider as inalienable.[2] He is willing to pause after so great an effort, and to enjoy what he has won. The fear of risking what he has already obtained damps the desire of acquiring what he has not got. Having conquered the first and greatest impediment which opposed his advancement, he resigns himself with less impatience to the slowness of his progress. His ambition will be more and more cooled in proportion as the increasing distinction of his rank teaches him that he has more to put in jeopardy. If I am not mistaken, the least warlike, and also the least revolutionary part, of a democratic army, will always be its chief commanders.

But the remarks I have just made on officers and soldiers are not applicable to a numerous class which in all armies fills the intermediate space between them—I mean the class of non-commissioned officers. This class of non-commissioned officers which have never acted a part in history until the present century is henceforward destined, I think, to play one of some importance. Like the officers, non-commissioned officers have broken, in their minds, all the ties which bound them to civil life; like the former, they devote themselves permanently to the service, and perhaps make it even more exclusively the object of all their desires: but non-commissioned officers are men who have not yet reached a firm and lofty post at which they may pause and breathe more freely ere they can attain further promotion. By the very nature of his duties, which is invariable, a non-commissioned officer is doomed to lead an obscure, confined, comfortless, and precarious existence; as yet he sees nothing of military life but its dangers; he knows nothing but its privations and its discipline— more difficult to support than dangers: he suffers the more from his present miseries, from knowing that the constitution of society and of the army allow him to rise above them; he may, indeed, at any time obtain his commission, and enter at once upon command, honours, independence, rights, and enjoyments. Not only does this object of his hopes appear to him of immense importance, but he is never sure of reaching it till it is actually his own; the grade he fills is by no means irrevocable; he is always entirely abandoned to the arbitrary pleasure of his commanding officer, for this is imperiously required by the necessity of discipline: a slight fault, a whim, may always deprive him in an instant of the fruits of many years of toil and endeavour; until he has reached the grade to which he aspires he has accomplished nothing; not till he reaches that grade does his career seem to begin. A desperate ambition can not fail to be kindled in a man thus incessantly goaded on by his youth, his wants, his passions, the spirit of his age, his hopes, and his fears. Non-commissioned officers are therefore bent on war—on war always, and at any cost; but if war be denied them, then they desire revolutions to suspend the authority of established regulations, and to enable them, aided by the general confusion and the political passions of the time, to get rid of their superior officers and to take their places. Nor is it impossible for them to bring about such a crisis, because their common origin and habits give them much influence over the soldiers, however different may be their passions and their desires.

It would be an error to suppose that these various characteristics of officers, non-commissioned officers, and men belong to any particular time or country; they will always occur at all times, and among all democratic nations. In every democratic army the non-commissioned officers will be the worst representatives of the pacific and orderly spirit of the country, and the private soldiers will be the best. The latter will carry with them into military life the strength or weakness of the manners of the nation; they will display a faithful reflection of the community: if that community is ignorant and weak, they will allow themselves to be drawn by their leaders into disturbances, either unconsciously or against their will; if it is enlightened and energetic, the community will itself keep them within the bounds of order.

Any army is in danger of being conquered at the outset of a campaign, after a long peace; any army which has long been engaged in warfare has strong chances of victory: this truth is peculiarly applicable to democratic armies. In aristocracies the military profession, being a privileged career, is held in honour even in time of peace. Men of great talents, great attainments, and great ambition embrace it; the army is in all respects on a level with the nation, and frequently above it. We have seen, on the contrary, that among a democratic people the choicer minds of the nation are gradually drawn away from the military profession, to seek by other paths distinction, power, and especially wealth. After a long peace—and in democratic ages the periods of peace are long—the army is always inferior to the country itself. In this state it is called into active service; and until war has altered it, there is danger for the country as well as for the army.

I have shown that in democratic armies, and in time of peace, the rule of seniority is the supreme and inflexible law of advancement. This is not only a consequence, as I have before observed, of the constitution of these armies, but of the constitution of the people, and it will always occur. Again, as among these nations the officer derives his position in the country solely from his position in the army, and as he draws all the distinction and the competency he enjoys from the same source, he does not retire from his profession, or is not superannuated, till toward the extreme close of life. The consequence of these two causes is, that when a democratic people goes to war after a long interval of peace all the leading officers of the army are old men. I speak not only of the generals, but of the non-commissioned officers, who have most of them been stationary, or have only advanced step by step. It may be remarked with surprise, that in a democratic army after a long peace all the soldiers are mere boys, and all the superior officers in declining years; so that the former are wanting in experience, the latter in vigour. This is a strong element of defeat, for the first condition of successful generalship is youth: I should not have ventured to say so if the greatest captain of modern times had not made the observation.

These two causes do not act in the same manner upon aristocratic armies: as men are promoted in them by right of birth much more than by right of seniority, there are in all ranks a certain number of young men, who bring to their profession all the early vigour of body and mind. Again, as the men who seek for military honours among an aristocratic people, enjoy a settled position in civil society, they seldom continue in the army until old age overtakes them. After having devoted the most vigorous years of youth to the career of arms, they voluntarily retire, and spend at home the remainder of their maturer years.

A long peace not only fills democratic armies with elderly officers, but it also gives to all the officers habits both of body and mind which render them unfit for actual service. The man who has long lived amid the calm and lukewarm atmosphere of democratic manners can at first ill adapt himself to the harder toils and sterner duties of warfare; and if he has not absolutely lost the taste for arms, at least he has assumed a mode of life which unfits him for conquest.

Among aristocratic nations, the ease of civil life exercises less influence on the manners of the army, because among those nations the aristocracy commands the army: and an aristocracy, however plunged in luxurious pleasures, has always many other passions besides that of its own well-being, and to satisfy those passions more thoroughly its well-being will be readily sacrificed.[3]

I have shown that in democratic armies, in time of peace, promotion is extremely slow. The officers at first support this state of things with impatience, they grow excited, restless, exasperated, but in the end most of them make up their minds to it. Those who have the largest share of ambition and of resources quit the army; others, adapting their tastes and their desires to their scanty fortunes, ultimately look upon the military profession in a civil point of view. The quality they value most in it is the competency and security which attend it: their whole notion of the future rests upon the certainty of this little provision, and all they require is peaceably to enjoy it. Thus not only does a long peace fill an army with old men, but it frequently imparts the views of old men to those who are still in the prime of life.

I have also shown that among democratic nations in time of peace the military profession is held in little honour and indifferently followed. This want of public favour is a heavy discouragement to the army; it weighs down the minds of the troops, and when war breaks out at last, they can not immediately resume their spring and vigour. No similar cause of moral weakness occurs in aristocratic armies: there the officers are never lowered either in their own eyes or in those of their countrymen, because, independently of their military greatness, they are personally great. But even if the influence of peace operated on the two kinds of armies in the same manner, the results would still be different. When the officers of an aristocratic army have lost their warlike spirit and the desire of raising themselves by service, they still retain a certain respect for the honour of their class, and an old habit of being foremost to set an example. But when the officers of a democratic army have no longer the love of war and the ambition of arms, nothing whatever remains to them.

I am therefore of opinion that, when a democratic people engages in a war after a long peace, it incurs much more risk of defeat than any other nation; but it ought not easily to be cast down by its reverses, for the chances of success for such an army are increased by the duration of the war. When a war has at length, by its long continuance, roused the whole community from their peaceful occupations and ruined their minor undertakings, the same passions which made them attach so much importance to the maintenance of peace will be turned to arms. War, after it has destroyed all modes of speculation, becomes itself the great and sole speculation, to which all the ardent and ambitious desires which equality engenders are exclusively directed. Hence it is that the self-same democratic nations which are so reluctant to engage in hostilities sometimes perform prodigious achievements when once they have taken the field. As the war attracts more and more of public attention, and is seen to create high reputations and great fortunes in a short space of time, the choicest spirits of the nation enter the military profession: all the enterprising, proud, and martial minds, no longer of the aristocracy solely, but of the whole country, are drawn in this direction. As the number of competitors for military honours is immense, and war drives every man to his proper level, great generals are always sure to spring up. A long war produces upon a democratic army the same effects that a revolution produces upon a people; it breaks through regulations, and allows extraordinary men to rise above the common level. Those officers whose bodies and minds have grown old in peace, are removed, or superannuated, or they die. In their stead a host of young men are pressing on, whose frames are already hardened, whose desires are extended and inflamed by active service. They are bent on advancement at all hazards, and perpetual advancement; they are followed by others with the same passions and desires, and after these are others yet unlimited by aught but the size of the army. The principle of equality opens the door of ambition to all, and death provides chances for ambition. Death is constantly thinning the ranks, making vacancies, closing and opening the career of arms.

There is, moreover, a secret connection between the military character and the character of democracies, which war brings to light. The men of democracies are naturally passionately eager to acquire what they covet, and to enjoy it on easy conditions. They for the most part worship chance, and are much less afraid of death than of difficulty. This is the spirit which they bring to commerce and manufactures; and this same spirit, carried with them to the field of battle, induces them willingly to expose their lives in order to secure in a moment the rewards of victory. No kind of greatness is more pleasing to the imagination of a democratic people than military greatness—a greatness of vivid and sudden lustre, obtained without toil, by nothing but the risk of life. Thus, while the interests and the tastes of the members of a democratic community divert them from war, their habits of mind fit them for carrying on war well; they soon make good soldiers, when they are roused from their business and their enjoyments. If peace is peculiarly hurtful to democratic armies, war secures to them advantages which no other armies ever possess; and these advantages, however little felt at first, can not fail in the end to give them the victory. An aristocratic nation, which in a contest with a democratic people does not succeed in ruining the latter at the outset of the war, always runs a great risk of being conquered by it.

It is a very general opinion, especially in aristocratic countries, that the great social equality which prevails in democracies ultimately renders the private soldier independent of the officer, and thus destroys the bond of discipline. This is a mistake, for there are two kinds of discipline, which it is important not to confound. When the officer is noble and the soldier a serf—one rich, the other poor—the former educated and strong, the latter ignorant and weak—the strictest bond of obedience may easily be established between the two men. The soldier is broken in to military discipline, as it were, before he enters the army; or rather, military discipline is nothing but an enhancement of social servitude. In aristocratic armies the soldier will soon become insensible to everything but the orders of his superior officers; he acts without reflection, triumphs without enthusiasm, and dies without complaint: in this state he is no longer a man, but he is still a most formidable animal trained for war.

A democratic people must despair of ever obtaining from soldiers that blind, minute, submissive, and invariable obedience which an aristocratic people may impose on them without difficulty. The state of society does not prepare them for it, and the nation might be in danger of losing its natural advantages if it sought artificially to acquire advantages of this particular kind. Among democratic communities, military discipline ought not to attempt to annihilate the free spring of the faculties; all that can be done by discipline is to direct it; the obedience thus inculcated is less exact, but it is more eager and more intelligent. It has its root in the will of him who obeys: it rests not only on his instinct, but on his reason; and consequently it will often spontaneously become more strict as danger requires it. The discipline of an aristocratic army is apt to be relaxed in war, because that discipline is founded upon habits, and war disturbs those habits. The discipline of a democratic army, on the contrary, is

51

strengthened in sight of the enemy, because every soldier then clearly perceives that he must be silent and obedient in order to conquer.

The nations which have performed the greatest warlike achievements knew no other discipline than that which I speak of. Among the ancients none were admitted into the armies but freemen and citizens, who differed but little from one another, and were accustomed to treat each other as equals. In this respect it may be said that the armies of antiquity were democratic, although they came out of the bosom of aristocracy; the consequence was that in those armies a sort of fraternal familiarity prevailed between the officers and the men. Plutarch's lives of great commanders furnish convincing instances of the fact: the soldiers were in the constant habit of freely addressing their general, and the general listened to and answered whatever the soldiers had to say: they were kept in order by language and by example, far more than by constraint or punishment; the general was as much their companion as their chief. I know not whether the soldiers of Greece and Rome ever carried the minutiæ of military discipline to the same degree of perfection as the Russians have done; but this did not prevent Alexander from conquering Asia—and Rome, the world.

When the principle of equality is in growth, not only among a single nation, but among several neighbouring nations at the same time, as is now the case in Europe, the inhabitants of these different countries, notwithstanding the dissimilarity of language, of customs, and of laws, nevertheless resemble each other in their equal dread of war and their common love of peace.[4] It is in vain that ambition or anger puts arms in the hands of princes; they are appeased in spite of themselves by a species of general apathy, and good-will, which makes the sword drop from their grasp, and wars become more rare. As the spread of equality, taking place in several countries at once, simultaneously impels their various inhabitants to follow manufactures and commerce, not only do their tastes grow alike, but their interests are so mixed and entangled with one another that no nation can inflict evils on other nations without those evils falling back upon itself; and all nations ultimately regard war as a calamity, almost as severe to the conqueror as to the conquered. Thus, on the one hand, it is extremely difficult in democratic ages to draw nations into hostilities; but, on the other hand, it is almost impossible that any two of them should go to war without embroiling the rest. The interests of all are so interlaced, their opinions and their wants so much alike, that none can remain quiet when the others stir. Wars, therefore, become more rare, but when they break out they spread over a larger field. Neighbouring democratic nations not only become alike in some respects, but they eventually grow to resemble each other in almost all.[5] This similitude of nations has consequences of great importance in relation to war.

If I inquire why it is that the Helvetic Confederacy made the greatest and most powerful nations of Europe tremble in the fifteenth century, while at the present day the power of that country is exactly proportioned to its population, I perceive that the Swiss are become like all the surrounding communities, and those surrounding communities like the Swiss: so that as numerical strength now forms the only difference between them, victory necessarily attends the largest army. Thus one of the consequences of the democratic revolution which is going on in Europe is to make numerical strength preponderate on all fields of battle, and to constrain all small nations to incorporate themselves with large States, or at least to adopt the policy of the latter. As numbers are the determining cause of victory, each people ought, of course, to strive by all the means in its power to bring the greatest possible number of men into the field. When it was possible to enlist a kind of troops superior to all others, such as the Swiss infantry or the French horse of the sixteenth century, it was not thought necessary to raise very large armies; but the case is altered when one soldier is as efficient as another.

The same cause which begets this new want also supplies means of satisfying it; for, as I have already observed, when men are all alike, they are all weak, and the supreme power of the State is naturally much stronger among democratic nations than elsewhere. Hence, while these nations are desirous of enrolling the whole male population in the ranks of the army, they have the power of effecting this object: the consequence is, that in democratic ages armies seem to grow larger in proportion as the love of war declines. In the same ages, too, the manner of carrying on war is likewise altered by the same causes. Machiavelli observes in " The Prince " that " it is much more difficult to subdue a people which has a prince and his barons for its leaders than a nation which is commanded by a prince and his slaves." To avoid offence, let us read public functionaries for slaves, and this important truth will be strictly applicable to our own time.

A great aristocratic people can not either conquer its neighbours, or be conquered by them, without great difficulty. It can not conquer them, because all its forces can never be collected and held together for a considerable period: it can not be conquered, because an enemy meets at every step small centres of resistance by which invasion is arrested. War against an aristocracy may be compared to war in a mountainous country; the defeated party has constant opportunities of rallying its forces to make a stand in a new position. Exactly the reverse occurs among democratic nations: they easily bring their whole disposable force into the field, and when the nation is wealthy and populous it soon becomes victorious; but if ever it is conquered, and its territory invaded, it has few resources at command; and if the enemy takes the capital, the nation is lost. This may very well be explained: as each member of the community is individually isolated and extremely powerless, no one of the whole body can either defend himself or present a rallying-point to others. Nothing is strong in a democratic country except the State; as the military strength of the State is destroyed by the destruction of the army, and its civil power paralyzed by the capture of the chief city, all that remains is only a multitude without strength or government, unable to resist the organized power by which it is assailed. I am aware that this danger may be lessened by the creation of provincial liberties, and consequently of provincial powers, but this remedy will always be insufficient. For after such a catastrophe not only is the population unable to carry on hostilities, but it may be apprehended that they will not be inclined to attempt it.

In accordance with the law of nations adopted in civilized countries, the object of wars is not to seize the property of private individuals, but simply to get possession of political power. The destruction of private property is only occasionally resorted to for the purpose of attaining the latter object. When an aristocratic country is invaded after the defeat of its army, the nobles, although they are at the same time the wealthiest members of the community, will continue to defend themselves individually rather than submit; for if the conqueror remained master of the country, he would deprive them of their political power, to which they cling even more closely than to their property. They therefore prefer fighting to subjection, which is to them the greatest of all misfortunes; and they readily carry the people along with them because the people has long been used to follow and obey them, and besides has but little to risk in the war. Among a nation in which equality of conditions prevails, each citizen, on the contrary, has but a slender share of political power, and often has no share at all; on the other hand, all are independent, and all have something to lose; so that they are much less afraid of being conquered, and much more afraid of war, than an aristocratic people. It will always be extremely difficult to decide a democratic population to take up arms, when hostilities have reached its own territory. Hence the necessity of giving to such a people the rights and the political character which may impart to every citizen some of those interests that cause the nobles to act for the public welfare in aristocratic countries.

It should never be forgotten by the princes and other leaders of democratic nations that nothing but the passion and the habit of freedom can maintain an advantageous contest with the passion and the habit of physical well-being. I can conceive nothing better prepared for subjection, in case of defeat, than a democratic people without free institutions.

Formerly it was customary to take the field with a small body of troops, to fight in small engagements, and to make long regular sieges: modern tactics consist in fighting decisive battles, and, as soon as a line of march is open before the army, in rushing upon the capital city, in order to terminate the war at a single blow. Napoleon, it is said, was the inventor of this new system; but the invention of such a system did not depend on any individual man, whoever he might be. The mode in which Napoleon carried on war was suggested to him by the state of society in his time; that mode was successful, because it was eminently adapted to that state of society, and because he was the first to employ it. Napoleon was the first commander who marched at the head of an army from capital to capital, but the road was opened for him by the ruin of feudal society. It may fairly be believed that, if that extraordinary man had been born three hundred years ago, he would not have derived the same results from his method of warfare, or, rather, that he would have had a different method.

I shall add but a few words on civil wars, for fear of exhausting the patience of the reader. Most of the remarks which I have made respecting foreign wars are applicable a fortiori to civil wars. Men living in democracies are not naturally prone to the military character; they sometimes assume it, when they have been dragged by compulsion to the field; but to rise in a body and voluntarily to expose themselves to the horrors of war, and especially of civil war, is a course which the men of democracies

are not apt to adopt. None but the most adventurous
members of the community consent to run into such risks;
the bulk of the population remains motionless. But even
if the population were inclined to act, considerable obstacles would stand in their way; for they can resort to no
old and well-established influence which they are willing
to obey—no well-known leaders to rally the discontented,
as well as to discipline and to lead them—no political powers subordinate to the supreme power of the nation, which
afford an effectual support to the resistance directed
against the government. In democratic countries the
moral power of the majority is immense, and the physical
resources which it has at its command are out of all proportion to the physical resources which may be combined
against it. Therefore the party which occupies the seat
of the majority, which speaks in its name and wields its
power, triumphs instantaneously and irresistibly over all
private resistance; it does not even give such opposition
time to exist, but nips it in the bud. Those who in such
nations seek to effect a revolution by force of arms have
no other resource than suddenly to seize upon the whole
engine of government as it stands, which can better be
done by a single blow than by a war; for as soon as there
is a regular war, the party which represents the State is
always certain to conquer. The only case in which a civil
war could arise is, if the army should divide itself into two
factions, the one raising the standard of rebellion, the other
remaining true to its allegiance. An army constitutes a
small community, very closely united together, endowed
with great powers of vitality, and able to supply its own
wants for some time. Such a war might be bloody, but
it could not be long; for either the rebellious army would
gain over the government by the sole display of its resources, or by its first victory, and then the war would be
over; or the struggle would take place, and then that
portion of the army which should not be supported by the
organized powers of the State would speedily either dis-
band itself or be destroyed. It may, therefore, be admitted

as a general truth, that in ages of equality civil wars will become much less frequent and less protracted.[6]

NOTES

[1] If I inquire what state of society is most favourable to the great revolutions of the mind, I find that it occurs somewhere between the complete equality of the whole community and the absolute separation of ranks. Under a system of castes generations succeed each other without altering men's positions: some have nothing more, others nothing better, to hope for. The imagination slumbers amid this universal silence and stillness, and the very idea of change fades from the human mind. When ranks have been abolished and social conditions are almost equalized, all men are in ceaseless excitement, but each of them stands alone, independent and weak. This latter state of things is excessively different from the former one; yet it has one point of analogy—great revolutions of the human mind seldom occur in it. But between these two extremes of the history of nations is an intermediate period—a period as glorious as it is agitated —when the conditions of men are not sufficiently settled for the mind to be lulled in torpor, when they are sufficiently unequal for men to exercise a vast power on the minds of one another, and when some few may modify the convictions of all. It is at such times that great reformers start up, and new opinions suddenly change the face of the world.

[2] The position of officers is indeed much more secure among democratic nations than elsewhere; the lower the personal standing of the man, the greater is the comparative importance of his military grade, and the more just and necessary is it that the enjoyment of that rank should be secured by the laws.

[3] See Appendix, V.

[4] It is scarcely necessary for me to observe that the dread of war displayed by the nations of Europe is not solely attributable to the progress made by the principle of equality among them; independently of this permanent cause several other accidental causes of great weight might be pointed out, and I may mention before all the rest the extreme lassitude which the wars of the Revolution and the Empire have left behind them.

[5] This is not only because these nations have the same social condition, but it arises from the very nature of that social condition which leads men to imitate and identify themselves with each other. When the members of a community are divided into castes and classes, they not only differ from one another, but they have no taste and no desire to be alike; on the contrary, every one endeavours, more and more, to keep his own opinions undisturbed, to retain his own peculiar habits, and to remain himself. The characteristics of individuals are very strongly marked. When the state of society among a people is democratic—that is to say, when there are no longer any castes or classes in the community, and all its members are nearly equal in education and in property—the human mind follows the opposite direction. Men are much alike, and they are annoyed, as it were, by any deviation from that likeness: far from seeking to preserve their own distinguishing singularities, they

endeavour to shake them off, in order to identify themselves with the general mass of the people, which is the sole representative of right and of might in their eyes. The characteristics of individuals are nearly obliterated. In the ages of aristocracy even those who are naturally alike strive to create imaginary differences between themselves : in the ages of democracy even those who are not alike seek only to become so, and to copy each other—so strongly is the mind of every man always carried away by the general impulse of mankind. Something of the same kind may be observed between nations : two nations having the same aristocratic social condition, might remain thoroughly distinct and extremely different, because the spirit of aristocracy is to retain strong individual characteristics ; but if two neighbouring nations have the same democratic social condition, they can not fail to adopt similar opinions and manners, because the spirit of democracy tends to assimilate men to each other.

[6] It should be borne in mind that I speak here of sovereign and independent democratic nations, not of confederate democracies ; in confederacies, as the preponderating power always resides, in spite of all political fictions, in the state governments, and not in the Federal Government, civil wars are in fact nothing but foreign wars in disguise.

CHAPTER XXXV

INFLUENCE OF DEMOCRATIC OPINIONS AND SENTIMENTS UPON POLITICAL SOCIETY

That equality naturally gives men a taste for free institutions—The notions of democratic nations on government are naturally favourable to the concentration of power—The sentiments of democratic nations accord with their opinions in leading them to concentrate political power—Certain peculiar and accidental causes which either lead a people to complete centralization of government, or which divert them from it—Among the European nations of our time the power of governments is increasing, although the persons who govern are less stable—What sort of despotism democratic nations have to fear—General survey of the subject.

I SHOULD imperfectly fulfil the purpose of this book if, after having shown what opinions and sentiments are suggested by the principle of equality, I did not point out, ere I conclude, the general influence which these same opinions and sentiments may exercise upon the government of human societies. To succeed in this object I shall frequently have to retrace my steps; but I trust the reader will not refuse to follow me through paths already known to him, which may lead to some new truth.

The principle of equality, which makes men independent of each other, gives them a habit and a taste for following, in their private actions, no other guide but their own will. This complete independence, which they constantly enjoy toward their equals and in the intercourse of private life, tends to make them look upon all authority with a jealous eye, and speedily suggests to them the notion and the love of political freedom. Men living at such times have a natural bias to free institutions. Take any one of them at a venture, and search if you can his most deep-seated instincts; you will find that of all governments he will soonest conceive and most highly value that government whose head he has himself elected, and whose administration he may control. Of all the political effects produced by the equality of conditions, this love of independence is the first to strike the observing, and to alarm the timid; nor can it be said that their alarm is wholly misplaced, for anarchy has a more formidable aspect in democratic countries than elsewhere. As the citizens have no direct influence on each other, as soon as the supreme power of the nation fails, which kept them all in their several stations, it would seem that disorder must instantly reach its utmost pitch, and that, every man drawing aside in a different direction, the fabric of society must at once crumble away.

I am, however, persuaded that anarchy is not the principal evil that democratic ages have to fear, but the least. For the principle of equality begets two tendencies: the one leads men straight to independence, and may suddenly drive them into anarchy; the other conducts them by a longer, more secret, but more certain road, to servitude. Nations readily discern the former tendency, and are prepared to resist it; they are led away by the latter, without perceiving its drift; hence it is peculiarly important to point it out. For myself, I am so far from urging as a reproach to the principle of equality that it renders men untractable, that this very circumstance principally calls forth my approbation. I admire to see how it deposits in the mind and heart of man the dim conception and instinctive love of political independence, thus preparing the remedy for the evil which it engenders; it is on this very account that I am attached to it.

The notion of secondary powers, placed between the sovereign and his subjects, occurred naturally to the imagination of aristocratic nations, because those communities contained individuals or families raised above the common level, and apparently destined to command by their birth, their education, and their wealth. This same

notion is naturally wanting in the minds of men in democratic ages, for converse reasons: it can only be introduced artificially, it can only be kept there with difficulty;
whereas they conceive, as it were, without thinking upon
the subject, the notion of a sole and central power which
governs the whole community by its direct influence.
Moreover, in politics, as well as in philosophy and in religion, the intellect of democratic nations is peculiarly open
to simple and general notions. Complicated systems are
repugnant to it, and its favourite conception is that of a
great nation composed of citizens all resembling the same
pattern, and all governed by a single power.

The very next notion to that of a sole and central
power, which presents itself to the minds of men in the
ages of equality, is the notion of uniformity of legislation.
As every man sees that he differs but little from those
about him, he can not understand why a rule which is
applicable to one man should not be equally applicable to
all others. Hence the slightest privileges are repugnant
to his reason; the faintest dissimilarities in the political
institutions of the same people offend him, and uniformity
of legislation appears to him to be the first condition of
good government. I find, on the contrary, that this same
notion of a uniform rule, equally binding on all the members of the community, was almost unknown to the human
mind in aristocratic ages; it was either never entertained,
or it was rejected. These contrary tendencies of opinion
ultimately turn on either side to such blind instincts and
such ungovernable habits that they still direct the actions
of men, in spite of particular exceptions. Notwithstanding
the immense variety of conditions in the Middle Ages, a
certain number of persons existed at that period in precisely similar circumstances; but this did not prevent the
laws then in force from assigning to each of them distinct
duties and different rights. On the contrary, at the present
time all the powers of government are exerted to impose
the same customs and the same laws on populations which
have as yet but few points of resemblance. As the condi-

tions of men become equal among a people, individuals
seem of less importance, and society of greater dimensions; or rather, every citizen, being assimilated to all the
rest, is lost in the crowd, and nothing stands conspicuous
but the great and imposing image of the people at large.
This naturally gives the men of democratic periods a lofty
opinion of the privileges of society, and a very humble
notion of the rights of individuals; they are ready to admit
that the interests of the former are everything, and those
of the latter nothing. They are willing to acknowledge
that the power which represents the community has far
more information and wisdom than any of the members
of that community; and that it is the duty, as well as the
right, of that power to guide as well as govern each private citizen.

If we closely scrutinize our contemporaries, and penetrate to the root of their political opinions, we shall detect
some of the notions which I have just pointed out, and
we shall perhaps be surprised to find so much accordance
between men who are so often at variance. The Americans hold that in every State the supreme power ought
to emanate from the people; but when once that power
is constituted, they can conceive, as it were, no limits to
it, and they are ready to admit that it has the right to do
whatever it pleases. They have not the slightest notion
of peculiar privileges granted to cities, families, or persons: their minds appear never to have foreseen that it
might be possible not to apply with strict uniformity the
same laws to every part, and to all the inhabitants. These
same opinions are more and more diffused in Europe; they
even insinuate themselves among those nations which most
vehemently reject the principle of the sovereignty of the
people. Such nations assign a different origin to the supreme power, but they ascribe to that power the same characteristics. Among them all, the idea of intermediate
powers is weakened and obliterated: the idea of rights
inherent in certain individuals is rapidly disappearing from
the minds of men; the idea of the omnipotence and sole

authority of society at large rises to fill its place. These ideas take root and spread in proportion as social conditions become more equal, and men more alike; they are engendered by equality, and in turn they hasten the progress of equality.

In France, where the revolution of which I am speaking has gone further than in any other European country, these opinions have got complete hold of the public mind. If we listen attentively to the language of the various parties in France, we shall find that there is not one which has not adopted them. Most of these parties censure the conduct of the government, but they all hold that the government ought perpetually to act and interfere in everything that is done. Even those which are most at variance are nevertheless agreed upon this head. The unity, the ubiquity, the omnipotence of the supreme power, and the uniformity of its rules, constitute the principal characteristics of all the political systems which have been put forward in our age. They recur even in the wildest visions of political regeneration: the human mind pursues them in its dreams. If these notions spontaneously arise in the minds of private individuals, they suggest themselves still more forcibly to the minds of princes. While the ancient fabric of European society is altered and dissolved, sovereigns acquire new conceptions of their opportunities and their duties; they learn for the first time that the central power which they represent may and ought to administer by its own agency, and on a uniform plan, all the concerns of the whole community. This opinion, which, I will venture to say, was never conceived before our time by the monarchs of Europe, now sinks deeply into the minds of kings, and abides there amid all the agitation of more unsettled thoughts.

Our contemporaries are therefore much less divided than is commonly supposed; they are constantly disputing as to the hands in which supremacy is to be vested, but they readily agree upon the duties and the rights of that supremacy. The notion they all form of government is that of a sole, simple, providential, and creative power. All secondary opinions in politics are unsettled; this one remains fixed, invariable, and consistent. It is adopted by statesmen and political philosophers; it is eagerly laid hold of by the multitude; those who govern and those who are governed agree to pursue it with equal ardour: it is the foremost notion of their minds, it seems connatural with their feelings. It originates, therefore, in no caprice of the human intellect, but it is a necessary condition of the present state of mankind.

If it be true that, in ages of equality, men readily adopt the notion of a great central power, it can not be doubted, on the other hand, that their habits and sentiments pre-dispose them to recognise such a power and to give it their support. This may be demonstrated in a few words, as the greater part of the reasons, to which the fact may be attributed, have been previously stated.[1] As the men who inhabit democratic countries have no superiors, no inferiors, and no habitual or necessary partners in their undertakings, they readily fall back upon themselves and consider themselves as beings apart. I had occasion to point this out at considerable length in treating of indi-vidualism. Hence such men can never, without an effort, tear themselves from their private affairs to engage in pub-lic business; their natural bias leads them to abandon the latter to the sole visible and permanent representative of the interests of the community—that is to say, to the State. Not only are they naturally wanting in a taste for public business, but they have frequently no time to attend to it. Private life is so busy in democratic periods, so excited, so full of wishes and of work, that hardly any energy or leisure remains to each individual for public life. I am the last man to contend that these propensities are uncon-querable, since my chief object in writing this book has been to combat them. I only maintain that at the present day a secret power is fostering them in the human heart, and that if they are not checked they will wholly over-grow it.

I have also had occasion to show how the increasing love of well-being, and the fluctuating character of property, cause democratic nations to dread all violent disturbance. The love of public tranquility is frequently the only passion which these nations retain, and it becomes more active and powerful among them in proportion as all other passions droop and die. This naturally disposes the members of the community constantly to give or to surrender additional rights to the central power, which alone seems to be interested in defending them by the same means that it uses to defend itself. As in ages of equality no man is compelled to lend his assistance to his fellow-men, and none has any right to expect much support from them, every one is at once independent and powerless. These two conditions, which must never be either separately considered or confounded together, inspire the citizen of a democratic country with very contrary propensities. His independence fills him with self-reliance and pride among his equals; his debility makes him feel from time to time the want of some outward assistance, which he can not expect from any of them, because they are all impotent and unsympathizing. In this predicament he naturally turns his eyes to that imposing power which alone rises above the level of universal depression. Of that power his wants and especially his desires continually remind him, until he ultimately views it as the sole and necessary support of his own weakness.[2] This may more completely explain what frequently takes place in democratic countries, where the very men who are so impatient of superiors patiently submit to a master, exhibiting at once their pride and their servility.

The hatred which men bear to privilege increases in proportion as privileges become more scarce and less considerable, so that democratic passions would seem to burn most fiercely at the very time when they have least fuel. I have already given the reason of this phenomenon. When all conditions are unequal, no inequality is so great as to offend the eye; whereas the slightest dissimilarity is odious in the midst of general uniformity: the more complete is this uniformity, the more insupportable does the sight of such a difference become. Hence it is natural that the love of equality should constantly increase together with equality itself, and that it should grow by what it feeds upon. This never-dying, ever-kindling hatred, which sets a democratic people against the smallest privileges, is peculiarly favourable to the gradual concentration of all political rights in the hands of the representative of the State alone. The sovereign, being necessarily and incontestably above all the citizens, excites not their envy, and each of them thinks that he strips his equals of the prerogative which he concedes to the crown. The man of a democratic age is extremely reluctant to obey his neighbour who is his equal; he refuses to acknowledge in such a person ability superior to his own; he mistrusts his justice, and is jealous of his power; he fears and he contemns him; and he loves continually to remind him of the common dependence in which both of them stand to the same master. Every central power which follows its natural tendencies courts and encourages the principle of equality; for equality singularly facilitates, extends, and secures the influence of a central power.

In like manner it may be said that every central government worships uniformity: uniformity relieves it from inquiry into an infinite number of small details which must be attended to if rules were to be adapted to men, instead of indiscriminately subjecting men to rules: thus the government likes what the citizens like, and naturally hates what they hate. These common sentiments, which, in democratic nations, constantly unite the sovereign and every member of the community in one and the same conviction, establish a secret and lasting sympathy between them. The faults of the government are pardoned for the sake of its tastes; public confidence is only reluctantly withdrawn in the midst even of its excesses and its errors, and it is restored at the first call. Democratic nations often hate those in whose hands the cen-

52

tral power is vested; but they always love that power itself.

Thus by two separate paths I have reached the same conclusion. I have shown that the principle of equality suggests to men the notion of a sole, uniform, and strong government: I have now shown that the principle of equality imparts to them a taste for it. To governments of this kind the nations of our age are therefore tending. They are drawn thither by the natural inclination of mind and heart; and in order to reach that result, it is enough that they do not check themselves in their course. I am of opinion that, in the democratic ages which are opening upon us, individual independence and local liberties will ever be the produce of artificial contrivance; that centralization will be the natural form of government.[3]

If all democratic nations are instinctively led to the centralization of government, they tend to this result in an unequal manner. This depends on the particular circumstances which may promote or prevent the natural consequences of that state of society—circumstances which are exceedingly numerous; but I shall only advert to a few of them. Among men who have lived free long before they became equal, the tendencies derived from free institutions combat, to a certain extent, the propensities superinduced by the principle of equality; and although the central power may increase its privileges among such a people, the private members of such a community will never entirely forfeit their independence. But when the equality of conditions grows up among a people which has never known, or has long ceased to know, what freedom is (and such is the case upon the continent of Europe), as the former habits of the nation are suddenly combined, by some sort of natural attraction, with the novel habits and principles engendered by the state of society, all powers seem spontaneously to rush to the centre. These powers accumulate there with astonishing rapidity, and the State instantly attains the utmost limits of its strength, while private persons allow themselves to sink as suddenly to the lowest degree of weakness.

The English who emigrated three hundred years ago to found a democratic commonwealth on the shores of the New World, had all learned to take a part in public affairs in their mother-country; they were conversant with trial by jury; they were accustomed to liberty of speech and of the press—to personal freedom, to the notion of rights and the practice of asserting them. They carried with them to America these free institutions and manly customs, and these institutions preserved them against the encroachments of the State. Thus among the Americans it is freedom which is old—equality is of comparatively modern date. The reverse is occurring in Europe, where equality, introduced by absolute power and under the rule of kings, was already infused into the habits of nations long before freedom had entered into their conceptions.

I have said that among democratic nations the notion of government naturally presents itself to the mind under the form of a sole and central power, and that the notion of intermediate powers is not familiar to them. This is peculiarly applicable to the democratic nations which have witnessed the triumph of the principle of equality by means of a violent revolution. As the classes which managed local affairs have been suddenly swept away by the storm, and as the confused mass which remains has as yet neither the organization nor the habits which fit it to assume the administration of these same affairs, the State alone seems capable of taking upon itself all the details of government, and centralization becomes, as it were, the unavoidable state of the country. Napoleon deserves neither praise nor censure for having centred in his own hands almost all the administrative power of France; for, after the abrupt disappearance of the nobility and the higher rank of the middle classes, these powers devolved on him of course: it would have been almost as difficult for him to reject as to assume them. But no necessity of this kind has ever been felt by the Americans, who, having passed through no revolution, and having governed themselves from the first, never had to call upon the State to act for a time as their guardian. Thus the progress of centralization among a democratic people depends not only on the progress of equality, but on the manner in which this equality has been established.

At the commencement of a great democratic revolution, when hostilities have but just broken out between the different classes of society, the people endeavours to centralize the public administration in the hands of the government, in order to wrest the management of local affairs from the aristocracy. Toward the close of such a revolution, on the contrary, it is usually the conquered aristocracy that endeavours to make over the management of all affairs to the State, because such an aristocracy dreads the tyranny of a people which has become its equal, and not infrequently its master. Thus it is not always the same class of the community which strives to increase the prerogative of the government; but as long as the democratic revolution lasts there is always one class in the nation, powerful in numbers or in wealth, which is induced, by peculiar passions or interests, to centralize the public administration, independently of that hatred of being governed by one's neighbour, which is a general and permanent feeling among democratic nations. It may be remarked that at the present day the lower orders in England are striving with all their might to destroy local independence, and to transfer the administration from all points of the circumference to the centre; whereas the higher classes are endeavouring to retain this administration within its ancient boundaries. I venture to predict that a time will come when the very reverse will happen.

These observations explain why the supreme power is always stronger, and private individuals weaker, among a democratic people which has passed through a long and arduous struggle to reach a state of equality than among a democratic community in which the citizens have been equal from the first. The example of the Americans completely demonstrates the fact. The inhabitants of the United States were never divided by any privileges; they have never known the mutual relation of master and inferior, and as they neither dread nor hate each other, they have never known the necessity of calling in the supreme power to manage their affairs. The lot of the Americans is singular: they have derived from the aristocracy of England the notion of private rights and the taste for local freedom; and they have been able to retain both the one and the other, because they have had no aristocracy to combat.

If at all times education enables men to defend their independence, this is most especially true in democratic ages. When all men are alike, it is easy to found a sole and all-powerful government, by the aid of mere instinct. But men require much intelligence, knowledge, and art to organize and to maintain secondary powers under similar circumstances, and to create amid the independence and individual weakness of the citizens such free associations as may be in a condition to struggle against tyranny without destroying public order.

Hence the concentration of power and the subjection of individuals will increase among democratic nations, not only in the same proportion as their equality, but in the same proportion as their ignorance. It is true, that in ages of imperfect civilization the government is frequently as wanting in the knowledge required to impose a despotism upon the people as the people are wanting in the knowledge required to shake it off; but the effect is not the same on both sides. However rude a democratic people may be, the central power which rules it is never completely devoid of cultivation, because it readily draws to its own uses what little cultivation is to be found in the country, and, if necessary, may seek assistance elsewhere. Hence, among a nation which is ignorant as well as democratic, an amazing difference can not fail speedily to arise between the intellectual capacity of the ruler and that of each of his subjects. This completes the easy concentration of all power in his hands: the administrative function of the State is perpetually extended, because the State alone is competent to administer the affairs of the country. Aristocratic nations, however unenlightened they may be, never afford the same spectacle, because in them instruction is nearly equally diffused between the monarch and the leading members of the community.

The Pasha, who now rules in Egypt, found the population of that country composed of men exceedingly ignorant and equal, and he has borrowed the science and ability of Europe to govern that people. As the personal attainments of the sovereign are thus combined with the ignorance and democratic weakness of his subjects, the utmost centralization has been established without impediment, and the Pasha has made the country his manufactory, and the inhabitants his workmen.

I think that extreme centralization of government ultimately enervates society, and thus after a length of time weakens the government itself; but I do not deny that a centralized social power may be able to execute great undertakings with facility in a given time and on a particular point. This is more especially true of war, in which success depends much more on the means of transferring all the resources of a nation to one single point, than on the extent of those resources. Hence it is chiefly in war that nations desire and frequently require to increase the powers of the central government. All men of military genius are fond of centralization, which increases their strength; and all men of centralizing genius are fond of war, which compels nations to combine all their powers in the hands of the government. Thus the democratic tendency which leads men unceasingly to multiply the privileges of the State, and to circumscribe the rights of private persons, is much more rapid and constant among those democratic nations which are exposed by their position to great and frequent wars, than among all others.

I have shown how the dread of disturbance and the love of well-being insensibly lead democratic nations to increase the functions of central government, as the only power which appears to be intrinsically sufficiently strong, enlightened, and secure, to protect them from anarchy. I would now add that all the particular circumstances which tend to make the state of a democratic community agitated and precarious, enhance this general propensity, and lead private persons more and more to sacrifice their rights to their tranquility. A people is therefore never so disposed to increase the functions of central government as at the close of a long and bloody revolution, which, after having wrested property from the hands of its former possessors, has shaken all belief, and filled the nation with fierce hatreds, conflicting interests, and contending factions. The love of public tranquility becomes at such times an indiscriminating passion, and the members of the community are apt to conceive a most inordinate devotion to order.

I have already examined several of the incidents which may concur to promote the centralization of power, but the principal cause still remains to be noticed. The foremost of the incidental causes which may draw the management of all affairs into the hands of the ruler in democratic countries is the origin of that ruler himself, and his own propensities. Men who live in the ages of equality are naturally fond of central power, and are willing to extend its privileges; but if it happens that this same power faithfully represents their own interests, and exactly copies their own inclinations, the confidence they place in it knows no bounds, and they think that whatever they bestow upon it is bestowed upon themselves.

The attraction of administrative powers to the centre will always be less easy and less rapid under the reign of kings who are still in some way connected with the old aristocratic order, than under new princes, the children of their own achievements, whose birth, prejudices, propensities, and habits appear to bind them indissolubly to the cause of equality. I do not mean that princes of aristocratic origin who live in democratic ages do not attempt to centralize; I believe they apply themselves to that object as diligently as any others. For them, the sole advantages of equality lie in that direction; but their opportunities are less great, because the community, instead of volunteering compliance with their desires, frequently obeys them with reluctance. In democratic communities the rule is that centralization must increase in proportion as the sovereign is less aristocratic. When an ancient race of kings stands at the head of an aristocracy, as the natural prejudices of the sovereign perfectly accord with the natural prejudices of the nobility, the vices inherent in aristocratic communities have a free course, and meet with no corrective. The reverse is the case when the scion of a feudal stock is placed at the head of a democratic people. The sovereign is constantly led, by his education, his habits, and his associations, to adopt sentiments suggested by the inequality of conditions, and the people tend as constantly, by their social condition, to those manners which are engendered by equality. At such times it often happens that the citizens seek to control the central power far less as a tyrannical than as an aristocratical power, and that they persist in the firm defence of their independence, not only because they would remain free, but especially because they are determined to remain equal. A revolution which overthrows an ancient regal family, in order to place men of more recent growth at the head of a democratic people, may temporarily weaken the central power; but however anarchical such a revolution may appear at first, we need not hesitate to predict that its final and certain consequence will be to extend and to secure the prerogatives of that power. The foremost or, indeed, the sole condition which is required in order to succeed in centralizing the supreme power in a democratic community, is to love equality, or to get men to believe you love it. Thus the science of despotism, which was once so complex, is simplified, and reduced as it were to a single principle.

On reflecting upon what has already been said, the reader will be startled and alarmed to find that in Europe everything seems to conduce to the indefinite extension of the prerogatives of government, and to render all that enjoyed the rights of private independence more weak, more subordinate, and more precarious. The democratic nations of Europe have all the general and permanent tendencies which urge the Americans to the centralization of government, and they are, moreover, exposed to a number of secondary and incidental causes with which the Americans are unacquainted. It would seem as if every step they make toward equality brings them nearer to despotism. And, indeed, if we do but cast our looks around, we shall be convinced that such is the fact. During the aristocratic ages which preceded the present time, the sovereigns of Europe had been deprived of, or had relinquished, many of the rights inherent in their power. Not a hundred years ago, among the greater part of European nations, numerous private persons and corporations were sufficiently independent to administer justice, to raise and maintain troops, to levy taxes, and frequently even to make or interpret the law. The State has everywhere resumed to itself alone these natural attributes of sovereign power; in all matters of government the State tolerates no intermediate agent between itself and the people, and in general business it directs the people by its own immediate influence. I am far from blaming this concentration of power, I simply point it out.

At the same period a great number of secondary powers existed in Europe, which represented local interests and administered local affairs. Most of these local authorities have already disappeared; all are speedily tending to disappear, or to fall into the most complete dependence. From one end of Europe to the other the privileges of the nobility, the liberties of cities, and the powers of provincial bodies, are either destroyed or upon the verge of destruction. Europe has endured, in the course of the last half century, many revolutions and counter-revolutions which have agitated it in opposite directions: but all these perturbations resemble each other in one respect—they have all shaken or destroyed the secondary powers of government. The local privileges which the French did not abolish in the countries they conquered, have finally succumbed to the policy of the princes who conquered the French. Those princes rejected all the innovations of the French Revolution except centralization: that is the only principle they consented to receive from such a source. My object is to remark, that all these various rights, which have been successively wrested, in our time, from classes, corporations, and individuals, have not served to raise new secondary powers on a more democratic basis, but have uniformly been concentrated in the hands of the sovereign. Everywhere the State acquires more and more direct control over the humblest members of the community, and a more exclusive power of governing each of them in his smallest concerns.[4] Almost all the charitable establishments of Europe were formerly in the hands of private persons or of corporations; they are now almost all dependent on the supreme government, and in many countries are actually administered by that power. The State almost exclusively undertakes to supply bread to the hungry, assistance and shelter to the sick, work to the idle, and to act as the sole reliever of all kinds of misery. Education, as well as charity, is become in most countries at the present day a national concern. The State receives, and often takes, the child from the arms of the mother, to hand it over to official agents: the State undertakes to train the heart and to instruct the mind of each generation. Uniformity prevails in the courses of public instruction as in everything else; diversity, as well as freedom, are disappearing day by day. Nor do I hesitate to affirm that among almost all the Christian nations of our days, Catholic as well as Protestant, religion is in danger of falling into the hands of the government. Not that rulers are over-jealous of the right of settling points of doctrine, but they get more and more hold upon the will of those by whom doctrines are expounded; they deprive the clergy of their property, and pay them by salaries;

they divert to their own use the influence of the priesthood, they make them their own ministers—often their own servants—and by this alliance with religion they reach the inner depths of the soul of man.[5]

But this is as yet only one side of the picture. The authority of government has not only spread, as we have just seen, throughout the sphere of all existing powers, till that sphere can no longer contain it, but it goes further, and invades the domain heretofore reserved to private independence. A multitude of actions, which were formerly entirely beyond the control of the public administration, have been subjected to that control in our time, and the number of them is constantly increasing. Among aristocratic nations the supreme government usually contented itself with managing and superintending the community in whatever directly and ostensibly concerned the national honour; but in all other respects the people were left to work out their own free will. Among these nations the government often seemed to forget that there is a point at which the faults and the sufferings of private persons involve the general prosperity, and that to prevent the ruin of a private individual must sometimes be a matter of public importance. The democratic nations of our time lean to the opposite extreme. It is evident that most of our rulers will not content themselves with governing the people collectively: it would seem as if they thought themselves responsible for the actions and private condition of their subjects—as if they had undertaken to guide and to instruct each of them in the various incidents of life, and to secure their happiness quite independently of their own consent. On the other hand, private individuals grow more and more apt to look upon the supreme power in the same light; they invoke its assistance in all their necessities, and they fix their eyes upon the administration as their mentor or their guide.

I assert that there is no country in Europe in which the public administration has not become not only more centralized, but more inquisitive and more minute: it everywhere interferes in private concerns more than it did; it regulates more undertakings, and undertakings of a lesser kind; and it gains a firmer footing every day about, above, and around all private persons, to assist, to advise, and to coerce them. Formerly a sovereign lived upon the income of his lands, or the revenue of his taxes; this is no longer the case now that his wants have increased as well as his power. Under the same circumstances which formerly compelled a prince to put on a new tax, he now has recourse to a loan. Thus the State gradually becomes the debtor of most of the wealthier members of the community, and centralizes the largest amounts of capital in its own hands. Small capital is drawn into its keeping by another method. As men are intermingled and conditions become more equal, the poor have more resources, more education, and more desires; they conceive the notion of bettering their condition, and this teaches them to save. These savings are daily producing an infinite number of small capitals, the slow and gradual produce of labour, which are always increasing. But the greater part of this money would be unproductive if it remained scattered in the hands of its owners. This circumstance has given rise to a philanthropic institution, which will soon become, if I am not mistaken, one of our most important political institutions. Some charitable persons conceived the notion of collecting the savings of the poor and placing them out at interest. In some countries these benevolent associations are still completely distinct from the State; but in almost all they manifestly tend to identify themselves with the government: and in some of them the government has superseded them, taking upon itself the enormous task of centralizing in one place, and putting out at interest on its own responsibility, the daily savings of many millions of the working classes. Thus the State draws to itself the wealth of the rich by loans, and has the poor man's mite at its disposal in the savings-banks. The wealth of the country is perpetually flowing around the government and passing through its hands; the accumulation increases in the same proportion as the equality of conditions; for in a democratic country the State alone inspires private individuals with confidence, because the State alone appears to be endowed with strength and durability.[6] Thus the sovereign does not confine himself to the management of the public treasury; he interferes in private money-matters; he is the superior, and often the master, of all the members of the community; and, in addition to this, he assumes the part of their steward and paymaster.

The central power not only fulfils of itself the whole of the duties formerly discharged by various authorities —extending those duties, and surpassing those authorities—but it performs them with more alertness, strength, and independence than it displayed before. All the governments of Europe have in our time singularly improved the science of administration: they do more things, and they do everything with more order, more celerity, and at less expense; they seem to be constantly enriched by all the experience of which they have stripped private persons. From day to day the princes of Europe hold their subordinate officers under stricter control, and they invent new methods for guiding them more closely, and inspecting them with less trouble. Not content with managing everything by their agents, they undertake to manage the conduct of their agents in everything; so that the public administration not only depends upon one and the same power, but it is more and more confined to one spot and concentrated in the same hands. The government centralizes its agency while it increases its prerogative—hence a twofold increase of strength.

In examining the ancient constitution of the judicial power, among most European nations, two things strike the mind—the independence of that power, and the extent of its functions. Not only did the courts of justice decide almost all differences between private persons, but in very many cases they acted as arbiters between private persons and the State. I do not here allude to the political and administrative offices which courts of judicature had in some countries usurped, but the judicial office common to them all. In most of the countries of Europe, there were, and there still are, many private rights, connected for the most part with the general right of property, which stood under the protection of the courts of justice, and which the State could not violate without their sanction. It was this semi-political power which mainly distinguished the European courts of judicature from all others; for all nations have had judges, but all have not invested their judges with the same privileges. Upon examining what is now occurring among the democratic nations of Europe which are called free, as well as among the others, it will be observed that new and more dependent courts are everywhere springing up by the side of the old ones, for the express purpose of deciding, by an extraordinary jurisdiction, such litigated matters as may arise between the government and private persons. The elder judicial power retains its independence, but its jurisdiction is narrowed; and there is a growing tendency to reduce it to be exclusively the arbiter between private interests. The number of these special courts of justice is continually increasing, and their functions increase likewise. Thus the government is more and more absolved from the necessity of subjecting its policy and its rights to the sanction of another power. As judges can not be dispensed with, at least the State is to select them, and always to hold them under its control; so that, between the government and private individuals, they place the effigy of justice rather than justice itself. The State is not satisfied with drawing all concerns to itself, but it acquires an ever-increasing power of deciding on them all without restriction and without appeal.[7]

There exists among the modern nations of Europe one great cause, independent of all those which have already been pointed out, which perpetually contributes to extend the agency or to strengthen the prerogative of the supreme power, though it has not been sufficiently attended to: I mean the growth of manufactures, which is fostered by the progress of social equality. Manufactures generally collect a multitude of men on the same spot, among whom new and complex relations spring up. These men are exposed by their calling to great and sudden alternations of plenty and want, during which public tranquility is endangered. It may also happen that these employments sacrifice the health, and even the life, of those who gain by them, or of those who live by them. Thus the manufacturing classes require more regulation, superintendence, and restraint than the other classes of society, and it is natural that the powers of government should increase in the same proportion as those classes.

This is a truth of general application; what follows more especially concerns the nations of Europe. In the centuries which preceded that in which we live, the aristocracy was in possession of the soil, and was competent to defend it: landed property was therefore surrounded by ample securities, and its possessors enjoyed great independence. This gave rise to laws and customs that have been perpetuated, notwithstanding the subdivision of lands and the ruin of the nobility; and, at the present time, land-owners and agriculturists are still those among the community who most easily escape from the control of the supreme power. In these same aristocratic ages, in which all the sources of our history are to be traced, personal property was of small importance, and those who possessed it were despised and weak: the manufacturing class formed an exception in the midst of those aristocratic communities; as it had no certain patronage, it was not outwardly protected, and was often unable to protect itself. Hence a habit sprang up of considering manufacturing property as something of a peculiar nature, not entitled to the same deference, and not worthy of the same securities as property in general; and manufacturers were looked upon as a small class in the bulk of the people, whose independence was of small importance, and who might with propriety be abandoned to the disciplinary passions of princes. On glancing over the codes of the Middle

Ages, one is surprised to see, in those periods of personal independence, with what incessant royal regulations manufactures were hampered, even in their smallest details: on this point centralization was as active and as minute as it can ever be. Since that time a great revolution has taken place in the world; manufacturing property, which was then only in the germ, has spread till it covers Europe: the manufacturing class has been multiplied and enriched by the remnants of all other ranks; it has grown and is still perpetually growing in numbers, in importance, in wealth. Almost all those who do not belong to it are connected with it at least on some one point; after having been an exception in society, it threatens to become the chief, if not the only, class; nevertheless, the notions and political precedents engendered by it of old still cling about it. These notions and these precedents remain unchanged, because they are old, and also because they happen to be in perfect accordance with the new notions and general habits of our contemporaries. Manufacturing property, then, does not extend its rights in the same ratio as its importance. The manufacturing classes do not become less dependent, while they become more numerous; but, on the contrary, it would seem as if despotism lurked within them, and naturally grew with their growth.[8] As a nation becomes more engaged in manufactures, the want of roads, canals, harbours, and other works of a semi-public nature, which facilitate the acquisition of wealth, is more strongly felt; and as a nation becomes more democratic, private individuals are less able, and the State more able, to execute works of such magnitude. I do not hesitate to assert that the manifest tendency of all governments at the present time is to take upon themselves alone the execution of these undertakings; by which means they daily hold in closer dependence the population which they govern.

On the other hand, in proportion as the power of a State increases, and its necessities are augmented, the State consumption of manufactured produce is always growing larger, and these commodities are generally made in the arsenals or establishments of the government. Thus, in every kingdom, the ruler becomes the principal manufacturer; he collects and retains in his service a vast number of engineers, architects, mechanics, and handicraftsmen. Not only is he the principal manufacturer, but he tends more and more to become the chief, or rather the master, of all other manufacturers. As private persons become more powerless by becoming more equal, they can effect nothing in manufactures without combination; but the government naturally seeks to place these combinations under its own control.

It must be admitted that these collective beings, which are called combinations, are stronger and more formidable than a private individual can ever be, and that they have less of the responsibility of their own actions; whence it seems reasonable that they should not be allowed to retain so great an independence of the supreme government as might be conceded to a private individual.

Rulers are the more apt to follow this line of policy, as their own inclinations invite them to it. Among democratic nations it is only by association that the resistance of the people to the government can ever display itself: hence the latter always looks with ill-favour on those associations which are not in its own power; and it is well worthy of remark that, among democratic nations, the people themselves often entertain a secret feeling of fear and jealousy against these very associations, which prevents the citizens from defending the institutions of which they stand so much in need. The power and the duration of these small private bodies, in the midst of the weakness and instability of the whole community, astonish and alarm the people; and the free use which each association makes of its natural powers is almost regarded as a dangerous privilege. All the associations which spring up in our age are, moreover, new corporate powers, whose rights have not been sanctioned by time; they come into existence at a time when the notion of private rights is weak, and when

53

the power of government is unbounded; hence it is not surprising that they lose their freedom at their birth. Among all European nations there are some kinds of associations which can not be formed until the State has examined their by-laws, and authorized their existence. In several others, attempts are made to extend this rule to all associations; the consequences of such a policy, if it were successful, may easily be foreseen. If once the sovereign had a general right of authorizing associations of all kinds upon certain conditions, he would not be long without claiming the right of superintending and managing them, in order to prevent them from departing from the rules laid down by himself. In this manner, the State, after having reduced all who are desirous of forming associations into dependence, would proceed to reduce into the same condition all who belong to associations already formed—that is to say, almost all the men who are now in existence. Governments thus appropriate to themselves, and convert to their own purposes, the greater part of this new power which manufacturing interests have in our time brought into the world. Manufactures govern us—they govern manufactures.

I attach so much importance to all that I have just been saying that I am tormented by the fear of having impaired my meaning in seeking to render it more clear. If the reader thinks that the examples I have adduced to support my observations are insufficient or ill-chosen—if he imagines that I have anywhere exaggerated the encroachments of the supreme power, and, on the other hand, that I have underrated the extent of the sphere which still remains open to the exertions of individual independence, I entreat him to lay down the book for a moment, and to turn his mind to reflect for himself upon the subjects I have attempted to explain. Let him attentively examine what is taking place in France and in other countries—let him inquire of those about him—let him search himself, and I am much mistaken if he does not arrive, without my guidance, and by other paths, at the point to which I have sought to lead him. He will perceive that for the last half century centralization has everywhere been growing up in a thousand different ways. Wars, revolutions, conquests, have served to promote it: all men have laboured to increase it. In the course of the same period, during which men have succeeded each other with singular rapidity at the head of affairs, their notions, interests, and passions have been infinitely diversified; but all have by some means or other sought to centralize. This instinctive centralization has been the only settled point amid the extreme mutability of their lives and of their thoughts.

If the reader, after having investigated these details of human affairs, will seek to survey the wide prospect as a whole, he will be struck by the result. On the one hand, the most settled dynasties shaken or overthrown—the people everywhere escaping by violence from the sway of their laws—abolishing or limiting the authority of their rulers or their princes—the nations, which are not in open revolution, restless at least, and excited—all of them animated by the same spirit of revolt: and, on the other hand, at this very period of anarchy, and among these untractable nations, the incessant increase of the prerogative of the supreme government, becoming more centralized, more adventurous, more absolute, more extensive—the people perpetually falling under the control of the public administration—led insensibly to surrender to it some further portion of their individual independence, till the very men, who from time to time upset a throne and trample on a race of kings, bend more and more obsequiously to the slightest dictate of a clerk. Thus, two contrary revolutions appear in our days to be going on; the one continually weakening the supreme power, the other as continually strengthening it: at no other period in our history has it appeared so weak or so strong.

But upon a more attentive examination of the state of the world, it appears that these two revolutions are intimately connected together, that they originate in the same source, and that after having followed a separate course, they lead men at last to the same result. I may venture once more to repeat what I have already said or implied in several parts of this book: great care must be taken not to confound the principle of equality itself with the revolution which finally establishes that principle in the social condition and the laws of a nation: here lies the reason of almost all the phenomena which occasion our astonishment. All the old political powers of Europe, the greatest as well as the least, were founded in ages of aristocracy, and they more or less represented or defended the principles of inequality and of privilege. To make the novel wants and interests, which the growing principle of equality introduced, preponderate in government, our contemporaries had to overturn or to coerce the established powers. This led them to make revolutions, and breathed into many of them that fierce love of disturbance and independence which all revolutions, whatever be their object, always engender. I do not believe that there is a single country in Europe in which the progress of equality has not been preceded or followed by some violent changes in the state of property and persons; and almost all these changes have been attended with much anarchy and license, because they have been made by the least civilized portion of the nation against that which is most civilized. Hence proceeded the twofold contrary tendencies which I have just pointed out. As long as the democratic revolution was glowing with heat, the men who were bent upon the destruction of old aristocratic powers hostile to that revolution displayed a strong spirit of independence; but as the victory or the principle of equality became more complete, they gradually surrendered themselves to the propensities natural to that condition of equality, and they strengthened and centralized their governments. They had sought to be free in order to make themselves equal; but in proportion as equality was more established by the aid of freedom, freedom itself was thereby rendered of more difficult attainment.

These two states of a nation have sometimes been con-

temporaneous: the last generation in France showed how
a people might organize a stupendous tyranny in the community, at the very time when they were baffling the authority of the nobility and braving the power of all kings
—at once teaching the world the way to win freedom, and
the way to lose it. In our days men see that constituted
powers are dilapidated on every side—they see all ancient
authority gasping away, all ancient barriers tottering to
their fall, and the judgment of the wisest is troubled at the
sight: they attend only to the amazing revolution which
is taking place before their eyes, and they imagine that
mankind is about to fall into perpetual anarchy: if they
looked to the final consequences of this revolution, their
fears would perhaps assume a different shape. For myself,
I confess that I put no trust in the spirit of freedom which
appears to animate my contemporaries. I see well enough
that the nations of this age are turbulent, but I do not
clearly perceive that they are liberal; and I fear lest, at
the close of those perturbations which rock the base of
thrones, the domination of sovereigns may prove more
powerful than it ever was before.

I had remarked during my stay in the United States
that a democratic state of society, similar to that of the
Americans, might offer singular facilities for the establishment of despotism; and I perceive, upon my return
to Europe, how much use had already been made by most
of our rulers of the notions, the sentiments, and the wants
engendered by this same social condition, for the purpose
of extending the circle of their power. This led me to
think that the nations of Christendom would perhaps
eventually undergo some sort of oppression like that which
hung over several of the nations of the ancient world. A
more accurate examination of the subject, and five years
of further meditations, have not diminished my apprehensions, but they have changed the object of them. No sovereign ever lived in former ages so absolute or so powerful
as to undertake to administer by his own agency, and
without the assistance of intermediate powers, all the parts

of a great empire: none ever attempted to subject all his subjects indiscriminately to strict uniformity of regulation, and personally to tutor and direct every member of the community. The notion of such an undertaking never occurred to the human mind; and if any man had conceived it, the want of information, the imperfection of the administrative system, and, above all, the natural obstacles caused by the inequality of conditions, would speedily have checked the execution of so vast a design. When the Roman emperors were at the height of their power, the different nations of the empire still preserved manners and customs of great diversity; although they were subject to the same monarch, most of the provinces were separately administered; they abounded in powerful and active municipalities; and although the whole government of the empire was centred in the hands of the emperor alone, and he always remained, upon occasions, the supreme arbiter in all matters, yet the details of social life and private occupations lay for the most part beyond his control. The emperors possessed, it is true, an immense and unchecked power, which allowed them to gratify all their whimsical tastes, and to employ for that purpose the whole strength of the State. They frequently abused that power arbitrarily to deprive their subjects of property or of life: their tyranny was extremely onerous to the few, but it did not reach the greater number; it was fixed to some few main objects, and neglected the rest; it was violent, but its range was limited.

But it would seem that if despotism were to be established among the democratic nations of our days, it might assume a different character; it would be more extensive and more mild; it would degrade men without tormenting them. I do not question that in an age of instruction and equality like our own, sovereigns might more easily succeed in collecting all political power into their own hands, and might interfere more habitually and decidedly within the circle of private interests, than any sovereign of antiquity could ever do. But this same principle of equality which facilitates despotism tempers its rigour. We have seen how the manners of society become more humane and gentle in proportion as men become more equal and alike. When no member of the community has much power or much wealth, tyranny is, as it were, without opportunities and a field of action. As all fortunes are scanty, the passions of men are naturally circumscribed —their imagination limited, their pleasures simple. This universal moderation moderates the sovereign himself, and checks within certain limits the inordinate stretch of his desires.

Independently of these reasons drawn from the nature of the state of society itself, I might add many others arising from causes beyond my subject; but I shall keep within the limits I have laid down to myself. Democratic governments may become violent and even cruel at certain periods of extreme effervescence or of great danger: but these crises will be rare and brief. When I consider the petty passions of our contemporaries, the mildness of their manners, the extent of their education, the purity of their religion, the gentleness of their morality, their regular and industrious habits, and the restraint which they almost all observe in their vices no less than in their virtues, I have no fear that they will meet with tyrants in their rulers, but rather guardians.[9] I think, then, that the species of oppression by which democratic nations are menaced is unlike anything which ever before existed in the world: our contemporaries will find no prototype of it in their memories. I am trying myself to choose an expression which will accurately convey the whole of the idea I have formed of it, but in vain; the old words despotism and tyranny are inappropriate: the thing itself is new; and since I can not name it, I must attempt to define it.

I seek to trace the novel features under which despotism may appear in the world. The first thing that strikes the observation is an innumerable multitude of men all equal and alike, incessantly endeavouring to procure the petty and paltry pleasures with which they glut their lives.

Each of them, living apart, is as a stranger to the fate of all the rest—his children and his private friends constitute to him the whole of mankind; as for the rest of his fellow-citizens, he is close to them, but he sees them not—he touches them, but he feels them not; he exists but in himself and for himself alone; and if his kindred still remain to him, he may be said at any rate to have lost his country. Above this race of men stands an immense and tutelary power, which takes upon itself alone to secure their gratifications, and to watch over their fate. That power is absolute, minute, regular, provident, and mild. It would be like the authority of a parent, if, like that authority, its object was to prepare men for manhood; but it seeks, on the contrary, to keep them in perpetual childhood: it is well content that the people should rejoice, provided they think of nothing but rejoicing. For their happiness such a government willingly labours, but it chooses to be the sole agent and the only arbiter of that happiness: it provides for their security, foresees and supplies their necessities, facilitates their pleasures, manages their principal concerns, directs their industry, regulates the descent of property, and subdivides their inheritances—what remains, but to spare them all the care of thinking and all the trouble of living? Thus it every day renders the exercise of the free agency of man less useful and less frequent; it circumscribes the will within a narrower range, and gradually robs a man of all the uses of himself. The principle of equality has prepared men for these things: it has predisposed men to endure them, and oftentimes to look on them as benefits.

After having thus successively taken each member of the community in its powerful grasp, and fashioned them at will, the supreme power then extends its arm over the whole community. It covers the surface of society with a network of small complicated rules, minute and uniform, through which the most original minds and the most energetic characters can not penetrate, to rise above the crowd. The will of man is not shattered, but softened, bent, and guided: men are seldom forced by it to act, but they are constantly restrained from acting: such a power does not destroy, but it prevents existence; it does not tyrannize, but it compresses, enervates, extinguishes, and stupefies a people, till each nation is reduced to be nothing better than a flock of timid and industrious animals, of which the government is the shepherd.

I have always thought that servitude of the regular, quiet, and gentle kind which I have just described might be combined more easily than is commonly believed with some of the outward forms of freedom; and that it might even establish itself under the wing of the sovereignty of the people. Our contemporaries are constantly excited by two conflicting passions; they want to be led, and they wish to remain free: as they can not destroy either one or the other of these contrary propensities, they strive to satisfy them both at once. They devise a sole, tutelary, and all-powerful form of government, but elected by the people. They combine the principle of centralization and that of popular sovereignty; this gives them a respite; they console themselves for being in tutelage by the reflection that they have chosen their own guardians. Every man allows himself to be put in leading-strings, because he sees that it is not a person or a class of persons, but the people at large, that holds the end of his chain. By this system the people shake off their state of dependence just long enough to select their master, and then relapse into it again. A great many persons at the present day are quite contented with this sort of compromise between administrative despotism and the sovereignty of the people; and they think they have done enough for the protection of individual freedom when they have surrendered it to the power of the nation at large. This does not satisfy me: the nature of him I am to obey signifies less to me than the fact of extorted obedience.

I do not, however, deny that a constitution of this kind appears to me to be infinitely preferable to one which, after having concentrated all the powers of government, should vest them in the hands of an irresponsible person or body of persons. Of all the forms which democratic despotism could assume, the latter would assuredly be the worst. When the sovereign is elective, or narrowly watched by a legislature which is really elective and independent, the oppression which he exercises over individuals is sometimes greater, but it is always less degrading; because every man, when he is oppressed and disarmed, may still imagine that while he yields obedience it is to himself he yields it, and that it is to one of his own inclinations that all the rest give way. In like manner I can understand that when the sovereign represents the nation, and is dependent upon the people, the rights and the power of which every citizen is deprived, not only serve the head of the state, but the state itself; and that private persons derive some return from the sacrifice of their independence which they have made to the public. To create a representation of the people in every centralized country is, therefore, to diminish the evil which extreme centralization may produce, but not to get rid of it. I admit that by this means room is left for the intervention of individuals in the more important affairs; but it is not the less suppressed in the smaller and more private ones. It must not be forgotten that it is especially dangerous to enslave men in the minor details of life. For my own part, I should be inclined to think freedom less necessary in great things than in little ones, if it were possible to be secure of the one without possessing the other. Subjection in minor affairs breaks out every day, and is felt by the whole community indiscriminately. It does not drive men to resistance, but it crosses them at every turn, till they are led to surrender the exercise of their will. Thus their spirit is gradually broken and their character enervated; whereas that obedience, which is exacted on a few important but rare occasions, only exhibits servitude at certain intervals, and throws the burden of it upon a small number of men. It is in vain to summon a people, which has been rendered so dependent on the central power, to choose from time to time the representatives of that power; this rare and brief exercise of their free choice, however important it may be, will not prevent them from gradually losing the faculties of thinking, feeling, and acting for themselves, and thus gradually falling below the level of humanity.[10]   I add that they will soon become incapable of exercising the great and only privilege which remains to them.   The democratic nations which have introduced freedom into their political constitution, at the very time when they were augmenting the despotism of their administrative constitution, have been led into strange paradoxes.   To manage those minor affairs in which good sense is all that is wanted —the people are held to be unequal to the task; but when the government of the country is at stake, the people are invested with immense powers; they are alternately made the playthings of their ruler, and his masters—more than kings, and less than men.   After having exhausted all the different modes of election, without finding one to suit their purpose, they are still amazed, and still bent on seeking further; as if the evil they remark did not originate in the constitution of the country far more than in that of the electoral body.   It is, indeed, difficult to conceive how men who have entirely given up the habit of self-government should succeed in making a proper choice of those by whom they are to be governed; and no one will ever believe that a liberal, wise, and energetic government can spring from the suffrages of a subservient people.   A constitution, which should be republican in its head and ultra-monarchical in all its other parts, has ever appeared to me to be a short-lived monster.   The vices of rulers and the ineptitude of the people would speedily bring about its ruin; and the nation, weary of its representatives and of itself, would create freer institutions, or soon return to stretch itself at the feet of a single master.

I believe that it is easier to establish an absolute and despotic government among a people in which the conditions of society are equal, than among any other; and I think that if such a government were once established among such a people, it would not only oppress men, but would eventually strip each of them of several of the highest qualities of humanity. Despotism, therefore, appears to me peculiarly to be dreaded in democratic ages. I should have loved freedom, I believe, at all times, but in the time in which we live I am ready to worship it. On the other hand, I am persuaded that all who shall attempt, in the ages upon which we are entering, to base freedom upon aristocratic privilege, will fail—that all who shall attempt to draw and to retain authority within a single class, will fail. At the present day no ruler is skilful or strong enough to found a despotism, by re-establishing permanent distinctions of rank among his subjects: no legislator is wise or powerful enough to preserve free institutions if he does not take equality for his first principle and his watchword. All those of our contemporaries who would establish or secure the independence and the dignity of their fellow-men, must show themselves the friends of equality; and the only worthy means of showing themselves as such, is to be so: upon this depends the success of their holy enterprise. Thus the question is not how to reconstruct aristocratic society, but how to make liberty proceed out of that democratic state of society in which God has placed us.

These two truths appear to me simple, clear, and fertile in consequences; and they naturally lead me to consider what kind of free government can be established among a people in which social conditions are equal.

It results from the very constitution of democratic nations and from their necessities that the power of government among them must be more uniform, more centralized, more extensive, more searching, and more efficient than in other countries. Society at large is naturally stronger and more active, individuals more subordinate and weak; the former does more, the latter less; and this is inevitably the case. It is not, therefore, to be expected that the range of private independence will ever be as extensive in democratic as in aristocratic countries—nor is this to be desired; for, among aristocratic nations, the

mass is often sacrificed to the individual, and the prosperity of the greater number to the greatness of the few.
It is both necessary and desirable that the government of
a democratic people should be active and powerful: and
our object should not be to render it weak or indolent, but
solely to prevent it from abusing its aptitude and its
strength.

The circumstance which most contributed to secure the
independence of private persons in aristocratic ages was,
that the supreme power did not affect to take upon itself
alone the government and administration of the community; those functions were necessarily partially left to the
members of the aristocracy: so that as the supreme power
was always divided, it never weighed with its whole weight
and in the same manner on each individual. Not only did
the government not perform everything by its immediate
agency; but as most of the agents who discharged its
duties derived their power not from the State, but from
the circumstance of their birth, they were not perpetually
under its control. The government could not make or
unmake them in an instant, at pleasure, nor bend them in
strict uniformity to its slightest caprice—this was an additional guarantee of private independence. I readily admit
that recourse can not be had to the same means at the
present time: but I discover certain democratic expedi-
ents which may be substituted for them. Instead of vest-
ing in the government alone all the administrative powers
of which corporations and nobles have been deprived, a
portion of them may be intrusted to secondary public
bodies, temporarily composed of private citizens: thus the
liberty of private persons will be more secure, and their
equality will not be diminished.

The Americans, who care less for words than the
French, still designate by the name of County the largest
of their administrative districts: but the duties of the count
or lord-lieutenant are in part performed by a provincial
assembly. At a period of equality like our own it would
be unjust and unreasonable to institute hereditary officers;

but there is nothing to prevent us from substituting elective public officers to a certain extent. Election is a democratic expedient which insures the independence of the public officer in relation to the government, as much and even more than hereditary rank can insure it among aristocratic nations. Aristocratic countries abound in wealthy and influential persons who are competent to provide for themselves, and who can not be easily or secretly oppressed: such persons restrain a government within general habits of moderation and reserve. I am very well aware that democratic countries contain no such persons naturally; but something analogous to them may be created by artificial means. I firmly believe that an aristocracy can not again be founded in the world; but I think that private citizens, by combining together, may constitute bodies of great wealth, influence, and strength, corresponding to the persons of an aristocracy. By this means many of the greatest political advantages of aristocracy would be obtained without its injustice or its dangers. An association for political, commercial, or manufacturing purposes, or even for those of science and literature, is a powerful and enlightened member of the community, which can not be disposed of at pleasure, or oppressed without remonstrance; and which, by defending its own rights against the encroachments of the government, saves the common liberties of the country.

In periods of aristocracy every man is always bound so closely to many of his fellow-citizens that he can not be assailed without their coming to his assistance. In ages of equality every man naturally stands alone; he has no hereditary friends whose co-operation he may demand— no class upon whose sympathy he may rely: he is easily got rid of, and he is trampled on with impunity. At the present time, an oppressed member of the community has therefore only one method of self-defence—he may appeal to the whole nation; and if the whole nation is deaf to his complaint, he may appeal to mankind: the only means he has of making this appeal is by the press. Thus the liberty of the press is infinitely more valuable among democratic nations than among all others; it is the only cure for the evils which equality may produce. Equality sets men apart and weakens them; but the press places a powerful weapon within every man's reach, which the weakest and loneliest of them all may use. Equality deprives a man of the support of his connections; but the press enables him to summon all his fellow-countrymen and all his fellow-men to his assistance. Printing has accelerated the progress of equality, and it is also one of its best correctives.

I think that men living in aristocracies may, strictly speaking, do without the liberty of the press: but such is not the case with those who live in democratic countries. To protect their personal independence I trust not to great political assemblies, to parliamentary privilege, or to the assertion of popular sovereignty. All these things may, to a certain extent, be reconciled with personal servitude —but that servitude can not be complete if the press is free: the press is the chiefest democratic instrument of freedom.

Something analogous may be said of the judicial power. It is a part of the essence of judicial power to attend to private interests, and to fix itself with predilection on minute objects submitted to its observation; another essential quality of judicial power is never to volunteer its assistance to the oppressed, but always to be at the disposal of the humblest of those who solicit it; their complaint, however feeble they may themselves be, will force itself upon the ear of justice and claim redress, for this is inherent in the very constitution of the courts of justice. A power of this kind is therefore peculiarly adapted to the wants of freedom, at a time when the eye and finger of the government are constantly intruding into the minutest details of human actions, and when private persons are at once too weak to protect themselves, and too much isolated for them to reckon upon the assistance of their fellows. The strength of the courts of law has ever been the greatest security which can be offered to personal independence; but this is more especially the case in democratic ages: private rights and interests are in constant danger, if the judicial power does not grow more extensive and more strong to keep pace with the growing equality of conditions.

Equality awakens in men several propensities extremely dangerous to freedom, to which the attention of the legislator ought constantly to be directed. I shall only remind the reader of the most important among them. Men living in democratic ages do not readily comprehend the utility of forms: they feel an instinctive contempt for them —I have elsewhere shown for what reasons. Forms excite their contempt and often their hatred; as they commonly aspire to none but easy and present gratifications, they rush onward to the object of their desires, and the slightest delay exasperates them. This same temper, carried with them into political life, renders them hostile to forms, which perpetually retard or arrest them in some of their projects. Yet this objection which the men of democracies make to forms is the very thing which renders forms so useful to freedom; for their chief merit is to serve as a barrier between the strong and the weak, the ruler and the people, to retard the one, and give the other time to look about him. Forms become more necessary in proportion as the government becomes more active and more powerful, while private persons are becoming more indolent and more feeble. Thus democratic nations naturally stand more in need of forms than other nations, and they naturally respect them less. This deserves most serious attention. Nothing is more pitiful than the arrogant disdain of most of our contemporaries for questions of form; for the smallest questions of form have acquired in our time an importance which they never had before: many of the greatest interests of mankind depend upon them. I think that if the statesmen of aristocratic ages could sometimes contemn forms with impunity, and frequently rise above them, the statesmen to whom the government of nations is now confided ought to treat the very least among them with respect, and not neglect them without imperious necessity. In aristocracies the observance of forms was superstitious; among us they ought to be kept with a deliberate and enlightened deference.

Another tendency, which is extremely natural to democratic nations and extremely dangerous, is that which leads them to despise and undervalue the rights of private persons. The attachment which men feel to a right, and the respect which they display for it, is generally proportioned to its importance, or to the length of time during which they have enjoyed it. The rights of private persons among democratic nations are commonly of small importance, of recent growth, and extremely precarious—the consequence is that they are often sacrificed without regret, and almost always violated without remorse. But it happens that at the same period and among the same nations in which men conceive a natural contempt for the rights of private persons, the rights of society at large are naturally extended and consolidated: in other words, men become less attached to private rights at the very time at which it would be most necessary to retain and to defend what little remains of them. It is therefore most especially in the present democratic ages that the true friends of the liberty and the greatness of man ought constantly to be on the alert to prevent the power of government from lightly sacrificing the private rights of individuals to the general execution of its designs. At such times no citizen is so obscure that it is not very dangerous to allow him to be oppressed—no private rights are so unimportant that they can be surrendered with impunity to the caprices of a government. The reason is plain: if the private right of an individual is violated at a time when the human mind is fully impressed with the importance and the sanctity of such rights, the injury done is confined to the individual whose right is infringed; but to violate such a right, at the present day, is deeply to corrupt the manners of the nation and to put the whole community in jeopardy, be-

cause the very notion of this kind of right constantly tends
among us to be impaired and lost.

There are certain habits, certain notions, and certain
vices which are peculiar to a state of revolution, and which
a protracted revolution can not fail to engender and to
propagate, whatever be, in other respects, its character,
its purpose, and the scene on which it takes place. When
any nation has, within a short space of time, repeatedly
varied its rulers, its opinions, and its laws, the men of whom
it is composed eventually contract a taste for change, and
grow accustomed to see all changes effected by sudden violence. Thus they naturally conceive a contempt for forms
which daily prove ineffectual; and they do not support
without impatience the dominion of rules which they have
so often seen infringed. As the ordinary notions of equity
and morality no longer suffice to explain and justify all
the innovations daily begotten by a revolution, the principle of public utility is called in, the doctrine of political
necessity is conjured up, and men accustom themselves to
sacrifice private interests without scruple, and to trample
on the rights of individuals in order more speedily to accomplish any public purpose.

These habits and notions, which I shall call revolutionary, because all revolutions produce them, occur in
aristocracies just as much as among democratic nations;
but among the former they are often less powerful and
always less lasting, because there they meet with habits,
notions, defects, and impediments, which counteract them:
they consequently disappear as soon as the revolution is
terminated, and the nation reverts to its former political
courses. This is not always the case in democratic countries, in which it is ever to be feared that revolutionary
tendencies, becoming more gentle and more regular, without entirely disappearing from society, will be gradually
transformed into habits of subjection to the administrative
authority of the government. I know of no countries in
which revolutions are more dangerous than in democratic
countries; because, independently of the accidental and

transient evils which must always attend them, they may always create some evils which are permanent and unending. I believe that there are such things as justifiable resistance and legitimate rebellion: I do not therefore assert, as an absolute proposition, that the men of democratic ages ought never to make revolutions; but I think that they have especial reason to hesitate before they embark in them, and that it is far better to endure many grievances in their present condition than to have recourse to so perilous a remedy.

I shall conclude by one general idea, which comprises not only all the particular ideas which have been expressed in the present chapter, but also most of those which it is the object of this book to treat of. In the ages of aristocracy which preceded our own, there were private persons of great power, and a social authority of extreme weakness. The outline of society itself was not easily discernible, and constantly confounded with the different powers by which the community was ruled. The principal efforts of the men of those times were required to strengthen, aggrandize, and secure the supreme power; and, on the other hand, to circumscribe individual independence within narrower limits, and to subject private interests to the interests of the public. Other perils and other cares await the men of our age. Among the greater part of modern nations, the government, whatever may be its origin, its constitution, or its name, has become almost omnipotent, and private persons are falling, more and more, into the lowest stage of weakness and dependence. In olden society everything was different; unity and uniformity were nowhere to be met with. In modern society everything threatens to become so much alike, that the peculiar characteristics of each individual will soon be entirely lost in the general aspect of the world. Our forefathers were ever prone to make an improper use of the notion that private rights ought to be respected; and we are naturally prone, on the other hand, to exaggerate the idea that the interest of a private individual ought always to bend to the interest of the many. The political world is metamorphosed: new remedies must henceforth be sought for new disorders. To lay down extensive, but distinct and settled limits, to the action of the government; to confer certain rights on private persons, and to secure to them the undisputed enjoyment of those rights; to enable individual man to maintain whatever independence, strength, and original power he still possesses; to raise him by the side of society at large, and uphold him in that position—these appear to me the main objects of legislators in the ages upon which we are now entering. It would seem as if the rulers of our time sought only to use men in order to make things great; I wish that they would try a little more to make great men; that they would set less value on the work, and more upon the workman; that they would never forget that a nation can not long remain strong when every man belonging to it is individually weak, and that no form or combination of social polity has yet been devised to make an energetic people out of a community of pusillanimous and enfeebled citizens.

I trace among our contemporaries two contrary notions which are equally injurious. One set of men can perceive nothing in the principle of equality but the anarchical tendencies which it engenders: they dread their own free agency—they fear themselves. Other thinkers, less numerous but more enlightened, take a different view: beside that track which starts from the principle of equality to terminate in anarchy, they have at last discovered the road which seems to lead men to inevitable servitude. They shape their souls beforehand to this necessary condition; and, despairing of remaining free, they already do obeisance in their hearts to the master who is soon to appear. The former abandon freedom, because they think it dangerous; the latter, because they hold it to be impossible. If I had entertained the latter conviction, I should not have written this book, but I should have confined myself to deploring in secret the destiny of mankind. I have sought to point out the dangers to which the principle of equality exposes the independence of man, because I firmly believe that these dangers are the most formidable, as well as the least foreseen, of all those which futurity holds in store: but I do not think that they are insurmountable. The men who live in the democratic ages upon which we are entering have naturally a taste for independence: they are naturally impatient of regulation, and they are wearied by the permanence even of the condition they themselves prefer. They are fond of power; but they are prone to despise and hate those who wield it, and they easily elude its grasp by their own mobility and insignificance. These propensities will always manifest themselves, because they originate in the groundwork of society, which will undergo no change: for a long time they will prevent the establishment of any despotism, and they will furnish fresh weapons to each succeeding generation which shall struggle in favour of the liberty of mankind. Let us then look forward to the future with that salutary fear which makes men keep watch and ward for freedom, not with that faint and idle terror which depresses and enervates the heart.

Before I close forever the theme that has detained me so long, I would fain take a parting survey of all the various characteristics of modern society, and appreciate at last the general influence to be exercised by the principle of equality upon the fate of mankind; but I am stopped by the difficulty of the task, and in presence of so great an object my sight is troubled and my reason fails. The society of the modern world which I have sought to delineate, and which I seek to judge, has but just come into existence. Time has not yet shaped it into perfect form: the great revolution by which it has been created is not yet over: and amid the occurrences of our time, it is almost impossible to discern what will pass away with the revolution itself, and what will survive its close. The world which is rising into existence is still half encumbered by the remains of the world which is waning into decay; and amid the vast perplexity of human affairs, none can say how much of ancient institutions and former manners will remain, or how much will completely disappear. Although the revolution that is taking place in the social condition, the laws, the opinions, and the feelings of men, is still very far from being terminated, yet its results already admit of no comparison with anything that the world has ever before witnessed. I go back from age to age up to the remotest antiquity; but I find no parallel to what is occurring before my eyes: as the past has ceased to throw its light upon the future, the mind of man wanders in obscurity.

Nevertheless, in the midst of a prospect so wide, so novel, and so confused, some of the more prominent characteristics may already be discerned and pointed out. The good things and the evils of life are more equally distributed in the world: great wealth tends to disappear, the number of small fortunes to increase; desires and gratifications are multiplied, but extraordinary prosperity and irremediable penury are alike unknown. The sentiment of ambition is universal, but the scope of ambition is seldom vast. Each individual stands apart in solitary weakness; but society at large is active, provident, and powerful: the performances of private persons are insignificant, those of the state immense. There is little energy of character; but manners are mild, and laws humane. If there be few instances of exalted heroism or of virtues of the highest, brightest, and purest temper, men's habits are regular, violence is rare, and cruelty almost unknown. Human existence becomes longer, and property more secure: life is not adorned with brilliant trophies, but it is extremely easy and tranquil. Few pleasures are either very refined or very coarse; and highly polished manners are as uncommon as great brutality of tastes. Neither men of great learning, nor extremely ignorant communities, are to be met with; genius becomes more rare, information more diffused. The human mind is impelled by the small efforts of all mankind combined together, not by the strenuous activity of certain men. There is less perfection, but more abundance, in all the productions of the arts. The ties of race, of rank, and of country are relaxed; the great bond of humanity is strengthened. If I endeavour to find out the most general and the most prominent of all these different characteristics, I shall have occasion to perceive that what is taking place in men's fortunes manifests itself under a thousand other forms. Almost all extremes are softened or blunted: all that was most prominent is superseded by some mean term, at once less lofty and less low, less brilliant and less obscure, than what before existed in the world.

When I survey this countless multitude of beings, shaped in each other's likeness, amid whom nothing rises and nothing falls, the sight of such universal uniformity saddens and chills me, and I am tempted to regret that state of society which has ceased to be. When the world was full of men of great importance and extreme insignificance, of great wealth and extreme poverty, of great learning and extreme ignorance, I turned aside from the latter to fix my observation on the former alone, who gratified my sympathies. But I admit that this gratification arose from my own weakness: it is because I am unable to see at once all that is around me that I am allowed thus to select and separate the objects of my predilection from among so many others. Such is not the case with that Almighty and Eternal Being, whose gaze necessarily includes the whole of created things, and who surveys distinctly, though at once, mankind and man. We may naturally believe that it is not the singular prosperity of the few, but the greater well-being of all, which is most pleasing in the sight of the Creator and Preserver of men. What appears to me to be man's decline is to his eye advancement; what afflicts me is acceptable to him. A state of equality is perhaps less elevated, but it is more just; and its justice constitutes its greatness and its beauty. I would strive, then, to raise myself to this point of the divine contemplation, and thence to view and to judge the concerns of men.

No man, upon the earth, can as yet affirm absolutely and generally that the new state of the world is better than its former one; but it is already easy to perceive that this state is different. Some vices and some virtues were so inherent in the constitution of an aristocratic nation, and are so opposite to the character of a modern people, that they can never be infused into it; some good tendencies and some bad propensities which were unknown to the former are natural to the latter; some ideas suggest themselves spontaneously to the imagination of the one which are utterly repugnant to the mind of the other. They are like two distinct orders of human beings, each of which has its own merits and defects, its own advantages and its own evils. Care must therefore be taken not to judge the state of society, which is now coming into existence, by notions derived from a state of society which no longer exists; for as these states of society are exceedingly different in their structure, they can not be submitted to a just or fair comparison. It would be scarcely more reasonable to require of our own contemporaries the peculiar virtues which originated in the social condition of their forefathers, since that social condition is itself fallen, and has drawn into one promiscuous ruin the good and evil which belonged to it.

But as yet these things are imperfectly understood. I find that a great number of my contemporaries undertake to make a certain selection from among the institutions, the opinions, and the ideas which originated in the aristocratic constitution of society as it was: a portion of these elements they would willingly relinquish, but they would keep the remainder and transplant them into their new world. I apprehend that such men are wasting their time and their strength in virtuous but unprofitable efforts. The object is not to retain the peculiar advantages which the inequality of conditions bestows upon mankind, but to secure the new benefits which equality may supply. We have not to seek to make ourselves like our progenitors, but to strive to work out that species of greatness and happiness which is our own. For myself, who now look back from this extreme limit of my task, and discover from afar, but at once, the various objects which have attracted my more attentive investigation upon my way, I am full of apprehensions and of hopes. I perceive mighty dangers which it is possible to ward off—mighty evils which may be avoided or alleviated; and I cling with a firmer hold to the belief, that for democratic nations to be virtuous and prosperous they require but to will it. I am aware that many of my contemporaries maintain that nations are never their own masters here below, and that they necessarily obey some insurmountable and unintelligent power, arising from anterior events, from their race, or from the soil and climate of their country. Such principles are false and cowardly; such principles can never produce aught but feeble men and pusillanimous nations. Providence has not created mankind entirely independent or entirely free. It is true that around every man a fatal circle is traced, beyond which he can not pass; but within the wide verge of that circle he is powerful and free: as it is with man, so with communities. The nations of our time can not prevent the conditions of men from becoming equal; but it depends upon themselves whether the principle of equality is to lead them to servitude or freedom, to knowledge or barbarism, to prosperity or to wretchedness.

NOTES

[1] See Appendix, W.

[2] In democratic communities nothing but the central power has any stability in its position or any permanence in its undertakings. All the members of society are in ceaseless stir and transformation. Now it is in the nature of all governments to seek constantly to enlarge their sphere of action ; hence it is almost impossible that such a government should not ultimately succeed, because it acts with a fixed principle and a constant will upon men whose position, whose notions, and whose desires are in continual vacillation. It frequently happens that the members of the community promote the influence of the central power without intending it. Democratic ages are periods of experiment, innovation, and adventure. At such times there are always a multitude of men engaged in difficult or novel undertakings, which they follow alone, without caring for their fellow-men. Such persons may be ready to admit, as

a general principle, that the public authority ought not to interfere in private concerns; but, by an exception to that rule, each of them craves for its assistance in the particular concern on which he is engaged, and seeks to draw upon the influence of the government for his own benefit, though he would restrict it on all other occasions. If a large number of men apply this particular exception to a great variety of different purposes, the sphere of the central power extends insensibly in all directions, although each of them wishes it to be circumscribed. Thus a democratic government increases its power simply by the fact of its permanence. Time is on its side; every incident befriends it; the passions of individuals unconsciously promote it; and it may be asserted, that the older a democratic community is, the more centralized will its government become.

[3] See Appendix, X.

[4] This gradual weakening of individuals in relation to society at large may be traced in a thousand ways. I shall select from among these examples one derived from the law of wills. In aristocracies it is common to profess the greatest reverence for the last testamentary dispositions of a man; this feeling sometimes even became superstitious among the elder nations of Europe: the power of the State, far from interfering with the caprices of a dying man, gave full force to the very least of them, and insured to him a perpetual power. When all living men are enfeebled, the will of the dead is less respected: it is circumscribed within a narrow range, beyond which it is annulled or checked by the supreme power of the laws. In the Middle Ages, testamentary power had, so to speak, no limits: among the French at the present day a man can not distribute his fortune among his children without the interference of the State: after having domineered over a whole life, the law insists upon regulating the very last act of it.

[5] In proportion as the duties of the central power are augmented, the number of public officers by whom that power is represented must increase also. They form a nation in each nation; and as they share the stability of the government, they more and more fill up the place of an aristocracy.

In almost every part of Europe the government rules in two ways: it rules one portion of the community by the fear which they entertain of its agents, and the other by the hope they have of becoming its agents.

[6] On the one hand the taste for worldly welfare is perpetually increasing, and on the other the government gets more and more complete possession of the sources of that welfare. Thus men are following two separate roads to servitude: the taste for their own welfare withholds them from taking a part in the government, and their love of that welfare places them in closer dependence upon those who govern.

[7] A strange sophism has been made on this head in France. When a suit arises between the government and a private person, it is not to be tried before an ordinary judge—in order, they say, not to mix the administrative and the judicial powers; as if it were not to mix those powers, and to mix them in the most dangerous and oppressive manner, to invest the government with the office of judging and administering at the same time.

[8] I shall quote a few facts in corroboration of this remark. Mines are the natural sources of manufacturing wealth : as manufactures have grown up in Europe, as the produce of mines has become of more general importance, and good mining more difficult from the subdivision of property which is a consequence of the equality of conditions, most governments have asserted a right of owning the soil in which the mines lie, and of inspecting the works ; which has never been the case with any other kind of property. Thus mines, which were private property, liable to the same obligations and sheltered by the same guarantees as all other landed property, have fallen under the control of the State. The State either works them or farms them ; the owners of them are mere tenants, deriving their rights from the State ; and, moreover, the State almost everywhere claims the power of directing their operations : it lays down rules, enforces the adoption of particular methods, subjects the mining adventurers to constant superintendence, and, if refractory, they are ousted by a government court of justice, and the government transfers their contracts to other hands ; so that the government not only possesses the mines, but has all the adventurers in its power. Nevertheless, as manufactures increase, the working of old mines increases also ; new ones are opened ; the mining population extends and grows up ; day by day governments augment their subterranean dominions, and people them with their agents.

[9] See Appendix, Y.

[10] See Appendix, Z.

APPENDIX

A. p. 4, note 2.—For information concerning all the
countries of the West which have not been visited by Europeans, consult the account of two expeditions undertaken at the expense of Congress by Major Long. This
traveller particularly mentions, on the subject of the great
American desert, that a line may be drawn nearly parallel
to the 20th degree of longitude (meridian of Washington),
beginning from the Red River and ending at the River
Platte. From this imaginary line to the Rocky Mountains, which bound the valley of the Mississippi on the
West, lie immense plains, which are almost entirely covered with sand, incapable of cultivation, or scattered over
with masses of granite. In summer, these plains are quite
destitute of water, and nothing is to be seen on them but
herds of buffaloes and wild horses. Some hordes of Indians are also found there, but in no great numbers. Major
Long was told that in travelling northward from the River
Platte you find the same desert lying constantly on the
left; but he was unable to ascertain the truth of this report.
However worthy of confidence may be the narrative of
Major Long, it must be remembered that he only passed
through the country of which he speaks, without deviating widely from the line which he had traced out for his
journey.

B. p. 5, note 4.—South America, in the regions between the tropics, produces an incredible profusion of
climbing plants, of which the flora of the Antilles alone

presents us with forty different species. Among the most graceful of these shrubs is the Passion-flower, which, according to Descourtiz, grows with such luxuriance in the Antilles as to climb trees by means of the tendrils with which it is provided, and form moving bowers of rich and elegant festoons, decorated with blue and purple flowers, and fragrant with perfume. The *Mimosa Scandens* (Acacia à grandes gousses) is a creeper of enormous and rapid growth, which climbs from tree to tree, and sometimes covers more than half a league.

C. p. 7, note 6.—The languages which are spoken by the Indians of America, from the Pole to Cape Horn, are said to be all formed upon the same model, and subject to the same grammatical rules; whence it may fairly be concluded that all the Indian nations sprang from the same stock. Each tribe of the American continent speaks a different dialect; but the number of languages, properly so called, is very small, a fact which tends to prove that the nations of the New World had not a very remote origin. Moreover, the languages of America have a great degree of regularity, from which it seems probable that the tribes which employ them had not undergone any great revolutions, or been incorporated, voluntarily or by constraint, with foreign nations. For it is generally the union of several languages into one that produces grammatical irregularities. It is not long since the American languages, especially those of the North, first attracted the serious attention of philologists, when the discovery was made that this idiom of a barbarous people was the product of a complicated system of ideas and very learned combinations. These languages were found to be very rich, and great pains had been taken at their formation to render them agreeable to the ear. The grammatical system of the Americans differs from all others in several points, but especially in the following:

Some nations of Europe, among others the Germans, have the power of combining at pleasure different expressions, and thus giving a complex sense to certain words. The Indians have given a most surprising extension to this power, so as to arrive at the means of connecting a great number of ideas with a single term. This will be easily understood with the help of an example quoted by Mr. Duponceau, in the " Memoirs of the Philosophical Society of America." "A Delaware woman playing with a cat or young dog," says this writer, "is heard to pronounce the word *kuligatschis*, which is thus composed: *k* is the sign of the second person, and signifies ' thou ' or ' thy '; *uli* is a part of the word *wulit*, which signifies ' beautiful,' ' pretty '; *gat* is another fragment of the word *wichgat*, which means ' paw '; and, lastly, *schis* is a diminutive giving the idea of smallness. Thus in one word the Indian woman has expressed ' Thy pretty little paw.' " Take another example of the felicity with which the savages of America have composed their words. A young man of Delaware is called *pilapé*. This word is formed from *pilsit*, chaste, innocent; and *lenapé*, man; viz., man in his purity and innocence. This facility of combining words is most remarkable in the strange formation of their verbs. The most complex action is often expressed by a single verb, which serves to convey all the shades of an idea by the modification of its construction. Those who may wish to examine more in detail this subject, which I have only glanced at superficially, should read:

1. The correspondence of Mr. Duponceau and the Rev. Mr. Hecwelder relative to the Indian languages, which is to be found in the first volume of the " Memoirs of the Philosophical Society of America," published at Philadelphia, 1819, by Abraham Small; vol. i.

2. The " Grammar of the Delaware or Lenape Language," by Geiberger, and the preface of Mr. Duponceau. All these are in the same collection; vol. iii.

D. p. 8, note 8.—See in Charlevoix the history of the first war which the French inhabitants of Canada carried on, in 1610, against the Iroquois. The latter, armed with bows and arrows, offered a desperate resistance to the French and their allies. Charlevoix is not a great painter, yet he exhibits clearly enough, in this narrative, the contrast between the European manners and those of savages, as well as the different way in which the two races of men understood the sense of honour. When the French, says he, seized upon the beaver-skins which covered the Indians who had fallen, the Hurons, their allies, were greatly offended at this proceeding; but without hesitation they set to work in their usual manner, inflicting horrid cruelties upon the prisoners, and devouring one of those who had been killed, which made the Frenchmen shudder. The barbarians prided themselves upon a scrupulousness which they were surprised at not finding in our nation, and could not understand that there was less to reprehend in the stripping of dead bodies than in the devouring of their flesh like wild beasts. Charlevoix, in another place, thus describes the first torture of which Champlain was an eye-witness, and the return of the Hurons into their own village. Having proceeded about eight leagues, says he, our allies halted; and having singled out one of their captives, they reproached him with all the cruelties which he had practised upon the warriors of their nation who had fallen into his hands, and told him that he might expect to be treated in like manner; adding, that if he had any spirit he would prove it by singing. He immediately chanted forth his death-song, and then his war-song, and all the songs he knew, "but in a very mournful strain," says Champlain, who was not then aware that all savage music has a melancholy character. The tortures which succeeded, accompanied by all the horrors which we shall mention hereafter, terrified the French, who made every effort to put a stop to them, but in vain. The following night, one of the Hurons having dreamed that they were pursued, the retreat was changed to a real flight, and the savages never stopped until they were out of the reach of danger. The moment they perceived the cabins of their own village, they cut themselves long sticks, to which they fastened the scalps which had fallen to their share, and carried them in triumph. At this sight, the women swam to the canoes, where they received the bloody scalps from the hands of their husbands, and tied them round their necks. The warriors offered one of these horrible trophies to Champlain; they also presented him with some bows and arrows—the only spoils of the Iroquois which they had ventured to seize—entreating him to show them to the King of France. Champlain lived a whole winter quite alone among these barbarians, without being under any alarm for his person or property.

E. p. 24, note 17.—Although the puritanical strictness which presided over the establishment of the English colonies in America is now much relaxed, remarkable traces of it are still found in their habits and their laws. In 1792, at the very time when the anti-Christian republic of France began its ephemeral existence, the legislative body of Massachusetts promulgated the following law, to compel the citizens to observe the Sabbath. We give the preamble and the principal articles of this law, which is worthy of the reader's attention. " Whereas," says the legislator, " the observation of the Sunday is an affair of public interest; inasmuch as it produces a necessary suspension of labour, leads men to reflect upon the duties of life, and the errors to which human nature is liable, and provides for the public and private worship of God, the creator and governor of the universe, and for the performance of such acts of charity as are the ornament and comfort of Christian societies: Whereas irreligious or light-minded persons, forgetting the duties which the Sabbath imposes, and the benefits which these duties confer on society, are known to profane its sanctity, by following their pleasures or their affairs; this way of acting being contrary to their own interest as Christians, and calculated to annoy those who do not follow their example; being also of great injury to society at large, by spreading a taste for dissipation and dissolute manners: Be it enacted and ordained by the Governor, Council, and Representatives convened in General Court of Assembly, that all and every person and persons shall on that day carefully apply themselves to the duties of religion and piety, that no tradesman or labourer shall exercise his ordinary calling, and that no game or recreation shall be used on the Lord's Day, upon pain of forfeiting ten shillings.

" That no one shall travel on that day, or any part thereof, under pain of forfeiting twenty shillings; that no vessel shall leave a harbour of the colony; that no persons shall keep outside the meeting-house during the time of public worship, or profane the time by playing or talking, on penalty of five shillings.

" Public-houses shall not entertain any other than strangers or lodgers, under penalty of five shillings for every person found drinking and abiding therein.

" Any person in health, who, without sufficient reason, shall omit to worship God in public during three months, shall be condemned to a fine of ten shillings.

" Any person guilty of misbehaviour in a place of public worship, shall be fined from five to forty shillings.

" These laws are to be enforced by the tything-men of each township, who have authority to visit public-houses on the Sunday. The innkeeper who shall refuse them admittance, shall be fined forty shillings for such offence.

" The tything-men are to stop travellers, and require of them their reason for being on the road on Sunday; any one refusing to answer, shall be sentenced to pay a fine not exceeding five pounds sterling. If the reason given by the traveller be not deemed by the tything-man sufficient, he may bring the traveller before the justice of the peace of the district." (Law of March 8, 1792; " General Laws of Massachusetts," vol. i.)

On March 11, 1797, a new law increased the amount of fines, half of which was to be given to the informer. (Same collection, vol. ii.) On February 16, 1816, a new law confirmed these same measures. (Same collection, vol. ii.) Similar enactments exist in the laws of the State

55

of New York, revised in 1827 and 1828. (See "Revised Statutes," Part I.) In these it is declared that no one is allowed on the Sabbath to sport, to fish, to play at games, or to frequent houses where liquor is sold. No one can travel, except in case of necessity.

And this is not the only trace which the religious strictness and austere manners of the first emigrants have left behind them in the American laws. In the "Revised Statutes of the State of New York," vol. i, is the following clause:

"Whoever shall win or lose in the space of twenty-four hours, by gaming or betting, the sum of twenty-five dollars, shall be found guilty of a misdemeanour, and, upon conviction shall be condemned to pay a fine equal to at least five times the value of the sum lost or won; which shall be paid to the inspector of the poor of the township. He that loses twenty-five dollars or more may bring an action to recover them; and if he neglects to do so the inspector of the poor may prosecute the winner, and oblige him to pay into the poor's box both the sum he has gained and three times as much besides." The laws we quote from are of recent date; but they are unintelligible without going back to the very origin of the colonies. I have no doubt that in our days the penal part of these laws is very rarely applied. Laws preserve their inflexibility long after the manners of a nation have yielded to the influence of time. It is still true, however, that nothing strikes a foreigner on his arrival in America more forcibly than the regard paid to the Sabbath. There is one, in particular, of the large American cities, in which all social movements begin to be suspended even on Saturday evening. You traverse its streets at the hour at which you expect men in the middle of life to be engaged in business, and young people in pleasure; and you meet with solitude and silence. Not only have all ceased to work, but they appear to have ceased to exist. Neither the movements of industry are heard, nor the accents of joy, nor even the confused murmur which arises from the midst of a great city. Chains are hung across the streets in the neighbourhood of the churches; the half-closed shutters of the houses scarcely admit a ray of sun into the dwellings of the citizens. Now and then you perceive a solitary individual who glides silently along the deserted streets and lanes. Next day, at early dawn, the rolling of carriages, the noise of hammers, the cries of the population, begin to make themselves heard again. The city is awake. An eager crowd hastens toward the resort of commerce and industry; everything around you bespeaks motion, bustle, hurry. A feverish activity succeeds to the lethargic stupor of yesterday; you might almost suppose that they had but one day to acquire wealth and to enjoy it.

F. p. 29, note 21.—It is unnecessary for me to say that, in the chapter which has just been read, I have not had the intention of giving a history of America. My only object was to enable the reader to appreciate the influence which the opinions and manners of the first emigrants had exercised upon the fate of the different colonies, and of the Union in general. I have therefore confined myself to the quotation of a few detached fragments. I do not know whether I am deceived, but it appears to me that, by pursuing the path which I have merely pointed out, it would be easy to present such pictures of the American republics as would not be unworthy the attention of the public, and could not fail to suggest to the statesman matter for reflection. Not being able to devote myself to this labour, I am anxious to render it easy to others; and, for this purpose, I subjoin a short catalogue and analysis of the works which seem to me the most important to consult.

At the head of the general documents which it would be advantageous to examine I place the work entitled "An Historical Collection of State Papers, and other Authentic Documents, intended as Materials for a History of the United States of America," by Ebenezer Hasard. The first volume of this compilation, which was printed at Philadelphia in 1792, contains a literal copy of all the charters granted by the Crown of England to the emigrants, as well as the principal acts of the colonial governments, during the commencement of their existence. Among other authentic documents, we here find a great many relating to the affairs of New England and Virginia during this period. The second volume is almost entirely devoted to the acts of the Confederation of 1643. This Federal compact, which was entered into by the colonies of New England with the view of resisting the Indians, was the first instance of union afforded by the Anglo-Americans. There were, besides, many other confederations of the same nature, before the famous one of 1776, which brought about the independence of the colonies.

Each colony has, besides, its own historic monuments, some of which are extremely curious; beginning with Virginia, the State which was first peopled. The earliest historian of Virginia was its founder, Captain John Smith. Captain Smith has left us an octavo volume, entitled " The generall Historie of Virginia and New England, by Captain John Smith, sometymes Governor in those Countryes, and Admirall of New England "; printed at London in 1627. The work is adorned with curious maps and engravings of the time when it appeared; the narrative extends from the year 1584 to 1626. Smith's work is highly and deservedly esteemed. The author was one of the most celebrated adventurers of a period of remarkable adventure; his book breathes that ardour for discovery, that spirit of enterprise which characterized the men of his time, when the manners of chivalry were united to zeal for commerce, and made subservient to the acquisition of wealth. But Captain Smith is most remarkable for uniting to the virtues which characterized his contemporaries several qualities to which they were generally strangers; his style is simple and concise, his narratives bear the stamp of truth, and his descriptions are free from false ornament. This author throws most valuable light upon the state and condition of the Indians at the time when North America was first discovered.

The second historian to consult is Beverley, who commences his narrative with the year 1585, and ends it with 1700. The first part of his book contains historical documents, properly so called, relative to the infancy of the colony. The second affords a most curious picture of the state of the Indians at this remote period. The third conveys very clear ideas concerning the manners, social conditions, laws, and political customs of the Virginians in the author's lifetime. Beverley was a native of Virginia, which occasions him to say at the beginning of his book, that he entreats his readers not to exercise their critical severity upon it, since, having been born in the Indies, he does not aspire to purity of language. Notwithstanding this colonial modesty, the author shows throughout his book the impatience with which he endures the supremacy of the mother-country. In this work of Beverley are also found numerous traces of that spirit of civil liberty which animated the English colonies of America at the time when he wrote. He also shows the dissensions which existed among them, and retarded their independence. Beverley detests his Catholic neighbours of Maryland even more than he hates the English Government: his style is simple, his narrative interesting, and apparently trustworthy.

I saw in America another work which ought to be consulted, entitled "The History of Virginia," by William Stith. This book affords some curious details, but I thought it long and diffuse.

The most ancient as well as the best document to be consulted on the history of Carolina is a work in small quarto, entitled "The History of Carolina," by John Lawson, printed at London in 1718. This work contains, in the first part, a journey of discovery in the west of Carolina; the account of which, given in the form of a journal, is in general confused and superficial; but it contains a very striking description of the mortality caused among the savages of that time both by the small-pox and the immoderate use of brandy; with a curious picture of the corruption of manners prevalent among them, which was increased by the presence of Europeans. The second part of Lawson's book is taken up with a description of the physical condition of Carolina, and its productions. In the third part, the author gives an interesting account of the manners, customs, and government of the Indians at that period. There is a good deal of talent and originality in this part of the work. Lawson concludes his history with a copy of the Charter granted to the Carolinas in the reign of Charles II. The general tone of this work is light, and often licentious, forming a perfect contrast to the solemn style of the works published at the same period in New England. Lawson's History is extremely scarce in America, and can not be procured in Europe. There is, however, a copy of it in the Royal Library at Paris.

From the southern extremity of the United States, I pass at once to the northern limit; as the intermediate space was not peopled till a later period. I must first point out a very curious compilation, entitled " Collection of the Massachusetts Historical Society," printed for the first time at Boston in 1792, and reprinted in 1806. The Collection of which I speak, and which is continued to the present day, contains a great number of very valuable documents relating to the history of the different States in New England. Among them are letters which have never been published, and authentic pieces which had been buried in provincial archives. The whole work of Gookin, concerning the Indians, is inserted there.

I have mentioned several times in the chapter to which this note relates the work of Nathaniel Norton, entitled " New England's Memorial "; sufficiently, perhaps, to prove that it deserves the attention of those who would be conversant with the history of New England. This book is in 8vo, and was reprinted at Boston in 1826.

The most valuable and important authority which exists upon the history of New England is the work of the Rev. Cotton Mather, entitled " Magnalia Christi Americana, or the Ecclesiastical History of New England, 1620–1698," 2 vols., 8vo, reprinted at Hartford, United States,

in 1820.[1] The author divided his work into seven books.
The first presents the history of the events which prepared
and brought about the establishment of New England.
The second contains the lives of the first governors and
chief magistrates who presided over the country. The
third is devoted to the lives and labours of the evangelical
ministers who, during the same period, had the care of
souls. In the fourth the author relates the institution and
progress of the University of Cambridge (Massachusetts).
In the fifth he describes the principles and the discipline
of the Church of New England. The sixth is taken up in
retracing certain facts, which, in the opinion of Mather,
prove the merciful interposition of Providence in behalf
of the inhabitants of New England. Lastly, in the seventh,
the author gives an account of the heresies and the troubles to which the Church of New England was exposed.
Cotton Mather was an evangelical minister who was born
at Boston, and passed his life there. His narratives are
distinguished by the same ardour and religious zeal which
led to the foundation of the colonies of New England.
Traces of bad taste sometimes occur in his manner of writing; but he interests, because he is full of enthusiasm. He
is often intolerant, still oftener credulous, but he never
betrays an intention to deceive. Sometimes his book contains fine passages, and true and profound reflections, such
as the following: " Before the arrival of the Puritans,"
says he, " there were more than a few attempts of the English to people and improve the parts of New England which
were to the northward of New Plymouth; but the designs
of those attempts being aimed no higher than the advancement of some worldly interests, a constant series of disasters has confounded them, until there was a plantation
erected upon the nobler designs of Christianity: and that
plantation, though it has had more adversaries than perhaps any one upon earth, yet, having obtained help from
God, it continues to this day." Mather occasionally relieves
the austerity of his descriptions with images full of tender
feeling: after having spoken of an English lady whose re-

ligious ardour had brought her to America with her husband, and who soon after sank under the fatigues and privations of exile, he adds, " As for her virtuous husband, Isaac Johnson,

" ' He tryed
To live without her, liked it not, and dyed.' "

Mather's work gives an admirable picture of the time and country which he describes. In his account of the motives which led the Puritans to seek an asylum beyond seas, he says:

" The God of Heaven served, as it were, a summons upon the spirits of his people in the English nation, stirring up the spirits of thousands which never saw the faces of each other, with a most unanimous inclination to leave all the pleasant accommodations of their native country, and go over a terrible ocean, into a more terrible desert, for the pure enjoyment of all his ordinances. It is now reasonable that, before we pass any further, the reasons of this undertaking should be more exactly made known unto posterity, especially unto the posterity of those that were the undertakers, lest they come at length to forget and neglect the true interest of New England. Wherefore I shall now transcribe some of them from a manuscript, wherein they were then tendered unto consideration:

" *General Considerations for the Plantation of New England.*

" First, It will be a service unto the Church of great consequence, to carry the Gospel unto those parts of the world, and raise a bulwark against the kingdom of Antichrist, which the Jesuits labour to rear up in all parts of the world.

" Secondly, All other Churches of Europe have been brought under desolations; and it may be feared that the like judgments are coming upon us; and who knows but God hath provided this place to be a refuge for many whom he means to save out of the general destruction?

" Thirdly, The land grows weary of her inhabitants, insomuch that man, which is the most precious of all creatures, is here more vile and base than the earth he treads upon; children, neighbours, and friends, especially the poor, are counted the greatest burdens, which, if things were right, would be the chiefest of earthly blessings.

" Fourthly, We are grown to that intemperance in all excess of riot, as no mean estate almost will suffice a man to keep sail with his equals, and he that fails in it must live in scorn and contempt: hence it comes to pass, that all arts and trades are carried in that deceitful manner and unrighteous course, as it is almost impossible for a good upright man to maintain his constant charge and live comfortably in them.

" Fifthly, The schools of learning and religion are so corrupted, as (beside the unsupportable charge of education) most children, even the best, wittiest, and of the fairest hopes, are perverted, corrupted, and utterly overthrown by the multitude of evil examples and licentious behaviours in these seminaries.

" Sixthly, The whole earth is the Lord's garden, and he hath given it to the sons of Adam, to be tilled and improved by them: why, then, should we stand starving here for places of habitation, and in the meantime suffer whole countries, as profitable for the use of man, to lie waste without any improvement?

" Seventhly, What can be a better or nobler work, and more worthy of a Christian, than to erect and support a reformed particular Church in its infancy, and unite our forces with such a company of faithful people, as by timely assistance may grow stronger and prosper; but for want of it, may be put to great hazards, if not be wholly ruined?

" Eighthly, If any such as are known to be godly, and live in wealth and prosperity here, shall forsake all this to join with this reformed Church, and with it run the hazard of an hard and mean condition, it will be an example of great use, both for the removing of scandal and to give more life unto the faith of God's people in their prayers for the plantation, and also to encourage others to join the more willingly in it."

Further on, when he declares the principles of the Church of New England with respect to morals, Mather inveighs with violence against the custom of drinking healths at table, which he denounces as a pagan and abominable practice. He proscribes with the same rigour all ornaments for the hair used by the female sex, as well as their custom of having the arms and neck uncovered. In another part of his work he relates several instances of witchcraft which had alarmed New England. It is plain that the visible action of the devil in the affairs of this world appeared to him an incontestable and evident fact.

This work of Cotton Mather displays, in many places, the spirit of civil liberty and political independence which characterized the times in which he lived. Their principles respecting government are discoverable at every page. Thus, for instance, the inhabitants of Massachusetts, in the year 1630, ten years after the foundation of Plymouth, are found to have devoted 400l. sterling to the establishment of the University of Cambridge. In passing from the general documents relative to the history of New England to those which describe the several States comprised within its limits, I ought first to notice " The History of the Colony of Massachusetts," by Hutchinson, Lieutenant-Governor of the Massachusetts Province, 2 vols., 8vo. The history of Hutchinson, which I have several times quoted in the chapter to which this note relates, commences in the year 1628, and ends in 1750. Throughout the work there is a striking air of truth and the greatest simplicity of style: it is full of minute details. The best history to consult concerning Connecticut is that of Benjamin Trumbull, entitled "A Complete History of Connecticut, Civil and Ecclesiastical," 1630–1764; 2 vols., 8vo, printed in 1818, at New Haven. This history contains a clear and calm account of all the events that happened in Connecticut during the period given in the title. The author drew from the best sources, and his narrative bears the stamp of truth. All that he says of the early days of Connecticut is extremely curious. See especially the Constitution of 1639, and also the " Penal Laws of Connecticut," vol. i.

" The History of New Hampshire," by Jeremy Belknap, is a work held in merited estimation. It was printed at Boston in 1792, in 2 vols., 8vo. The third chapter of the first volume is particularly worthy of attention for the valuable details it affords on the political and religious principles of the Puritans, on the causes of their emigration, and on their laws. The following curious quotation is given from a sermon delivered in 1663: " It concerneth New England always to remember that they are a plantation religious, not a plantation of trade. The profession of the purity of doctrine, worship, and discipline, is written upon her forehead. Let merchants, and such as are increasing cent. per cent., remember this, that worldly gain was not the end and design of the people of New England, but religion. And if any man among us make religion as twelve, and the world as thirteen, such an one hath not the spirit of a true New Englishman." The reader of Belknap will find in his work more general ideas, and more strength of thought, than are to be met with in the American historians even to the present day.

Among the Central States which deserve our attention for their remote origin, New York and Pennsylvania are the foremost. The best history we have of the former is entitled " A History of New York," by William Smith, printed at London in 1757. Smith gives us important details of the wars between the French and English in America. His is the best account of the famous confederation of the Iroquois.

With respect to Pennsylvania, I can not do better than point out the work of Proud, entitled " The History of Pennsylvania, from the original Institution and Settlement of that Province, under the first Proprietor and Governor, William Penn, in 1681, till after the year 1742," by Robert Proud, 2 vols., 8vo, printed at Philadelphia in 1797. This work is deserving of the especial attention of the reader; it contains a mass of curious documents concerning Penn, the doctrine of the Quakers, and the character, manners, and customs of the first inhabitants of Pennsylvania. I need not add that among the most important documents relating to this State are the works of Penn himself, and those of Franklin.

G. p. 38, note 4.—We read in Jefferson's " Memoirs " as follows:

" At the time of the first settlement of the English in Virginia, when land was to be had for little or nothing, some provident persons having obtained large grants of it, and being desirous of maintaining the splendour of their families, entailed their property upon their descendants. The transmission of these estates from generation to generation, to men who bore the same name, had the effect of raising up a distinct class of families, who, possessing by law the privilege of perpetuating their wealth, formed by these means a sort of patrician order, distinguished by the grandeur and luxury of their establishments. From this order it was that the King usually chose his councillors of state." [2]

In the United States, the principal clauses of the English law respecting descent have been universally rejected. The first rule that we follow, says Mr. Kent, touching inheritance, is the following: If a man dies intestate, his property goes to his heirs in a direct line. If he has but one heir or heiress, he or she succeeds to the whole. If there are several heirs of the same degree, they divide the inheritance equally among them, without distinction of sex. This rule was prescribed for the first time in the State of New York by a statute of February 23, 1786. It has since then been adopted in the Revised Statutes of the same State. At the present day this law holds good throughout the whole of the United States, with the exception of the State of Vermont, where the male heir inherits a double portion. Kent gives an historical account of American legislation on the subject of entail: by this we learn that, previous to the Revolution, the colonies followed the English law of entail. Estates tail were abolished in Virginia in 1776, on a motion of Mr. Jefferson. They were suppressed in New York in 1786, and have since been abolished in North Carolina, Kentucky, Tennessee, Georgia, and Missouri. In Vermont, Indiana, Illinois, South Carolina, and Louisiana, entail was never introduced. Those States which thought proper to preserve the English law of entail, modified it in such a way as to deprive it of its most aristocratic tendencies. " Our general principles on the subject of government," says Mr. Kent, " tend to favour the free circulation of property."

It can not fail to strike the French reader who studies the law of inheritance that on these questions the French legislation is infinitely more democratic even than the American. The American law makes an equal division of the father's property, but only in the case of his will not being known; " for every man," says the law, " in the State of New York has entire liberty, power, and authority to dispose of his property by will, to leave it entire, or divided in favour of any persons he chooses as his heirs, provided he do not leave it to a political body or any corporation." The French law obliges the testator to divide his property equally, or nearly so, among his heirs. Most of the American republics still admit of entails, under certain restrictions; but the French law prohibits entail in all cases. If the social condition of the Americans is more democratic than that of the French, the laws of the latter are the most democratic of the two. This may be explained more easily than at first appears to be the case. In France, democracy is still occupied in the work of destruction; in America, it reigns quietly over the ruins it has made.

H. p. 46, note 1.—Summary of the qualifications of voters in the United States as they existed in 1832: All the States agree in granting the right of voting at the age of twenty-one. In all of them it is necessary to have resided for a certain time in the district where the vote is given. This period varies from three months to two years.

As to the qualification: in the State of Massachusetts it is necessary to have an income of three pounds sterling or a capital of sixty pounds.

In Rhode Island, a man must possess landed property to the amount of one hundred and thirty-three dollars.

In Connecticut, he must have a property which gives an income of seventeen dollars. A year of service in the militia also gives the elective privilege.

In New Jersey, an elector must have a property of fifty pounds a year.

In South Carolina and Maryland, the elector must possess fifty acres of land.

In Tennessee, he must possess some property.

In the States of Mississippi, Ohio, Georgia, Virginia, Pennsylvania, Delaware, and New York, the only necessary qualification for voting is that of paying the taxes; and in most of the States, to serve in the militia is equivalent to the payment of taxes.

In Maine and New Hampshire any man can vote who is not on the pauper list.

Lastly, in the States of Missouri, Alabama, Illinois, Louisiana, Indiana, Kentucky, and Vermont, the conditions of voting have no reference to the property of the elector.

I believe there is no other State beside that of North Carolina in which different conditions are applied to the voting for the Senate and the electing the House of Representatives. The electors of the former, in this case, should possess in property fifty acres of land; to vote for the latter, nothing more is required than to pay taxes.

I. p. 82, note 46.—The small number of custom-house officers employed in the United States, compared with the extent of the coast, renders smuggling very easy; notwithstanding which, it is less practised than elsewhere, because everybody endeavours to repress it. In America there is no police for the prevention of fires, and such accidents are more frequent than in Europe; but in general they are more speedily extinguished, because the surrounding population is prompt in lending assistance.

K. p. 84, note 47.—It is incorrect to assert that centralization was produced by the French Revolution; the revolution brought it to perfection, but did not create it. The mania for centralization and government regulations dates from the time when jurists began to take a share in the Government, in the time of Philippe-le-Bel; ever since which period they have been on the increase. In the year 1775, M. de Malesherbes, speaking in the name of the Cour des Aides, said to Louis XIV:

". . . Every corporation and every community of citizens retained the right of administering its own affairs; a right which not only forms part of the primitive constitution of the kingdom, but has a still higher origin; for it is the right of nature and of reason. Nevertheless, your subjects, Sire, have been deprived of it; and we can not refrain from saying that in this respect your government has fallen into puerile extremes. From the time when powerful ministers made it a political principle to prevent the convocation of a national assembly, one consequence has succeeded another, until the deliberations of the inhabitants of a village are declared null when they have not been authorized by the Intendant. Of course, if the community has an expensive undertaking to carry through, it must remain under the control of the sub-delegate of the Intendant, and, consequently, follow the plan he proposes, employ his favourite workmen, pay them according to his pleasure; and if an action at law is deemed necessary, the Intendant's permission must be obtained. The cause must be pleaded before this first tribunal, previous to its being carried into a public court; and if the opinion of the Intendant is opposed to that of the inhabitants, or if their adversary enjoys his favour, the community is deprived of the power of defending its rights. Such are the means, Sire, which have been exerted to extinguish the municipal spirit in France; and to stifle, if possible, the opinions of the citizens. The nation may be said to lie under an interdict, and to be in wardship under guardians." What could be said more to the purpose at the present day, when the revolution has achieved what are called its victories in centralization?

In 1789, Jefferson wrote from Paris to one of his friends, " There is no country where the mania for over-governing has taken deeper root than in France, or been the source of greater mischief." (Letter to Madison, August 28, 1789.) The fact is, that for several centuries past the central power of France has done everything it could to extend central administration; it has acknowledged no other limits than its own strength. The central power to which the revolution gave birth made more rapid advances than any of its predecessors, because it was stronger and wiser than they had been; Louis XIV committed the welfare of such communities to the caprice of an Intendant; Napoleon left them to that of the Minister. The same principle governed both, though its consequences were more or less remote.

L. p. 93, note 1.—The immutability of the Constitution of France is a necessary consequence of the laws of that country. To begin with the most important of all the laws, that which decides the order of succession to the Throne; what can be more immutable in its principle than a political order founded upon the natural succession of father to son? In 1814, Louis XVIII had established the perpetual law of hereditary succession in favour of his own family. The individuals who regulated the consequences of the Revolution of 1830 followed his example; they merely established the perpetuity of the law in favour of another family. In this respect they imitated the Chancellor Meaupou, who, when he erected the new Parliament upon the ruins of the old, took care to declare in the same ordinance that the rights of the new magistrates should be as inalienable as those of their predecessors had been. The laws of 1830, like those of 1814, point out no way of changing the Constitution: and it is evident that the ordinary means of legislation are insufficient for this purpose. As the King, the Peers, and the Deputies, all derive their authority from the Constitution, these three powers united can not alter a law by virtue of which alone they govern. Out of the pale of the Constitution they are nothing: where, when, could they take their stand to effect a change in its provisions? The alternative is clear: either their efforts are powerless against the Charter, which continues to exist in spite of them, in which case they only reign in the name of the Charter; or they succeed in changing the Charter, and then the law by which they existed being annulled, they themselves cease to exist. By destroying the Charter, they destroy themselves. This is much more evident in the laws of 1830 than in those of 1814. In 1814, the royal prerogative took its stand above and beyond the Constitution; but in 1830, it was avowedly created by, and dependent on, the Constitution. A part, therefore, of the French Constitution is immutable, because it is united to the destiny of a family; and the body of the Constitution is equally immutable, because there appear to be no legal means of changing it. These remarks are not applicable to England. That country having no written Constitution, who can assert when its Constitution is changed?

M. p. 93, note 1.—The most esteemed authors who have written upon the English Constitution agree with each other in establishing the omnipotence of the Parliament. Delolme says, " It is a fundamental principle with the English lawyers that Parliament can do everything except making a woman a man, or a man a woman." Blackstone expresses himself more in detail, if not more energetically, than Delolme, in the following terms: " The power and jurisdiction of Parliament, says Sir Edward Coke, is so transcendent and absolute that it can not be confined, either for causes or persons, within any bounds." And of this High Court, he adds, may be truly said, " ' Si antiquitatem spectes, est vetustissima; si dignitatem, est

honoratissima; si jurisdictionem, est capacissima.' It hath
sovereign and uncontrollable authority in the making, con-
firming, enlarging, restraining, abrogating, repealing, re-
viving, and expounding of laws, concerning matters of all
possible denominations; ecclesiastical or temporal; civil,
military, maritime, or criminal; this being the place where
that absolute despotic power which must, in all Governments, reside somewhere, is intrusted by the Constitution
of these kingdoms. All mischiefs and grievances, operations and remedies, that transcend the ordinary course of
the laws, are within the reach of this extraordinary tribunal.
It can regulate or new-model the succession to the Crown;
as was done in the reign of Henry VIII and William III.
It can alter the established religion of the land; as was
done in a variety of instances in the reigns of King Henry
VIII and his three children. It can change and create
afresh even the Constitution of the kingdom, and of Par-
liaments themselves; as was done by the Act of Union
and the several statutes for triennial and septennial elections. It can, in short, do everything that is not naturally
impossible to be done; and, therefore, some have not
scrupled to call its power, by a figure rather too bold, the
omnipotence of Parliament."

N. p. 105, note 3.—There is no question upon which
the American Constitutions agree more fully than upon
that of political jurisdiction. All the Constitutions which
take cognizance of this matter, give to the House of Delegates the exclusive right of impeachment; excepting only
the Constitution of North Carolina, which grants the same
privilege to grand juries. (Article 23.) Almost all the Constitutions give the exclusive right of pronouncing sentence
to the Senate, or to the Assembly which occupies its place.

The only punishments which the political tribunals can
inflict are removal, or the interdiction of public functions
for the future. There is no other Constitution but that
of Virginia which enables them to inflict every kind of
punishment. The crimes which are subject to political

jurisdiction are, in the Federal Constitution (Section 4, Art. 1); in that of Indiana (Art. 3, paragraphs 23 and 24); of New York (Art. 5); of Delaware (Art. 5), high treason, bribery, and other high crimes or offences. In the Constitution of Massachusetts (Chap. 1, Section 2); that of North Carolina (Art. 23); of Virginia (p. 252), misconduct and maladministration. In the Constitution of New Hampshire (p. 105), corruption, intrigue, and maladministration. In Vermont (Chap. 2, Art. 24), maladministration. In South Carolina (Art. 5); Kentucky (Art. 5); Tennessee (Art. 4); Ohio (Art. 1, Sections 23, 24); Louisiana (Art. 5); Mississippi (Art. 5); Alabama (Art. 6); Pennsylvania (Art. 4), crimes committed in the non-performance of official duties. In the States of Illinois, Georgia, Maine, and Connecticut, no particular offences are specified.

O. p. 168, note 41.—It is true that the powers of Europe may carry on maritime wars with the Union; but there is always greater facility and less danger in supporting a maritime than a continental war. Maritime warfare only requires one species of effort. A commercial people which consents to furnish its Government with the necessary funds, is sure to possess a fleet. And it is far easier to induce a nation to part with its money, almost unconsciously, than to reconcile it to sacrifices of men and personal efforts. Moreover, defeat by sea rarely compromises the existence or independence of the people which endures it. As for continental wars, it is evident that the nations of Europe can not be formidable in this way to the American Union. It would be very difficult to transport and maintain in America more than 25,000 soldiers; an army which may be considered to represent a nation of about 2,000,000 men. The most populous nation of Europe contending in this way against the Union, is in the position of a nation of 2,000,000 inhabitants at war with one of 12,000,000. Add to this, that America has all its resources within reach, while the European is at 4,000 miles distance from his; and that the immensity of the Ameri-

can continent would of itself present an insurmountable
obstacle to its conquest.

P. p. 193, note 2.—The first American journal appeared
in April, 1704, and was published at Boston. See " Collection of the Historical Society of Massachusetts," vol. vi.
It would be a mistake to suppose that the periodical press
has always been entirely free in the American colonies: an
attempt was made to establish something analogous to a
censorship and preliminary security. Consult the Legislative Documents of Massachusetts of January 14, 1722.
The Committee appointed by the General Assembly (the
Legislative body of the province) for the purpose of examining into circumstances connected with a paper entitled " The New England Courier," expresses its opinion that " the tendency of the said journal is to turn religion into derision and bring it into contempt; that it
mentions the sacred writers in a profane and irreligious
manner; that it puts malicious interpretations upon the
conduct of the ministers of the Gospel; and that the Government of his Majesty is insulted, and the peace and tranquility of the province disturbed by the said journal. The
Committee is consequently of opinion that the printer and
publisher, James Franklin, should be forbidden to print
and publish the said journal or any other work in future,
without having previously submitted it to the Secretary
of the province; and that the justices of the peace for the
county of Suffolk should be commissioned to require bail
of the said James Franklin for his good conduct during
the ensuing year." The suggestion of the Committee was
adopted and passed into a law, but the effect of it was null,
for the journal eluded the prohibition by putting the name
of Benjamin Franklin instead of James Franklin at the
bottom of its columns, and this manœuvre was supported
by public opinion.

Q. p. 303, note 6.—The Federal Constitution has introduced the jury into the tribunals of the Union in the

same way as the States had introduced it into their own
several courts; but as it has not established any fixed rules
for the choice of jurors, the Federal Courts select them
from the ordinary jury-list which each State makes for
itself. The laws of the States must therefore be examined
for the theory of the formation of juries. See " Story's
Commentaries on the Constitution," " Sergeant's Constitutional Law." See also the Federal Laws of the years
1789, 1800, and 1802, upon the subject. For the purpose
of thoroughly understanding the American principles with
respect to the formation of juries, I examined the laws of
States at a distance from one another, and the following
observations were the result of my inquiries: In America,
all the citizens who exercise the elective franchise have the
right of serving upon a jury. The great State of New
York, however, has made a slight difference between the
two privileges, but in a spirit quite contrary to that of the
laws of France; for in the State of New York there are
fewer persons eligible as jurymen than there are electors.
It may be said in general that the right of forming part
of a jury, like the right of electing representatives, is open
to all the citizens: the exercise of this right, however, is
not put indiscriminately into any hands. Every year a
body of municipal or county magistrates—called selectmen
in New England, supervisors in New York, trustees in
Ohio, and sheriffs of the parish in Louisiana—choose for
each county a certain number of citizens who have the
right of serving as jurymen, and who are supposed to be
capable of exercising their functions. These magistrates,
being themselves elective, excite no distrust; their powers,
like those of most republican magistrates, are very extensive and very arbitrary, and they frequently make use of
them to remove unworthy or incompetent jurymen. The
names of the jurymen thus chosen are transmitted to the
County Court; and the jury who have to decide any affair
are drawn by lot from the whole list of names. The Americans have contrived in every way to make the common
people eligible to the jury, and to render the service as

little onerous as possible. The sessions are held in the chief town of every county, and the jury are indemnified for their attendance either by the State or the parties concerned. They receive in general a dollar per day, besides their travelling expenses. In America, the being placed upon the jury is looked upon as a burden, but it is a burden which is very supportable. See " Brevard's Digest of the Public Statute Law of South Carolina "; " The General Laws of Massachusetts, revised and published by authority of the Legislature," vol. ii; " The Revised Statutes of the State of New York," vol. ii; " The Statute Law of the State of Tennessee," vol. i; " Acts of the State of Ohio "; and " Digeste général des Actes de la Législature de la Louisiane."

R. p. 307, note 7.—If we attentively examine the constitution of the jury as introduced into civil proceedings in England, we shall readily perceive that the jurors are under the immediate control of the judge. It is true that the verdict of the jury, in civil as well as in criminal cases, comprises the question of fact and the question of right in the same reply; thus—a house is claimed by Peter as having been purchased by him: this is the fact to be decided. The defendant puts in a plea of incompetency on the part of the vendor: this is the legal question to be resolved. But the jury do not enjoy the same character of infallibility in civil cases, according to the practice of the English courts, as they do in criminal cases. The judge may refuse to receive the verdict; and even after the first trial has taken place, a second or new trial may be awarded by the Court. See " Blackstone's Commentaries," book iii.

S. p. 690, note 3.—I find in my travelling journal a passage which may serve to convey a more complete notion of the trials to which the women of America, who consent to follow their husbands into the wilds, are often subjected. This description has nothing to recommend it to the reader but its strict accuracy:

A JURY.

Photogravure from an engraving after a painting by J. Morgan.

". . . From time to time we come to fresh clearings; all these places are alike; I shall describe the one at which we have halted to-night, for it will serve to remind me of all the others.

" The bell which the pioneers hang round the necks of their cattle, in order to find them again in the woods, announced our approach to a clearing, when we were yet a long way off; and we soon afterward heard the stroke of the hatchet, hewing down the trees of the forest. As we came nearer, traces of destruction marked the presence of civilized man: the road was strewn with shattered boughs; trunks of trees, half consumed by fire, or cleft by the wedge, were still standing in the track we were following. We continued to proceed till we reached a wood in which all the trees seemed to have been suddenly struck dead; in the height of summer their boughs were as leafless as in winter; and upon closer examination we found that a deep circle had been cut round the bark, which, by stopping the circulation of the sap, soon kills the tree. We were informed that this is commonly the first thing a pioneer does; as he can not in the first year cut down all the trees which cover his new parcel of land, he sows Indian corn under their branches, and puts the trees to death in order to prevent them from injuring his crop. Beyond this field, at present imperfectly traced out, we suddenly came upon the cabin of its owner, situated in the centre of a plot of ground more carefully cultivated than the rest, but where man was still waging unequal warfare with the forest; there the trees were cut down, but their roots were not removed, and the trunks still encumbered the ground which they so recently shaded. Around these dry blocks, wheat, suckers of trees, and plants of every kind, grow and intertwine in all the luxuriance of wild, untutored Nature. Amid this vigorous and various vegetation stands the house of the pioneer, or, as they call it, the log-house. Like the ground about it, this rustic dwelling bore marks of recent and hasty labour; its length seemed not to exceed thirty feet, its height fifteen; the walls as well as the roof were formed of rough trunks of trees, between which a little moss and clay had been inserted to keep out the cold and rain.

" As night was coming on, we determined to ask the master of the log-house for a lodging. At the sound of our footsteps, the children who were playing among the scattered branches sprang up and ran toward the house, as if they were frightened at the sight of man; while two large dogs, almost wild, with ears erect and outstretched nose, came growling out of their hut, to cover the retreat of their young masters. The pioneer himself made his appearance at the door of his dwelling; he looked at us with a rapid and inquisitive glance, made a sign to the dogs to go into the house, and set them the example, without betraying either curiosity or apprehension at our arrival.

" We entered the log-house: the inside is quite unlike that of the cottages of the peasantry of Europe: it contains more that is superfluous, less that is necessary. A single window with a muslin blind; on a hearth of trodden clay an immense fire, which lights the whole structure; above the hearth a good rifle, a deer's skin, and plumes of eagles' feathers; on the right hand of the chimney a map of the United States, raised and shaken by the wind through the crannies in the wall; near the map, upon a shelf formed of a roughly hewn plank, a few volumes of books—a Bible, the first six books of Milton, and two of Shakespeare's plays; along the wall, trunks instead of closets; in the centre of the room a rude table, with legs of green wood, and with the bark still upon them, looking as if they grew out of the ground on which they stood; but on this table a tea-pot of British ware, silver spoons, cracked tea-cups, and some newspapers.

" The master of this dwelling has the strong angular features and lank limbs peculiar to the native of New England. It is evident that this man was not born in the solitude in which we have met with him: his physical constitution suffices to show that his earlier years were spent in the midst of civilized society, and that he belongs to that

restless, calculating, and adventurous race of men, who do
with the utmost coolness things only to be accounted for
by the ardour of the passions, and who endure the life
of savages for a time, in order to conquer and civilize the
backwoods.

"When the pioneer perceived that we were crossing
his threshold, he came to meet us and shake hands, as is
their custom; but his face was quite unmoved; he opened
the conversation by inquiring what was going on in the
world; and when his curiosity was satisfied, he held his
peace, as if he were tired by the noise and importunity of
mankind. When we questioned him in our turn, he gave
us all the information we required; he then attended sedulously, but without eagerness, to our personal wants.
While he was engaged in providing thus kindly for us,
how came it that in spite of ourselves we felt our gratitude
die upon our lips? It is that our host, while he performs
the duties of hospitality, seems to be obeying an irksome
necessity of his condition: he treats it as a duty imposed
upon him by his situation, not as a pleasure. By the side
of the hearth sits a woman with a baby on her lap: she
nods to us without disturbing herself. Like the pioneer,
this woman is in the prime of life; her appearance would
seem superior to her condition, and her apparel even betrays a lingering taste for dress; but her delicate limbs appear shrunken, her features are drawn in, her eye is mild
and melancholy; her whole physiognomy bears marks of
a degree of religious resignation, a deep quiet of all passions, and some sort of natural and tranquil firmness, ready
to meet all the ills of life, without fearing and without braving them. Her children cluster about her, full of health,
turbulence, and energy: they are true children of the
wilderness; their mother watches them from time to time
with mingled melancholy and joy: to look at their strength
and her languor, one might imagine that the life she has
given them has exhausted her own, and still she regrets
not what they have cost her. The house inhabited by
these emigrants has no internal partition or loft. In the

one chamber of which it consists the whole family is gathered for the night. The dwelling is itself a little world—an ark of civilization amid an ocean of foliage: a hundred steps beyond it the primeval forest spreads its shades, and solitude resumes its sway."

T. p. 691, note 4.—It is not the equality of conditions that makes men immoral and irreligious; but when men, being equal, are at the same time immoral and irreligious, the effects of immorality and irreligion easily manifest themselves outwardly, because men have but little influence upon each other, and no class exists which can undertake to keep society in order. Equality of conditions never engenders profligacy of morals, but it sometimes allows that profligacy to show itself.

U. p. 713, note 2.—Setting aside all those who do not think at all, and those who dare not say what they think, the immense majority of the Americans will still be found to appear satisfied with the political institutions by which they are governed; and, I believe, really to be so. I look upon this state of public opinion as an indication, but not as a demonstration, of the absolute excellence of American laws. The pride of a nation, the gratification of certain ruling passions by the law, a concourse of circumstances, defects which escape notice, and more than all the rest, the influence of a majority which shuts the mouth of all cavillers, may long perpetuate the delusions of a people as well as those of a man. Look at England throughout the eighteenth century. No nation was ever more prodigal of self-applause, no people was ever more self-satisfied; then every part of its constitution was right—everything, even to its most obvious defects, was irreproachable: at the present day a vast number of Englishmen seem to have nothing better to do than to prove that this constitution was faulty in many respects. Which was right?—the English people of the last century, or the English people of the present day?

The same thing has occurred in France. It is certain that during the reign of Louis XIV the great bulk of the nation was devotedly attached to the form of government which, at that time, governed the community. But it is a vast error to suppose that there was anything degraded in the character of the French of that age. There might be some sort of servitude in France at that time, but assuredly there was no servile spirit among the people. The writers of that age felt a species of genuine enthusiasm in extolling the power of their king; and there was no peasant so obscure in his hovel as not to take a pride in the glory of his sovereign, and to die cheerfully with the cry " Vive le Roi! " upon his lips. These very same forms of loyalty are now odious to the French people. Which are wrong? —the French of the age of Louis XIV, or their descendants of the present day?

Our judgment of the laws of a people must not then be founded exclusively upon its inclinations, since those inclinations change from age to age; but upon more elevated principles and a more general experience. The love which a people may show for its laws proves only this—that we should not be in too great a hurry to change them.

V. p. 768, note 3.—In the chapter to which this note relates I have pointed out one source of danger: I am now about to point out another kind of peril, more rare, indeed, but far more formidable if it were ever to make its appearance. If the love of physical gratification and the taste for well-being, which are naturally suggested to men by a state of equality, were to get entire possession of the mind of a democratic people, and to fill it completely, the manners of the nation would become so totally opposed to military tastes that perhaps even the army would eventually acquire a love of peace, in spite of the peculiar interest which leads it to desire war. Living in the midst of a state of general relaxation, the troops would ultimately think it better to rise without efforts, by the slow but com-

modious advancement of a peace establishment, than to
purchase more rapid promotion at the cost of all the toils
and privations of the field. With these feelings, they would
take up arms without enthusiasm, and use them without
energy; they would allow themselves to be led to meet
the foe, instead of marching to attack him. It must not
be supposed that this pacific state of the army would render
it adverse to revolutions; for revolutions, and especially
military revolutions, which are generally very rapid, are attended, indeed, with great dangers, but not with protracted
toil; they gratify ambition at less cost than war; life only
is at stake, and the men of democracies care less for their
lives than for their comforts. Nothing is more dangerous
for the freedom and the tranquility of a people than an
army afraid of war, because, as such an army no longer
seeks to maintain its importance and its influence on the
field of battle, it seeks to assert them elsewhere. Thus it
might happen that the men of whom a democratic army
consists should lose the interests of citizens without acquiring the virtues of soldiers; and that the army should cease
to be fit for war without ceasing to be turbulent. I shall
here repeat what I have said in the text: the remedy for
these dangers is not to be found in the army, but in the
country: a democratic people which has preserved the
manliness of its character will never be at a loss for military prowess in its soldiers.

W. p. 785, note 1.—Men connect the greatness of
their idea of unity with means, God with ends: hence this
idea of greatness, as men conceive it, leads us into infinite
littleness. To compel all men to follow the same course
toward the same object is a human notion—to introduce
infinite variety of action, but so combined that all these
acts lead by a multitude of different courses to the accomplishment of one great design, is a conception of the Deity.
The human idea of unity is almost always barren; the divine idea pregnant with abundant results. Men think they
manifest their greatness by simplifying the means they use;

but it is the purpose of God which is simple—his means are infinitely varied.

X. p. 788, note 3.—A democratic people is not only led by its own tastes to centralize its government, but the passions of all the men by whom it is governed constantly urge it in the same direction. It may easily be foreseen that almost all the able and ambitious members of a democratic community will labour without ceasing to extend the powers of government, because they all hope at some time or other to wield those powers. It is a waste of time to attempt to prove to them that extreme centralization may be injurious to the State, since they are centralizing for their own benefit. Among the public men of democracies there are hardly any but men of great disinterestedness or extreme mediocrity who seek to oppose the centralization of government: the former are scarce, the latter powerless.

Y. p. 809, note 9.—I have often asked myself what would happen if, amid the relaxation of democratic manners, and as a consequence of the restless spirit of the army, a military government were ever to be founded among any of the nations of the present age. I think that even such a government would not differ very much from the outline I have drawn in the chapter to which this note belongs, and that it would retain none of the fierce characteristics of a military oligarchy. I am persuaded that, in such a case, a sort of fusion would take place between the habits of official men and those of the military service. The administration would assume something of a military character, and the army some of the usages of the civil administration. The result would be a regular, clear, exact, and absolute system of government; the people would become the reflection of the army, and the community be drilled like a garrison.

Z. p. 813, note 10.—It can not be absolutely or generally affirmed that the greatest danger of the present age is license or tyranny, anarchy or despotism. Both are equally to be feared; and the one may as easily proceed as the other from the self-same cause, namely, that general apathy, which is the consequence of what I have termed Individualism: it is because this apathy exists that the executive government, having mustered a few troops, is able to commit acts of oppression one day, and the next day a party, which has mustered some thirty men in its ranks, can also commit acts of oppression. Neither one nor the other can found anything to last; and the causes which enable them to succeed easily prevent them from succeeding long: they rise because nothing opposes them, and they sink because nothing supports them. The proper object, therefore, of our most strenuous resistance is far less either anarchy or despotism than that apathy which may almost indifferently beget either the one or the other.

NOTES

[1] A folio edition of this work was published in London in 1702.

[2] This passage is extracted and translated from M. Conseil's work upon the life of Jefferson, entitled "Mélanges Politiques et Philosophiques de Jefferson."

INDEX

Volume II begins with page 419

Able men rarely in office, 208.
Abstract terms, 554.
Activity of Americans, 265.
Advantages from democratic government, 251.
Ambition, 737.
Anglo-Americans, origin of, 11.
Archives, absence of, 221.
Armies in democratic countries, 756.
Association, liberty of, 200.
Associations, public, 593.

Balance of power between the nation and the States, 110.
Baltimore, riots in, 288.
Bank of the United States, 182, 449, 465.
Bankruptcy, 240.
Beverly, 839.
Bibliography, 837 et seq.
Black voters, 288.
Blue laws, the, 23.
Books, American, 539.
British race, preponderance of the, 479.

Calhoun, John C., quoted, 451.
Capitol of the United States, 537.
Centralization, 72, 791, 849, 863.
Character, difference of, North and South, 434.
Charlevoix, quoted, 832.

Cherokee petition, 377.
China, original condition of, 530.
Cities, large, 356.
Climbing plants, 830.
Colonies, government of the, 21.
Colonization Society, the, 402.
Commerce, North and South, 464.
Commercial prosperity, 467.
Commercial statistics, 475, 476.
Congress, composition of, 112; contrast in the personnel of the two houses, 213.
Constitution, the American, 106, 852; powers of, 94.
Constitution, the English, 851.
Courage, American, 725.
Court of Sessions, 65.
Courts, the Federal, 137.

Dangers to democracy, 150.
Dartmouth College case, 172.
Democratic government in America, 207.
Democratic institutions, main evil of, 278.
Democratic opinions and sentiments, influence of, 780.
Democratic republic, how maintained, 309.
Despotism, 588.
Division of labour, 645.
Duration of the Union, 419.

Eastern and Western States compared, 346.

Education, public, 26.

Election of President, 128.

Elective system, vices of the, 124.

English colony, first, 15.

English critics of America, 705.

Equality, political and social, 41.

Europe, condition of, in the seventeenth century, 27.

Expenditure, public, 230.

Family relations, 683.

Federal systems, evil of all, 161.

" Federalist," the, 169.

Foreign policy, 244.

France, prediction as to, 356.

Freedom of the press, 854.

Frontier, the Western, life there, 341, 857; movement of the, 437.

Gambling, 836.

Governor, powers of the, 71.

Hamilton, Alexander, quoted, 215, 237, 287.

Hints, American obliviousness to, 659.

Home missions, 330.

Honour, 718.

Impeachment, 100.

Indians, North American, 6, 361 et seq, 408 et seq.

Individualism in democratic countries, 580.

Inheritance, laws of, 35.

Interest, principle of, 608.

Jackson, Andrew, newspaper attack on, 188; influence and conduct of, 453.

Jefferson, Thomas, quoted, 216, 244, 287.

Journalists of the United States, 192, 540.

Judicial power, 90, 97, 307.

Jury, trial by, 301, 854.

Justices of the peace, 62.

Land-owners and tenants, 674.

Lands, sale of public, 448.

Language and literature, influence of democracy upon, 539; in America, 549; free use of, 711.

Languages, Indian, 831.

Lawson, John, 839.

Lawyers, 292.

Legislators, 574.

Legislatures, State, 70.

Liberty of opinion, 281.

Liquors, intoxicating, 240.

Long's expedition, 830.

Majority, power of the, 271, 493; tyranny of the, how mitigated, 290.

Manners, influence of democracy on, 650.

Manufactures, growth of, 800.

Maritime warfare, 853.

Marriage, 688.

Marshall, John, quoted, 250.

Mather, Cotton, his Magnalia, 840 et seq.

Mines, 829.

Mississippi Valley, the, 3; importance of, 439.

Morals, American, 691.

Mounds, 8.

Negro, the, 360 et seq.

New England, emigration from, 315; principles, 16.

Newspapers, 598.

North America, exterior form of, 1.

Novels, American, why few, 708.

Nullification, 450.

Occupations and business callings, 639.
Officers, public, simplicity of, 216; pay of, 227.
Ohio Valley, 386.

Parties, political, in the United States, 177.
Patriotism, peculiarity of American, 712.
People, the, real governors, 175.
Periodicals, number of, 191.
Philosophy in America and in Europe, 484.
Pilgrims of Plymouth, 18.
Poets and poetic ideas, 559.
Poles, assistance for the, 325.
Political associations, 197.
Political jurisdiction in the United States, 99.
Population, increase of, 463–465.
Presidency, the, its functions and power, 114 et seq.
Press, liberty of the, 185, 817; power of the, 188.
Primogeniture, 390.
Principles that actuate Americans, 432.
Prisons, condition of the, 275.
Private rights, 819.
Procedure, legal, in America, 30.
Prospects of the United States, 477.
Prosperity, danger of, 442.
Public relations, 709.
Puritans, the, 17.

Races, the three, 358.
Religion, its influence on politics, 326; in America, 488, 502 et seq.; influences of democracy upon, 502.
Representation, ratio of, 170.
Republic and Union, distinction between, 456.

Roman Catholics, 323; in America, 510 et seq.
Russian growth parallel with American, 483.

Sabbath in America, 628.
Salaries of officials, 248.
Science and the arts, influence of democracy upon, 517.
Selectmen, duties of, 51.
Servants, treatment of, 664.
Sévigné, Madame, quoted, 652.
Sexes, duties and rights of the two, 698.
Ships, American, 469.
Slavery, first introduction of, 15; effects of, 385, 433; predictions concerning, 400.
Slaves, legislation concerning, 405.
Small nations, the peculiarities of, 154.
Smith, Captain John, 834.
Social and domestic relations, influence of democracy upon, 664.
Social conditions of the Anglo-Americans, 33.
Society, growth of, in America, 12.
South America, relation of United States to, 473.
South, uneasiness in the, 440.
Sovereignty, 117; division of, 420; of mankind, 276; of the people, 43.
Stage, literature of the, 564.
Stith, William, 839.
Suffrage, universal, 208.
Sunday laws, 834.
Supreme Court, the, 136, 144.

Tariff, trouble caused by the, 450.
Townships and municipal bodies, 47.
Township independence, 25.

Tyranny of the majority, how mitigated, 290.

Union, the usefulness of the, 427; losing strength, 443.
Unrest, spirit of, 622, 731.

Voters, qualifications of, in the United States, 847.

War, effect of, 167; civil, 776.
Warfare and revolutions among democratic peoples, 741.

Washington, George, quoted, 242.
Weakness, supposed, of the Federal Government, 425.
Wealth, pursuit of, 316; desire for, 615.
Winthrop, John, quoted, 27.
Women, position of, in America, 699; education of, 686.
Workmen, intelligence of American, 471.
Writers, American, 339.

THE END